CLARENDON LAW SERIES

Introduction to Roman Law
BARRY NICHOLAS

Natural Law and Natural Rights
JOHN G. FINNIS

Conflicts of Law and Morality
KENT GREENWALT

Bentham and the Common Law
Tradition
GERALD J. POSTEMA

Public Law and Democracy
P. P. CRAIG

Precedent in English Law
4th edition
SIR RUPERT CROSS AND
J. W. HARRIS

Playing by the Rules
FREDERICK SCHAUER

Labour Legislation and Public Policy:
A Contemporary History
PAUL DAVIES AND
MARK FREEDLAND

Legal Reasoning and Legal Theory
NEIL MACCORMICK

The Concept of Law 2nd edition
H. L. A. HART

An Introduction to Constitutional
Law
ERIC BARENDT

Discrimination Law
SANDRA FREDMAN

The Conflict of Laws
ADRIAN BRIGGS

The Law of Property
3rd edition
F. H. LAWSON AND BERNARD
RUDDEN

Introduction to Company Law
PAUL L. DAVIES

Personal Property Law
3rd edition
MICHAEL BRIDGE

An Introduction to the Law of Trusts
2nd edition
SIMON GARDNER

Employment Law
HUGH COLLINS

Public Law
ADAM TOMKINS

Contract Theory
STEPHEN A. SMITH

Administrative Law
4th edition
PETER CANE

Criminal Justice
LUCIA ZEDNER

An Introduction to Family Law
2nd edition
GILLIAN DOUGLAS

Unjust Enrichment
2nd edition
PETER BIRKS

Atiyah's Introduction to the
Law of Contract
6th edition
STEPHEN A. SMITH

Equity
2nd edition
SARAH WORTHINGTON

An Introduction to Tort Law
2nd edition
TONY WEIR

Continued on next page

CLARENDON LAW SERIES

THE CONFLICT
OF LAWS

Second Edition

ADRIAN BRIGGS

St Edmund Hall,
University of Oxford

OXFORD
UNIVERSITY PRESS

OXFORD
UNIVERSITY PRESS

Great Clarendon Street, Oxford OX2 6DP

Oxford University Press is a department of the University of Oxford.
It furthers the University's objective of excellence in research, scholarship,
and education by publishing worldwide in

Oxford New York

Auckland Cape Town Dar es Salaam Hong Kong Karachi
Kuala Lumpur Madrid Melbourne Mexico City Nairobi
New Delhi Shanghai Taipei Toronto

With offices in

Argentina Austria Brazil Chile Czech Republic France Greece
Guatemala Hungary Italy Japan Poland Portugal Singapore
South Korea Switzerland Thailand Turkey Ukraine Vietnam

Oxford is a registered trade mark of Oxford University Press
in the UK and in certain other countries

Published in the United States
by Oxford University Press Inc., New York

British Library Cataloguing in Publication Data
Data available

Library of Congress Catologing in Publication Data
Data available

Typeset by Newgen Imaging Systems (P) Ltd., Chennai, India
Printed in Great Britain
on acid-free paper by
Antony Rowe Ltd, Chippenham

ISBN 978–0–19–953966–6 (Hbk)
ISBN 978–0–19–953967–3 (Pbk)

1 3 5 7 9 10 8 6 4 2

Preface to the Second Edition

The innocent enquirer may ask what the point of the conflict of laws is. It is a good question; and there are three ways to answer it. The first is that it poses the challenge of constructing a theory of law which accounts for the foreign components in a legal question, and which results in a single *corpus iuris* which is logical, impersonal, and entire. Such a version of private international law tends to be made in universities and institutes, rather than the courts, and it reflects the manner in which civilian lawyers have gone about their business. The second is that it tries to ensure that the where and how of litigation does the least possible damage and distortion to the rights and obligations of the persons who may find themselves in court. To this end it assembles a toolkit of principles, rules, and above all, techniques, which is made available to litigants and judge alike. The law can be described and shown to be predictable (it must be so; the choice of English law to govern consensual relationships does not happen by accident), but forces which are not immediately visible play a large part in the overall scheme. This is how the common law has discharged its responsibility in the field of private international law.

We should pause here for a moment. The common law is not without its theory, but it is fairly uncomplicated. It is assumed that the law is made for man, not man for the law, so it looks around for ways to get to the right answer to the question on which the parties join issue before the judge. Its doctrinal rules of jurisdiction and of choice of law get it off to a good start. What gives them strength, however, is the complex of procedure and technique and which makes the end product more subtle and sensitive than anything a set of textual rules ever could produce. The aim is that this amalgam of rule and technique will sort out the rights and obligations of the parties with the minimum of fuss. Of course a court will know that the particular legal dispute may be part of a bigger story, and that the things an English court may do may ramify, if indirectly, in the world outside. But courts adjudicate on the issues brought before them, with the judge acting as umpire. The remoter consequences of the decision are not really a matter for them. This combination of doctrine and technique, law and tactic, is what English private international law offers to the world. It illustrates, perhaps more than any other area of law, the proposition that the common law is not a map but a maze. And it is stimulating, fun even.

The third way is a product of our times: to capture the whole of private international law and administer a series of lethal injections. The European Union has assumed responsibility for abolishing private international laws and setting up, in their place, of a row of lifeless, grey statutes. In a triumph of bureaucracy over individualism, these are to be known as Brussels I, Rome II, etc: the echo of bad 1970s science fiction, describing a world in which personal names are no longer needed, is never far away. One thing must be made clear. It is not that the individual rules which these Regulations enact are bad: such an assertion would be as wrong as it would be absurd. Some of the new provisions show just how badly the common law got itself, or Parliament froze the law, into a muddle or a knot. Some of them show that, if English law had got round to developing a rule along the lines of one found in a particular Regulation, it would have been able to do justice much better and more efficiently. What is so dispiriting is the deliberate snapping of the sinews and tendons which make the law work, and which allow courts to honour legal principles— that agreements should not be broken and that ways may be found to prevent it; that the result of litigation should be as it would have been if it had been taking place in the place where it really belonged; and that some legal values are more important than legal rules—which animate the private international laws of each of the Member States: it is, after all, not just the common law's private international law which is being legislated out of existence.

And why is this? Because the completion of the single market requires it. Of course, no empirical research sustains so implausible an assertion, but we are here in the realm of faith rather than reason. The one market in which there is to be no competition, no freedom of (or point in) movement, is that of dispute resolution. Good law is not to be allowed to drive out bad. And while the European Union intones its message of dreary uniformity, one might just try totting up the official languages in which this single market is being completed. At the last count there were 23, plus three half-languages, with the promise of many more to come as the European Bureau for Lesser Used Languages (*sic*) gets busy with the funding of Project Babel. But where private international law is concerned, a nightmarish, sterile, monoculture prevails. In 2008, private international law is still—just—an amalgam of common law and European law, but we are in a transitional phase. So this book seeks to show how it all works, and to convey just why it was, and still is, that the subject is so rewarding and such fun. Fun, of course, is about to be given an autonomous interpretation, and then that will be that.

There was never a discussion about private international law which was not worth having; never a seminar which was not worth attending; never a paper which was not worth reading; never a book which was not worth reviewing. The benefits derived and pleasure to be had from talking to colleagues and co-workers in other jurisdictions—common law and civilian alike—are numberless. It still is a privilege to collaborate with people who share, for the passing moment or for a working lifetime, an interest in this complex and beautiful subject. Whatever one may think of the raw material with which we all have to deal, it is the sense of having been working together even while working apart for which the law makes us truly thankful. Although, in the end, this book can only be one person's impression of English private international law, it owes much to the many, whose contributions are now acknowledged: with pleasure and with respect for their absolute right to privacy. All errors, of doctrine and judgment, are mine, of course. But if they stimulate the reader to think and see that he or she knows better, their presence will not be unjustified.

Oxford, New Year's Day, 2008.

Contents

Decisions of National Courts

Decisions of European Courts

United Kingdom Legislation

EU Legislation

International Agreements and Conventions

I

The Structure of the Subject

A. THE NATURE OF THE SUBJECT

The title of this book suggests that it is concerned with the conflict of laws, but this should not be taken too seriously, for our subject has nothing to do with conflict, legal or otherwise. Once some very important preliminaries are out of the way, in the chapters which follow, our fields of inquiry will be three in number. First, we will examine the rules which define whether an English court has jurisdiction to hear a claim where one or more of the parties, or some other aspect of the story, may be foreign to England or to English law: the conflict of jurisdictions.[1] Secondly, we will examine whether and how a foreign judgment may have an effect in the English legal order.[2] And thirdly, we will consider the rules and principles which tell an English court hearing a case with a foreign element whether to apply English law or a foreign law or a combination of laws to resolve the dispute: the conflict of laws.[3]

The common law label for this collection of material is the conflict of laws, because in the third category just mentioned there may be a conflict between the answers which would be given by the various potentially applicable systems of law, and a choice between them has to be made. This nomenclature only ever made sense[4] when the subject confined its attention to the question of choice of law: whether a claim for damages for breach of contract was governed by English or French law; whether an alleged tort was governed by English or German law; whether the succession to an estate was governed by English or Spanish law; whether the validity of a marriage or effect of a divorce was governed by English or Mexican law, and so on. These were the questions which dominated the subject in the period of its classical development, from the 19th to the middle of the

[1] Ch 3.
[2] Ch 4.
[3] Chs 5–10.
[4] Dr Morris considered that it never did: Dicey's *Conflict of Laws* (6th edn, 1949) at 7, a view endorsed by the majority of the High Court of Australia in *John Pfeiffer Pty Ltd v Rogerson* [2000] HCA 36, (2000) 203 CLR 503 at [43].

20th centuries. But in more recent times this focus has changed. For one thing, substantial legislation has diminished the domain of the common law conflict of laws. For another, much greater attention is paid to whether English (or foreign) courts have and will exercise jurisdiction in a given case, at least if a count of reported cases is any guide. The principal cause of the former development is the harmonization of European law, and the perception, perhaps more apparent to some than to others, that diversity among national choice of laws rules serves to impede the completion of the single market by making litigation scary and unpredictable. The principal reason for the latter was the realization that the question where a trial takes place is of critical importance to the outcome of litigation; that once parties have skirmished on the question of jurisdiction the case may well settle. Developments in this area took place within the common law, but also by means of harmonization of laws across Europe.

One can improve on the nomenclature of the conflict of laws. The traditional alternative, private international law is better, for the subject matter is almost entirely private law, and its concern is with international elements and points of contact. And it is under the label of *droit international privé* that French lawyers think about our subject. But this title may suggest that there is a relationship with public international law, which describes or regulates relations between states; and this would be misleading. Rather little public international law infiltrates the subject. For example, when dealing with the confiscation or nationalization of private property by states, there may well be rules of public international law which specify whether the property of a foreign citizen may be seized, whether compensation has to be paid, and so forth. But the conflict of laws has little concern with this: as long as the property was within the territory of the seizing state, title acquired by seizure will usually be effective in private international law, whatever public international law may say about the steps taken to acquire it. Nor is there a private international law of crime, an archetypal matter of public law: the international aspect of criminal law is dealt with by specific local legislation, or by extradition.

'International private law' would be best of all; it is also reflected in the German conception of the subject, as *internazionales Privatrecht*. It concerns private law—the law of contracts, torts, property, status—in those contexts when a foreign element is present within the factual matrix. One day a writer in the common law world will publish a book under this title and, when this happens, the label will, once again, describe the contents of the box. But this has not happened yet.

Private international law is made up of statute and case law. In two respects the source material is, however, distinctively different. First, much of the common law material has been overlaid with legislation, the larger part of which results from the United Kingdom's membership of the European Union. The challenges posed by the assimilation of this material into a subject constructed on common law foundations have yet to be fully met. Second is the influence of a single textbook on the judicial development of the subject. Dicey's *Conflict of Laws*[5] tends to be treated by the judiciary as authoritative to a degree still unusual in England.

B. FOREIGN LAW APPLIED BY AN ENGLISH JUDGE

The principal characteristic of the conflict of laws is that it will sometimes lead to a judge being asked to apply foreign law to the dispute.[6] In the ordinary course, an English judge will apply English domestic law: common law, equity, and statute. The judge will apply only English law, and cannot and will not apply a foreign law, to a question unless four conditions are satisfied. First, the choice of law rules of English law must provide that a foreign law is in principle applicable to the issue in question; secondly, English legislation must not supervene to forbid the application of foreign law; thirdly, the party who relies on foreign law must plead and establish its applicability; and, fourthly, the party relying on foreign law must adduce evidence which proves its content to the satisfaction of the court. Meeting these four conditions means that the judge will be enabled and obliged to apply a rule of foreign law.

As regards the first point, we will consider in Chapters 4 to 9 the rules of choice of law which may lead the court to the point where it may be required to apply a foreign law: to the conclusion that the law which governs a contract is French, or that the law applicable to an alleged tort is German, and so forth. As regards the second point, however, the rules of choice of law may in certain circumstances be overridden by contradictory English legislation which directs the court not to apply a rule of foreign law. So, for example, a contract admittedly governed by French law may contain a provision limiting or excluding the liability of the defendant in circumstances where this would not be permitted were the contract governed by English law. In such a case, English legislation may stipulate that the rules of English law on exemption clauses are to be applied even

---

[5] The 8th to 13th editions appeared as Dicey & Morris; the 14th edition (2006) appears as Dicey Morris & Collins. In this book it is referred to as 'Dicey'.

[6] See generally Fentiman, *Foreign Law in English Courts* (1998).

though English law is not otherwise the governing law.[7] This being so, the judge will, to that extent, be precluded from applying foreign law.

As regards the third point, the party or parties seeking to rely on foreign law must plead its applicability. It follows that if neither party does, the judge will be obliged to apply English domestic law to the issues in dispute: the judge has neither right nor power to apply foreign law *ex officio*. So in the example of personal injury or damage to property taking place overseas, a claimant may consider that the law of the place where he was injured affords him a cause of action, whereas English domestic law would not: it will be up to him to plead the applicability of foreign law to the claim.[8] Again, a defendant may consider that the law of the place where the alleged tort happened furnishes her with a defence which would not be available as a matter of English law: it will be up to her to plead the applicability of foreign law to the issue raised by way of defence. But neither party is obliged to do this, and a judge will therefore be left to apply English domestic law when the parties do not invoke foreign law. According to the English way of thinking, this is so even when an international convention stipulates that an issue *shall* be governed by a particular law.[9] As a matter of observable fact, overseas tort cases litigated in England will frequently be decided by application of English domestic law. This may reflect the truth that the principles of the law of obligations are all very similar, meaning that there is usually little point in proving foreign law; and it may also be driven by the practical problem, and expense, of actually proving foreign law, as will be seen below. However, it results in English private international law taking a pragmatic, rather than a dogmatic, view of the role of the courts: the parties are entitled to establish a common position on the applicability or not of foreign law, and once they have done that, it is not for a judge to take a contrary view. This is fair enough where a court is called on to adjudicate a matter in the law of obligations: the question whether a contract was valid or broken, or whether a defendant was the victim of negligence or *volens* to the risk, is a matter of interest to the two parties alone,[10] and if they agree to the application of English domestic law to their dispute, there is no third

---

[7] eg Unfair Contract Terms Act 1977, s 27(2); cf Rome Convention (Contracts (Applicable Law) Act 1990, Sch 1) Art 7(2).

[8] Private International Law (Miscellaneous Provisions) Act 1995, s 11(2)(a); Regulation (EC) 864/2007, [2007] OJ L199/40, Art 4(1).

[9] But it certainly can be argued that the traditional English approach is part and parcel of the common law, and is in formal conflict with, and inapplicable in relation to, the particular conventions.

[10] And their insurers.

party interest to disagree with this. But in cases where the court is called on to decide an issue which may have an effect *in rem*, such as whether B obtained good title to a car from S, or whether H and W were validly married, this *laissez-faire* approach is less attractive, for a ruling on status may well affect non-parties, such as a subsequent purchaser or an intending spouse. In this context the decision of the original parties to have an adjudication by reference only to English domestic law affects other interested persons who were not privy to the agreement. Yet English law has never taken the view that in questions of status the court is obliged to apply foreign law in defiance of the wishes of the litigants.

As regards the fourth point, the content and effect of an applicable foreign law are matters of fact, to be proved by the parties as a question of fact.[11] Every pleaded proposition of fact requires to be proved; and as foreign law is a question of fact, evidence will have to be given by experts, usually one for each side and evaluated by the judge.[12] Expertise in foreign law is, however, easier to describe than to define. There is no register of individuals who are qualified, still less authorized, to give such evidence to an English court; there is no reliable way to evaluate the expert or his evidence; it may not be clear whether an expert's knowledge is practical and up to date. Nor is it always clear that the content of a foreign law as derived from statute and code will be consistent in every respect with the result which would result from its application by a foreign judge; and anyway, is Ruritanian law the law as derived from the written sources of Ruritanian law, or the outcome which would be reached by a Ruritanian judge called upon to apply it? The answer appears to be that the expert is required to testify to what the law means, if this is distinct from what the legislative text appears to say. An expert who has written books may have had little or no practical experience of how the law he has described would be applied in a court; the fact that a lawyer is in private practice or judicial office may nevertheless leave her wholly unsuitable to give evidence of an area of law of which she has no direct experience. An English court may be more impressed by the reported decisions of a foreign court than a local court would be; it may be less persuaded by the writings of scholars than a foreign court would be. These are not trivial points, for as English private international law has committed itself to this particular view, it is

[11] It might be thought to follow that a decision on foreign law is not subject to reversal on appeal, unless the primary judge's conclusion was so unreasonable that no judge could properly have reached the conclusion he did. But foreign law is a fact of a rather peculiar kind, and appeals are more frequent, and the substitution of an appellate court's own conclusion more common, than its formal status as a question of fact might suggest.
[12] See generally *Glencore International AG v Metro Trading Inc* [2001] 1 Lloyd's Rep 283.

legitimate to question whether the approach is suitable for the ends it is designed to serve. There are many cases in which the judge has had to pick his way through baffling and contradictory bodies of evidence of foreign law, with the result that one may applaud the effort yet still lack confidence in the outcome; and the financial cost to the parties can be quite disproportionate to the substance of the claim.

If the party seeking to prove the content of an applicable foreign law fails to satisfy the judge, it is sometimes said that the judge will apply the foreign law, but will do so in the sense that foreign law is taken to be the same as English law as the contrary was not proved. This is not very edifying. In default of proof of the content of foreign law, an English judge still has to adjudicate; and although the traditional default position was that English law would be applied, *faute de mieux*, courts are increasingly prepared to dismiss a claim or defence as unproven if foreign law pleaded as its support has not been established by evidence.[13]

The proposition that the judge may go off on a frolic of his own and inquire into foreign law for himself has no place in an English court. The same principle should prevent a judge from founding on his own personal recollection of a particular foreign law,[14] even if he was trained and qualified in that system, for the law may have changed, and memory is fallible even when bewigged; and, in any event, for a judge to usurp the privilege of the parties would be to ignore the limits on judicial power: the principle that *curia novit jus*, that the court knows the law, begins and ends with English domestic law.

It may be thought that the practical difficulties in the English system reveal so many shortcomings that the model of other systems, in which the judge must investigate and apply foreign law as well as his own, is to be preferred. But this proposition does not stand up to inspection. A national judge manifestly does not know foreign law; a report on it must be commissioned. Whether it will be possible for a court to locate a competent expert from whom to obtain a report must be doubtful, at least where the law in question is specialized or exotic; and where the reporter will require close and detailed knowledge of the entire dispute, in order to be sure that he has seen all the issues which bear on the legal analysis, it is improbable that a court-commissioned expert will be able to do this. And even if the report is signed off by an authoritative figure, the chances will be that it was researched and written by someone very much more

---

[13] *Damberg v Damberg* (2001) 52 NSWLR 492; *Global Multimedia International Ltd v Ara Media Services* [2006] EWHC 3107 (Comm), [2007] 1 All ER (Comm) 1160.
[14] Examples exist, but are best left unidentified.

junior. So despite the claims sometimes heard, that the continental system of establishing and applying foreign law is superior to the English one, the truth is that the application of foreign law by a judge is fraught with difficulty of a general complexity which will not go away unless the trial is made to go away. This in turn may point to the real truth, that a court should have the power to decline to hear certain cases if it is persuaded that a court elsewhere would be better placed to give the parties the adjudication they deserve.

A final question, to which we return when examining the doctrine of *renvoi*, is what it means to apply foreign law: that is, what exactly is the judge asked to do? The common law understanding is that a judge, called upon to apply French or Ruritanian domestic law, should apply it as a French or Ruritanian judge, trying the case, would interpret and apply it. In other words, 'French law' means 'French domestic law as a local judge would apply it'. If the judge would apply this rule to this particular contract, or would not apply that rule to that claim or claimant, then an English judge, in applying foreign law, should do likewise, for this is the truest sense in which foreign law is applied. This technique is particularly helpful when a court is called upon to apply foreign statute law. In deciding whether and how the statute applies, the relevant question is whether, and if so to what effect, a judge trying the case in the foreign court would apply the particular statutory provision. If he would not apply it to the case in question, it is, for present purposes, not part of the foreign law which an English judge may be invited to apply. So if an Australian judge would not apply a provision of the Trade Practices Act 1974 to conduct taking place outside Australia, an English court, if applying Australian law as *lex causae*, should not apply it either. If a New Zealand judge would interpret and apply the Accident Rehabilitation and Compensation Insurance Act 1992 as precluding a civil claim for damages arising from an industrial injury, an English court, applying New Zealand law as *lex causae*, should hold that there is no civil liability under the law of New Zealand,[15] and should not be tempted to hold that whilst a New Zealand judge might be required to apply the Act, a non-New Zealand judge need not do so. The other side of the coin is that where a statute is intended by its legislator to be applied, but the *lex causae* is the law of another country, it will be ignored by an English court. So, if an English borrower and a Victorian lender enter into a contract of loan governed by English law, Victorian legislation reducing interest rates will be irrelevant to an English court, even if designed by the

---

[15] *James Hardie & Co Pty Ltd v Hall* (1998) 43 NSWLR 554 (CA); *James Hardie Industries Pty Ltd v Grigor* (1998) 45 NSWLR 20 (CA).

Victorian legislator to apply to the contract,[16] and even though a Victorian judge would have been required to apply the Act.[17] The simple point is that where a statute is part of the *lex causae*, it should[18] be applied by the English judge, along with all other substantive provisions of the *lex causae*, in the way the foreign judge would have applied it; and if it is not part of the *lex causae* it is to be ignored.

A significant point of principle arises if the foreign judge would not have applied his own domestic law at all, but would instead have used his choice of law rules to point to a different substantive law which he would then have applied. Whether the parties are entitled to invite an English judge to go down that path depends on the impact of the doctrine of *renvoi*, which is examined below.

C. BASIC CHOICE OF LAW REASONING: THE FOUR ANALYTICAL TOOLS

We have seen that a judge may be asked and required to apply a foreign law in the determination of a dispute. But there is a framework for the analysis, which keeps the exercise under reasonably manageable or reviewable control. We have also seen, and will frequently observe, that the grammar of the conflict of laws is assembled from propositions which connect issues to a particular law. So we say that the material validity of a contract is governed by its applicable law; liability in tort may be governed by the law of the place where the person was when injured; the effect of a transfer of movable property is governed by the law of the place where the thing was when transferred; the capacity of an individual to marry another is governed by the law of his or her domicile at the time of the marriage; the ranking of claims and distribution of assets in an insolvency is governed by the law of the court hearing the case; and so on.

The simplicity of these propositions is deceptive, for they contain three legal ideas, and suggest a fourth. The first is the concept of an 'issue': how do we know whether to frame our question in terms of the material validity of a contract as opposed to its formal validity, or just its validity? How do we know whether to ask the question in terms of the capacity of persons to marry as opposed to the validity of the marriage? The answer

---

[16] cf *Mount Albert Borough Council v Australasian Temperance and General Mutual Life Assurance Society* [1938] AC 224 (PC) (where the borrower was a New Zealander).
[17] *Akai Pty Ltd v People's Insurance Co Ltd* (1997) 188 CLR 418.
[18] Unless there is some rule of English law which overrides and instructs the English judge to do differently.

is that we *characterize* an issue, or issues, as being presented for decision. The second is the concept of a law: how do we know whether the applicable law means the domestic law of the relevant country, or, if this is different, the national law which would be applied by the judge trying the case in the courts of that country? How do we know whether the law of the domicile means the domestic law of the country in which the person is domiciled or if this is different, the law which would be applied by a judge trying the case in the courts of that country? The answer[19] is that the principles of *renvoi* tell us whether our rule of decision is one pointing to a domestic law only or includes a reference to the private international law rules of that country. The third is this: suppose the facts are characterized as giving rise to two issues, each having a choice of law rule, and for each of which English law and the foreign law would prescribe different solutions. Do we approach them independently, and try to combine the answers at the end, or does one play a dominant role, applying its rules to the determination of the other issue? This raises the *incidental question*, to which a solution must be found. Fourth and last is the identification of the rule of connection, the 'law of the …' rule. These are the *connecting factors*, and once the appropriate one has been found, the process of choice of law is over, and the proof of foreign law may begin. But these four elements of the choice of law process now need to be examined in a little more detail.

I. CHARACTERIZATION OF ISSUES

A choice of law rule is formulated by reference to connecting factors. This requires the facts to be accommodated within one, or perhaps more, legal categories to which a choice of law rule may be applied. The definition of these categories, and the location of facts within them, comprises the process of characterization.[20]

Both aspects of the process of characterization are undertaken by reference to English law: the available categories are those created by English private international law; and the placing of the facts within one or more of them is done according to English private international law: for those who find analogies helpful, English law designs the pigeonholes, and an English sorter decides which facts belong in which pigeonhole. This exercise has to be undertaken by reference to English law, for at this stage we are far from having explained why, still less which, foreign law is going to be relevant.

---

[19] Unless the choice of rule is a statutory one, and the statute itself answers the question.
[20] Dicey, ch 2.

As regards the definitional list of the available categories or characterizations, these are established in part by authority, and in part by principle.[21] As we look at different substantive areas of law we will identify them: the capacity to contract, the proprietary effect of a transfer, the formal validity of marriage, the capacity of a corporation to do an act, and so on. Although the categories are established, there is no reason of principle why the law may not develop a new one, and every reason why it should. So, for example, it has been proposed that the category of essential validity of marriage should be broken down into capacity to marry and the quintessential validity of marriage, for which separate choice of laws rules would be prescribed;[22] it has been proposed that the category of capacity to marry should be broken down into the capacity to contract a polygamous marriage and the remainder of capacity to marry.[23] And again, the choice of law rules for the transfer of intangible movables may yet divide so that certain complex cases, as arise in the system for indirect holding of financial instruments, are dealt with separately from other intangibles. It is to be expected that the process of change in this context will be slow and measured: the certainty of the law would be damaged if new categories were created willy-nilly. Moreover, an alternative response might be to make exceptions in individual cases, rather than the creation of new categories of general application. For all that, it is clear that the creation of new characterization categories is not impossible, but is sometimes overdue. For example, there might be a characterization category for equitable claims, for which the choice of law rule is the *lex fori*, the law of the court hearing the claim. Quite apart from the point, considered below,[24] that this might not be a desirable choice of law rule, it is doubtful that 'equitable claims' represents a coherent characterization category in the first place. Similar doubts have been expressed whether there should be a characterization category for 'receipt-based restitutionary claims'.[25] Though these ideas may[26] be indispensable as a matter of domestic English law, it does not follow that there is any use for them in the conflict of laws.

As regards whether a particular issue raised for decision in a case should be fitted into one or another of these categories, the usual explanation is that this is done by using English law as the point of departure, and treating

---

[21] *Raiffeisen Zentralbank Österreich AG v Five Star Trading LLC* [2001] EWCA Civ 68, [2001] QB 825.

[22] *Vervaeke v Smith* [1983] 1 AC 145.

[23] *Radwan v Radwan (No 2)* [1973] Fam 35.

[24] Ch 7.

[25] *Macmillan Inc v Bishopsgate Investment Trust plc (No 3)* [1996] 1 WLR 387 (CA).

[26] But which is not admitted.

an issue as one would treat its nearest English equivalent: the exercise is undertaken 'in a broad internationalist spirit in accordance with the principles of the conflict of laws of the forum'.[27] So, for example, an argument that a contract was unenforceable because it was not notarized concerns the formal validity of contracts, even though English law does not require contracts to be notarized; an argument that a promise is enforceable as a contract even though not given for consideration will raise a question of the material validity of a contract, even though English law would not see a gratuitous promise as a contract at all;[28] an action claiming damages for insult or for breach of confidence, will be treated as tortious even though English domestic law knows no such tort of insult and regards the breach of confidence as an equitable wrong; and a polygamous marriage will be treated as a marriage, even though English domestic law does not allow for polygamy. Occasionally this will lead to a result which appears unsatisfactory. After a marriage celebrated in England between English and French persons, it was alleged[29] that it was invalid because the French parents had not given their consent. One[30] analysis adopted by the court was that the need for third party consent raised a question of the formal validity of a marriage, which was governed by the law of the place (England) of celebration, under which law the lack of consent was immaterial. It is argued by some that the issue should instead have been treated as one of capacity to marry and governed by the domestic law of the person (French) alleged to lack marital capacity.[31] There is some force in the alternative view, especially if the court really did reason that as third party consent is a matter of formal validity in domestic English law it must be the same in the conflict of laws. Quite apart from the fact that the categories of the two (domestic, private international) systems of law are not obliged to be strictly congruent, it is sensible that the allocation of an issue to one or another of the characterization categories is done with a degree of flexibility. Even so, it is hard to see why the capacity solution is intrinsically better than the formality alternative; and the truth may be that some cases are inescapably hard ones. More novel cases can be expected in the future, as domestic laws are refashioned and reshaped to meet changing social conditions. In the

---

[27] *Raiffeisen Zentralbank Österreich AG v Five Star Trading LLC* [2001] EWCA Civ 68, [2001] QB 825, at [27].

[28] *Re Bonacina* [1912] 2 Ch 394.

[29] *Ogden v Ogden* [1908] P 46 (CA).

[30] The other was that if the facts raised an issue of capacity, it was still governed by English law, under the principle in *Sottomayor v De Barros (No 2)* (1879) 5 PD 94.

[31] Although under the rule in *Sottomayor v De Barros (No 2)*, this would not in fact have been the outcome.

context of family law, foreign legislative provision for marriage between persons of the same sex, and the creation of legal regimes for the registration of a civil partnership between persons whether of opposite or the same sex, might have required the courts to have to decide whether these unions are to be characterized as marriage, or as contract, or as requiring an entirely new characterization category, in order to provide a framework for litigation about their international validity and consequences.[32]

As for what represents the object of characterization, the 'thing' characterized, the usual understanding is that issues, rather than rules of law, are characterized.[33] The initial justification for this is that the language of the subject is written in terms which connect categories of legal issue with a choice of law. It also has the immense practical advantage that a single law is identified to provide the solution to the single issue. If, by contrast, one were to adopt the approach of characterizing the individual rules of law found in the legal systems having some connection to the dispute, aiming to apply the one which was framed so as to apply in the given context, one could end up with two contradictory solutions or none at all. Take the case of marriage without parental consent, discussed above. Suppose it had been held that the English rule that parental consent was not required was a rule about the formal validity of marriage, and hence applicable to a marriage taking place in England; and the French rule requiring parental consent was held to be a rule about capacity to marry, and hence applicable to the marriage of a French domiciliary. Both rules would have been 'characterized' as applicable; the result of their combined application is an impossible contradiction. Or, taking the opposite possibility in each case, each rule might have been characterized as being inapplicable. This does not seem sensible; the ends condemn the means. Accordingly, the judge is required to identify an issue and apply the law which governs that issue. In the only case to have confronted the issue directly,[34] a mother and daughter, domiciled in Germany but refugees in England, had been killed in an air raid. The court had to decide who succeeded to the estate of the mother. Where it was unknown which victim died first, both English law and German law would apply a presumption: English law presuming that the older died first, German law that they died simultaneously. The judge deduced that he had to decide an issue of inheritance or succession, which was governed by German law and not a question of evidence governed by English law. He therefore applied the German rule. But whether he was right

---

[32] But Civil Partnership Act 2004, Sch 20, provides a statutory answer.

[33] However, as will be seen in ch 2 below, the rule of private international law that an English court will not enforce a foreign penal or revenue law will require characterization of the particular law, and not of an issue.

[34] *Re Cohn* [1945] Ch 5.

or wrong about this, his technique of identifying *an* issue raised by the facts is the critical point to notice. Had he simply characterized the competing rules of German and English law, he might have found that both applied or neither applied: this would have been so self-defeating that, whatever else may be said in its defence, the solution could not be right.[35]

A final question concerns exactly what happens after characterization has pointed the court to a particular law in which to find the answer. Suppose a marriage has taken place in France, without the parental consent required by the French domiciliary law of one of the parties. An English court will characterize the issue as one of formal validity, and look to French law for an answer. But an answer to what question? If the question is 'is this marriage formally valid as a matter of French law despite the absence of parental consent?' the answer may be a rather puzzled 'yes': puzzled because, in the eye of the French expert, this is not the right question. If, by contrast, the question is 'is this marriage valid as a matter of French law despite the lack of parental consent?' the reasoning may be more complex, but the answer will be 'no': the French expert will explain that this issue is seen by French law as raising an issue of capacity, governed by the national (French) law of the allegedly incapable party, and according to which the marriage is invalid. To take another example, suppose that the requirement of consideration or a seal is regarded by English law as going to the material validity of the contract, but that Italian law would regard it as relevant to the formal validity of the contract. If the law applicable to the contract is Italian, is the expert required to state his view on the material validity of the contract, or is he allowed to address the issue of seals in the very way an Italian judge would? It will be seen that the outcome of the case may depend on the manner in which the question is formulated: put shortly, is the question as formulated for the expert to answer one expressed in and bounded by the precise terms of the characterization which led there in the first place, or is characterization defunct and forgotten once it has served to make a connection to a law? The answer may well require an understanding of the principles of *renvoi*, and the suggested solution will be found at the end of the next section.

2. THE MEANING OF LAW: *RENVOI*

If an issue is governed by the *law* of a particular country, what is the meaning to be given to the word *law*? Does it mean the rules of domestic law,

---

[35] For a different view, see Forsyth (1998) 114 LQR 141.

as these would apply to a wholly internal case, or does it refer to law in a wider sense, including, perhaps, the private international law rules of that legal system? This question can be formulated another way: is the issue to be resolved by applying the domestic law, or by permitting a reference on—a *renvoi*—from that law to another, if that law would make one? The answer is that there is no short answer: sometimes it will be the former, othertimes the latter. Which is which is mostly a matter of authority; why this represents the approach of English private international law is more controversial.[36]

We can illustrate the operation of the principle of *renvoi* by taking an example. Suppose a woman has died without leaving a will, and the question arises concerning succession to her estate.[37] Suppose she died domiciled in Spain, but still a British citizen. As a matter of English private international law, succession to her movable estate would be governed by Spanish law as the law of her domicile. Suppose that according to Spanish domestic law, X would succeed to the estate, but that according to Spanish private international law, succession would be governed by the law of the nationality, which would be taken to be English; and as a matter of English domestic law, Y would succeed. What is the judge to do?

He faces three possibilities, at least in principle. He may interpret his choice of law rule as pointing him to Spanish domestic law, and hold in favour of X. Or he may interpret his choice of law rule as pointing to Spanish law as including its rules of private international law, follow the path by which this points to English law, interpret this as meaning English domestic law, and find for Y. Or he may interpret his choice of law rule as pointing to Spanish law, follow the path by which this points to English law, interpret this as meaning 'English law including its conflicts rules', which point back to Spain, ask what the Spanish judge would do when informed that English law would look back to Spanish law, and accept whatever answer the Spanish judge would then give. As a matter of common law authority, the English judge will not take the second of these three possibilities. Sometimes he will take the first, and interpret the 'law' as meaning the domestic rules of the chosen law; but on other occasions, which include issues of succession, he will take the third, and interpret the 'law' as meaning what the foreign judge, hearing the case in the court whose law has been chosen, would do.[38] In other words, he will, so far as

---

[36] Dicey, ch 4.
[37] For the rules on intestate succession, see ch 8, below.
[38] *Re Annesley* [1926] Ch 692; *Re Ross* [1930] 1 Ch 377; *Re Askew* [1930] 2 Ch 259; *Re Duke of Wellington* [1947] Ch 506.

the evidence of the content of foreign law allows him to do so, ask what a Spanish judge would do if he were deciding the case himself, and adopt that answer as his own, whatever it may be. For this reason the English approach to *renvoi* is sometimes called the 'foreign court theory' of *renvoi*; sometimes 'total *renvoi*'; and sometimes as involving the 'impersonation' of the foreign judge. Is this not all very difficult? Should the judge not simply have applied Spanish domestic law and left it at that?

Judges and writers have suggested so, and legislators may be tempted to say so. But before looking at the authority and the arguments, it is well to be reminded that *renvoi* applies only in certain areas of private international law; and that, as the proof of foreign law lies primarily in the hands of the parties, a court will have neither need nor opportunity to examine the principles of *renvoi* unless the parties choose to raise them on the pleadings. One criticism of *renvoi*, that it can make life very difficult for the parties and for the judge, may be overstated. Another, that choice of law rules were inherently formulated without any thought for *renvoi* but as pointers to a domestic system of law, is simply a rejection of the principle without separate justification. A third, which is that *renvoi* subordinates English choice of law rules to those of a foreign system, is misconceived, particularly if English law decides for itself to choose to follow a foreign court's pattern of reasoning. A fourth is that the English 'impersonation' approach works only if the judge who is being impersonated is not himself trying at the same time to do the very thing which the English judge would do, which just goes to show that the very idea is flawed.[39] But this creation of the febrile academic imagination has never arisen for decision;[40] and were it to do so, the rational answer is that if the foreign court looks back to English law, *renvoi* has shot its bolt, and English domestic law applies.[41]

The arguments in favour of *renvoi* are stronger. Rules of private international law in general, and of *renvoi* in particular, are rules of a foreign legal system: if this foreign law is selected for application, it is odd that material parts of that law are sheared off and ignored when it comes to be applied. It may be convenient to imagine the rules of private international law as separate

---

[39] It is said that it is hardly a recommendation that the English doctrine of *renvoi* works only if other states reject it. This is nonsense: one may as well say that one should never hold a door open for another to pass through, for if the other person is equally polite neither will make any progress at all.

[40] But the worry of it prompted the dissent of McHugh J in *Neilson v Overseas Projects Corp of Victoria* [2005] HCA 54, (2005) 233 CLR 331: he was frightened by a paper tiger.

[41] *Casdagli v Casdagli* [1918] P 89, Scrutton LJ. Other answers may be imagined, but there is no sense in looking for an answer which is impossible to work with.

and distinct, but this is a pedagogic device which risks damaging the coherence and integrity of the law. If one is to apply foreign law, it seems right to apply all of it; and equally right to apply it in the same way, and to the same effect (so far as this is possible) as the foreign judge would: realism teaches, and common sense understands, that the law is what a judge will say it is. Moreover, although in our example it may not matter very much whether X or Y succeeds to the movable estate, it would seem very strange that an English court could consider and declare that one person is entitled to foreign land when, as a matter of that foreign law, the register of title will not be amended in conformity with this view. If[42] it is ever right for an English court to make a judgment about title to foreign land, it should surely do so in conformity with what it understands to be the law which the local courts would themselves apply; and if this aligns English choice of law rules to those of another system, so much the better for that.

There is another justification for the general operation of the principle of *renvoi*.[43] When applied by an English court, its aim is to ensure that the case is decided as it would be if the action were brought in the courts which are probably the closest to the facts of the dispute. Consider a case in which a claimant is injured in a traffic accident in Malta, under the domestic law of which state he would have no claim for damages for pain and suffering, but only for pecuniary losses.[44] Suppose he sues in England, hoping to rely on English domestic law which would not so limit his claim. An English court might see this as a case of forum shopping: suing in a court in which the claimant has no legitimate expectation of being allowed to proceed, so as to avoid a hard judgment from the courts at the place where the action really did belong. To prevent this, an English court may decide to apply Maltese law, as the law of the place where the tort occurred; but to accomplish what it sets out to achieve, it will have to interpret 'Maltese law' as meaning that law—all of it, including its conflicts rules—which a Maltese judge would have brought to bear on the adjudication. The doctrine of *renvoi* would, on this view of the matter, have a supporting role to play in the prevention of forum shopping,[45] and in refining a choice of law rule which seeks to apply the law of the place where the tort occurred.[46]

---

[42] See further below, ch 8.

[43] See further Briggs (1998) 47 ICLQ 877.

[44] cf *Boys v Chaplin* [1971] AC 356.

[45] If it is said that this need is now met by the doctrine of *forum conveniens* (discussed in ch 3), the reply is that modern reform of the rules on civil jurisdiction removes the possibility from courts in a large number of cases.

[46] *Neilson v Overseas Projects Corp of Victoria*. But in England, the Private International Law (Miscellaneous Provisions) Act 1995, s 9(5) and Regulation (EC) 864/2007, Art 24, exclude the application of *renvoi* from the statutory choice of law for tort.

The objection that *renvoi* serves to subordinate English conflicts rules to foreign ones is unimpressive, not least because any adoption of *renvoi* is done as part of, and not to contradict, English choice of law. Common law rules for choice of law evidently come in two patterns. In one, the choice of law rule is expressed as the choice of a domestic law to determine the issue. So the material validity of a contract is governed by the domestic law chosen and expressed by the parties or, in default of such expression, by that domestic law with which it is most closely connected: the rule is formulated in terms of a choice of a domestic law, and *renvoi* is irrelevant. In other cases, the choice of law rule is expressed indirectly, or formula-ically, as the choice of the law which would be applied by a judge holding court at the relevant place. So a question of title to land is governed by the law which would be applied by a judge sitting at the place where the land is; succession to movable property is governed by that law which would be applied by a judge sitting in the place where the defendant died domiciled. Expressed in those terms the principle of *renvoi* does not lead to the upset-ting of choice of law, but reflects the intellectual diversity of common law choice of law rules.

It is necessary to admit, however, that *renvoi* is viewed in some quarters with a dislike which borders on pathological. It is often legislated against, although without much thought evidently being given to the disruption which this may bring about. Statute now provides that it has no applica-tion to the choice of law for contract[47] and tort,[48] and this was arguably the view of the common law which has now been largely superseded. It does, in principle and if pleaded and proved by the parties, apply to ques-tions of title to property, whether by *inter vivos* transaction or on death, and whether movable[49] or immovable.[50] It also applies to the validity of marriage,[51] and therefore applies to the invalidity of marriage; it does not apply to divorce for the reason that choice of law rule for granting and rec-ognizing divorces is for the law of the forum.[52] Although some have ques-tioned whether it still does apply in these cases, the answer must be that it does, although the failure of the parties to plead or prove it will lead to its absence from the analysis. In other words, when the court is being asked to give a judgment which will have its effect only on the litigants themselves,

---

[47] Contracts (Applicable Law) Act 1990, Sch 1, Art 15.
[48] See above, n 46.
[49] This proposition was denied in *Iran v Berend* [2007] EWHC 132 (QB), [2007] 2 All ER (Comm) 132, but the decision is insupportable.
[50] See, ch 8 below.
[51] *Taczanowska v Taczanowski* [1957] P 301 (CA); *R v Brentwood Superintendent Registrar of Marriages, ex p Arias* [1968] 2 QB 956.
[52] See, ch 9 below.

renvoi does not apply. But when it is asked to give a judgment on status, either the ownership of a thing or the marriageability of an individual, which will have a potential impact on third parties the court will, if invited to do so, interpret the law in the *renvoi* sense. If this increases the chance that the view reached by an English court will align with that which might be reached by a potentially-involved other law so much the better.

One may now return to the point left open at the end of the examination of characterization: how to formulate the question which is to be referred to and answered by the expert on foreign law. The answer should be along the following lines. In a legal context where the principle of *renvoi* has no application, there is no compelling need to reach the same answer as would be given by the foreign judge. The question may therefore be asked in terms of the English characterization: 'was the contract formally valid?' etc. But in a case where the principle of *renvoi* does apply, and where the aim is to reach the same conclusion as would be stated by a judge in the local court, it will impair the chances of success if the law is not interpreted in a *renvoi* sense: only by allowing the expert to use the characterization and choice of law rules of his own system will it be possible for him and for the court to produce an answer of the quality sought. So in the case of the absence of parental consent, the question put should be whether the absence of parental consent makes the marriage invalid, without regard to the way that the issue was earlier characterized by the English judge or would be characterized by the foreign judge. But in the case of the absence of consideration or seal, the question should be whether this affects the material validity of the contact, even though the foreign law would have regarded the absence of a seal as a question of formal validity.

3. INTERLOCKING ISSUES AND THE INCIDENTAL QUESTION

We have seen how the machinery for isolating the law to be applied to determine an issue identifies an issue and attaches a law to it. But a set of facts may contain more issues than one, and characterization may refer these to separate laws. So, for example, a claim for damages for an alleged tort may be defended by pointing to a contractual promise not to sue; a claim for the delivery up of goods over which a seller has reserved his title may be met by a defence that they were sold to the defendant who bought them in good faith and thereby destroyed the title of the claimant; the validity of a marriage may be impugned by the alleged incapacity of one of the parties, the factual basis for this lying in a disputed prior divorce. The problem arises if there is a conflict between the laws which English private international law chooses for the two issues. To take the first example, English law will apply the *lex delicti* to a claim in tort, but the *lex contractus* to the contractual defence; how it combines them can be left for later.[53] But it may happen that the private international law of the *lex delicti* has its own view, which differs from that of English private international law, of what the *lex contractus* is. On any view the intrinsic validity of the contractual defence depends on first identifying the *lex contractus*: so is this done by the rules of English private international law or by the conflicts rules of the *lex delicti*? Or do the conflicts rules of the law which governs the earlier-made contract identify the *lex delicti*? Again, the capacity of a person to marry will be affected by the recognition or otherwise of the anterior divorce: is the law which governs the validity of the divorce chosen by the conflicts rules of English law or by those of the law which governs capacity? Or is the capacity of the party to marry determined by the conflicts rules of the law which governs the validity of the earlier divorce?

Although it may seem complicated, the law reports suggest that it rarely arises for application and decision in practice. In the end, the considerations which underpin the doctrines of characterization and *renvoi* probably allow a coherent result to be reached. The starting point is that the prevailing view of the common law is to regard one of the issues, if possible, as the main one. The conflicts rules of the law chosen to govern that main question will then choose the law which governs the incidental question, so that the overall result is generated by the law (including its conflicts rules) which governs the main question. This assumes that a question can be identified as the main one; in many cases this will be the question which arises or occurs later in time, because in the end this is the decision which counts. By this reasoning, the effectiveness of the ultimate sale of the goods is the main question, the incidental one being that of the validity and effect of the prior reservation of title; the law governing the later sale will be the *lex causae* whose conflicts rules identify the law which governs the earlier reservation of title. Again, personal capacity to (re)marry is the main question, the incidental one being that of the validity and effect of the prior divorce;[54] the law governing capacity to marry will be the *lex causae* whose conflicts rules identify the law which governs the earlier divorce. In neither case does English private international law take a simple chronological approach, applying its choice of law rules to

[53] Chapter 6, below.
[54] *Schwebel v Ungar* (1964) 48 DLR (2d) 644 (Ont CA), but only to the extent that statute has not provided otherwise.

the issues individually and sequentially and then seeking to combine the results.

But title to property and personal status are two areas in which the principles of *renvoi* apply, and where the court aims to replicate the result which would be reached by the foreign judge if he were trying the case; the focus is immediately on the final or main question, and therefore any prior or incidental questions should be dealt with as if by the judge in the final court. A different analysis may be called for in a case where the principles of *renvoi* have no acknowledged part to play in the choice of law, and where the dominance of the final judge's perspective is absent. So in the case of a contractual defence to a tort claim, the *lex delicti* will determine whether there is a claim in tort. But if a contractual defence is pleaded, the first step is to decide whether the conflicts rules of the *lex delicti* or of English law identify the *lex contractus*. There being no necessity to decide the overall question as a judge of the *lex delicti* would, there is no reason to prefer the conflicts rules of the *lex delicti* to those of English law. Accordingly, the law which governs the contract and assesses the intrinsic validity of the defence is determined by applying English conflicts rules. If according to the law thus identified the defence is intrinsically valid, whether it works to defeat the claimant is a matter for the *lex delicti*, but the *lex delicti* has to take the validity of the contract as given, and does not make that judgment for itself.

The incidental question is therefore integrated into the common law methodology for choice of law. But it can be overridden by statute,[55] for Parliament may have enacted a law in such a way that it precludes the possibility of assessing, say, the validity of a divorce by anything other than English law. To that extent, the solution given above will be displaced, and the validity of the divorce conclusively determined, in accordance with Parliamentary intention, by English law.[56]

4. CONNECTING FACTORS

The identifier which appears at the end of the 'law of the...' formula is traditionally known as a 'connecting factor', on the ground that these points of contact are what connect an individual or an event to a system of the law which will, in principle, then be applied to determine the issue. They are almost all defined by exclusive reference to English, and not foreign, law: this is inevitable, for until the choice of law machinery has

---

[55] For further consideration of statute law, see below.
[56] *Lawrence v Lawrence* [1985] Fam 106; Family Law Act 1986, s 50.

identified a foreign law to apply to a dispute, there is no rational basis for using any law other than English for definitional purposes. For example, if as a matter of English law X is domiciled in France, this attribution of domicile is unaffected by the possibility that French law may not agree, and would, if it were relevant to know it, regard him as being domiciled in England instead.[57] If English law considers the law applicable to a contract to be Swiss law, it is irrelevant that a Swiss court, applying Swiss private international law, would have come to a different conclusion.

For it to be functional, the connecting factor will need to point to a territory having *a* system of law, as opposed to indicating a larger political unit which may have many systems of law or have none. For example, an individual may be found to be domiciled in England, but not in the United Kingdom: there is English law on his capacity to marry, but no 'United Kingdom law' on the point; and if a statute has been enacted to apply in England, Scotland, and Northern Ireland, and may in some sense be considered as the law of the United Kingdom, it will apply because it is part of English law, rather than for any other reason. An individual may be domiciled in Florida, but not in the United States, with the result that the law of Florida, as distinct from the law of the United States, will be applied; although where the relevant law of Florida is in fact a federal rule of the law of the United States, the federal rule will be applied as part of the law in the state of Florida. But by contrast, in true cases where a federal state has defined itself as a single legal unit for certain purposes, the connecting factor may point to that law. So a person may be regarded as domiciled in Australia for the purpose of capacity to marry, for Australia is constituted by its own legislation a single law district so far as concerns the law of marriage,[58] but in Queensland for the purpose of making a will, for the law of testamentary succession is a matter on which state law is sovereign, and state laws are several. An occasional form of expression for this special sense of a 'country' is a 'law district'.[59]

Connecting factors fall into two broad categories: those which define the law in terms of a personal connection, and those which define the law in terms of a state of affairs. For ease of exposition they need to be examined separately.

---

[57] *Re Annesley* [1926] Ch 692. But if choice of law rules refer to French law in a *renvoi* sense, and as a matter of French law he is domiciled in England, this detail will form part of the overall decision, and will not be contradicted.

[58] And, according to *John Pfeiffer Pty Ltd v Rogerson* [2000] HCA 36, (2000) 203 CLR 503, for all matters which fall within the federal jurisdiction.

[59] In *John Pfeiffer*, referred to as a 'law area'.

(a) Personal connecting factors

The personal connecting factors are domicile, habitual (or ordinary or usual) residence, (simple) residence, and nationality. As far as the common law is concerned, domicile is the most significant, and it is the law of the domicile which, to a greater or lesser extent, determines the status and capacities of an individual.

Domicile

At common law, the fundamental personal connecting factor is domicile.[60] As a matter of legal definition, every person has a domicile and, subject to what appears below,[61] no person can have more than one domicile at any time. The domiciliary law—the *lex domicilii*—still has a significant role in family and in property law, but it may also define the capacity of persons, especially companies,[62] to make contracts; and it plays a part in the law of taxation. From this very general introduction two points may emerge: the concept of domicile regulates a wide but diverse range of matters, and it may be that its meaning should take its colour from its context. It is also desirable that it represent a rational connection to a particular law. In these two respects the English law of domicile scores very badly indeed. On the first, although it has been suggested from time to time that domicile should adjust its definition to its context, there is no trace in English law of its having done so. So a case on UK tax liability, in which it was held that a person had not acquired an English domicile despite 40 years' residence,[63] will be authoritative on whether and how a person may acquire an English domicile for the purpose of his or her capacity to marry or make a will, as also will be the decision on whether a fugitive member of a German terrorist group, or an illegal immigrant or overstayer,[64] has acquired a domicile in England.[65] One imagines that the policies which underpin the individual decisions in these various contexts will not be identical and may even be contradictory, but this fact, if it is

---

[60] Dicey, ch 7.

[61] The persistence of the domicile of origin constitutes a general half-exception to the rule; the jurisdictional domicile which forms the backbone of the Civil Jurisdiction and Judgments Act 1982 and the Civil Jurisdiction and Judgments Order 2001 (SI 2001/3929) is a completely separate concept, irrelevant to the common law of domicile.

[62] Where it means the law of the place of incorporation: see, p 267 below.

[63] *IRC v Bullock* [1976] 1 WLR 1178 (CA).

[64] *Mark v Mark* [2005] UKHL 42, [2006] 1 AC 98.

[65] *Puttick v AG* [1980] Fam 1: she did not. But the decision probably cannot stand with *Mark v Mark*.

a fact, is not reflected in the definition of domicile, for domicile has, as a matter of common law, a common definition.

A particular difficulty, on which authority is surprisingly sparse, is how to determine the domicile of a person who, in some sense, belonged to a territory whose borders have moved. A woman once domiciled in Czechoslovakia will now face the impossibility of being domiciled in a non-country, in something which has no law and is no longer a law district. At a guess, she will be held to have acquired a domicile of choice in the part in which she was resident on the date on which the country severed itself, but this will be more difficult to defend as a conclusion if she had not, on that date, made up her mind whether to remain, and hence to reside, in the part-country. A person who was domiciled in the USSR or Yugoslavia, both of which disappeared by disintegration, is in much the same position; likewise one who was domiciled in East Germany, which country disappeared by voluntary absorption. In all these cases there are practical problems in defining domicile in terms which look backward to an earlier set of facts, but there is no easy solution to the problem created by the fact that, not only do people change their domiciles, but domiciles change their people.[66]

On the question whether the concept of domicile yields rational responses to the need for a personal connecting factor, it is necessary to distinguish three *genera* of the single domiciliary *species*.

The *domicile of origin* is the domicile of one's father (or mother, for one who is born out of wedlock or after the death of the father) at the date of one's birth. The domicile of origin will therefore be the first domicile of a child. It will prevail as the actual domicile until superseded by the acquisition of another, either a domicile of choice or a domicile of dependency. But it is only ever superseded, with the result that when a later-acquired domicile is lost, then unless at the same moment a new domicile is acquired, the domicile of origin reasserts itself as the person's actual domicile. It is therefore a characteristic of the domicile of origin that it can never be shaken off; and if it revives at a point late in a person's life it has the potential to connect him to a legal system which may be far and remote from the circumstances of his present life.[67] It is sometimes said that this potential to reassert itself goes to illustrate why the domicile of origin should be abolished by legislation, but the truth is less clear-cut. After all, if a refugee flees from the country in which she has had a domicile of choice, it may be more offensive to hold that she remains domiciled

[66] *Re O'Keefe* [1940] Ch 124.
[67] *Udny v Udny* (1869) LR 1 Sc & Div 441. See also *Re O'Keefe* [1940] Ch 124.

in a country now engaged in genocide against her ethnic group than to revive her domicile of origin until she is able to establish a new domicile of choice somewhere less awful.

A *domicile of choice* is acquired by taking up residence in a particular country and intending to reside there permanently or indefinitely. Both conditions must be satisfied in relation to the law district in which the domicile is to be established before acquisition is complete. The *intention* must be geographically specific, unconditional, and deliberate in order to meet the restrictive conditions of the law. As regards the first of these, if a person emigrates to the United States and has an intention to remain there but has not yet settled on which state she will, permanently or indefinitely, reside in, she will not have established a domicile of choice in any American state;[68] by parity of reasoning, if she intends to reside in Texas but has not yet taken up residence there she will not have established a domicile in Texas. As regards the second, the intention must be one of permanent or indefinite residence. So, an intention to reside for a defined period, or until the occurrence of a certain specific event, such as retirement or the death of a spouse, does not suffice either,[69] although if the condition upon which the residence would terminate is vague and unspecific it may be disregarded.[70] It can follow from this that residence even of several decades will not necessarily establish a domicile of choice, a fact which certain overpaid foreign nationals living and working in London have exploited shamelessly.[71] As regards the third, a number of cases have regarded a person's intention as insufficient because the residence was, in a sense, unintended. A fugitive from justice who intends to remain only until the passing of time has prescribed his offence will not acquire a domicile of choice,[72] but this was controversially extended to a German terrorist who fled to England but whose intention to remain was apparently unconditional.[73] A wastrel who came to England to sponge off his relatives forever was held to be too indolent to have an intention to establish an English domicile;[74] and an American citizen who was advised on medical grounds to remain in England, but who spent his time planning the destruction of the British maritime empire by various lunatic schemes,

---

[68] *Bell v Kennedy* (1868) LR 1 Sc & Div 307 (England and Scotland).
[69] *IRC v Bullock* [1976] 1 WLR 1178 (CA) (unless wife died first).
[70] *Re Fuld's Estate (No 3)* [1968] P 675; *Re Furse* [1980] 3 All ER 838.
[71] *IRC v Bullock* [1976] 1 WLR 1178 (CA).
[72] *Re Martin* [1900] P 211.
[73] *Puttick v AG* [1980] Fam 1.
[74] *Ramsay v Liverpool Royal Infirmary* [1930] AC 588.

was held not to have the requisite intention either.[75] It is hard to regard these colourful authorities as cases of conditional intention, but what they add to the requirements for the acquisition of a domicile of choice is difficult to define with specificity. What constitutes *residence* is hard to say; and the definition of 'present as a resident' hardly advances matters very much. The view that residence in England originating in unlawful entry was incapable of sustaining an English domicile of choice has now been abandoned.[76] A person can remain resident in a country although absent from it, but it is unclear whether he can be a resident upon the instant of his arrival.[77] In principle one can be resident in two countries at once, but to avoid the inadmissible result of this leading to there being two domiciles of choice, it is probable that the residence requirement identifies the principal residence if there is more than one contender.[78]

The domicile of choice can be lost by being abandoned, by the person ceasing to reside and to intend to reside indefinitely—both elements, not one, must be brought to an end—or lost on the acquisition of a new domicile of choice on the basis of the rules set out above. But if the abandonment is not contemporaneous with the acquisition of a new domicile of choice, the domicile of origin will reassert itself to prevent any domiciliary hiatus.[79]

A child's *domicile of dependency* is that, from time to time, of the parent upon whom, until the age of 16 or lawful marriage under this age, the child is dependent.[80] In principle, therefore, a child may supplant its domicile of origin with a domicile of dependency as soon as the cord is cut. When the age of independence is reached, it is debatable whether the domicile of dependency is lost by operation of law, so that the domicile of origin, if different, revives unless a domicile of choice is immediately acquired, or whether instead the domicile had from dependency continues as a 'deemed' domicile of choice. Statute suggests that the latter is possible,[81] but principle, and the balance of authority, suggests that it is not, and that the domicile of dependence ceases and is defunct on the

---

[75] *Winans v AG* [1904] AC 287.
[76] *Mark v Mark* [2005] UKHL 42, [2006] 1 AC 98.
[77] In the case of habitual residence, this will not suffice: *Re J (a Minor) (Abduction: Custody Rights)* [1990] 2 AC 562.
[78] *Plummer v IRC* [1988] 1 WLR 292.
[79] *Udny v Udny* (1869) LR 1 Sc & Div 441.
[80] Domicile and Matrimonial Proceedings Act 1973, s 3.
[81] ibid, s 1.

attaining of majority.[82] The domicile of dependency of married women was abolished in 1974.[83]

It will have become apparent that the rules of domicile, comprising as they do some implausible rules and peculiar authorities, are capable of producing a capricious answer in a given case, and all the more so in Europe as political states and boundaries move and change.[84] But repeated proposals for reform have been ignored or rejected,[85] and the cause of reform is now lost. The reasons for this probably lie in the substantial fiscal (historically adverse) consequences of having a domicile in England and the political clout of those who would stand to lose out if domicile were aligned more closely to simple residence. One particular consequence of this inability to rationalize the common law of domicile was that it was manifestly unsuitable to identify a court in which a person should be liable to be sued in a civil or commercial action. For this reason the term 'domicile' in the Civil Jurisdiction and Judgments Act 1982 and the Civil Jurisdiction and Judgments Order 2001[86] is statutorily defined to make it separate and distinct from its common law homonym; it is examined in Chapter 3.

Residence (habitual, ordinary, usual, simple)

Habitual residence, for which expression ordinary residence and usual residence are practically synonymous, is more usually employed as a personal connecting factor in laws which derive from international conventions; but its use will increase each time the cause of reform of the law of domicile is defeated. At one time it would indicate a person's usual residence, but with few of the technical complications of the common law of domicile. But its use in areas liable to generate high emotional stress—child abduction being the most notable[87]—has increasingly meant that courts have to be increasingly precise about its meaning. It is probable that it indicates only one place, although regular absence will not by itself deprive a residence of its habitual or usual character.[88] It is also probable that it is not significantly affected by a party's intention, though where it is contended that a new habitual residence has been acquired, there will

[82] See Wade (1983) 32 ICLQ 1.

[83] Domicile and Matrimonial Proceedings Act 1973, s 1.

[84] cf *Re O'Keefe* [1940] Ch 124.

[85] Most recently in Law Commission Report No 168 *The Law of Domicile* (1987).

[86] SI 2001/3929.

[87] Chapter 9, below.

[88] *R v London Borough of Barnet, ex p Shah* [1983] 2 AC 309. But one does not become habitually resident in a single day: *Re J (a Minor)(Abduction: Custody Rights)* [1990] 2 AC 562; *Nessa v Chief Immigration Officer* [1998] 2 All ER 728.

need to be evidence of a settled intention to remain there on a long-term basis.[89] By contrast, (simple) *residence* may be found to exist in more than one place. It and the concept of presence play a significant part in the rules of the common law dealing with jurisdiction and the recognition of judgments, although the relationship between residence and presence in these contexts can sometimes be obscure. Because its relevance is so closely related to these jurisdictional questions, it is examined in Chapter 3.

Nationality

As a connecting factor, nationality features only rarely in the English conflict of laws, by contrast with civilian jurisdictions where it is the dominant personal connecting factor. The reasons for its non-use in English private international law are pragmatic but compelling. To begin with, a person's status as a national of a particular country is determined by the law of the proposed state: no rule of English law can determine whether someone is or is not a national of Russia, for example. Nationality is therefore immune to the judicial refinement and control which can be brought to bear on other connecting factors. Although it plays a significant part in the law of the European Union, it may be supposed that the Member States are content for this purpose to accept each other's ascription of nationality; it does not follow that it would be a useful tool outside that context. Moreover, a person may retain a nationality long after ceasing to have any practical connection to the state in question, retaining it, perhaps, for emotional or other idiosyncratic reasons: in such a case it may not be the most appropriate law to serve as the person's personal law. Most tellingly, instances of dual nationality, or of nationality in a federal or complex state, such as the United States or the United Kingdom, or statelessness, would cause formidable difficulties for any person for whom nationality was a personal connecting factor; it is unclear how those jurisdictions which employ nationality deal with these practical objections, and convenient that English law rarely has to.

(b) Causal connecting factors

Those terms which describe a connection between a fact or an event and a law are also defined by reference to English law; where the meaning is not obvious it will be explained in the particular area of the law where it is utilized. Those which will be encountered in the conflict of laws are summarized here. Even though latinate expression is considered by some

---

[89] *Re J (a Minor) (Abduction: Custody Rights)* [1990] 2 AC 562; *Re S (a Minor) (Abduction: European Convention)* [1998] AC 750.

to add to the obscurity of the law, with the result that the usage is less frequent than before, the definitional concepts of the conflict of laws are still rendered, across the world, in classical forms. Up to this point in this chapter the attempt has been made to express connecting factors in an English language paraphrase, but it is undeniable, except by those with tin ears, that these lack the elegance and the economy of the traditional usages. From this point on, therefore, these connecting factors will generally be referred to in the form in which they appear in the authorities and as they are used internationally in the discourse of the conflict of laws. In addition to the *lex domicilii*, the law of the domicile, they include the *lex fori*, the law of the court in which the trial is taking place; the *lex contractus*, the law which governs a contract, whether determined under the rules of the common law (in contracts made before 2 April 1991, the 'proper law') or the Rome Convention (contracts made after 1 April 1991, the 'governing law'); the *lex loci contractus*, the law of the place where the contract was made; the *lex delicti*, the law which governs liability in tort, whether determined under the rules of the common law or statute; the *lex loci delicti commissi*, the law of the place of the tort, which is a component of the *lex delicti* under the rules of the common law; the *lex situs*, the law of the place where land, or other thing, is; the *lex loci actus*, the law of the place where a transaction was carried out; the *lex loci celebrationis*, the law of the place of celebration of marriage; the *lex incorporationis*, the law of the place of incorporation; the *lex protectionis*, the law under which legal protection of an intellectual property right is conferred; and the *lex causae*, which is used to refer generically to the law applicable to the dispute.

D.   ALTERNATIVES TO THE TRADITIONAL APPROACH

It is accurate to describe the traditional approach of the common law as 'jurisdiction-selecting': the choice of law process selects a legal system whose rule will govern the issue, and this legal system, more or less automatically, provides the answer. Although it has proved remarkably durable in England and much of the common law world, and although it appears to be found in most civilian systems as well, it is certainly open to criticism. Several points may be suggested. First, the creation of characterization categories is to some extent an artificial process, an attempt to impose order on a market of conflicting legal rules and tending, unless care is taken, to be rigid and blinkered.[90] Secondly, the idea that within

---

[90]   cf *Raiffeisen Zentralbank Österreich AG v Five Star Trading LLC* [2001] EWCA Civ 68, [2001] QB 825.

each of these categories—material validity of contract, personal capacity to marry—there is an intellectual unity which justifies grouping all the sub-issues within the single category not always plausible: should the one law really determine the age at which a person may marry, whether a blood or other relative may be married, whether polygamy or same-sex union is permitted, and the effect of inability or refusal to consummate the marriage? Is this really a single and coherent group of issues? Thirdly, and tellingly, little interest is shown in whether the rule of law actually chosen for application was developed or enacted with the intention that it be applied in the instant case. Fourthly, little or no attempt is made to compare and evaluate the result which would be produced by the rules of law from the various systems which connect to the facts, still less to choose between them. For these among other reasons American jurists,[91] and some others drawing their inspiration from these, have proposed a variety of alternative approaches. These are varied in their content; have received some, but not substantial, judicial support; are more prominent in litigation about inter-state torts than elsewhere; and are more complex, and may be more subtle, than the more mechanical traditional approach. Take for example the case of an inter-state traffic accident, involving cars registered in and drivers and passengers resident in, different states, and let it be supposed that the laws of some, but not all, of these states restrict the type and extent of damages which can be recovered. The mechanical application of a *lex delicti*, probably the law of the place where the tort occurred, may appear too insensitive to the actual and personal facts of the case.[92] One alternative solution would propose that the law having the closest and most real connection to the particular claim be applied. Another would be to ask whether each of the various rules contained in the competing systems were intended by their legislators to be applied to a case with this combination of international elements: a 'rule-selecting' approach. It may be that only one can, in fact, be shown to be designed to apply; if so, there will have been a false or illusory conflict of laws, and the one concerned law will be applied. It may be that more than one was intended to apply to the given facts, at which point the court may settle the conflict of laws by applying its own domestic law, or the 'better' law. The scientific analysis of these alternatives to traditional choice of law is too uncertain to be susceptible to concise analysis, but if and in so far as the approach involves construing conflicting statutes to discern what they

---

[91] Especially Cavers, *The Choice of Law Process* (1965) and (1970) III Hague Recueil 143; Currie, *Selected Essays on the Conflict of Laws* (1963); American Law Institute, *Restatement Second of the Conflict of Laws* (1971).

[92] cf *Babcock v Jackson* 191 NE 2d 279 (1963).

really intend, it taps into an ancient and respectable tradition. But it also works better in a system where the majority of actual rules from which the selection must be made are contained in codes or statutes. For the common law has no legislator and his purpose is, therefore, unknown and unknowable; this contrasts with a statute where *travaux préparatoires* and constitutional theory may shine light on the actual or deemed legislative intention by a process called, if rather curiously, 'governmental interest analysis': call it instead 'searching for the intentions of the legislatures' and it seems much less alien. Whether it could ever be made to work in England is open to doubt;[93] and as English choice of law rules are increasingly contained in legislation, there is relatively little scope for an English judge to follow whatever he may take to be the American way ahead.

E. NEW TECHNOLOGIES AND THE CONFLICT OF LAWS

If private international law is to continue to use connecting factors which select a law to be applied, the greater challenge may yet come from those new technologies which make the operation of a 'law of the place of...' rule seem inappropriate. The growth of the internet as a medium for communication, publicity, trade, and defamation, has yet to be properly examined in the context of the conflict of laws. Opinions vary. At one extreme, there are those who consider that these new media mean that a rethinking of jurisdiction and choice of law cannot be avoided, and the sooner the better; at the other, it is suggested that just as the conflict of laws came to terms with the telephone, telex, and fax, it will simply adapt its basic ideas to the factual challenges of this electronic technology. It is too early to announce the death of the traditional conflict of laws; rules tailor made for new technology risk rapid obsolescence.

If the past is any guide to the future, specific choice of law rules which have reached the end of their shelf life may be superseded by more flexible ones. A couple of examples may illustrate the point. In the private international law of restitution, there is authority for the view that certain claims will be governed by the law of the place of the enrichment.[94] But when claims result from the electronic transfer—except that nothing is transferred—of funds by banks, the place of enrichment may be so fortuitous or artificial that the choice of law rule may become a more

---

[93] Kahn-Freund (1974) III Hague Recueil 147; Fawcett (1982) 31 ICLQ 189.
[94] Dicey, Rule 230(2)(c).

flexible proper law of the obligation to make restitution.[95] In the private international law of intangible property, dealings with negotiable instruments are traditionally governed by the law of the place where the document is. But widely-used, international electronic dealing or settlement systems, and the custodianship of securities, would risk being defeated by the rigid application of this venerable rule of law to such novel methods of dealing. It may be anticipated that new choice of law rules will evolve to apply the most appropriate law to the issues raised by this new technology.

It may be that something similar will be required for general electronic commerce and communication. When contracts are made over the internet, it may be necessary to decide where a contract was made or was broken,[96] or whether a supplier directed his professional or commercial activities to the place of a consumer's domicile.[97] It seems unlikely that a technical analysis of the locations of the customer's computer and internet server, or of the server which hosts the supplier's website, the supplier's computer, and of the various ways in which this information is read or downloaded, and so forth, can offer a solution which is scientifically respectable, comprehensible for the people involved, and jurisprudentially rational. Where it is alleged that a claimant has been defamed by a statement displayed on a web page accessible by computer users from China to Peru, it may be necessary to ask where the tort or torts occurred, or where the damage occurred or where was the event which gave rise to the damage;[98] and the points of contact listed above are now multiplied by the number of people who may have had access to the information. For the purpose of jurisdiction[99] or the recognition of foreign judgments,[100] it may be necessary to ask whether the defendant was present (or carrying on business) in or at a particular place; and the same basic facts of electronic exchange of information may make this a difficult question to answer. For the purposes of regulation of deposit takers and investment businesses, it may be necessary to determine whether an individual carried on business in the United Kingdom.[101] The conflict of laws must adapt itself to this brave new world.

---

[95]   cf *El Ajou v Dollar Land Holdings plc* [1993] 3 All ER 717 (reversed on other grounds [1994] 2 All ER 685 (CA)).

[96]   See CPR r 6.20(5), (6).

[97]   Council Regulation (EC) 44/2001, [2001] OJ L12/1, Art 15.

[98]   ibid Art 5(3). cf *Gutnick v Dow Jones & Co Inc* [2002] HCA 56, (2002) 210 CLR 375.

[99]   CPR r 6.5(6).

[100]   *Adams v Cape Industries plc* [1990] Ch 433 (CA).

[101]   Financial Services and Markets Act 2000, s 418.

A tentative guess may be that the place where the individuals, or their office premises, are located will prove to be more significant than where the hardware is, and that both will be more significant than the notional places where links in the chain of communication may be found. After all, domestic law and the conflict of laws deal with communication and contracts made by telephone, and it appears to be assumed that the place of the telephone subscriber is decisive. It appears not to matter that the offeree left a message on an answering machine on the premises, or in a voicemail box maintained by a telephone company; or that either caller used a mobile phone. Rough and ready locations are ascribed to the persons who communicate, and the legal analysis proceeds from there. For defamation, the eye of the reader is significant, and not the place where or from which his computer 'reads' the information in question.[102] For presence or the carrying on of business, it seems probable that this can indicate only where living, breathing, individuals do what they do, rather than a notional place where information is transferred. This is not to say coming to terms with conflicts issues presented by the new technology will be plain sailing, or that no legislation will be required. But calm creativity from commercial judges may well be all that is required to reach rational solutions.

F. NEW SOURCES OF LAW AND THE CONFLICT OF LAWS

Much the most difficult question is the one which we now address. The system of private international law which we have just described was developed by the common law and clarified by Dicey. To the extent that it was required to accommodate rules of statute law,[103] it generally did so by treating them as though they were no different from rules of common law. English legislation would therefore be applied when, but only when, English law was the *lex causae*; foreign law would be applied when that foreign law was the *lex causae*, and so on. Although an occasional English statute might be applied in a case in which the *lex causae* was not English, the mechanism for this was understood to be that the legislative instruction to the judge overrode and to that extent displaced the result which would have been derived from the ordinary process of choice of

---

[102] *Gutnick v Dow Jones & Co Inc*, n 98, above.

[103] That is, rules of domestic law in statutory form. There was very little legislation of rules of choice of law.

law.[104] There is no doubt that such a direct instruction from legislator to judge may have this effect on an English judge. But this effect could be attributed only to English legislation, and then only where the terms in which the legislation was drafted made it sufficiently clear[105] that it was made as a legislative instruction directed to the judge, by-passing the rules for choice of law. In the great majority of cases, English legislation was simply fitted into the established pattern for choice of law.

But legislation is not only made in England, and instructions to judges do not come only from Westminster. Increasingly, rules of law, including private international law, are established by the organs of the European Union. These rules of law take effect in the English legal order under the authority of the European Communities Act 1972.[106] The law on jurisdiction and the recognition of foreign judgments is, in part at least, governed by such European (which means pan-European) legislation. This applies to civil and commercial matters,[107] and to some issues of family law,[108] and insolvency,[109] but the legislative ambition of the European Union is to widen its area of authority still further. So far as concerns choice of law, contract[110] and tort[111] are subject to such legislation; wills, succession, and matrimonial property are evidently not far behind; and legislation for choice of law for the dissolution of marriage is also on the cards. All this legislation is made with the open and important aim of putting in place a common, pan-European, rule for the matters which it governs. This aim requires that the legislation be given, wherever possible, a common interpretation, and applied to the same effect and in the same circumstances, across the Member States. After all, it would be self-defeating to produce a single legislative text but which was subject to 27 different interpretations or modes of application.

Where the European Union has legislated rules for choice of law, therefore, there is a threshold question whose importance is not always noticed: does the statutory rule apply within the framework of, or independently

---

[104] The traditional terminology of private international law was therefore to refer to these as 'overriding' statutes. A more modern usage is to refer to them as 'mandatory' laws.

[105] Which rarely happened.

[106] Which gave a blank cheque to what is now the European Union to make legislation within the scope of the Treaty of Rome, as amended from time to time.

[107] See chs 3 and 4.

[108] See ch 9.

[109] See ch 10.

[110] See ch 5. Strictly speaking, the Rome Convention is not made under the authority of the European Communities Act 1972, but is a parallel instrument. However, negotiations to replace it with a Regulation which would take effect under the 1972 Act are well advanced.

[111] Including unjust enrichment: see chs 6 and 7, below.

of, the common law structure for choice of law? For example, do the statutory rules for choice of law in contract and tort apply only to issues which the common law rules of characterization regard as issues of contract or tort, or does it apply despite, and without regard to, them? The answer, almost inevitably, must be the latter: these legislative instruments are not made subject to the national rules of private international law of the different Member States, but are designed to operate without regard to them. In other words, the statutory choice of law rule for contracts applies to whatever the European instrument defines as a contractual issue, and without regard to whether the common law rules for choice of law would have regarded the issue as a contractual one. If this is right, the common law principles of characterization, which form the point of departure for the application of the common law principles of choice of law, are themselves displaced and overridden in a case covered by direct legislation of rules of pan-European choice of law. The common law doctrine of *renvoi* has no necessary application, either; but to be on the safe side, European legislation for choice of law usually legislates for its exclusion in express terms.

But what else? Two issues come to mind. One is that there is, as we shall see, a principle of the common law, including its private international law, that a claimant who wishes to do so may formulate his claim against a defendant in contract (and take advantage of the choice of law rules for contracts), and in tort (using the choice of law rules for tort), and as a claim for breach of equitable or fiduciary duty, and so on: and as long as he wins under one of these, he wins overall. We will examine below[112] this really very peculiar state of affairs: but is it equally applicable where the choice of law rules from which the claimant seeks to pick and choose include, or are all, these legislative European ones? The second is that common law private international law only applies a rule of foreign law, indicated as applicable by its rules for choice of law, if it is pleaded and proved by the party seeking to rely on it. Is that relaxed approach consistent with a legislative instruction from the European Union that the law indicated by a statutory choice of law rule 'shall be applied'? Is it really correct to understand this as though it actually said 'shall not be applied unless the party relying on it succeeds in pleading and proving it'? At first sight, that would be a surprising interpretation.

Of course, there is a limit to how far this legislation can be understood to go. Usually it will disclaim any intention to regulate issues of evidence

---

[112] See pp 162–3.

and procedure,[113] but the precise meaning of these expressions, as used in such European legislation, is subject to the same problem of interpretation. The current position is neither clear nor uncontroversial. As matters are understood at present, it is prudent to say this. The common law methodology of private international law is still a sensible starting point for the analysis of issues, and in many cases it will not mislead. But where it becomes entangled with European statutory rules for choice of law, it is necessary to ask whether a particular aspect of that common law methodology would, if applied insensitively, damage the legislative aim of the particular provision. If the answer is that it would, the rule of the common law may be expected to yield to the contrary or contradictory statutory rule. In the end, this is the solution most faithful to the intention of Parliament as conveyed in the European Communities Act 1972; for the identified exercise of Parliamentary sovereignty is the end of every legal debate.

G. THE NATURE OF ADJUDICATION

Already we have seen, and at various points hereafter we will see, that the essence of an adjudication by an English judge is to decide on the issues submitted to him, on the evidence placed before him and, in general if not in absolute terms, between the legal submissions made to him. If he is not asked to decide questions of foreign law, he will not. If he is not asked to apply a foreign law, he will not. If parties bring a dispute before him he will adjudicate without stopping to question whether either might have objected to his jurisdiction. If they argue about whether they made a jurisdiction agreement by which they should be bound, he will deal with that contention and will decree the consequences which follow from it. If a defendant does not appear to a summons, or does not file a defence, there is nothing for the judge to adjudicate, with the result that the claimant, not the judge, enters judgment. In this sense the common law judge is an umpire, not an inquisitor. In fact, the tennis analogy is unexpectedly accurate: the trial judge is the umpire, adjudicating fact and law; the appellate court is referee, leaving the umpire's finding of fact intact, but reviewing his application of law. If there is no dispute, there is nothing to decide. Within the common law this is unremarkable. It is when we enter the realm of private international law that it begins to perturb.

---

[113] Which might well extend to the manner and proof of foreign law.

It is clear that the role of the judiciary in civilian systems is not so confined. The proposition that a judge is confined by the four corners of the facts and matters placed before him does not easily translate into a system in which the judge is a functionary who has been vested with authority, by the legislator, to apply the law. It seems probable that the divergent treatment of foreign law can be traced back to this fundamental difference of approach; but the extent to which the parties are bound by their agreement and will be ordered by a judge to obey its terms will be seen to be another issue on which the common law approach, and the civilian view which underpins the various European Regulations with which we will deal, are at odds with each other. The treatment of jurisdiction agreements is one such area, but what of default judgments? To allow the claimant to enter judgment because the defendant did not oppose the claim is quite different, quite distinct, from the manner in which a judge in a civilian system will still adjudicate, and will give judgment. Too frequently, perhaps, the modern problems of private international law arise from unarticulated assumptions about what judges do and do not do. It may be helpful to bear this in mind, even if it will only add to the sense that it is not just the law, but the fundamentals of procedure, which divide England from the rest of Europe. It is not clear that more and more legislation is aimed at the real target.

Reflecting on the nature of adjudication suggests one further development which may be taking place on the commercial side of private international law. There is an increasing awareness that contractual terms which specify a choice of court, choice for arbitration, or choice of law, or a combination of these, form a discrete agreement laying down the rules for the resolution of disputes, and which should be applied by the court or tribunal in question with a minimum of fuss.[114] They remain valid and binding on the parties even though the legal relationship between them may be contested, and are probably intended to be applied without reference to the general rules for choice of law which might deny their effect. If this development were to become entrenched in the law, choice of law rules would be seen to divide into two groups: choice of law by the parties, and choice of law by the court where the parties have not expressed a choice: traditional choice of law rules, as examined in this book, would apply to the second, but not to the first, category of cases. At present, however, this may be regarded as a tendency, although not yet as established doctrine.[115]

---

[114] See, for example, *Premium Nafta Products Ltd v Fili Shipping Co Ltd* [2007] UKHL 40 at [26], [27].
[115] See further, Briggs, *Agreements on Jurisdiction and Choice of Law* (2008).

2

The Role of the *Lex Fori*

It has been indicated, and will be seen, that the rules for choice of law will sometimes select the *lex fori* to govern the issue in question. The choice of law for divorce,[1] for the distribution of assets in an insolvency,[2] and until recently (and it has not been completely eliminated, even today) for liability in tort[3] was to apply the *lex fori*: these will be examined in the chapters dealing with these subjects. Moreover, questions of trial and pre-trial procedure are governed by the *lex fori*, and the scope of this principle is examined immediately below. It is sometimes said that the application of English domestic law to these substantial areas results in English private international law making less recourse to the doctrine of public policy than it otherwise might. This seems plausible. But in addition to these areas where the *lex causae* is the *lex fori*, there are other instances in which the *lex fori* supervenes, to contradict and negate a choice of law rule pointing to an otherwise-applicable foreign law. A partial summary of the role of the *lex fori* is now given: it examines the role of the *lex fori* in relation to procedural issues, and two areas in which English law will simply apply the *lex fori* in contradiction of any conflicting choice of law.

A. MATTERS REGARDED AS PROCEDURAL

Issues characterized as procedural are governed by English law, and a rule of the *lex causae* which conflicts with it will not be applied, for the *lex causae* governs issues of substance, but not those of procedure. Thus the first level of characterization in any case is to ask whether the issue is one of substance or of procedure.[4] So the question whether an intending litigant has such personality and other competence as to allow it to sue in an English court is a matter of procedure and governed by English law. That said, however, English law will be applied with a measure of flexibility. It does not follow, for example, that juristic persons unfamiliar or unknown to English law may not litigate: although the curator, appointed

---

[1] Ch 9, below.
[2] Ch 10, below.
[3] Ch 6, below.
[4] Dicey, ch 8.

by a Lebanese court, of a disappeared person has been denied *locus standi,*[5] a ruined Hindu temple, which enjoyed legal personality under Indian law, has been recognized as competent to sue.[6] But the trial process is governed by English law. So its nature and form will be as provided by English law and, in principle at least, the question whether or upon what matters witnesses may or may be compelled to give evidence is a matter for English law. It has been held that where English law requires evidence to be in writing, this applies equally in cases where the *lex causae* would not have imposed a similar requirement; but this may be due for reconsideration.[7] More flexibility may apply to the acquisition of evidence for use at trial. There is no rule which prevents the acquisition of evidence by lawful means not known to English law, so the product of depositions taken under United States federal procedure is admissible at trial,[8] as will be documents obtained by disclosure under rules which are more liberal than those of English law. If it is objected that this distorts the balance which each system of civil procedure establishes between the parties to litigation, the answer is that in an extreme case the court may use its inherent power to regulate the trial to prevent it.

If the admissibility of evidence is a procedural issue, it may also be argued that the burden of proof must be also; and that if this is so, the operation of presumptions must also be included within the category. The law is not so clear. Although the meagre balance of authority holds that the burden of proof is a matter for English law as *lex fori,*[9] insistence on this as a matter of principle may distort or denature the substantive right to which it relates. If the *lex contractus* provides that a particular loss will be held to have been caused by the breach unless the defendant proves that it was not, or the *lex delicti* provides that the impairment will be presumed to be attributable to the tortfeasor's breach of duty unless it is proved that it was not, it will appreciably alter the rights of the parties if an English court applies its rules on the burden of proof and disregards the foreign presumption. The present state of the law is uncertain,[10] but its future direction should be to the contraction of the category of

---

[5] *Kamouh v Associated Electrical Industries International Ltd* [1980] QB 199.

[6] *Bumper Development Corp v Commissioner of Police of the Metropolis* [1991] 1 WLR 1362 (CA).

[7] *Leroux v Brown* (1852) 12 CB 801.

[8] *South Carolina Insurance Co v Assurantie Maatschappij De Zeven Provincien NV* [1987] 1 AC 24.

[9] *Re Fuld's Estate (No 3)* [1968] P 675.

[10] In the case of contracts, however, see the Contracts (Applicable Law) Act 1990, Sch 1, Art 14(1).

procedure, at least where this would enhance the effect of the *lex causae* and it can be accomplished without significant adverse effect on the management of the trial process. In this regard, recent decisions of the High Court of Australia are instructive. That court had held that limitation of actions was in general a procedural matter, governed by the *lex fori*, and also that rules of law which fixed a statutory cap on the amount of recoverable damages were procedural, both decisions[11] being in line with traditional common law conflict of laws. It followed that in a tort case, therefore, the impact of these two critical factors would be determined by the accident of where the claimant succeeded in bringing the defendant to court, and not by the location of the accident itself. This was indefensible: there was no reason why the local court should be bound or entitled to apply its rule on these issues to the exclusion of the corresponding rules of the *lex delicti*; and seeing the point the High Court overruled its earlier decisions.[12] There had been a theoretical justification for the earlier decisions, but the ends condemned the means, and the High Court changed its mind. By contrast, the decision of the House of Lords[13] that the assessment of damages was a procedural question, to which provisions of the *lex delicti* capping damages were irrelevant, was regrettable. The judgment purported to find this answer in the legislation.[14] Had this been a tenable reading of what Parliament had actually said, it would have been justifiable, but it was not and is not. All the statute did was to preserve the rule that matters which were procedural before the Act was passed were not affected by its being passed, which should have encouraged the court to consider whether the procedural characterization of assessment of damages was still justifiable as a matter of common law private international law. It is therefore necessary to look a little more closely at the relationship between damages and the category of procedure.

Although the matters in respect of which damages may be recovered are seen as a substantive issue for the *lex causae*,[15] the assessment or quantification of the sums due under each of those heads was traditionally done in accordance with English law.[16] Accordingly, whether a tortfeasor was

[11] *McKain v RW Miller & Co (SA) Pty Ltd* (1991) 174 CLR 1 (limitation); *Stevens v Head* (1993) 176 CLR 433 (financial cap on damages).

[12] *John Pfeiffer Pty Ltd v Rogerson* [2000] HCA 36, (2000) CLR 203 at [97]–[103].

[13] *Harding v Wealands* [2006] UKHL 32, [2007] 2 AC 1.

[14] Private International Law (Miscellaneous Provisions) Act 1995, s 14(3).

[15] *Boys v Chaplin* [1971] AC 356.

[16] ibid; also *D'Almeida Araujo Lda v Becker & Co Ltd* [1953] 2 QB 329. But in the case of contract claims, the Rome Convention (given effect by the Contracts (Applicable Law) Act

liable to pay damages for loss of earnings, loss of earning capacity, medical expenses, pain and suffering, and loss of amenity, and so on, was a heads of damage question answered by the *lex delicti*, but for those heads available under the *lex delicti*, the calculation—both its basis and the arithmetic— was done by reference to English law methods. Whilst that guarded an English court from having to award damages at astronomic[17] or miserly levels, the dislocation was undeniable, especially if English rules of quantification were ever applied to a head of damages unknown to English law. It also depended upon a line of division which was not always straight-forward. For example, French law allows the victim of a tort to return to court for a further assessment of damages if the original injury turns out to be more severe than was predicted and compensated at trial. If such a claim is brought before an English court, it may be necessary to ask whether this is to be regarded as a substantive or a procedural issue; but it would be better by far if the question did not need to be asked at all. For a court ought to be able to quantify according to the principles of the *lex causae* where evidence of foreign law allows it to,[18] and subject to its right to disapply foreign law and apply its own, on the ground of public policy, wherever this appears to be a necessary corrective. So far as the law of tort was concerned, the House of Lords held that the division of damages into substance and procedure was confirmed and petrified by statute.[19] But when Regulation (EC) 864/2007 is in force,[20] the extent of tortious damages will be determined by the *lex delicti*.[21] As the statutory choice of law rule for contracts now encourages the court to allow the *lex contractus* to govern the grant of remedies to the maximum extent possible,[22] where there still is a residual rule of common law private international law that the assessment of damages is a procedural matter, these legislative developments may yet embolden a court to reconsider it.

The same general approach applies to other remedies. It was sometimes said that an English court would grant remedies only when English law, *qua* procedural *lex fori*, considers them to be available, but would not do

---

1990), provides by art 10(1)(c) that the *lex contractus* should be applied so far as the assessment of damages is governed by rules of law.

[17] *Mitchell v McCulloch* 1976 SC 1.

[18] However, if under the *lex causae*, damages would be fixed by a jury award, it may be impossible to give evidence of the foreign law on quantum to an English court.

[19] *Harding v Wealands* [2006] UKHL 32, [2007] 2 AC 1, so interpreting Private International Law (Miscellaneous Provisions) Act 1995, s 14(3).

[20] See, ch 6 below. The date of coming into force is explained at ch 6, p 201, below.

[21] Article 15(a), (c).

[22] Contracts (Applicable Law) Act 1990, Sch 1, art 10(1)(c).

so if the English remedy did not dovetail with the particular right under the *lex causae* for which it is claimed, nor if the remedy, though notionally existing in the *lex causae* and the *lex fori* would not in the particular case be granted as a matter of English law. Thus an English court dismissed a claim brought by a Greek daughter for an order that her father constitute a dowry for her, as no English remedy even remotely corresponded to so foreign a right;[23] and at common law, an English court would not order specific performance of a foreign contract in circumstances where English law would not grant it for an English one, even though no such objection were found in the *lex causae*. On the other hand, the statutory choice of law rule for contracts now encourages the court to allow the *lex contractus* to govern the grant of remedies to the maximum extent possible[24] and Regulation (EC) 864/2007 will do likewise for tort and unjust enrichment claims to which it applies. Moreover, the constructive approach taken by the Court of Appeal to litigation by entities not known to English law[25] may also be prayed in aid of a constructive and flexible application of English remedies beyond the bounds of their usual limits. It is probably accurate, if not entirely helpful, to say that the law is in a transitional phase.

I. INTERLOCUTORY PROCEDURE

An important sub-category of procedure is that of interim and interlocutory relief: this is ordered by an English court according to English law and represents one of the main prizes at stake when issues of jurisdiction are fought.[26] An English court has no power to make orders unknown to English civil procedural law; but equally, it will not withhold relief even if the only connection to England is that the trial is taking place there. Certain specific limitations on the power of the court may be imposed by international agreement or by the principles of comity. For example, an order freezing a defendant's assets worldwide, the making of which is within the power of an English court, should probably not be made in relation to assets within the territorial jurisdiction of another Member State bound by the Brussels Regulation[27] unless the English court is seised of the substantive proceedings,[28] or (perhaps) unless the respondent is

---

[23] *Phrantzes v Argenti* [1960] 2 QB 19 (CA).
[24] Contracts (Applicable Law) Act 1990, Sch 1, art 10(1)(c).
[25] *Bumper Development Corp v Commissioner of Police of the Metropolis* [1991] 1 WLR 1362 (CA).
[26] See generally Collins, *Essays in International Litigation and the Conflict of Laws* (1994), ch 1.
[27] Council Regulation (EC) 44/2001, on which see ch 3, below.
[28] Case C–391/95 *Van Uden Maritime BV v Deco-Line* [1998] ECR I–7091.

resident in England. And an injunction ordering a respondent to discontinue an action in a foreign court, which is no more than an instance of the power of an English court to make procedural orders against someone within its personal jurisdiction, will be made with a measure of restraint which reflects the competing interest of the foreign court in the matter.[29] But in all cases the relief is governed wholly by English procedural law.

B. MATTERS FORMERLY REGARDED AS PROCEDURAL

Because of their potential to apply a disproportionately English gloss to a case not substantively governed by English law, certain issues which were once regarded as procedural have lost that characterization. To this list might be added the assessment of damages in matters falling within the European rules for choice of law for contract, tort, and unjust enrichment, but these have already been examined[30] and are not repeated here.

I. THE CURRENCY OF JUDGMENT

The first results from a judge-made alteration to the common law. Until 1976 an English court had no power to award damages in a foreign currency, even if the loss was sustained in that currency: the rule of English law, regarded as procedural, was that the claim was quantified in sterling as at the date of the claim and judgment, years afterwards, would be for that sterling sum.[31] This began to endanger the role of England as a centre for commercial litigation when the currency began to devalue. Consequently, in two cases in the 1970s, it was held that if, in effect, the loss was sustained in a foreign currency, an English court should be able to give judgment in that foreign currency or in its sterling equivalent as at the date of judgment.[32] A claimant cannot simply ask a court to give judgment in a foreign currency of his choice, but if the loss is sustained in that currency, there is no longer any reason for reluctance to acknowledge it. It is a good illustration of how a court was prepared to re-examine the characterization of an issue as procedural when the interests of justice demanded it. It stands in sharp contrast to the decision in *Harding v Wealands*.[33]

---

[29] *Airbus Industrie GIE v Patel* [1999] 1 AC 119.

[30] p 39 above.

[31] Although the judgment would carry interest, and interest rates will bear some relationship to local currency values.

[32] *Miliangos v George Frank (Textiles) Ltd* [1976] AC 443; *Services Europe Atlantique Sud (SEAS) v Stockholms Rederaktiebolag Svea of Stockholm (The Despina R)* [1979] AC 685.

[33] [2006] UKHL 32, [2007] 2 AC 1.

2. LIMITATION OF ACTIONS

Until the Foreign Limitation Periods Act 1984, the approach to time bars
and their impact on litigation was complicated. A provision which acted
by extinguishing the claim, by prescribing it, was regarded as substantive, and such a provision found that the *lex causae* was applicable in an
English court. By contrast, a provision which prevented the bringing of
proceedings, by limiting the right to being an action, was regarded as procedural, with the result that such a provision of the *lex fori* was applied by
an English court, but such a provision contained in the *lex causae* would
not be. English time-bar provisions are enacted in the form of limitation
statutes, not prescriptions. As a result, English limitation periods, and
foreign rules of prescription, were applied cumulatively, with the shorter
of the two having decisive effect. The justification for this, otherwise than
as the outcome of an arid exercise in theory, was impossible to see. The
Foreign Limitation Periods Act 1984[34] pre-empted reform by the courts,
by providing that time-bar provisions are governed by the *lex causae* and
not by English law unless it is the *lex causae*. This does not make time-bars
substantive; it applies a statutory rule without regard to characterization.
English law will still define the point at which proceedings were begun,
even where the period is measured by a foreign law.[35] English law will also
define the time period in cases where the application of the new statutory
rule would be contrary to public policy.[36] Public policy, as defined by the
Act, includes cases where the operation of the new rule would do undue
hardship to a party, actual or potential. So a period which is too short, and
especially one which does not allow for postponement if the claimant is too
ill to make the decision to litigate, may offend public policy; conversely, a
period which is excessively long, given that an English trial relies on oral
testimony, may also be offensive to public policy. Although the wording
of the Act is hardly pellucid, it has been held that the effect of the public
policy provision, when applicable, is that the English time period applies
without further ado.[37] The lamentable provision that there is no recourse
to *renvoi* on questions of limitation[38] is a dim-witted absurdity. One may
charitably suppose that its purpose was to ensure that once the rules for
choice of law, including any *renvoi* which they may make and the evidence
of foreign law allows, have identified a domestic law for application to the

---

[34] Section 1.
[35] Section 4.
[36] Section 2.
[37] *Arab Monetary Fund v Hashim* [1996] 1 Lloyd's Rep 589, 599–600 (CA).
[38] Section 1(5).

merits, the time-bar provisions of that law will also apply. But if that is what was meant, it is regrettable that the Act does not say so. For it can be read as providing that the law to govern limitation is identified and fixed before any question arises of *renvoi* to another law on the issues of substance may be addressed. Such dissociation of limitation from rules which actually resolve the substantive question is bereft of rational justification.

C. PENAL LAWS AND REVENUE CLAIMS

The second broad area in which English private international law applies the *lex fori* and disregards any provision of the *lex causae* is in the area of penal, revenue, and other public laws: the rule is usually stated as providing that an English court will not enforce a foreign penal law or a foreign revenue law; the status of the third category of other public laws is less secure but, subject to careful definition, is wholly sound in principle.[39] The identification of a penal or revenue law is generally straightforward, although it is to be observed that it is an area in which the law arguably requires the process of classification to focus on a rule of law and not on an issue; but more difficulty is encountered in understanding the limits of enforcement, which is prohibited, as distinct from recognition, which is not.

A penal law is one which imposes a fine or forfeit or other obligation upon a lawbreaker and is ordered to be made to the state. Its identification as penal is a matter for English law as *lex fori*.[40] It is improbable that a law which requires a payment to be made to a private individual is a penal law, even if the avowed purpose of the law is to punish wrongdoing by ordering a payment which is a multiple of any loss suffered, or which is unrelated to any loss: on this basis the Roman law action which the owner had against a thief for twice or fourfold the value of the thing stolen, or the award of damages trebling the loss inflicted on the victim by violation of US anti-trust laws, would not be considered as penal laws whose enforcement is prohibited by the common law.[41] It appears to follow that where a regulatory body brings a civil action on behalf of a class of persons who have sustained losses at the hands of a criminal wrongdoer, this will not involve the enforcement of a penal law. But it is irrelevant that the defendant has agreed to make the payment, so the forfeit of a voluntary bail bond

---

[39] Dicey, Rule 3.

[40] *Huntington v Attrill* [1893] AC 150.

[41] But in the case of multiple damages, statute precludes enforcement: Protection of Trading Interests Act 1980, s 5; *Lewis v Eliadis* [2003] EWCA Civ 1758, [2004] 1 WLR 692.

involves enforcement of a penal law;[42] and the payment of an agreed sum to prevent prosecution will be treated likewise.

It is not very illuminating to define a revenue law as a tax law, but it is hard to improve on it; and in this context the rule is sometimes described as the 'revenue rule'. Income and capital taxes, sales and service taxes will be revenue laws, and their enforcement cannot be by action in the English courts. More marginal cases may arise from the collection of state medical insurance payments from employees, for it may be thought that if the state provides a benefit in return for the payment, the demand is not a tax but a charge for services; the same analysis may be applied to payments made to a state monopoly utility. But such an argument would be misconceived, not least because it is capable, if with a little strain, of being applied to all income taxes: every taxpayer is said to get something—national defence, social security, that sort of thing—in return for his payment. The more incisive question is whether the payment is voluntary in the sense that the law, which imposes the charge on a person who satisfies the criterion for payment, permits the person to avoid liability to pay by renouncing the benefit. Whatever the practicalities otherwise may be, if a person is not entitled to disclaim the right to take advantage of the hospitals, national defence, and state television channels etc, which are paid for and provided to him from his income taxes and national health insurance and licence fee, and thereby obtain release from liability to pay for them, the laws will be revenue laws. Likewise, if he is not entitled to renounce whatever it is which is provided to the public from value added tax takings and thereby be released from liability to pay VAT, this identifies the law as a revenue law. The same principle applies to a state utility supply. If a homeowner is legally entitled to tell the water utility that he does not want its services, and may as a result avoid the liability to pay a charge, any payment is not made under a revenue law, no matter how unlikely it is that the person could take advantage of his technical freedom of contract. But if the owner of a television remains liable in law to pay the licence fee even though he forswears any reception of the state broadcasting service, the payment is demanded under a revenue law. It is nothing to the point that a householder can avoid liability for payment by having no television, or that an employee can avoid income tax by giving up his job, or that a customer can avoid VAT by not buying shoes, for on that basis only death duties would be true revenue laws. Rather, the question is whether the person may satisfy the condition which renders him liable to tax, but still

---

[42] *United States of America v Inkley* [1989] QB 255 (CA).

renounce the benefit which is offered in return for the payment. If he cannot, it is a tax law and not a contractual liability. Or if there is a better test, no-one has yet identified it.

English private international law prevents only the enforcement of such laws; it does not deny them recognition[43] unless they are so offensive that even to notice that they have been enacted would be repellent to public policy.[44] It is easy to see the action as an enforcement one when a foreign attorney general sues for sums due on a dishonoured bail bond, or when a foreign collector of taxes sues for unpaid taxes.[45] As the exclusionary rule also applies to indirect enforcement, the analysis is no different if the state first obtains a judgment in regular civil form from its courts, and then seeks recognition of the judgment and enforcement of the judgment debt: a coat of whitewash will not deceive the court.[46] By contrast, recognition of a penal or revenue law is unobjectionable, so that if performance of a contract is made illegal under the criminal law of the place where performance is due, that will render the contract unenforceable in the English courts: a result which would be impossible if the penal law were to be denied even recognition.[47] The problematic cases arise where indirect enforcement rubs up against recognition, not least because some loosely-reasoned authorities have stated that if judgment in the action 'would increase the likelihood' that a tax would be paid, the action is prohibited by this rule.[48] This is silly. For example, a claim brought by a seller or provider of services upon an invoice which contained an element of value added or service tax might be thought to involve the indirect (because brought at the instance of a person obliged by law to levy the charge and collect the dues on behalf of the state, to which an account must be made) enforcement (because it seeks an order to pay money which in law belongs to the defendant) of a revenue law. But it has also been used to justify the dismissal of a claim, brought by a company against a director who looted its assets, on the spurious ground that sums recovered would be used to discharge a corporation tax liability.[49] For the supposed rule to license

---

[43] *Re Emery's Investment Trusts* [1959] Ch 410.
[44] cf *Kuwait Airways Corp v Iraqi Airways Co (Nos 4 and 5)* [2002] UKHL 19, [2002] 2 AC 883, where the court refused to recognize Iraqi legislation purporting to dissolve Kuwait and to seize the assets of the Kuwaiti state airline, in flagrant breach of international law.
[45] *Government of India v Taylor* [1955] AC 491.
[46] *United States of America v Harden* (1963) 41 DLR (2d) 721 (Can SC).
[47] *Ralli Bros v Compania Naviera Sota y Aznar* [1920] 2 KB 287; *Regazzoni v K C Sethia (1944) Ltd* [1958] AC 301.
[48] *Rossano v Manufacturers' Life Insurance Co Ltd* [1963] 2 QB 352; *QRS 1 ApS v Fransden* [1999] 1 WLR 2169 (CA).
[49] ibid.

theft from a company is anarchic, revolting even.[50] It could not possibly have been correct, quite apart from its defiance of clear and contradictory authority.[51] If it had been correct, and the court were to deduct the tax element from the judgment sum, the claimant would presumably still have to account to the state for the due percentage of this reduced sum, which would then have to be further reduced, and so on, *ad absurdam*; a similar analysis would make impossible an action to be brought by an employee for any sum due as unpaid but taxable wages. *Res tota ridicula est.* A simple test would simply ask whether the right upon which the claim is founded, the *jus actionis*, was a revenue law, or upon some other, such as a contractual promise to pay, or the liability of a thief or other wrongdoer that he account for his wrong, or for the delivery up of property. If the claim may be pleaded and sustained without mention of any tax law, it is very hard indeed to see that it will involve the enforcement of a revenue law. Similar care, and a similar approach, will be required in relation to governmental seizure of property, where close attention needs to be paid to whether law which provided for the seizure is being pleaded as due for enforcement[52] or is merely part of the history of an accomplished fact, with the claim being based on a property right.[53]

To understand this material as enshrining a rule where the *lex fori* supervenes to defeat a claim which was otherwise well founded under a foreign *lex causae* may not, however, be helpful. It may be more instructive to reformulate the rule as providing that penal and revenue claims are governed by the *lex fori*: if the claim is a penal or revenue one, it must be founded on the domestic law of the court in which it is brought. So liability for a crime may be enforceable under the English law of extradition, or under those rare English laws which criminalize conduct taking place overseas, or under those even rarer English laws which give effect in England to the criminal laws of another state. A revenue claim may be enforceable by recourse to the provisions of a treaty with the foreign state given effect in England by domestic legislation. Seen in these terms the application of the *lex fori* in this context is part of, and does not contradict, the rules for choice of law in the conflict of laws; and the critical question would be whether the *claim* should be characterized as a penal or a revenue one, and not whether the *law* relied on is a penal or a revenue one. Acceptance of this reformulation would have the beneficial effect of

---

[50] *Williams & Humbert Ltd v W & H Trade Marks (Jersey) Ltd* [1986] AC 368.
[51] *Re Norway's Application (Nos 1 and 2)* [1990] 1 AC 723.
[52] *Banco de Vizcaya v Don Alfonso de Borbon y Austria* [1935] 1 KB 140.
[53] *Williams & Humbert Ltd v W & H Trade Marks (Jersey) Ltd* [1986] AC 368; *Islamic Republic of Iran v Barakat Galleres Ltd* [2007] EWCA Civ 1374.

integrating this collection of cases into the mainstream of the conflict of laws, and would end their having to be regarded as some sort of overriding exception to the general scheme for choice of law.

As indicated above, some authority maintains that there is a third category, of 'other public laws'.[54] It seems rational that claims based on and calling for the enforcement of foreign laws which are analogous to penal and revenue laws, such as confiscation and nationalization, exchange control, laws regulating the duties of those employed in the security services, and so forth should be dealt with similarly, although whether it is beneficial to call these 'other public laws' must be open to doubt. On the other hand, if a householder is obliged by law to pay water or other utility charges, whether he wishes to take the service or not, to a private or privatized company, it would be unfortunate if the private character of the payee meant the payment was not under a revenue law. If it may be treated as quasi-revenue, or as an other public law, the difficulty goes away.

However, some difficulty still remains if the rule is stated as one which asks whether the right or relationship relied on is a private law right or a public one. For example, such an approach would allow a foreign state to sue one of its spies who, in breach of his service agreement or fiduciary duty, has spilled the beans and made a profit. It would allow a repressive government to sue the liberation movement which had caused physical damage to the infrastructure of the state, relying on the ordinary law of tort. There is an understandable reluctance to allow courts to be used by a foreign secret service,[55] or to allow a state to sue those who seek to cause it harm;[56] and the fact that the claim may be got up as a private law action of the kind any master could bring against a disloyal servant, or any property owner against a trespasser who did damage, or any victim of a conspiracy to injure its economic interests by unlawful means, is nothing to the particular point. For this reason, the High Court of Australia[57] has declined to adjudicate on claims brought to vindicate a foreign 'governmental interest', an expression which is usefully flexible. Although the English courts have not yet adopted it, it seems that it will only be a matter of time before they find themselves driven to the same conclusion.[58]

---

[54] *AG (UK) v Heinemann Publishers Australia Pty Ltd* (1988) 165 CLR 30; *AG of New Zealand v Ortiz* [1984] AC 1 (CA); Private International Law (Miscellaneous Provisions) Act 1995, s 14(3).

[55] *AG (UK) v Heinemann Publishers Australia Pty Ltd* (1988) 165 CLR 30.

[56] *Mbasogo v Logo Ltd* [2006] EWCA Civ 1370, [2007] QB 846.

[57] *AG (UK) v Heinemann Publishers Australia Pty Ltd* (1988) 165 CLR 30.

[58] *Equatorial Guinea v Bank of Scotland International Ltd* [2006] UKPC 7; also *Islamic Republic of Iran v Barakat Galleries Ltd* [2007] EWCA Civ 1374.

D. PUBLIC POLICY AND RELATED DOCTRINES

At various points in our examination of private international law we will encounter the proposition that a particular result otherwise provided by choice of law will be departed from by reason of public policy. It is helpful to set out some lines of distinction to demarcate what properly is regarded as public policy and what is not. The public policy engaged is only ever that of English law, but where it is engaged it overrides the application of a foreign *lex causae*. As an illustration which relates to the previous material, if an English court is called upon to recognize a foreign law which is so repellent to English standards that even to take notice of it is intolerable, it will be ignored. So if a defendant resists a claim for the return of property by relying on a law which divested the claimant on grounds of race or religion, the defence will be struck out on the ground that, as a matter of English public policy, the law is too wicked even to be recognized as datum.[59] Less dramatically, if it is alleged that a contract is unenforceable as illegal in the place of performance, the illegality being one which prevents the performance of acts on openly racial grounds, the law may be denied recognition and the contract enforced according to its terms. With that introduction, we may examine three separate, although linked, issues: where English public policy overrides a foreign rule; where an English statute precludes the application of a foreign rule; and the public policy of a foreign law.

I. ENGLISH PUBLIC POLICY

As indicated above, where foreign rules are picked out for application by choice of law rules, a rule of the *lex causae* will not be applied if its content is repugnant to English public policy, or if the result of its application in the given context is contrary to English public policy. 'Public policy' in this sense refers to the fundamental values of English law. although it is often said that it generally has a restrictive meaning, the Human Rights Act 1998 will broaden the scope of, but also provide a clearer and more precise definitional basis for, English public policy.[60] The history of

---

[59] *Oppenheimer v Cattermole* [1976] AC 249; *Kuwait Airways Corp v Iraq Airways Co (Nos 4 and 5)* [2002] UKHL 19, [2002] 2 AC 883.

[60] Although it may be more correct to understand the Human Rights Act 1998 as applying part of the *lex fori*, by virtue of a direct instruction from legislature to judge, rather than as something which is dependent on the common law doctrine of public policy.

prejudice has given a few ghastly illustrations. A law depriving a racial group of its property,[61] or one invalidating marriage between members of a dominant ethnic group and a subjugated ethnic group will, or should, be regarded as so offensive to English public policy that it will be treated as if it did not exist and had never been enacted, no matter the context in which it arises; alternatively, a court will refuse to receive evidence of such foreign law and will therefore not be in a position to apply it. Iraqi laws purporting to seize Kuwaiti assets in time of war and in defiance of United Nations sanctions which demanded to have mandatory effect have also been denied recognition.[62] To take a less obvious example, it has been held that although a contract containing a covenant restricting the freedom of a party to take employment may be valid and enforceable according to the *lex causae*, it may still conflict with the English doctrine that such agreements are illegal restraints of trade;[63] and the English rule of freedom may prevail. It has yet to be held that a rule of foreign 'religious' law, which entitled a husband to repudiate his marriage and divorce his wife, or to refuse his wife a divorce on religious grounds, should not be recognized, but discrimination on grounds of sex is peculiarly offensive when 'justified' by the obscurantist nonsense of religion.

By contrast with unconditionally immoral or evil laws, others may need to be evaluated in their context and the facts shown to have a sufficient connection to England before any similar conclusion can be drawn about them. For instance, to recognize a law giving a husband, but not a wife, a unilateral right to divorce should be considered to be contrary to public policy when said to apply to a wife who is resident in England[64] but may, just possibly, be regarded differently, and not disqualified from application, when applied to parties who have no material connection with England. Likewise, a law which allows marriage of uncle and niece will not be regarded as so objectionable that it will be overridden by English public policy when the marriage has nothing to do with England.[65] Much confusion is reduced when the two senses of public policy—the first absolute, the second contextual—are distinguished; and it may be that the restraint of trade example considered above would be better seen as falling into the contextual category.

---

[61] *Oppenheimer v Cattermole* [1976] AC 249.

[62] *Kuwait Airways Corp v Iraq Airways Co (Nos 4 and 5)* [2002] UKHL 19, [2002] 2 AC 883.

[63] *Rousillon v Rousillon* (1880) 14 Ch D 351.

[64] cf *Chaudhary v Chaudhary* [1985] Fam 19 (CA).

[65] *Cheni v Cheni* [1965] P 85.

Another way to express this idea might be that the first category of public policy applies whatever the *lex causae* or connection to England, whereas the second applies only if the issue has a real and substantial connection with England. This could be seen either as a disguised choice of law rule, or as analogous to the 'sufficient connection' principle which must be satisfied before an English court will grant certain forms of equitable relief. And if this were to be accepted, attention could be focused on the question which ought to lie at the heart of the analysis, namely what degree of connection with England ought to be required before this contextual form of public policy would be invoked.

2. ENGLISH STATUTES WITH OVERRIDING EFFECT

The operation of public policy amounts to the superimposition of a rule of common law on the choice of law process. The statutory equivalent is superficially similar, but actually very different. Where English legislation is framed in such a way that it instructs the judge to apply it to any case which falls within its terms, without regard to choice of law, it applies by virtue of parliamentary sovereignty: the legislator has in this specific instance overridden the general rules of the conflict of laws.[66] Now what Parliament can do expressly it can also do by implication, albeit that deducing the intention where Parliament has been delphic is difficult. As a very general guide to the identification of parliamentary intention, a rule which may be interpreted as one of absolutely fundamental importance and insistence may be held to override in every case falling within its terms; one which may be thought of as less imperative applies only if the facts disclose enough of a connection to England for it to be supposed that this is what the legislator had in mind. Whether the Human Rights Act 1998 will be applicable in an English court regardless of the connection of the matter to England, or only if the facts have a sufficient connection to England, remains uncertain. On the face of it, its standards are universal, and should be applied by an English judge even though there was no significant connection to England. However, the House of Lords has held that it does not apply in full force to prevent the recognition of an American judgment obtained by proceedings which, had they taken place in England, would plainly have violated the right to a fair trial guaranteed by Article 6 of the European Convention on Human Rights.[67] It is difficult

---

[66] eg Carriage of Goods by Sea Act 1971.
[67] *Barnette v United States* [2004] UKHL 37, [2004] 1 WLR 2241.

to accept this as correct,[68] as the judicial decision to enforce a foreign judgment is one by which an English public authority affects the civil rights of a person. But as the United States is not party to the Convention, it would undeniably be odd to treat its judgments as though it were.

3. PUBLIC POLICY OF FOREIGN COUNTRIES

No mechanism exists at common law for applying the rules of public policy of a country whose law is not the *lex causae*, or one of the *leges causae*. It is true that statute may provide what the common law cannot reach: in the contractual context, Article 7(1) of the Rome Convention[69] offered the opportunity to do this very thing. Problems of uncertainty laid aside, there is a good case to be made for such a statutory provision. The *lex causae* may be such by reason of the parties' choice; and they may have made the choice for the very purpose of avoiding the law which would otherwise have applied, and a particular provision of that law which is regarded as of mandatory effect, such as one protecting consumers from unfair or unequal contractual terms, or protecting investors from unauthorized providers of financial services. One way of dealing with such evasive choices of law is to annul the right to choose, or to limit the right to choose,[70] the law. But another would have been to maintain the choice of law (which may have been for a variety of reasons, not all of them improper), while allowing the public policy of another country to be applied. But perhaps because it would have been an unprecedented novelty for English judges, and a disconcerting novelty for litigants, Article 7(1) was not enacted into English law.[71] Of course, where a provision of the *lex causae* is described under that law as, or as enshrining, a rule of public policy, there is no reason whatever for an English court to decline to give it effect, for it is still part of the *lex causae*, whatever else it may be.

---

[68] It appears to contradict *Pellegrini v Italy* (2002) 35 EHRR 2 (ECtHR).

[69] Contracts (Applicable Law) Act 1990, Sch 1.

[70] By providing, as in some circumstances the Rome Convention does for the additional application of certain laws from third countries, often called 'mandatory rules'.

[71] Contracts (Applicable Law) Act 1990, s 2(2).

3

Jurisdiction of English Courts

A. TYPES OF JURISDICTION

To say that a court has jurisdiction means that the law has conferred on it the power to hear and determine a case against a defendant.[1] It must have jurisdiction over the subject matter of the claim, and personal jurisdiction over the defendant to it. But in English law, it does not follow that, just because a court has jurisdiction, it will invariably exercise it at the behest of the claimant. A pervasive characteristic of the common law approach to the conflict of jurisdictions is that a court may on application by the defendant decline to exercise the jurisdiction which it admittedly has, with the result that the claimant, if he wishes to sue, may have to have recourse to a foreign court. By contrast with this common law flexibility, where jurisdiction is conferred on the courts by the Brussels Regulation, Council Regulation (EC) 44/2001,[2] this discretion is mostly excluded. Such discretionary matters, however, impinge only on the complex rules which govern the personal jurisdiction of the court. By contrast with this, the topic of subject matter jurisdiction, which is not usually a problem in English private international law, contains no element of discretion. It needs to be examined at the outset of any account of jurisdiction.

I. SUBJECT MATTER JURISDICTION

There are few instances in which an English court lacks jurisdiction over the subject matter of a claim, but where this is so it is irrelevant that the parties may be willing to submit to the personal jurisdiction of the court: absence of subject matter jurisdiction lies beyond their power or control. A potentially difficult question, however, will arise where the common law denies subject matter jurisdiction, but the Regulation nevertheless ascribes personal jurisdiction over the defendant.

---

[1] See generally Dicey, chs 11 and 12; Briggs and Rees, *Civil Jurisdiction and Judgments* (4th edn, 2005) *passim*.
[2] [2001] OJ L12/1. See the next section below for details of these jurisdictional instruments.

At common law a court had no jurisdiction to determine title to foreign land, and therefore no jurisdiction to hear claims which involved determining a question of title.[3] This view is shared by many systems. Statute has modified the common law rule, so that a court may now hear a claim in tort which relates to foreign land unless it is principally concerned with title to that land.[4] The result is that if the defence to an allegation of trespass is that the defendant had a licence to enter, or the defence to a claim for nuisance is that the claimant had no title to the land, the court will be unable to adjudicate the claim. It is unnecessary to ask whether the exclusionary rule would apply where no question arises of legal title but equitable title is disputed, such as a claim about shares in the beneficial ownership of land subject to a trust. As a matter of ancient authority, where there was a contract or an equity between the parties, the court had jurisdiction to adjudicate on and enforce the personal obligations arising from it, even if the subject of this personal right was foreign land.[5] So a court may determine the shares in a tenancy in common in foreign land arising from the trust of that land and require the parties to behave accordingly, and may decree the specific enforcement of a contract to mortgage or to convey foreign land. Indeed, the statutory reform mentioned above was required because there is no contract or equity between tortfeasors, and this principle could not be used in the context of a tort committed in relation to foreign land. Sparse but persuasive authority[6] also held that a court lacked jurisdiction at common law to adjudicate the validity of foreign patents or copyright, especially where issues of validity were raised for, save where covered by international treaty, the grant or extent of such rights was a matter for the foreign sovereign alone. The better view may, however, be that the court does not lack jurisdiction, so that its adjudication would be a nullity, but should accede to an application to decline to exercise its jurisdiction.

Where the Brussels Regulation gives the court personal jurisdiction over the defendant, it is hard to say whether the court is still at liberty to find that it lacks subject matter jurisdiction, and to dismiss the proceedings for that reason. Analysis of the question is best postponed until the

---

[3] *British South Africa Co v Companhia de Moçambique* [1893] AC 602; *Hesperides Hotels Ltd v Aegean Turkish Holidays Ltd* [1979] AC 508; cf Civil Jurisdiction and Judgments Act 1982, s 30.

[4] ibid.

[5] *Penn v Baltimore* (1750) 1 Ves Sen 444.

[6] *Potter v Broken Hill Pty Ltd* (1906) 3 CLR 479; *Norbert Steinhardt & Son v Meth* (1961) 105 CLR 440; *Tyburn Productions Ltd v Conan Doyle* [1991] Ch 75.

scheme of the Regulation has been examined, but even then the answer will not be completely clear to see.[7]

2. PERSONAL JURISDICTION

The principles of state and diplomatic immunity limit the exercise of jurisdiction over non-commercial claims brought against states and diplomats.[8] Indeed, in these cases it may be subject-matter jurisdiction, rather than personal jurisdiction, which is lacking, on the footing that once the immunity is pleaded, scrutiny of the act of a foreign sovereign lies beyond the competence of the English court. In relation to international organizations, the instrument establishing the organization as a juridical person for the purposes of English law will usually also define the extent of any immunity from the processes of the court.[9] If the organization is not accorded personality by English legislation, its personality may still be recognized if this has been conferred under the law of another state, rather as if it were a corporation created under the law of that state.[10]

Subject to that exception, a court will have jurisdiction over a defendant when process has been or is deemed to have been served on him, and rules of jurisdiction *in personam* are therefore rules which specify whether and when it is lawful to serve the defendant.[11] As a matter of common law, any defendant present within the territorial jurisdiction of the court was liable to be served with process by or on behalf of the claimant, who might do so as of right; but no defendant was liable to be served if he was outside England. To overcome this difficulty, Rules of Court permitted a claimant to apply for permission to serve process on a defendant out of the jurisdiction: the cases in which this may be done are currently set out in Part 6 of the Civil Procedure Rules (CPR).[12] For convenience, these provisions are referred to as 'traditional' rules of jurisdiction, even though some are very recent indeed.

Since 1987, a series of European instruments, taking effect in English law and operating alongside the traditional rules, has radically altered the jurisdiction of English courts in civil and commercial matters. In such

[7] See, p 89 below.

[8] State Immunity Act 1978; *Holland v Lampen-Wolfe* [2000] 1 WLR 1573 (HL).

[9] International Organisations Act 1968.

[10] *Arab Monetary Fund v Hashim (No 3)* [1991] 2 AC 114. What happens if it is given legal personality under the laws of more than one state is not very clear.

[11] For the procedure for effecting service see Civil Procedure Rules 1998 (CPR) Pt 6. Personal service is still the most common method.

[12] In force from 2 May 2000, replacing Rules of the Supreme Court, Order 11. Care must be taken to notice alterations to the wording of these provisions from one incarnation to the next.

cases, a claimant must first consider whether these instruments confer jurisdiction on, or withhold it from, an English court. Only if these instruments are wholly inapplicable, or if they themselves make reference to the traditional jurisdictional rules, will the latter apply. For civil or commercial disputes, these European rules are at the heart of the subject, the traditional rules left to apply only in the gaps which they leave. The coexistence between these jurisdictional systems, each complex and founded on assumptions which are not always articulated, leaves a number of tricky issues unresolved.

In this chapter we examine jurisdiction over defendants in civil or commercial matters, this being the principal issue of the conflict of jurisdictions. Jurisdiction in family matters, the administration of estates, bankruptcy and insolvency, and so on is more conveniently treated alongside choice of law in the chapters which deal with those substantive topics. In summary, where the dispute arises as a civil or commercial matter, the rules set out in the Brussels Regulation, which at one point incorporates by reference the traditional rules of jurisdiction, will determine the jurisdiction of an English court, or its lack.

B. THE BRUSSELS REGULATION

1. HISTORY

The interest of the European Community in civil jurisdiction grew from Article 293[13] of the EC Treaty, which committed the six original Member States[14] to develop a system for the mutual recognition and enforcement of judgments in civil and commercial matters. It was decided that the best way to ensure an uncomplicated enforcement of sister-state judgments—creating a free market in judgments, as some call it—was to limit the power of the judge to review the judgment of which enforcement was sought; and that the best way to achieve that result was to adopt a uniform set of rules for the taking of jurisdiction in the first place. The Brussels Convention of 27 September 1968[15] was adopted to perform this dual function.

As new states joined the European Community, they acceded to the Brussels Convention, which was successively amended on the accession of the United Kingdom,[16] Denmark, and Ireland; Greece; Portugal,

---

[13] Formerly Art 220 EC.
[14] Belgium, France, Germany, Italy, Luxembourg, and the Netherlands.
[15] In force in the six states from 1 January 1973.
[16] Enacted as Sch 1 to the Civil Jurisdiction and Judgments Act 1982 (the 1982 Act), which has been amended on each subsequent accession.

and Spain; and Austria, Finland, and Sweden. By the end of 2000, the re-re-re-amended text[17] of the Brussels Convention served as the common jurisdictional text of the 15 Member States. In addition, a parallel Convention, signed at Lugano on 16 April 1988,[18] bound the states of the European Union and of the European Free Trade Area (Austria, Finland, and Sweden), which later acceded to the Brussels Convention, and thereby ceased to be 'Lugano states'; and Iceland, Norway, and Switzerland, which remained, and remain, outside the European Union, as 'Lugano states'.

But the process of amending an international convention is slow and cumbersome. To avoid sclerosis, therefore, it was agreed to allow the European Union to legislate directly, to transform the Brussels Convention into a European Regulation, which became known, rather predictably, as the Brussels Regulation.[19] It came into effect on 1 March 2002. It supplanted the Convention in the then-Member States, except for Denmark which elected to stand aside. The 10 states which joined the European Union in 2004,[20] and the two which joined in 2007,[21] were bound by the Regulation from the date of their accession; and Denmark came in from the cold in 2007 as well.[22] Not only that, but the remaining three Lugano states agreed with the European Union to amend the Lugano Convention to bring it into line with the Brussels Regulation, a step which will take place in 2008. The result of all this effort is that, in effect, a single legislative text governs jurisdiction and the enforcement of judgments in civil and commercial matters in the 27 Member States and the three Lugano states. By any reckoning, and notwithstanding any unease about the way the rules actually work, it is a remarkable achievement. For present purposes, and to avoid clumsiness, we will refer to the Brussels Regulation as shorthand for it and for the superseded and related instruments. Where there is a material difference in the wording, this will be dealt with individually. References to 'the Court' are to the Court of Justice of the European Communities, or European Court. Although almost all the reported cases were decided under the provisions of the Brussels and Lugano Conventions, the account which follows has

---

[17] SI 2000/1824, in force from 1 January 2001.
[18] Civil Jurisdiction and Judgments Act 1982, Sch 3C, as inserted by Civil Jurisdiction and Judgments Act 1991, Sch 1.
[19] Regulation (EC) 44/2001, [2002] OJ L12/1.
[20] Cyprus, Czech Republic, Estonia, Hungary, Latvia, Lithuania, Malta, Poland, Slovakia, and Slovenia.
[21] Bulgaria and Romania.
[22] SI 2007/1655.

its focus on the Regulation, and terminology, and numbering of Articles, has been adjusted accordingly. It may be unhistorical, but that is too bad.

2. GENERAL SCHEME

The regulation deals with jurisdiction in civil or commercial matters. It is the basic jurisdictional statute for the Member States, and national courts may make references to the European Court for a preliminary ruling on its interpretation.[23] It is drafted in many languages, although these versions are not, perhaps, in every nuance and respect, identical, and occasionally parties may exploit the differences. The Brussels Convention had the same scope, but the wording has evolved. Where the Regulation confers jurisdiction on an English court, process may be served on the defendant as of right, whether in England or (with the appropriate certification of the court's jurisdiction under the Regulation) outside it.[24]

Where the Regulation confers international jurisdiction upon the courts of a Member State, it confers it on the courts of the United Kingdom, not England, for England is not a state. To deal with this, internal rules of national jurisdiction, resembling but sometimes deliberately diverging from the Regulation, sub-allocate jurisdiction as between the courts of England, Scotland, and Northern Ireland.[25] These rules of internal United Kingdom law are not the concern of the European Court.[26]

Most definitional terms used in the Regulation bear 'autonomous' meanings, distinct from those accorded to the same terms in national law. They were mostly developed in the jurisprudence of the Court on references under the Brussels Convention, which remain authoritative.[27] The meanings of 'contract' and 'tort', used for the jurisdictional purpose of the Regulation,[28] for example, do not mirror these terms when

---

[23] Article 234 (ex Art 177) EC; but by Art 68 EC, the power is confined to courts from which no further appeal lies. The Lugano Convention is not subject to the interpretation of the Court.

[24] CPR r 6.19. For the form of the certification, see the Practice Direction to CPR Pt 6.

[25] 1982 Act, Sch 4, as amended by Civil Jurisdiction and Judgments Order 2001, Sch 2.

[26] Case C–364/93 *Kleinwort Benson Ltd v City of Glasgow DC* [1995] ECR I–415. The extent to which preliminary rulings from the Court are conclusive on the interpretation of the internal UK rules is uncertain, but they must at least be influential: *Kleinwort Benson Ltd v Glasgow City Council* [1999] 1 AC 153; *Agnew v Länsförsäkringsbolagens AB* [2001] 1 AC 223, 245.

[27] So, except where the provisions have been materially altered, will the expert reports on the various conventions: Jenard Report [1979] OJ C59/1; Schlosser Report [1979] OJ C59/71; Evrigenis Report [1986] OJ C298/1; Cruz Report [1989] OJ C189/35; Jenard and Möller Report [1990] OJ C189/61.

[28] Article 5.

used in English private international law to characterize issues and choose laws. The former is a jurisdictional matter of European law; the latter a substantive matter of national law. It follows that a court which has special jurisdiction on the basis of the 'contract' rule may proceed to determine the merits by using its private international law of tort.[29] In addition, certain general canons of interpretation have emerged over the years. First, as the basic principle is that a defendant shall be sued in the courts of the Member State where he is domiciled, a provision of the Regulation derogating from this rule will tend to receive a restrictive construction.[30] This was established by the Court in its jurisprudence on the Brussels Convention, and it continues to underpin the interpretation of the Regulation.[31] Secondly, as the Regulation seeks to make judgments obtained in one Member State freely enforceable in other Member States, rules which mandate non-recognition of judgments will be given restrictive construction, whereas those which prevent parallel litigation will be construed amply.[32] Thirdly, the courts of the Member States are mutually trusted to be of equal competence, and it is inadmissible to invite the courts of one Member State to conclude that the courts of another Member State erred in considering that they have or had jurisdiction.[33]

Where a claim falls within the domain of the Regulation, this instrument determines the jurisdiction of an English court. Its application is not dependent on the claimant being domiciled in a Member State, for it is not a statute which is available to be taken advantage of by only a chosen few.[34] If the defendant is out of the jurisdiction, service of process does not require the permission of the court.[35] The hierarchy of its provisions is reflected in the order in which they are examined below.

---

[29] Case C–26/91 *Soc Jakob Handte GmbH v Soc Traîtements Mécano-chimiques des Surfaces* [1992] ECR I–3967, 3984. But as choice of law is increasingly legislated by the European Union, such divergence in the meaning of terms will diminish.

[30] eg Case C–220/88 *Dumez France SA v Hessische Landesbank* [1990] ECR I–49; Case C–364/93 *Marinari v Lloyds Bank plc* [1995] ECR I–2719.

[31] Now see recitals 10 and 11 to the Regulation.

[32] Recital 15. See also Case 144/86 *Gubisch Machinenfabrik KG v Palumbo* [1987] ECR 4861.

[33] Case C–351/89 *Overseas Union Insurance Ltd v New Hampshire Insurance Co* [1991] ECR I–3317; Case C–116/02 *Erich Gasser GmbH v Misat srl* [2003] ECR I–14693.

[34] Case C–412/98 *Universal General Insurance Co v Groupe Josi Reinsurance Co SA* [2000] ECR I–5925.

[35] CPR r 6.19(1).

3. THE DOMAIN OF THE REGULATION:
ARTICLES 1, 66–68, AND 71

The point of departure is to define the domain of the Regulation in its three elements, that is to say, its material, or subject matter scope; its temporal scope; and its relationship with other legal instruments.

(a) Material scope

Article 1 of the Regulation applies, like its forerunners, in 'civil and commercial matters'. It will often be obvious whether the claim falls within this expression, but where it is not obvious it will be measured against an autonomous interpretation of the terms. It may include claims made by or against public authorities where the obligations which are enforced are imposed on persons generally, no matter who is enforcing them. So proceedings against a town council which has failed to pay a contractor who did work on the town hall will be brought in a civil and commercial matter; proceedings brought to stop a contractor using unfair terms in consumer contracts are brought in a civil or commercial matter, even though the claimant is a public body charged with the enforcement of the law.[36] Only if the obligation enforced is one peculiar to public law will the matter not be civil or commercial.[37] So where a claim for repayment of sums advanced by a state by way of financial assistance is founded on the ordinary law of subrogation or restitution, the fact that the claim is brought by a state in relation to its administrative or public law duty of support does not prevent the claim being seen as civil or commercial.[38] This interpretation of Article 1, which pays attention to the specific legal obligation which founds the claim, or more specifically, the defendant's liability, has superseded an earlier view, that a matter was identified as civil or commercial only after looking at the laws of the Member States generally to see whether they would, in their own systems of law, regard comparable claims as civil or commercial.[39] Such an approach was particularly difficult where, for example, a claim was brought against a body which has emerged from the denationalization of public utilities. Whether a claim against the body which now supplies water, or owns the railway tracks, and which has caused damage by its negligence, would be civil or commercial, would be almost impossible to say if the laws of all 27 Member States had to be surveyed. Placing the focus of attention on the actual legal

[36] Case C–167/00 *VfK v Henkel* [2002] ECR I–8111.
[37] Case C–265/02 *Frahuil SA v Assitalia SpA* [2004] ECR I–1543.
[38] Case C–433/01 *Freistaat Bayern v Blijdenstein* [2004] ECR I–981.
[39] Case 814/79 *Netherlands v Rüffer* [1980] ECR 3807.

obligation which it is sought to enforce will ensure that the answer will be easier to arrive at, although it will make for greater variation from one law to another. And it is the claim which identifies the matter as civil or commercial; the nature of the defence to it is, apparently, immaterial.[40]

A claim is also outside the domain of the Regulation if it concerns customs, revenue, or administrative matters;[41] likewise status or legal capacity of natural persons, matrimonial property, or succession; bankruptcy and the winding up of insolvent companies or other legal persons; or social security.[42] It is still uncertain whether, if such an issue arises only incidentally, the claim as a whole may be outside the Regulation. English authority[43] holds that the Regulation will apply unless the excluded matter forms the principal component in the dispute, this following from the need to construe exceptions to the Regulation restrictively. Even if this is right, the justification is dubious, for although the perimeter of the Regulation must be well defined, it is not necessary that it be far flung; and there is an apparent distinction between the Regulation 'not applying to X' and 'not applying to a matter principally concerned with X'. The point may be illustrated by examination of 'arbitration' which, as a single and unelucidated word, is excluded from the Regulation.[44] All agree that arbitration as a means of dispute resolution, and judicial measures which regulate and control it, and the judicial enforcement of arbitral awards, fall outside the Regulation.[45] But what of the enforcement of judgments obtained in breach of an agreement to arbitrate, or proceedings to obtain an injunction to restrain a party from breaching an arbitration agreement by suing in a foreign court?[46] On the one hand, if the subject matter of the dispute, and hence the judgment, is civil or commercial, it falls within the domain of the Regulation. But on the other, for a court to be obliged to recognize the judgment would mean it having to contradict its own law on arbitration, a matter untouched by the Regulation. The cases conflict. In one, it was held that a Dutch court was not bound to recognize a German order for maintenance (a matter within the scope of the Regulation) where this would mean it had to contradict its own law on the marital status of

---

[40] Case C–266/01 *Préservatrice Foncière TIARD v Netherlands* [2003] ECR I–4867.
[41] Article 1(1).
[42] Article 1(2)(a)–(c).
[43] *Ashurst v Pollard* [2001] Ch 595 (CA) (bankruptcy); *The Ivan Zagubanski* [2002] 2 Lloyd's Rep 106 (arbitration).
[44] Article 1(2)(d).
[45] Case C–190/89 *Marc Rich & Co AG v Soc Italiana Impianti PA* [1991] ECR I–3855.
[46] Case C–185/07 *West Tankers Inc v Riunione Adriatica di Sicurtà SpA* (pending); referred by the House of Lords: [2007] UKHL 4, [2007] 1 Lloyd's Rep 391.

the parties (a matter excluded from the Regulation).[47] But another supports the contention that if a court in another Member State has heard and given judgment in a case, having rejected a jurisdictional defence based on an arbitration clause, it has given judgment in a civil or commercial matter.[48] Whatever the answer is held to be, it is unlikely to be significantly more persuasive than the alternative.

Proceedings for enforcement of a judgment from a non-Member State are not within the Regulation, nor are ancillary or incidental procedures which arise in the course of such proceedings, such as the trial of an issue whether the judgment creditor obtained his non-Member State judgment by fraud.[49] This same reasoning confirms the exclusion of judgments which make an order in terms of an arbitral award:[50] the exclusion reflects the fact that the adjudication from which enforcement follows was not that of a judge of a Member State.

In all cases falling outside the domain of the Regulation, the jurisdiction of the English courts over the defendant is a matter for the traditional jurisdictional rules of English law, and the Regulation can thereafter be ignored.

(b) Temporal scope

Article 66 provides that the Regulation applies to the taking of jurisdiction by courts in legal proceedings instituted after 1 March 2002. In England, at least, the institution of proceedings will mean the issue of process, rather than its service on a defendant.[51] The transitional provisions in respect of states which joined the European Union after 2002 are complex, and utterly devoid of interest.

(c) Other conventions

As regards the relationship with other conventions, one might have expected that existing international agreements, especially those which implicate non-Member States, would remain unaffected by the Regulation. The reality is not quite so rational. Although Article 71 provides that the Regulation 'shall not affect any Conventions . . . which

---

[47] Case 145/86 *Hoffmann v Krieg* [1988] ECR 645.

[48] The question is examined in ch 4 below. The effect of Case C–391/95 *Van Uden Maritime BV v Deco Line* [1998] ECR I–7091 is that agreement to arbitrate means that a state has no jurisdiction to adjudicate, even though the dispute is within the scope of the Regulation; jurisdictional error is no basis for denying recognition to a judgment.

[49] Case C–129/92 *Owens Bank plc v Bracco* [1994] ECR I–117.

[50] Schlosser Report [1979] OJ C59/71.

[51] *Canada Trust Co v Stolzenberg (No 2)* [2002] 1 AC 1.

in relation to particular matters, govern jurisdiction' it goes on, rather ineptly, to explain that this means that if a convention allows for the taking of jurisdiction, that provision shall continue to be effective, even though the defendant is domiciled in a Member State which is not party to it. Accordingly, if another convention, such as those in maritime law which deal with the arrest of sea-going ships, and with cargo claims, authorize the taking of jurisdiction, the Regulation shall not impede it. But unless the particular convention also makes express provision to deal with parallel litigation, the provisions of the Regulation[52] will apply 'to fill the gap'. It is as if the particular convention is absorbed into the Regulation, with the result that it may then be modified in its operation.[53] The result is hard to reconcile with the proposition that the Regulation does not affect the assumption of jurisdiction under the particular convention; and Article 71(2) of the Regulation is misleading. Even so, what Article 71 completely fails to say is that, where a convention forbids the taking of jurisdiction, that provision shall continue to be effective, whatever the Regulation would otherwise have decreed. The international obligations of the United Kingdom in relation to specific matters include obligations to *refuse* to accept jurisdiction, rather than to exercise it, and for this to be ignored by the Regulation is inexplicable. In the context of arbitration, where the New York Convention lays negative jurisdictional obligations on Contracting States, this is crucial.

In relation to community instruments which make provision for jurisdiction in relation to specific matters, Article 67 provides that these are not prejudiced in their application by the Regulation. So Directive 96/71/EC[54] on workers temporarily posted abroad, and Directive 93/13/EC on unfair terms in consumer contracts,[55] will to this extent prevail over the Regulation.

4. DOMICILE

Many of the provisions contained in the Regulation turn upon whether the defendant is domiciled in the United Kingdom or another Member State. It is necessary to distinguish natural persons from companies or other legal persons or associations of persons, and from trusts, for the definition of domicile is not uniform. To decide whether an individual is

---

[52] Articles 27–30, below.
[53] Case C–406/92 *The Tatry* [1994] ECR I–5439.
[54] [1997] OJ L18/1, Art 6 of which deals with jurisdiction.
[55] Unfair Terms in Consumer Contracts Regulations 1999, SI (1999/2083), applicable to arbitration and jurisdiction agreements: Case C–240/98 *Océano Grupo Editorial SA v Quintero* [2000] ECR I–4941. The directive can be found at [1993] OJ L95/29.

domiciled in the United Kingdom, Article 59(1) of the Regulation tells a court to apply the law of the United Kingdom. In this context, domicile in the United Kingdom is defined by statutory instrument[56] rather than by the common law. According to this, an individual is domiciled in the United Kingdom if he is resident in the United Kingdom, and this residence indicates that he has a substantial connection with the United Kingdom, a fact which may be presumed from three months' residence. Similar rules, *mutatis mutandis*, determine whether an individual is domiciled in a part of the United Kingdom. But to determine whether an individual is domiciled in another Member State, Article 59(2) tells a court to apply the law of the Member State of the proposed domicile. So whether she is domiciled in France is a matter of French law; in Italy, a matter of Italian law, and so on. It follows that an individual may have a domicile in more than one Member State. This is unproblematic, for whereas it would be very inconvenient for concurrent domiciliary laws to determine capacity to marry, for example, it is much less surprising that a person's connections with each of two Member States are sufficient for either to be a proper place in which to sue him in matters of general[57] jurisdiction.

There has been pressure to provide a single autonomous definition of domicile, or to abandon it *holus bolus* and move instead to the concept of habitual residence, not least because of variation in the separate national law definitions of domicile. But in the absence of a public register of status, however defined, it is difficult to see that such a change would accomplish very much of value. There will be occasional difficult cases, typically where a person maintains a residence or some other establishment, but manages to cast a veil of secrecy over his movements.[58] In such a case his domicile would probably be no more difficult to ascertain than his habitual residence, and it is unlikely that the change would have brought much about.

For a *company*, *other legal person*, or *association of natural persons*, Article 60(1) provides that it has a domicile in any one or more of three places: where it has its statutory seat, or its central administration, or its principal place of business. For the purposes of the United Kingdom, 'statutory seat' is defined as the registered office or, where there is none anywhere, the place of incorporation or, where there is none anywhere, the place under the law of which the formation took place. The purpose[59]

---

[56] Civil Jurisdiction and Judgments Order 2001 (SI 2001/3929) Sch 1, para 9.
[57] Chapter II, Sect 1 of the Regulation is entitled 'General provisions'.
[58] cf *Canada Trust Co v Stolzenberg (No 2)* [2002] 1 AC 1.
[59] Recital 11.

of Article 60 is to nudge the law towards a more uniform definition of the domicile of a corporation or other legal person. Previously each national law had supplied its own definition of the domicile of a company, etc, and the result was a complexity which served no useful purpose.

By contrast, to ascertain whether a *trust* is domiciled in the United Kingdom, Article 60(3) provides that the court will apply the law of the United Kingdom. Accordingly, a trust is domiciled in England if English law is that with which the trust has its closest and most real connection.[60] It is never necessary to determine whether a trust is domiciled in another Member State, for no jurisdictional rule is formulated on this basis.

C. JURISDICTIONAL RULES OF THE REGULATION

Where proceedings are brought in a civil or commercial matter, the Regulation alone serves to determine whether the court has, or does not have, jurisdiction; to put it another way, the answers must be found within this Section of this Chapter. To obtain a reliable answer, it is necessary to examine the provisions of the Regulation, and preferably, in the order in which they are set out below.

I. EXCLUSIVE JURISDICTION, REGARDLESS OF DOMICILE: ARTICLE 22

Article 22 of the Regulation[61] gives exclusive jurisdiction, regardless[62] of domicile, to the courts of a Member State, in five areas. In the rare case where it confers exclusive jurisdiction on the courts of two Member States, Article 29 provides that the first court seised alone has exclusive jurisdiction. Where Article 22 confers exclusive jurisdiction on a court, no other court has jurisdiction, even if both parties purport to submit to it;[63] and a judgment which conflicts with Article 22 must be denied recognition.[64] For Article 22 to be engaged, the material connection must lie with a Member State. If the land, or public register etc, is in a non-Member State, Article 22 has no application; the relevant question is whether the Regulation gives a court with jurisdiction under some other

---

[60] 2001 Order, Sch 1, para 12, re-enacting 1982 Act, s 45.
[61] Section 6 of Chapter II; cf Art 16 BC, from which it slightly departs.
[62] That is to say, whether the defendant is domiciled in any Member State or none.
[63] Article 23(5).
[64] Article 35(1).

Article a discretion to decline it by pointing to a non-Member State. The issue is not straightforward, and is considered below.

Article 22(1) covers proceedings which have as their (principal[65]) object rights *in rem* in, or tenancies of, immovable property in a Member State, and gives exclusive jurisdiction to the state where the land is situated. To this two ancillary rules are added. First, where the proceedings have as their object a tenancy of immovable property concluded for temporary private use for no more than six consecutive months, Article 22(1) provides that the courts of the Member State in which the defendant is domiciled also[66] have exclusive jurisdiction, provided that the tenant is a natural person, and landlord and tenant are domiciled in the same Member State, which is useful if the dispute is a small one concerned with a holiday letting in another Member State. Secondly, Article 6(4) allows a contractual action to be combined with the action *in rem* against the same defendant, which is useful in a mortgage action.

It is not enough that the proceedings concern or are even fought over land or a tenancy of immovable property; the words 'have as their object' do not simply mean that the claim is concerned with land; they must be concerned with the extent, content, ownership or possession of land.[67] Most Member States treat the determination of title to land as a matter for only the courts of the *situs*; and in any event, land law, and especially tenancy law, is complicated and is better applied by a local court. And as the Article derogates from the jurisdiction of the defendant's domicile, it will be understood restrictively. This last point has been taken to mean that proceedings in which a tenancy forms only part of the background to the dispute, or comprises only a minor part of a more complex contract, such as an all-inclusive holiday,[68] or timeshare club membership,[69] do not come under Article 22(1). Likewise, claims to enforce obligations contained in or associated with leases but which are not themselves peculiar to tenancies, such as a covenant to pay for the business goodwill in a lease of commercial premises[70] or the statutory obligations of the provider of consumer credit after the landlord has defaulted,[71] fall outside it as well.

---

[65] This word does not appear in the text of the Art, but was read in: Case C–280/90 *Hacker v Euro-Relais GmbH* [1992] ECR I–1111; cf *Ashurst v Pollard* [2001] Ch 595 (CA).

[66] Joint exclusive jurisdiction may occasion the use of Art 29.

[67] Case C–343/04 *ČEZ v Land Oberösterreich* [2006] ECR I–4557.

[68] Case C–280/90 *Hacker v Euro-Relais GmbH* [1992] ECR I–1111.

[69] Case C–73/04 *Klein v Rhodos Management Ltd* [2005] ECR I–8667.

[70] Case 73/77 *Sanders v Van der Putte* [1977] ECR 2383.

[71] *Jarrett v Barclays Bank plc* [1999] QB 1 (CA).

By contrast, a claim in respect of unpaid rent or utility charges,[72] or for the cost of cleaning up behind departing tenants who made a ruin of the premises,[73] are founded on obligations natural to a tenancy, and no matter how narrow the interpretation of Article 22(1), these fall within it.

Proceedings do not 'have as their object rights *in rem*' if the claimant does not assert that he is already legal proprietor who is suing as such but claims, for example as contractual purchaser, to be entitled to be made legal owner[74] or claims, for example, as beneficiary under a resulting trust of the land already to be equitable owner of the land. The conclusion of the Court in such a case[75] that a beneficiary under a resulting trust has only an interest *in personam* and not one *in rem* was wrong, at least as a matter of English law, by several centuries;[76] and its further holding that a suit does not have a right *in rem* as its object when brought to acquire legal title from a resulting trustee is almost inexplicable: if an action brought to acquire a conveyance of legal title does not have legal title as its object, what on earth does it have?[77] If, as Article 27 makes clear, 'the object of proceedings' means 'the end in view':[78] the end in the beneficiary's view is the acquisition of legal title to the land. On the other hand, the outcome, if not the reasoning, can be defended from two very different points of view. Where the substantive law which the court will apply is not specifically land law or tenancy law, there is no need to engage Article 22(1), any more than if the same principles under which a right to conveyance were demanded were to be deployed against the owner of a yacht or of shares. Moreover, the common law drew an analogous jurisdictional distinction between determining legal title to foreign land, which it had no power to do, and enforcing a contract or other equity between the parties concerning foreign land, which it would.[79] This just goes to illustrate the manner in which the various policies behind Article 22(1), all sensible in themselves, can collide, and that their reconciliation is not always possible.

Article 22(2) covers proceedings which have as their object the validity of the constitution, the dissolution or winding up of companies, or the

---

[72] Case 241/83 *Rösler v Rottwinkel* [1985] ECR 99.

[73] Case C–8/98 *Dansommer A/S v Götz* [2000] ECR I–393.

[74] Or as contractual seller, seeking rescission of unperformed contract of sale: Case C–518/98 *Gaillard v Chekili* [2001] ECR I–2771.

[75] Case C–294/92 *Webb v Webb* [1994] ECR I–1717.

[76] The interest of the beneficiary can be enforced against all the world except the *bona fide* purchaser for value without notice; it is unreal to see this as a mere right *in personam*.

[77] Not least because it is brought on the basis that the claimant beneficiary does have pre-existing (and exclusive) equitable title.

[78] Case C–406/92 *The Tatry* [1994] ECR I–5439.

[79] *Penn v Baltimore* (1750) 1 Ves Sen 444.

decisions of their organs. Exclusive jurisdiction is given to the Member State of the seat of the company, but this means the seat as defined by national law, as distinct from that in Article 60(2).[80] Where winding up is a hoped-for remedy, perhaps as a remedy for minority shareholder oppression,[81] rather than an ongoing process, Article 22(2) is probably inapplicable.[82] Authority suggests that claims that an organ of the company has acted without authority will fall under the Article, at least where this is the principal component of the claim; but that allegations of abuse of authority will not.[83] Such a distinction is not easy to defend.

Article 22(3) gives exclusive jurisdiction to the Member State in which a public register is kept if the proceedings have as their object the validity of an entry in that register. An action to rectify an entry on a land register will be covered;[84] and there is no rational[85] reason to exclude any action which seeks the amendment of an entry in such a register. The Article may also apply to a register maintained by a public limited company if it is open for inspection by the public, but the point is debatable.[86]

Article 22(4) gives exclusive jurisdiction to the Member State in which a patent or trade mark is registered or deposited if the proceedings have as their object the registration or validity of that right. A simple action for infringement will not fall within the Article.[87] Where, as frequently happens, the validity of the patent is challenged by way of defence to such the action, the court seised with the infringement claim is forbidden to enter upon the question of validity.[88] Most unhelpfully, though, the Court disdained to say whether the infringement proceedings were to be stayed pending another court's ruling on validity, or could be transferred to the court with exclusive jurisdiction to rule on validity.

Article 22(5) gives exclusive jurisdiction to the Member State in which a judgment from a Member State is being enforced if the proceedings are concerned with that enforcement. There must have been a judgment: proceedings which seek to pave the way for enforcing a prospective judgment, such as

---

[80] Final sentence of Art 22(2); see SI 2001/3929, Sch 1, para 10.

[81] Companies Act 2006 s 994 (replacing Companies Act 1985, s 459).

[82] cf Case C–294/92 *Webb v Webb* [1994] ECR I–1717.

[83] *Grupo Torras SA v Sheikh Fahad Mohammed al Sabah* [1996] 1 Lloyd's Rep 7 (CA).

[84] *Re Hayward* [1997] Ch 45.

[85] The decision in *Ashurst v Pollard* [2001] Ch 595 (CA) that an application to procure amendment to the register of land ownership in Portugal was not within the predecessor of Art 22(3) is beyond comprehension.

[86] *Re Fagin's Bookshop plc* [1992] BCLC 118.

[87] Case 288/82 *Duijnstee v Goderbauer* [1983] ECR 3663.

[88] Case C–4/03 *Gesellschaft für Antriebstechnik mbH & Co KG v Lamellen- und Kupplungsbau Beteiligungs KG* [2006] ECR I–6509.

by obtaining a freezing injunction, are outside the Article.[89] It is possible that applications against a non-party for an order that there be a contribution to payment of the winning party's costs fall within this provision, for these are concerned with the enforcement of the court's original judgment.[90]

2. JURISDICTION BY APPEARANCE: ARTICLE 24

Unless Article 22 applies, where the defendant enters an appearance before a court, Article 24[91] provides that the court has jurisdiction. Any prior agreement on jurisdiction will be considered to have been waived or varied by consent.[92] But if the appearance was entered[93] to contest the jurisdiction of the court, which in England will mean following the procedure in CPR Part 11, the appearance will not confer jurisdiction under this rule. One of the bedrock principles of the Regulation is that a defendant must be allowed to appear, without prejudice, to argue for its proper application to his case, and that he must do this *in limine litis* rather than by opposing recognition of the judgment after the event. So long as he does what is necessary to contest the jurisdiction at the first opportunity which the procedural law of the court allows him, he will not lose this protection if he is required in practice to plead his defence to the merits of the claim at the same time.[94] But if he takes a step towards defending the claim on the merits, which was not in this sense required, he will have thrown away the shield which Article 24 would have given him.[95]

3. INSURANCE, CONSUMER, AND EMPLOYMENT CONTRACTS

Where disputes arise out of insurance contracts,[96] certain consumer contracts,[97] or individual contracts of employment,[98] and where the insurer,

---

[89] Case C–261/90 *Reichert v Dresdner Bank (No 2)* [1992] ECR I–2149.

[90] cf *The Ikarian Reefer* [2000] 1 WLR 603 (CA) where the point was not taken. But the Art does not require it to be a judgment from *another* Member State.

[91] Section 7 of Chapter II.

[92] Case C–150/80 *Elefanten Schuh GmbH v Jacqmain* [1981] ECR 1671.

[93] The predecessor to Art 24 (Art 18 of the Conventions) required, in the English language at least, that the appearance be *solely* to contest the jurisdiction. If the law was ever that restrictive, it is not now.

[94] Case 27/81 *Rohr SA v Ossberger* [1981] ECR 2431.

[95] cf (in a case not governed by the Regulation) *Marc Rich & Co AG v Soc Italiana Impianti PA* [1992] 2 Lloyd's Rep 624 (CA).

[96] Articles 8–14; Sect 3 of Chapter II; cf Arts 7–12A BC, from which some divergence has been made.

[97] Articles 15–17; Sect 4 of Chapter II; cf Arts 13–15 BC, from which some divergence has been made.

[98] Arts 18–21; Sect 5 of Chapter II. This had no immediate precursor in the Conventions, although Arts 5(1) and 17 BC did make piecemeal provision for these contracts.

supplier, or employer is domiciled in a Member State (or is not, but made the contract by a local branch or agency which is so domiciled[99]), there may well have been such inequality between the parties that the insured or policyholder, consumer, and employee will need special jurisdictional privileges if their rights are to be effectively safeguarded. These three Sections of Chapter II conform to a template which the policyholder,[100] consumer, or employee may insist on being sued in the Member State of his domicile and may, which is the real novelty, sue in his 'own' Member State: that is, the domicile in the case of insureds, etc, and consumers; the place where the work is done for employees. In certain cases the policyholder or insured, consumer, or employee may elect to sue in a Member State other than that of his domicile or workplace; but the insurer, supplier, or employer is generally restricted to suing where the defendant is domiciled. Jurisdiction agreements are generally binding only if entered into after the dispute arose, or if they widen the choice given to the policyholder,[101] consumer,[102] or employee.[103] By way of reinforcement, a judgment which violates any of the jurisdictional provisions governing insurance and consumer contracts will be denied recognition, though for no obvious reason this safeguard does not extend to employment contracts.[104] Where the insurer, supplier, or employer neither has, nor is deemed by reason of his having a branch or agency to have, a domicile in a Member State, Article 4 will apply to claims against it.[105] It is to be observed that these rules do not depend on proof of a relationship of actual inequality; this fact may have contributed to the view that they are to be construed restrictively.[106]

More particularly, the *insurance* provisions do not apply to reinsurance, which is not a relationship of inherent inequality,[107] but they do apply to

---

[99] For the definition of domicile in the UK in this context see Civil Jurisdiction and Judgments Order 2001, Sch 1, para 11.

[100] In addition to those general rules described in the text there is specific provision for co-insurance (Art 9(1)(c)), liability insurance or insurance of immoveables (Art 10), direct actions by an injured party against an insurer (Art 11), joinder of parties (Art 11), counterclaims (Art 12). Jurisdiction agreements are regulated by Arts 13 and 14.

[101] Article 13.

[102] Article 17; and see Unfair Terms in Consumer Contracts Regulations 1999 (SI 1999/2083), enacting Directive (EC) 93/13 on unfair terms in consumer contracts [1993] OJ L95/29; Case C–240/98 *Océano Grupo Editorial SA v Quintero* [2000] ECR I–4941.

[103] Article 21.

[104] Article 35(1), which omits reference to Sect 5 of Chapter II.

[105] Case C–412/98 *Universal General Insurance Co v Groupe Josi Reinsurance Co SA* [2000] ECR I–5925.

[106] Case C–464/01 *Gruber v Bay Wa AG* [2005] ECR I–439.

[107] Case C–412/98 *Universal General Insurance Co v Groupe Josi Reinsurance Co SA* [2000] ECR I–5925.

direct actions by the injured party against the insurer.[108] The restrictions on jurisdiction agreements are relaxed in the cases of marine insurance and in the case of large risks.[109] A *consumer* contract is one in which an individual concludes the contract for a purpose which is wholly[110] outside his trade or profession and is one which in general secures the needs of an individual in terms of private consumption.[111] Cases in which a consumer seeks to enforce the offer of a prize will be within this Section if the prize offer required the offeree to buy goods,[112] but not if no such condition was imposed.[113] There is no exclusion of investment or other middle-class contracts so long as they fall within the definition,[114] for any rule which sought to differentiate between weak consumers and strong consumers would be terribly subjective. Within that general definition, the types of consumer contracts actually covered by Section 4 of Chapter II are more restrictive than might be expected: Article 15(1) applies only to (a) a contract for the sale of goods on instalment credit terms, or (b) a contract for a loan repayable by instalments, or other credit, made to finance the sale of goods, or (c) a contract concluded with a person who pursues commercial or professional activities in the Member State of the consumer's domicile or, by any means, directs such activities to that Member State or to several states including that Member State, and contracts falling within the scope of such activities. And in any event Article 15(3) excludes contracts of transport except for package holiday contracts. Point (c) replaces an earlier version which focused on targeted invitations or advertising; and it remains to be seen what this more general wording will cover. Prior to the adoption of the Regulation there had been much discussion of whether contracts made by computer-literate consumers from the comfort of their spare bedrooms would be routinely included or excluded. But it seems entirely plausible that the intention is for a supplier, who uses the internet as the way to bring his goods and services to the attention of potential customers in a Member State or elsewhere as well, to be someone whose contracts may fall within (c) above. The suggestion earlier heard, that this

---

[108] Article 11(2). In England this will most commonly arise under the Third Parties (Rights Against Insurers) Act 1930.

[109] Articles 13(5) and 14.

[110] Case C-464/01 *Gruber v Bay Wa AG* [2005] ECR I-439.

[111] Case C-269/95 *Benincasa v Dentalkit Srl* [1997] ECR I-3767; and see also Case C-99/96 *Mietz v Intership Yachting Sneek BV* [1999] ECR I-2277.

[112] Case C-96/00 *Gabriel v Schlank & Schick GmbH* [2002] ECR I-6367

[113] Case C-27/02 *Engler v Janus Versand GmbH* [2004] ECR I-481.

[114] Case C-318/93 *Brenner v Dean Witter Reynolds Inc* [1994] ECR I-4275. But if the consumer has assigned his rights to a body which is not itself a consumer, the jurisdictional privilege is lost: Case C-89/91 *Shearson Lehmann Hutton v TVB* [1993] ECR I-139.

will so discourage suppliers that it will, at a stroke, put an end to electronic commerce in the European Union has shown itself to be the utter nonsense it always appeared to be.

The *employment* contract provisions of Section 5 are substantively new. They represent the culmination of a series of steps, judicial and legislative, to protect workers from some of the inevitable inequalities under contracts written by the bosses. The employee may sue where the employer is domiciled or in the Member State in which the worker habitually carries out his work, so as to secure the benefits of local[115] employment law. Where the employment involves duties in more Member States than one, they are sorted out on a common sense, centre-of-gravity, basis, which works well enough in most cases.[116]

4. AGREEMENTS ON JURISDICTION: ARTICLE 23

Apart from the cases mentioned above, where their effect is restricted, agreements on jurisdiction for the courts of a Member State are validated by Article 23.[117] A compliant agreement is required to be respected both by the court chosen and by the courts whose jurisdiction is excluded: the agreement serves to prorogate and derogate. Only if no party to the agreement is domiciled in a Member State may it be overridden, and then not before the nominated court has declined jurisdiction. But there is otherwise no discretion to override a valid jurisdiction agreement, say on grounds of overall trial convenience.[118] An agreement to confer jurisdiction on the courts of the United Kingdom is effective so far as the Regulation is concerned, but raises some practical difficulties: it probably gives jurisdiction to the courts in any part of the United Kingdom unless it can be construed as being more particular than first appears.[119] An agreement nominating the courts of two Member States will probably be effective;[120] one which is construed as giving non-exclusive jurisdiction to a court will do exactly what it says.[121] But an agreement for the courts of a non–Member State is outside Article 23, not least because the Regulation cannot bind such a court to accept jurisdiction. For them,

---

[115] There is not much likelihood of this attracting much litigation business to the UK.

[116] Case C–125/92 *Mulox IBC v Geels* [1993] ECR I–4075; Case C–37/00 *Weber v Universal Ogden Services Ltd* [2002] ECR I–2013.

[117] Section 7 of Chapter II; cf Art 17 BC, from which some departure has been made.

[118] *Hough v P&O Containers Ltd* [1999] QB 834.

[119] cf *The Komninos S* [1991] 1 Lloyd's Rep 370 (CA).

[120] Case 23/78 *Meeth v Glacetal Sàrl* [1978] ECR 2133 (but each court had exclusive jurisdiction over particular actions; there was no overlapping of competences).

[121] Article 23(1), which thereby removes the uncertainty about such clauses under Art 17 BC.

the relevant question is whether this gives a court with jurisdiction under some other provision of the Regulation a discretion to decline it in favour of a non-Member State. The issue is considered below.

To ensure that the parties have a proper opportunity to be aware of the effect of the agreement they are making, the agreement must be in writing or evidenced in writing (which includes electronic means which provide a durable record in writing[122]), or in a form which accords with the parties' established practice, or in a form which is well known to accord with international trade usage of which the parties were or should have been aware. So a printed term in standard conditions of business will be ineffective unless the party to be bound has written his agreement to it;[123] but a settled course of dealing or a trade usage will establish a binding form. There is an inevitable tension between the desire to prevent unfair dealing by strict application of the rules on form, and awareness that this may be inappropriate where both parties were perfectly well aware that they were dealing on the basis of an agreement on jurisdiction. Although the Court has insisted on strict interpretation of these formalities,[124] it has also approved a more flexible approach where a party pleading the formal invalidity would be doing so in bad faith.[125] More radically, a shareholder was bound by a jurisdiction agreement contained in the company's constitution on the ground that he knew or should have known of it, and had assented to be bound by his becoming a shareholder.[126] Whether this principle, which looks rather like constructive notice, will be extended to other contexts remains to be seen. Problems arise where the written consent was provided by the original contracting parties, but the proceedings involve a third party who has become involved in the legal relationship. If the third party has succeeded to the contractual rights or liabilities of one of the parties, as under a bill of lading,[127] he may be held to the agreement on jurisdiction, even though his own original consent was not separately written.[128] But where a third party acquires rights or obligations under

---

[122] Which certainly includes fax, and presumably includes a printed or printable message by e-mail.

[123] Case 24/76 *Estasis Salotti v RÜWA Polstereimaschinen GmbH* [1976] ECR 1831, a proposition reiterated in Case C–159/97 *Trasporti Castelletti Spedizioni Internazionali SpA v Hugo Trumpy SpA* [1999] ECR I–1517 (a case decided on an earlier version of Art 17 BC).

[124] Case 24/76 *Estasis Salotti v RÜWA* [1976] ECR 1831, reiterated in Case C–105/95 *MSG v Les Gravières Rhénanes Sàrl* [1997] ECR I–911.

[125] Case 221/84 *Berghofer v ASA SA* [1985] ECR 2699; Case 313/85 *Iveco Fiat v Van Hool* [1986] ECR 3337 (previous course of dealing).

[126] Case C–214/89 *Powell Duffryn plc v Petereit* [1992] ECR I–1745.

[127] Case 71/83 *The Tilly Russ* [1984] ECR 2417.

[128] Case C–387/98 *Coreck Maritime GmbH v Handelsveem BV* [2000] ECR I–9337.

the contract otherwise than by means of succession, he can be bound to the agreement on jurisdiction only by virtue of his own satisfaction of the formalities of writing or the alternative.[129]

An agreement which complies with the formalities may not be impeached on the ground that it fails to comply with some provision, whether as to form[130] or substance,[131] of national (as distinct from European[132]) law which would otherwise deprive it of effect. A contention that the contract containing the agreement on jurisdiction is ineffective or void is irrelevant to the jurisdiction agreement, for the latter is to be regarded as distinct from the substantive contract to which it relates.[133] Indeed, if Article 23 is understood to operate upon the basis that a party has waived or renounced the general jurisdictional rule contained in Article 2, there is no reason to assess his acts in contractual terms: no contract is required to make a binding declaration or renunciation. But if a party claims that his writing was procured by force, fear, or fraud, a court must be allowed to find that there was no 'agreement' to the jurisdiction of the named court. In all probability it will have to do this by notional reference to an autonomous conception of what amounts to an agreement,[134] which may be more easily said than done.

The jurisdiction given by Article 23 is exclusive unless the agreement stipulated otherwise, but it is intended to be of a lower degree of potency than that conferred by Article 22. For example, a judgment which violates Article 23 may not be denied recognition.[135] English courts for many years refused to treat jurisdiction agreements so lightly. To that end they would accept jurisdiction even though a court in another Member State had been seised first, and were prepared to restrain by injunction a party to an agreement on jurisdiction who, in breach of that agreement, launched proceedings in a foreign court.[136] But the European Court held each conclusion to be inconsistent with the scheme of the Regulation.[137]

---

[129] Case C–112/03 *Soc Financière & Industrielle de Peloux v Soc AXA Belgium* [2005] ECR I–3707.

[130] Case 150/80 *Elefanten Schuh GmbH v Jacqmain* [1981] ECR 1671 (wrong language).

[131] Case 25/79 *Sanicentral GmbH v Collin* [1979] ECR 3423 (ousting the jurisdiction of the local employment tribunal).

[132] Article 67; cf the Unfair Terms in Consumer Contracts Regulations 1999 (SI 1999/2083), enacting Directive (EC) 93/13 on unfair terms in consumer contracts [1993] OJ L95/29.

[133] Case C–269/95 *Benincasa v Dentalkit Srl* [1997] ECR I–3767.

[134] The point was left wide open in *Benincasa*.

[135] Article 35(1) makes no reference to Sect 7 of Chapter II.

[136] *Continental Bank NA v Aeakos Compania Naviera SA* [1994] 1 WLR 588 (CA); *The Angelic Grace* [1995] 1 Lloyd's Rep 87 (CA).

[137] Case C–116/02 *Erich Gasser GmbH v Misat srl* [2003] ECR I–14693 (exercising jurisdiction although seised second; referred from an Austrian court); Case C–159/02 *Turner v Grovit* [2004] ECR I–3565 (anti-suit injunction).

In doing so it made plain that the principle that each court must decide for itself, and only for itself, whether it has jurisdiction, prevailed over any sense that the most important concern was to hold parties to their agreements on jurisdiction and to prevent chicanery. Whatever else one may be tempted to think of it, it is hard to assert that the conclusion of the Court was based on a misreading of the legislative text; and a strict application of the first seised does avoid taking sides between two parties, one who alleges that there was a material agreement on jurisdiction, while the other contends the opposite.

5. GENERAL JURISDICTION: DEFENDANTS DOMICILED IN THE UNITED KINGDOM: ARTICLE 2

If none of the provisions examined so far serves to confer or deny the jurisdiction of the court, the rule in Article 2,[138] that general jurisdiction exists where the defendant is domiciled, will apply: 'general jurisdiction' means that it is not limited by reference to its subject matter or the form of the action. The definition of domicile in the United Kingdom, and in England, has been given above. It is striking that although this is always said to be the fundamental rule on which the Regulation is constructed, its place in the hierarchy of rules is relatively low.

6. SPECIAL JURISDICTION: DEFENDANTS DOMICILED IN ANOTHER MEMBER STATE: ARTICLES 5–7

If none of the provisions examined so far serves to confer or deny the jurisdiction of the court, the defendant will be domiciled somewhere other than the United Kingdom. Articles 5 to 7[139] confer special jurisdiction over defendants who are domiciled in another Member State. Article 5 reflects an indirect awareness of *forum conveniens*, but jurisdiction based on the wording of Article 5 may not be contested by showing that the court is, in the particular case, not a *forum conveniens*: the relevance of *forum conveniens* was exhausted when the Article was drafted. Article 5 may not be used as the hook upon which to hang claims against defendants over which the court would not otherwise have had jurisdiction: such general jurisdiction is conferred only by Article 2, and this may limit the attraction

---

[138] Section 1 of Chapter II.
[139] Section 2 of Chapter II; cf Arts 5 and 6 BC, from which some departure has been made.

of Article 5.[140] Article 6 deals with some forms of multipartite litigation; and Article 7 with proceedings to limit liability in maritime claims.

(a) Matters relating to a contract: Article 5(1)

In matters relating to a contract, Article 5(1)(a) gives special jurisdiction to the courts for the place of performance[141] of the obligation in question. A matter does not relate to a contract for the purpose of this jurisdictional rule unless it involves obligations freely entered into with regard to another,[142] but if it does it is not relevant that it would not be regarded as substantively contractual by a court applying its national law. So a claim to enforce the rules of a club,[143] or the obligation of a shareholder to a company[144] is contractual even though a national law may disagree; a claim by a sub-buyer against a manufacturer is not contractual, even if it is regarded as contractual under national law;[145] it is uncertain whether it covers claims by someone who received negligent advice from another who had voluntarily assumed responsibility, and whose liability in English law is regarded as tortious.[146] If the validity of the contract is disputed, the Article may still apply,[147] and this is so even if the claimant is asserting, contrary to the submission of the defendant, that an alleged contract is ineffective or that it has been rescinded for misrepresentation, non-disclosure, or duress.[148] But it may well be different if both parties

---

[140] It has been persuasively shown that where parties to a contract sue on it, all associated claims should be 'channelled' into that one action, in the interests of efficiency and because the contract rule is of a higher order: Case 189/87 *Kalfelis v Bankhaus Schröder Münchmeyer Hengst & Co* [1988] ECR 5565, where this was proposed by the AG, but rejected by the Court.

[141] The French text renders this as the place where the obligation was or should have been performed, and this is the sense in which it must be understood.

[142] Case C–26/91 *Soc Jakob Handte GmbH v Soc Traîtements Mécano-chimiques des Surfaces* [1992] ECR I–3967.

[143] Case 34/82 *Peters v ZNAV* [1983] ECR 987.

[144] Case C–214/89 *Powell Duffryn plc v Petereit* [1992] ECR I–1745.

[145] Case C–26/91 *Soc Jakob Handte GmbH v Soc Traîtements Mécano-chimiques des Surfaces* [1992] ECR I–3967. But the French cour de cassation has now accepted that the claim of the sub-buyer is not contractual as a matter of French law, after all: *Soc Donovan Data Systems Europe v Soc Dragon Rouge Holding*, Cass civ 1ère, 6 July 1999; [2000] Rev Crit 67.

[146] Under the principle in *Hedley Byrne & Co v Heller & Partners* [1964] AC 465. There may be a difference between two- and three-party cases. In *Hedley Byrne* and *Smith v Eric S Bush* [1990] 1 AC 831, reliance is predictable and the identity of the relier is known. In three party cases, such as *Caparo Industries plc v Dickman* [1990] 2 AC 605, this is not so. Cases founded on misrepresentation by a contracting party are not completely straightforward, and are examined below.

[147] Case 38/81 *Effer SpA v Kantner* [1982] ECR 825.

[148] *Agnew v Länsförsäkringsbolagens AB* [2001] 1 AC 223; *Boss Group Ltd v Boss France SA* [1997] 1 WLR 351 (CA). If the case falls within Art 5(1)(c), the obligation in question will be the one not to misrepresent or to coerce.

accept that a supposed contract is invalid and are parties to a claim only for unjust enrichment.[149] However, once the issue of special jurisdiction has been settled, the national court will apply its own substantive law to dispose of the merits of the claim.[150]

The place of performance of the obligation in question, which pinpoints the court with special jurisdiction, has to be selected from a menu of four items. The first three are given by Article 5(1)(b): in a contract for the sale of goods it is where under the contract the goods were or should have been delivered; in a contract for the provision of services it is where under the contract the services were or should have been provided; and in either of these two classes of contract, it will be the place of performance which the parties otherwise agreed if this is what they did. The application of these rules calls for no more than careful analysis of the contract itself.

The fourth choice is given by Article 5(1)(c): in the case of other contracts, it is the place of performance of the primary[151] obligation on the basis of which the claimant brings the claim: this means the obligation whose non-performance forms the basis of his claim.[152] Despite the possibility of disagreement, which will probably be reinforced by the wording of Article 5(1)(b),[153] the obligation referred to by Article 5(1)(c) need not be one created by the contract and required by the terms of the contract to be performed: an obligation not to use misrepresentation or non-disclosure to procure a contract of reinsurance, for example, is not created by the contract but will be covered by the rule.[154] If the contract does not specify the place of performance of the relevant obligation, it must be identified by the court first applying its choice of law rules to ascertain the law which governs the contract, and then using this to specify the place of performance.[155] Although it is sometimes said that this can make the location of special jurisdiction unpredictable, all Member States have the same choice of law rule for contracts,[156] and it is unlikely that this

---

[149] *Kleinwort Benson Ltd v Glasgow City Council* [1999] 1 AC 153 (a case on the intra-UK provisions, and a decision whose scope is curtailed by *Agnew*).

[150] Case C–26/91 *Soc Jakob Handte GmbH v Soc Traîtements Mécano-chimiques des Surfaces* [1992] ECR I–3967, 3984. But as choice of law is increasingly governed by European Regulation, the opportunity for such dissonance will reduce.

[151] That is to say, a performance obligation as distinct from a secondary obligation to compensate for breach of a primary obligation.

[152] Case 14/76 *De Bloos Sprl v Bouyer SA* [1976] ECR 1497.

[153] Which refers to obligations 'under the contract', as if to exclude reference to those arising outside it.

[154] *Agnew v Länsförsäkringsbolagens AB* [2001] 1 AC 223 (HL).

[155] Case 12/76 *Industrie Tessili Italiana Como v Dunlop AG* [1976] ECR 1473; Case C–440/97 *GIE Groupe Concorde v Master of the Vessel 'Suhediwarno Panjan'* [1999] ECR I–6307.

[156] The Rome Convention, examined in ch 5, is common to all pre-2004 Member States.

criticism needs to be taken too seriously. And after all, if the parties have not troubled to specify the place of performance of an obligation, the only safe assumption is that they are content to have the default option provided by the governing law.

Although in many cases it will produce an easy answer, Article 5(1)(b) is cast in this complex form because of the perceived need to depart from its predecessor in the conventions, which invariably looked to the obligation on which the claimant founded his claim.[157] Where the claimant was an unpaid seller, the obligation in question would therefore be the payment of the price, which was not always due somewhere with a close connection to the facts giving rise to the dispute.[158] In the case of a seller under a contract governed by English law, this would allow the action to be brought in the seller's home courts, as under English law a debt is payable where the creditor resides,[159] and this challenged the principle that it was defendants, not claimants, who were intended to play with home advantage. So for these two major classes of contract, sale of goods and supply of services, the obligation is defined as the performance one, not the payment one, no matter how the claim arises. If the parties have not specified the place of delivery or provision, it will be necessary to fall back on the technique of identifying the law which governs the contract, and then using it to determine the place for performance. So if a contract for the sale of goods is governed by English law, the general rule is that the place of delivery is the manufacturer's place of business.[160] And it is unclear what is intended by the provision in Article 5(1)(b) which allows for contrary agreement, for the place of performance of these obligations is always a matter of agreement between the parties. However, although an agreement on place of performance need not be reduced to writing,[161] a wholly artificial stipulation of a place of performance will be treated as if it were a jurisdiction agreement, and required to comply with Article 23.[162]

The law has therefore embarked on the task of sub-classifying contracts, as opposed to having an omnibus special jurisdictional rule for them all. Article 5(1)(b) will include contracts for the supply of goods, for example on hire or hire purchase, and the supply of goods and services,

---

[157] That is, on the provision which is now Art 5(1)(c).
[158] Case C–288/92 *Custom Made Commercial Ltd v Stawa Metallbau GmbH* [1994] ECR I–2913.
[159] *The Eider* [1893] P 119.
[160] Sale of Goods Act 1979, s 29(2).
[161] Case 56/79 *Zelger v Salinitri* [1980] ECR 89.
[162] Case C–106/95 *MSG v Les Gravières Rhénanes Sàrl* [1997] ECR I–911 (contract for carriage by barge; place of performance specified as a place not on a waterway).

as in a contract for work and materials. But there will be others which do not so easily conform to the assumed pattern of a payment of money[163] in return for a transfer of property: commission agency, a barter contract, contracts of reinsurance, goods paid for by cheque, distributorship, and many arrangements in the realm of financial services will fit only uneasily within Article 5(1)(b); and it may be expected that considerable difficulties of definition will arise as the law is hammered out.

The relevant obligation may be performed in more Member States than one: delivery to sites in Belgium and the Netherlands, sales representation[164] in the United Kingdom and Ireland, and so on. One asks where this obligation was principally to be performed, and locates it there;[165] likewise in a case within Article 5(1)(c), if two obligations are relied on, that which is principal will be the critical one.[166] But if it is not possible to regard one as ancillary to the other as principal, there will be special jurisdiction over only a portion of the claim.[167] A wise judge will avoid so inconvenient a result.

(b) Matters relating to tort, delict, or quasi-delict: Article 5(3)

Article 5(3) gives special jurisdiction to the courts for the place where the harmful event occurred or may occur. The addition of the words 'or may occur' is new and welcome; the place where a harmful event may occur will be subject to the same interpretation as that which identifies where it did occur, differing only in chronology. The place where the harmful event occurred means the place where the damage occurred, or of the event giving rise to it: the claimant may elect between them if they diverge.[168] So when a waterway was polluted and the water used by a gardener downstream with disastrous consequences, the damage occurred where the crop was ruined; the event giving rise to the damage was the discharge of poison into the river; and the claimant was entitled to elect between them.[169] Ascribing a place to damage can be an artificial exercise, but the cases offer

---

[163] See the definition in Sale of Goods Act 1979, s 61.

[164] But if this were seen as a contract of employment, it would have fallen under Arts 18–21.

[165] Case C–125/92 *Mulox IBC v Geels* [1993] ECR I–4075; Case C–383/95 *Rutten v Cross Medical Ltd* [1997] ECR I–57.

[166] Case 266/85 *Shenavai v Kreischer* [1987] ECR 239.

[167] Case C–420/97 *Leathertex Divisione Sintetici SpA v Bodetex BVBA* [1999] ECR I–6747.

[168] Case 21/76 *Handelskwekerij GJ Bier BV v Mines de Potasse d'Alsace* [1976] ECR 1875; Case C–364/93 *Marinari v Lloyds Bank plc* [1995] ECR I–2719; Case C–68/93 *Shevill v Presse Alliance SA* [1995] ECR I–415.

[169] *Handelskwekerij Bier.*

some guidance. In principle, damage occurs where the damage or loss first materializes, and not, if this is different, where it or its consequence is subsequently felt.[170] So if property is wrongfully taken, the damage occurs where the taking occurred, as distinct from where the claimant's financial records of the loss are kept;[171] or—assuming the case does not fall within Article 5(1)—where the negligent advice is acted on so as to result in loss, as distinct from where it was initially received and read,[172] and as further distinct from where the adverse financial consequences of acting on it are eventually felt;[173] where damaged goods were delivered rather than where the damage later eventually came to light;[174] where people read defamatory material and lower their opinion of the victim, as distinct from where the victim lives.[175] But in identifying and locating the damage, an autonomous interpretation of the cause of action must be used, as distinct from one which is taken from the national tort law of the court seised; a similar principle applies to identify the event giving rise to it. So the event giving rise to the damage caused by defamation in the press is the production of the newspaper and not (as it would be seen in English domestic law) the sale of the newspaper to its readership;[176] the compilation of negligent advice and not (as it would be seen in English domestic law) its receipt by the person who acts on it.[177] Any uniformity of jurisdictional result which this may eventually produce will be preceded by an era of uncertainty while it is decided whether, for example, it is the failure properly to test, or the marketing without adequate warning, which gives rise to the damage in product liability cases.[178] In effect, an entire book of tort will need to be written to fill in the blanks created by the preference for autonomous definitions of causes of action, all to be paid for by hapless litigants.

A 'matter relating to tort' means any action which seeks to establish the liability of a defendant and which is not a matter relating to a contract within Article 5(1).[179] There is no difficulty in using it to encompass

---

[170] Case C–220/88 *Dumez France SA v Hessische Landesbank* [1990] ECR I–49.
[171] Case C–364/93 *Marinari v Lloyds Bank plc* [1995] ECR I–2719. It is probable that this also excludes the jurisdiction of the place where the claimant's shares are traded.
[172] ibid.
[173] *Domicrest Ltd v Swiss Bank Corporation* [1999] QB 548.
[174] Case C–51/97 *Réunion Européenne SA v Spliethoff's Bevrachtingskantoor BV* [1998] ECR I–6511.
[175] Case C–68/93 *Shevill v Presse Alliance SA* [1995] ECR I–415.
[176] ibid.
[177] *Domicrest Ltd v Swiss Bank Corporation* [1999] QB 548.
[178] cf *Distillers & Co Ltd v Thompson* [1971] AC 458 (PC).
[179] Case 189/87 *Kalfelis v Bankhaus Schröder, Münchmeyer, Hengst & Co* [1988] ECR 5565.

equitable wrongs such as dishonest assistance of a breach of trust,[180] or breach of confidence, or statutory wrongs such as patent infringement or occupiers' liability.[181] Despite the width of this formulation, and despite the fact that there is no clear line which separates it from restitutionary claims,[182] especially in respect of wrongs, it was probably limited to cases where the claim is based on some semblance of wrongdoing and probably did not extend to claims for restitution which allege the injustice of retaining a gain made at the expense of another: there would not usually be special jurisdiction over such claims which are only casually connected to a particular place. So a claim for the repayment of money handed over in the mistaken belief that there was a contract would not be within Article 5(3).[183] If this is indeed correct, it proceeds not from a theological view about the nature of restitution in English domestic law, but from the fact that other language versions of what in English is rendered as 'liability' connote rather more clearly the sense of liability for doing wrong or inflicting loss.[184] But as Regulation (EC) 864/2007[185] aligns torts and unjust enrichment for the purposes of choice of law, this restriction in the interpretation of Article 5(3) may need to be reconsidered.

Claims founded on pre-contractual misrepresentation are notoriously tricky. Insofar as they seek the rescission of the contract, authority suggests that they would fall within Article 5(1);[186] where the claim is for damages, it has been held that the matter is within Article 5(3).[187] But as the measure of damages in the latter case is designed to place the parties in the same financial position as if the contract had not been made, it may be seen as the financial equivalent of rescission; and on that basis, Article 5(1) would be its more natural home. A claim based on the proposition that the failure to conclude a contract was actionable is not within Article 5(1),[188] but proceedings founded on the disputed validity of a contract would appear to be within Article 5(1). However, as Regulation (EC) 864/2007

---

[180] *Casio Computer Co Ltd v Sayo* [2001] EWCA Civ 661, [2001] ILPr 594.

[181] *Mecklermedia Corp v DC Congress GmbH* [1998] Ch 40.

[182] Indeed, the AG in Case C–89/91 *Shearson Lehmann Hutton Inc v TVB* [1993] ECR I–139 was clear (at 178) that the effect of *Kalfelis* was to include claims alleging unjust enrichment within Art 5(3).

[183] *Kleinwort Benson Ltd v Glasgow City Council* [1999] 1 AC 153.

[184] In *Kalfelis*, the language of which was German, the term is '*Schadenshaftung*', where the sense of loss caused by wrong is more palpable.

[185] [2007] OJ L199/40.

[186] *Agnew v Länsförsäkringsbolagens AB* [2001] 1 AC 223.

[187] *Alfred Dunhill Ltd v Diffusion Internationale de Maroquinerie de Prestige Sarl* [2001] CLC 949.

[188] Case C–334/00 *Fonderie Officine Mecchaniche Tacconi SpA v Heinrich Wagner Sinto Maschinenfabrik GmbH* [2002] ECR I-7357.

treats pre-contractual liability as falling within the choice of law rules for tort,[189] this may lead to the reassignment of claims based on pre-contractual misrepresentation to Article 5(3). Whatever the answer is, it proceeds from the fact that the strict separation of Article 5(1) and 5(3) is easier to state in principle than to apply in practice where the complaint is that a tort induced the victim to enter into a contract.

(c) Other cases of special jurisdiction under Article 5

In relation to *maintenance claims*, Article 5(2) gives special jurisdiction to the maintenance creditor's place of domicile or habitual residence; the term maintenance creditor includes an original applicant for maintenance.[190] In England, a court dealing with the aftermath of a failed marriage will usually make an order for a single, undifferentiated, sum by way of financial provision. But for the purposes of the Regulation, maintenance, which falls within its domain, needs to be separated from the adjudication of rights in property arising out of a matrimonial relationship, which does not. It therefore behoves a judge to mark this distinction within the order which he makes, especially if the creditor may need to enforce it in another Member State.[191] For *civil claims in criminal proceedings*, Article 5(4) allows a court hearing a criminal claim to order damages or restitution to a claimant who, in accordance with the procedure of the court, has intervened as a 'civil party'. This has little practical relevance in England where this is not a common form of procedure.

Article 5(5) deals with *liability arising out of the operation of a branch, agency, or other establishment*: such claims may be brought in the place where it is situated. The concept of a branch, agency, or establishment has to occupy a slippery patch of territory between being too dependent to be anything at all, and too independent to be a branch or agency.[192] A useful test is probably to ask whether it has power on its own account to make contracts which will bind its principal. If it does, it will probably be a branch.[193] It is worth noting that the jurisdictional exposure of the defendant is only to the extent that the claim arises out of the operations of the branch, but it is not implicit that the acts of the defendant must have been performed in that place.[194] The equivalent common law rule

---

[189] Regulation (EC) 864/2007, Art 2(1).
[190] Case C–295/95 *Farrell v Long* [1997] ECR I–1683.
[191] Case C–220/95 *Van den Boogaard v Laumen* [1997] ECR I–1147.
[192] Case 218/86 *SAR Schotte GmbH v Parfums Rothschild Sàrl* [1987] ECR 4905.
[193] Opinion of the AG in Case C–89/91 *Shearson Lehmann Hutton Inc v TVB* [1993] ECR I–139, 169.
[194] Case C–439/93 *Lloyds Register of Shipping v Soc Campenon Bernard* [1995] ECR I–961.

asks whether the defendant is present within the jurisdiction; and, if he is, allows the bringing of any claim against him, whether or not connected to activities undertaken in that place. There is much to be said for the more limited rule contained in Article 5(5).

In relation to *trusts*, Article 5(6) gives special jurisdiction over a settlor, trustee, or beneficiary who is sued as such to the courts of the Member State where the trust is domiciled. For this provision to apply, the trust must be created by the operation of a statute, or by a written instrument, or created orally but evidenced in writing. In relation to claims for payment in respect of *salvage of cargo or freight*, Article 5(7) gives special jurisdiction to the place of the court under the authority of which the freight was arrested to secure payment or could have been arrested but for the fact that bail or other security was given.

(d) Multipartite litigation and consolidated claims: Articles 6 and 7

The Regulation does not permit special jurisdiction over a claim on the simple basis that the court has jurisdiction over another claim to which the first is connected. If a claimant wishes to join separate claims against a single defendant in a single proceeding, this has to be done under the general domiciliary jurisdiction of Article 2. Articles 6 and 7[195] go some way towards allowing the consolidation of separate claims in the interest of coordinating the judicial function and avoiding inconsistent judgments, but the limits on their operation are rigid, and at this point the Regulation operates less than perfectly. There are five cases to consider.

Where a claim is brought against *multiple defendants*, Article 6(1) allows them all to be joined in the one action if it is brought where one of them is domiciled and it is necessary to join the defendants so as to avoid the risk of irreconcilable judgments resulting from separate trials. It is not a requirement that the defendant who is sued where he is domiciled be the principal target of the claim; indeed, it may even be that there is no actual intention to proceed against him at all once he has performed his jurisdictional function. Of course, it is unsatisfactory that a defendant who could have challenged the jurisdiction of the court over him[196] can prejudice the position of co-defendants by declining to do so;[197] but on the other hand, if it were required that the local defendant be the main defendant, there would be endless scope for argument. As for the degree of connection

---

[195] Section 2 of Chapter II; cf Art 6 BC.
[196] eg, on the ground that he is not actually domiciled in that state.
[197] cf *Canada Trust Co v Stolzenberg (No 2)* [2002] 2 AC 1.

between the claims, an exercise in judgment is called for. The predominant need to avoid irreconcilable judgments should incline a court to err on the side of joinder, and against taking a restrictive view.[198] There is, however, no analogous right to join co-defendants into proceedings in a court having only special jurisdiction under Article 5, or having jurisdiction by agreement or submission under Articles 23 or 24. It is difficult to see the rational[199] policy which excludes these cases from Article 6(1), probably because there is none. It goes without saying that there is no joinder by Article 6(1) where jurisdiction is founded on Article 4.[200]

Article 6(2) allows a claim against a *third party* for a warranty, guarantee, contribution, or indemnity, or brought in some other third party proceeding, to be brought in the court hearing the original action unless the original action[201] was instituted with the sole object of allowing the defendant to ensnare the third party with special jurisdiction. It seems probable that the original action must still be live[202] but, by contrast with Article 6(1), the jurisdictional basis of the original action is irrelevant to the operation of Article 6(2). The court may refuse joinder of the third party if this is not done for reasons which, in effect, contradict the general scheme of the Regulation.[203] But if there is an Article 23 jurisdiction agreement between defendant and third party, this will prevent reliance on Article 6(2) by the defendant, no matter how inconvenient the overall result may be, for, by contrast with the common law position, there is no discretion to override Article 23.[204]

Article 6(3) allows a *counterclaim* to be brought in the court in which the original action is pending. The Article is limited to claims which arise out of the same relationship or other essential facts as the original claim, but a pleaded set-off which will not overtop the claim is a defence, not a counterclaim, and need not be justified by reference to this rule.[205] It is not clear whether Article 6(3) extends to a counterclaim against a party other

---

[198] Case C–98/06 *Freeport plc v Arnoldsson* (11 October 2007), reinterpreting Case C–51/97 *Réunion Européenne SA v Spliethoff's Bevrachtingskantoor BV* [1998] ECR I–6511.

[199] There is an irrational one of seeking at all costs to promote the jurisdiction of the domicile.

[200] Case C–51/97 *Réunion Européenne SA v Spliethoff's Bevrachtingskantoor BV* [1998] ECR I–6511.

[201] According to Jenard. But according to Case C–77/04 *GIE Réunion Européenne v Zurich España* [2005] ECR I–4509, the third party claim (instead? as well?) must not have this bad motivation.

[202] *Waterford Wedgwood plc v David Nagli Ltd* [1999] 3 All ER 185; cf *The Ikarian Reefer* [2000] 1 WLR 603 (CA).

[203] Case C–365/88 *Kongress Agentur Hagen GmbH v Zeehaghe BV* [1990] ECR I–1845.

[204] *Hough v P&O Containers Ltd* [1999] QB 834.

[205] Case C–431/93 *Danvaern Productions A/S v Schuhfabriken Otterbeck GmbH & Co* [1995] ECR I–2053.

than the original claimant, but in the context of insurance, at least, it has been held that it does not where to allow it would deprive an insured or policyholder of his special jurisdictional privileges.[206] Article 6(4), which deals with contract actions joined with actions against the same defendant in *matters relating to rights in rem in immovable property*, has already been mentioned. It is obviously sensible that an action against a mortgagor should be able to enforce the security right as well as the personal covenant to repay and this is, in effect, what Article 6(4) allows. (Article 7 allows a court which has jurisdiction 'by virtue of this Regulation'[207] in an action relating to liability from the use or operation of a ship to entertain a claim for the limitation of such liability.)

Article 6 still takes too few steps in the direction of the efficient coordination of claims, and if its provisions are to be given a restrictive interpretation, it will be even less successful than currently it is. Rules which operate in this area need to trust the judge to be sensible, something which is alien to much of the modern legal tradition on the continent of Europe. If it is now expected that courts will trust each other to interpret the Regulation properly, it may be time to allow judges more general flexibility in this area, and the provisions for the coordination and consolidation of claims be made a little more generous.

7. RESIDUAL JURISDICTION OVER DEFENDANTS NOT DOMICILED IN A MEMBER STATE: ARTICLE 4

If none of the rest of the Regulation has applied, the defendant must be someone who has no domicile in a Member State. At this point, the Regulation does not prescribe in detail when jurisdiction may be taken over a defendant whose only connection is with a non-Member State. Article 4 therefore expressly authorizes the claimant to rely on the traditional jurisdictional rules of the court[208] in which he wishes to sue: service of process on an Australian defendant present in England, service out of the jurisdiction on an American defendant with the permission of the court under the CPR, Part 6, and so on. But the Regulation has not washed its hands of the dispute. Article 4 is an integral part of Chapter II, and it is expressly provided that Articles 22[209] and 23[210] prevail over it.

---

[206] *Jordan Grand Prix Ltd v Baltic Insurance Group* [1999] 2 AC 127.
[207] Which presumably includes a reference to other conventions by way of Art 66.
[208] Some of which are set out in Annex I to the Regulation.
[209] Exclusive jurisdiction regardless of domicile.
[210] Jurisdiction agreements for the courts of a Member State: this specific provision did not appear in Art 4 BC.

Moreover, as Article 4 will result in a judgment enforceable under Chapter III of the Regulation, its operation is also subject to Article 27[211] on *lis alibi pendens*. So a claimant may not rely on Article 4 if proceedings between the same parties and involving the same cause of action were instituted in a court which was seised earlier in time, not even if that court has based its jurisdiction on Article 4 as well.[212] It is therefore wrong to picture Article 4 as opening a door back into the world outside the Regulation. It is better understood as incorporating by reference traditional jurisdictional rules; and the effect of their incorporation into the Regulation means that they have to be tweaked to fit into their new surroundings. Even so, there is room for unease at the combination of traditional jurisdictional rules, many of which will appear to defendants as being outrageously wide in their sweep, and the automatic recognition under Chapter III, of judgments based on such provisions. The point will be examined when we look at the recognition of foreign judgments.

8. LOSS OF JURISDICTION: *LIS ALIBI PENDENS* AND RELATED ACTIONS: ARTICLES 27–30

The aim of the Regulation, that judgments should be enforceable in other Member States without impediment, would be jeopardized by concurrent litigation of identical or similar disputes. Articles 27 to 30[213] accordingly provide the means of control. Where the *same action, between the same parties*, is brought before the courts of two Member States, Article 27 requires the court seised second to dismiss its action; its only alternative is to stay while any challenge to the jurisdiction of the first court is dealt with (and to dismiss proceedings once it is confirmed). The rule is simple and clear, entirely dependent on which action was first out of the starting blocks. It takes no account of considerations of comparative appropriateness, for all courts with jurisdiction[214] under the Regulation are equally appropriate. It takes no account of the particular rule relied on by each claimant, for despite their hierarchy, all jurisdictional rules[215] applicable under the Regulation are equally proper. Moreover, the court seised second is absolutely forbidden to investigate whether, still less decide that, the first erred in concluding that it had jurisdiction: all courts are

---

[211] And presumably Art 28 on related actions.

[212] Case C–351/89 *Overseas Union Insurance Ltd v New Hampshire Insurance Co* [1991] ECR I–3317.

[213] Section 9 of Chapter II; cf Arts 21–23 BC; although Art 30 had no precursor.

[214] Including Art 4 jurisdiction.

[215] Including Art 4.

equally competent to apply the Regulation, and where the competences are equal, the first in time prevails.[216] A possible exception exists where the second court has exclusive jurisdiction under Article 22,[217] but this has not been confirmed. Only if the defendant in the first court has contested its jurisdiction is the second court permitted to stay its hand; but once the first court has confirmed its jurisdiction the second court must dismiss the action. This abrupt solution to the problem may produce an unseemly rush to commence litigation and seise the court of a party's choice; it may be catastrophic to tell the opposite party that proceedings will be commenced after a period of days.[218] 'Speak softly and hurry a big writ',[219] as Theodore Roosevelt nearly said.

For its operation, Article 27 requires three 'identities': identity of parties (but procedural differences between the formulation of the claimants and defendants are not decisive); identity of object (the two actions must have the same end in view); and identity of cause (they must be based on the same facts and rules of law).[220] So in relation to the identity of parties, an action brought *in rem* against a vessel may still be between the same parties as one *in personam* against those with an interest in the vessel; the critical test is whether the interests of the parties are identical and indissociable.[221] As regards object and cause, an action for damages for breach of contract shares identity with one for a declaration that the contract had been lawfully rescinded;[222] an action by a cargo-owner in respect of damage to cargo shares identity with one against the cargo-owner for a declaration of non-liability.[223] But an action for damages for breach of warranty of quality is not identical to an action for the price of goods delivered, and Article 27 will not apply to it.[224]

Prior to the Regulation, the Conventions made only a general attempt to define the point at which a court was seised for the purpose of these Articles. The Court held that the date on which a court was seised was determined by asking on what date the matter was 'definitively pending' in the particular court, and the question was answered by recourse to the

---

[216] Case C–351/89 *Overseas Union Insurance Ltd v New Hampshire Insurance Co* [1991 ECR I–3317.

[217] ibid.

[218] *Messier Dowty Ltd v Sabena SA* [2000] 1 WLR 2040 (CA).

[219] That is, one drafted with such width that it is not possible for the opponent to construct a claim of argument which takes advantage of a gap in the claims made.

[220] Case C–406/92 *The Tatry* [1994] ECR I–5439.

[221] Case C–351/96 *Drouot Assurances SA v CMI* [1998] ECR I–3075.

[222] Case 144/86 *Gubisch Maschinenfabrik KG v Palumbo* [1987] ECR 4861.

[223] *The Tatry.*

[224] Article 28 may apply, though.

procedural laws of the several courts in which the actions were brought.[225] As a matter of English law, it was held that a court was not seised, even though the action had been commenced, until the writ had been served on the particular defendant.[226] Service on a co-defendant would not suffice to seise the court in relation to an unserved defendant,[227] neither did the obtaining of interlocutory relief prior to service of process.[228] In other states the rules were different, and in some a court would be seised prior to service of process. The result was chaotic and confusing, not least because it could be difficult for litigants to obtain reliable advice about the seisin of foreign courts for the purpose of this jurisdictional rule: this is not the daily business of the average practitioner. Responding to this concern, Article 30 provides a solution to cases governed by the Regulation: (a) in countries where the claimant lodges a document at court before serving it, it is the date of lodging (assuming the claimant has not failed to take the subsequent steps he needs to take for service to be effected); (b) in countries where the document has to be served before being lodged with the court, at the time when it is received by the authority responsible for service (assuming the claimant has not failed to take the subsequent steps he needs to take for lodging to take place). England is a category (a) country, and the date stamped on the claim form by the court will identify the date of seisin. There may be cases which do not fit easily into this framework at all, such as where an amendment is made to add a fresh claim, or a new cause of action, or an additional defendant, into proceedings which are already pending *inter alios*. Difficulty may yet also arise in cases in which a claimant is required to institute a process of mediation before being permitted to litigate a claim. But it would be ungrateful to cavil. The confusion which preceded this reform was indefensible, and if problems emerge with Article 30, they can be addressed when within five years[229] the operation of the Regulation is reviewed.

If Article 27 is inapplicable, Article 28 may apply if there are *related actions* in the two courts: that is, actions which are so closely connected that it is expedient to hear them together to avoid the risk of irreconcilable judgments resulting from separate proceedings. If the actions are related, the second court may dismiss its action if it may be consolidated with the proceedings pending in the first court; it may stay its proceedings to

---

[225] Case 129/83 *Zelger v Salinitri (No 2)* [1984] ECR 2397.
[226] *Dresser UK Ltd v Falcongate Freight Management Ltd* [1992] QB 502 (CA).
[227] *Grupo Torras SA v Sheikh Fahad Mohammed al Sabah* [1996] 1 Lloyd's Rep 7 (CA).
[228] *Neste Chemicals SA v DK Line SA (The Sargasso)* [1994] 3 All ER 180 (CA). But see also *Phillips v Symes* [2008] UKHL 1.
[229] Article 68.

await the outcome in the first court; or it may do neither. Where Article 28 applies, the English preference is to prefer dismissal for consolidation in the first court.[230] This may well be appropriate if the two actions involve different parties but have essentially the same cause of action: to bind all concerned into the one hearing and one judgment is sensible, and if the cause of action is substantially the same, the joinder of parties may not lengthen the trial in the first court. But if the same parties are litigating different causes of action in the two Member States, it may be more efficient to stay the second action to await the outcome of the first, and apply Chapter III of the Regulation to curtail the second action. By contrast, if the second action is dismissed for consolidation with the first, the effect will be to lengthen the first trial by the length of the second; had there instead been a stay, the second trial may never need to take place.

Where two courts have exclusive jurisdiction regardless of domicile, Article 29 provides that the court seised second must decline jurisdiction in favour of the first court. Although a court with jurisdiction under a jurisdiction agreement is said by Article 23 to have exclusive jurisdiction, it has never been considered that Article 29, as opposed to Article 27, is applicable to such cases.

9. PROCEDURAL MODIFICATION OF REGULATION JURISDICTION

A troublesome set of questions concerns the extent to which an English court may supplement or modify the jurisdictional scheme of the Regulation by recourse to its rules on *forum conveniens*, anti-suit injunctions, and so forth. To this question there is no clear and easy answer; much avoidable confusion has arisen from the search for wide and general solutions. The picture must be painted with a fine brush. But it is also important to bear in mind the 'judge as umpire' nature of common law adjudication,[231] for it explains (although cannot eradicate) some of the difficulties which this area of law has thrown up.

(a) Disputes about jurisdiction

When contesting jurisdiction *in limine*, a defendant may deny that the court has the jurisdiction asserted by the claimant. In general, factual doubt on any material point is resolved by requiring a 'good arguable case' to be shown that the ground on which reliance is placed is satisfied. This

---

[230] *Sarrio SA v Kuwait Investment Authority* [1999] 1 AC 32.
[231] Above, p 35.

is the reason a simple denial by the defendant of the existence of the contract, or whatever, is not conclusive against the existence of jurisdiction.
Although this has been established by the House of Lords,[232] later cases
have refined it to mean that the party seeking to disturb the jurisdiction
which would otherwise exist must have 'much the better of the argument'
on the material before the court.[233] For example, if the claimant seises the
English court, but the defendant asserts that the case is covered by a jurisdiction agreement for the courts of another Member State, he must have
the better of the argument on the point or points in dispute. If the claimant seises the English court by reference to what he alleges is a choice of
court agreement for the English court, but which the defendant does not
admit, the claimant must have the better of the argument on the point or
points in dispute. If the claimant could get away with a lower standard of
showing, it would mean a court would exercise jurisdiction even though it
believed that, on balance, it did not have jurisdiction. This would make no
sense, and would jeopardize the practical effect of the Regulation.

(b) *Forum non conveniens*

When the claimant relies on a jurisdictional rule other than Article 4, a
court has no discretion to stay its proceedings and encourage the claimant
to proceed instead in another Member State on the ground that it is the
natural forum.[234] It makes no difference that the claimant is not domiciled
in a Member State.[235] But where the natural forum is in a non-Member
State, the original view[236] of the Court of Appeal was that nothing in the
Regulation stood in the way of an English court acceding to a defendant's
application for a stay of proceedings on the ground of *forum non conveniens*.
This followed from the perception that the Regulation had no application
to a question which arose, not as between the courts of Member States,
but as between one Member State and a non-Member State. Eventually
this view was decisively rejected by the European Court.[237] A claim was
brought in England after a very serious personal injury was sustained
in Jamaica. One of the six defendants was domiciled in England;[238]

---

[232] *Canada Trust Co v Stolzenberg (No 2)* [2002] 1 AC 1.

[233] *Bols Distilleries BV v Superior Yacht Services Ltd* [2006] UKPC 45, [2007] 1 WLR 12;
Konkola Copper Mines plc v Coromin Ltd [2006] EWCA Civ 5, [2006] 1 Lloyd's Rep 410.

[234] Schlosser Report [1979] OJ C59/71 at para 78.

[235] For the Regulation draws no distinction: Case C–412/98 *Universal General Insurance Co
v Groupe Josi Reinsurance Co SA* [2000] ECR I–5925.

[236] *Re Harrods (Buenos Aires) Ltd* [1992] Ch 72 (CA).

[237] Case C–281/02 *Owusu v Jackson* [2005] ECR I–1383 (a decision on the Brussels
Convention, but directly applicable to the Regulation).

[238] The other five in Jamaica.

the natural forum was undoubtedly in Jamaica. The Court ruled that as Article 2 gave the English court jurisdiction, and as the Regulation made no reference to a power to stay proceedings on the ground of *forum non conveniens*, the exercise of such a power was inconsistent with the Regulation. The Court laboured under the startling misapprehension that an English court could order a stay even though the defendant had not applied for it, but this schoolboy howler cannot justify ignoring the rest of the judgment. And from the perspective of the European Court, it must have seemed incredible that, eight years after he had been rendered quadriplegic, a claimant could be ordered by an English court to start from scratch in the courts of a third world country, several thousand miles from where he was receiving constant medical care. That the Court of Appeal made the reference is beyond belief, but it did so; and if the judgment of the European Court is a wound, it is entirely self-inflicted.

The Court rested its conclusion on the principle of legal certainty, and on the fact that the legislative text made no reference to the doctrine of *forum non conveniens*. But it refused to answer the second question referred, namely whether there was a power to stay in response to a jurisdiction agreement for the courts of a non-Member State, or where there were proceedings already pending before the courts of a non-Member State, or where the claim concerned title to land, the validity of patents, and so forth, in a non-Member State. A superficial reading of the judgment might suggest that such connections to a non-Member State, not being mentioned in the Regulation, are irrelevant and furnish no basis for jurisdictional relief, but this is plainly wrong. The Court had made it clear, only a few years earlier, that a jurisdiction agreement for a non-Member State took whatever effect it had according to the national law of the court seised.[239] There is no reason to suppose that the Court had changed its mind, and less to suggest that the principle of legal certainty is best served by ignoring agreements on jurisdiction. Neither is legal certainty much advanced by pretending that proceedings pending in the courts of a non-Member State are not happening at all, or by ruling on the validity of a non-Member State patent, or on title to land in a non-Member State. The real surprise is that anyone[240] would interpret the new judgment as leading to such ludicrous results. The reason that there is no mention in the Regulation of these particular connections to non-Member States is that the Regulation cannot, any more than the Convention could, direct a non-Member State court to hear or not hear a case. It therefore left these issues

---

[239] Case C–387/98 *Coreck Maritime GmbH v Handelsveem BV* [2000] ECR I–9337.
[240] Those who have done so are not cited here.

unregulated because it lacked the legal power to harmonize them.[241] But there is no serious doubt about it: a court seised with jurisdiction under Article 2 may still apply its own law to give effect to a choice of court for a non-Member State; it may still take the appropriate notice of a *lis pendens* in a non-Member State; and it is not obliged to adjudicate title to land in New York or the validity of patents granted under the law of Japan, just because the defendant to the claim is domiciled in England.

One explanation for this general conclusion, and which finds some support in French doctrinal writing, is that a national court may give 'reflexive effect' to Articles 22, 23, and 27 of the Regulation.[242] But this is not how the Court dealt with jurisdiction agreements for a non-Member State,[243] and it is not an ideal solution if it suggests that the 'reflexive effect' is as obligatory as the Articles are when they operate within the Regulation. This is not as satisfactory as a remission to the more flexible and sensitive approach of the doctrine of *forum non conveniens*. But none of this challenges the decision of the Court in *Owusu*.

Where jurisdiction is founded on Article 4, a court may take into account issues of *forum conveniens* in determining whether to grant or to set aside permission to serve out of the jurisdiction, for, as a matter of English jurisdictional law, service out may only be made, and jurisdiction will only therefore exist, if England is the natural forum.[244] It has also been held that a stay of proceedings commenced as of right under Article 4 may be granted on the basis of *forum non conveniens*. Where the natural forum is a non-Member State, this makes sense as the doctrine of *forum non conveniens* is an integral part of the jurisdictional rules which Article 4 absorbs into the Regulation. It has also been held to apply where the natural forum is another Member State, which is more controversial,[245] not least because if the English court grants a stay of proceedings it still remains seised of them,[246] and may at a later stage lift the stay. That and Article 27 may prevent the courts of the natural forum, seised second, exercising jurisdiction at all. It has been suggested that this may be overcome by the English court dismissing the action rather than staying it,[247] but this would be a novelty, and one which contradicts the proposition

---

[241] Opinion C–1/03 *Lugano* [2006] ECR I–1145.

[242] The argument was first advanced by Mr Droz. See [1990] RCDIP 1 at 14.

[243] Case C–387/98 *Coreck Maritime GmbH v Handelsveem BV* [2000] ECR I–9337.

[244] CPR r 6.21(2A).

[245] *Haji-Ioannou v Frangos* [1999] 2 Lloyd's Rep 337 (CA).

[246] *Rofa Sport Management AG v DHL International (UK) Ltd* [1989] 1 WLR 902 (CA).

[247] *Haji-Ioannou v Frangos* [1999] 2 Lloyd's Rep 337 (CA).

that a stayed action is still pending, and that the stay can be lifted in an appropriate case.[248]

(c) Anti-suit injunctions

Given that a court seised second has no right to assess the jurisdiction of a court seised first,[249] it may appear that it has no right to order a respondent who is suing as claimant in another Member State to discontinue his action, for this would involve not only ruling on the foreign court's jurisdiction, but granting relief on the back of a finding that it was lacking. For a while the English courts simply overlooked such objections, and ordered injunctions to enforce agreements on jurisdiction without regard to the status of proceedings before the courts of other Member States.[250] Despite the fact that there was much to be said for summary enforcement of such commercial agreements,[251] reconciling this with the scheme of the Regulation was quite impossible; and as soon as it was given the opportunity to do so, the Court declared that anti-suit injunctions were inconsistent with the scheme of the Regulation.[252] To the submission that an anti-suit injunction did not depend on a finding that the foreign court lacked jurisdiction, but simply sought to enforce the parties' personal rights and obligations, the Court responded that the effect of the order was to interfere with proceedings before a judge in another Member State, and that the interference was indirect was no justification for it. In this respect it seems to have departed from an earlier approach to equitable rights and duties, which were understood as operating *in personam* only,[253] but it is undeniable that a judge in a Member State is unlikely to appreciate the subtlety of the distinction between direct and indirect interference with the proceedings before his court: his judicial oath is unlikely to oblige him to abide by instructions from a foreign judge whether these come directly or via one of the parties at the bar.

The law may have been declared by the European Court, but it is worth observing the misunderstanding, on all sides, which gave rise to it. When an English judge says 'on the application before me I am not asked to

---

[248] It is also complicated if undertakings have been given by the defendant in support of his application for a stay, and it is later sought to enforce these.

[249] Case C–351/89 *Overseas Union Insurance Ltd v New Hampshire Insurance Co* [1991] ECR I–3317.

[250] *Continental Bank NA v Aeakos Compania Naviera SA* [1994] 1 WLR 588 (CA); *The Angelic Grace* [1995] 1 Lloyd's Rep 87 (CA).

[251] *OT Africa Line Ltd v Hijazy* [2001] 1 Lloyd's Rep 76.

[252] Case C–159/02 *Turner v Grovit* [2004] ECR I–3565 (a case on the Brussels Convention).

[253] Case C–294/92 *Webb v Webb* [1994] ECR I–1717.

decide whether the foreign court has jurisdiction, which I won't; I am asked to decide whether the parties bound themselves so that the respondent is in beach of his agreement by invoking it, which I will' he is performing the judge as umpire role which common law procedure, wittingly or unwittingly, ascribes to him. It is quite misleading to say that he is doing indirectly that which he may not do directly; he is doing what the parties ask him to do, by acting as umpire in relation to a particular dispute, giving his decision, decreeing the legal consequences of it, and leaving it to the parties to work out what happens next. Any litigator will instantly recognize the way it happens. It is perverse or untruthful to assert that a judge in such circumstances is deciding whether a foreign court has jurisdiction. He is simply drawing the legal conclusions which flow from his decision as umpire of the dispute which the parties formulate for his decision. If this offends the scheme of the Brussels Regulation, well, that is as may be; but the real basis of the objection, as it is submitted, lies in the failure to understand the 'judge as umpire', or limited, nature of judicial adjudication in the common law. It is far from clear that this has ever been explained; it is unclear whether it would have led to any different outcome if it had been; and it may now all be too late. Even so, the course of the modern law has been charted under a cloud of ignorance for which no-one and everyone is to blame.

The immediate consequence is that an English court may not restrain a wrongdoer, who is subject to its personal jurisdiction, from committing his litigational wrong before a foreign court. Whatever justifies this result, there is no doubt that it weakens the power of an English court to do effective justice according to the law. This is especially noticeable where a party to a binding agreement on jurisdiction brings proceedings in another Member State, which are designed to frustrate reliance on the jurisdiction agreement for so long as the spoiling action may be dragged out in the foreign court. So notorious has this tactic become that it has acquired a name of its own: the 'Italian torpedo' describes the institution of proceedings in Italy, the court that time forgot, to prevent the enforcement of a jurisdiction agreement.[254] Even so, there appears to be nothing to stand in the way of an action brought to obtain damages for breach of contract, and while this will not be as effective as the injunction in holding parties to their obligations, it may be a reasonable second best. Such claims are increasingly common outside the scope of the Regulation,[255]

---

[254] Case C–116/02 *Erich Gasser GmbH v Handelsveem BV* [2003] ECR I–14693. The terminology of torpedo is that of Mr Franzosi: [1997] 7 Eur Int Prop R 382.

[255] *Union Discount Co v Zoller* [2001] EWCA Civ 1755, [2002] 1 WLR 1517.

but as they make no judgment about, and have no effect upon, the jurisdiction of the court in another Member State, they may yet come to be used to enforce agreements. The battle to forum shop and to prevent forum shopping simply moves onto new ground: *plus ça change, plus c'est la même chose*.

10. APPLICATIONS FOR PROVISIONAL OR PROTECTIVE MEASURES: ARTICLE 31

Provisional or protective measures obtained before the trial may critically affect the way the dispute is resolved: measures freezing assets and ordering disclosure of their whereabouts, orders for an interim payment, and so on, will affect the balance of power prior to the trial. Yet the jurisdictional control of these measures is touched only lightly by Article 31[256] of the Regulation, which contents itself with the principle that so long as they are guaranteed to be provisional and reversible, there is no need to impose any jurisdictional restriction on where, nor on in how many states at the same time, they may be obtained. Where the substantive claim to which they are ancillary falls within the domain of the Regulation, that is, within Article 1, it is necessary to distinguish two types of case in which provisional, including protective, measures may be applied for. If the court applied to has jurisdiction over the merits, there is no external limit upon the relief it may order, provisional or otherwise.[257] But if it does not, an application may still be made under Article 31 of the Regulation. The only jurisdictional requirement to be satisfied is any which national law places upon the applicant, and there is no objection to the use, in this context, of traditional or exorbitant grounds of personal jurisdiction. In England, therefore, all that is needed is to serve the respondent with the claim form by which the relief is sought: within the jurisdiction as of right, or out of it with the prior permission of the court[258] (although in deciding whether to grant permission to serve, the court may take account of the fact that the trial will not be taking place in England and may ask whether this makes it inexpedient to grant the relief applied for[259]). But Article 31 has been held[260] to impose two further limitations, not strictly jurisdictional in

---

[256] Section 10 of Chapter II; cf Art 24 BC.
[257] Case C–391/95 *Van Uden Maritime BV v Deco Line* [1998] ECR I–7091 (where the court did not have merits jurisdiction, an agreement to arbitrate having denied every court merits jurisdiction).
[258] CPR r 6.20(4).
[259] Civil Jurisdiction and Judgments Act 1982, s 25(2). For analysis of this, see *Crédit Suisse Fides Trust SA v Cuoghi* [1998] QB 818 (CA).
[260] Case C–391/95 *Van Uden Maritime BV v Deco Line* [1998] ECR I–7091.

nature. First, the measure must be one which is truly provisional, in that it is guaranteed to be reversible if it turns out not to have been warranted once the merits have been tried. An English freezing order, which will require an undertaking in damages often fortified by a bank guarantee, is a good example of what is meant. Secondly, its scope may not extend to assets within the territorial jurisdiction of another Member State. This is more problematic, for although this limitation makes sense if the order is expressed to take effect directly against assets,[261] an English freezing order does not do so, but merely orders an individual who is or has been brought within the personal jurisdiction of the court not to dissipate his assets. It remains unclear whether the presence or residence of the respondent within England immunizes such an order from this limitation,[262] or whether the order must instead be taken as one which, in substance and notwithstanding its form,[263] does affect assets in another Member State so that, to that extent, it may not be sought under cover of Article 31.

D. COMMON LAW JURISDICTION AND JURISDICTION UNDER RULES OF COURT

It is now necessary to examine the traditional rules of jurisdiction. These apply where the Regulation does not, or where the Regulation states that they do. A fundamental distinction is drawn between cases where the defendant is and is not within the territorial jurisdiction of the court when the proceedings are commenced.

1. DOMAIN OF THE TRADITIONAL RULES

If the dispute is not a civil or commercial matter, the traditional rules of English law, as established by common law and legislation, alone determine the jurisdiction of the court. In such a case the Regulation has no bearing on the existence or the exercise of jurisdiction, even in the event of a *lis alibi pendens*; and the judgment will not qualify for recognition in other Member States under Chapter III of the Regulation.

If the dispute is in a civil or commercial matter in which Article 4 of the Regulation specifies that the traditional rules of English law are to

---

[261] Which is understood to be the way in which a French order of *saisie conservatoire* operates.

[262] This appears to have been the view in *Crédit Suisse Fides Trust SA v Cuoghi*.

[263] For an analogous refusal by the Court to accept that the precise form of an English admiralty action *in rem* renders it different from an action *in personam* in the context of Art 27 see Case C–406/92 *The Tatry* [1994] ECR I–5439.

be applied, it is, as was explained above, misleading to contend that the Regulation is inapplicable. The control of parallel litigation in the courts of Member States and the recognition of judgments will still be governed by the Regulation, as will an application for provisional or protective measures. This context may require the traditional rules to 'receive shape from the subject matter and wording of the Convention itself'.[264] But with that proviso we can proceed to examine the traditional approach to the jurisdiction of an English court.

2. ESTABLISHING JURISDICTION BY SERVICE OF PROCESS WITHIN ENGLAND

Jurisdiction is established by the service of process. A person who is present in England may be served with process as of the claimant's right; and this simple fact serves to establish the jurisdiction of the court over him. The manner of service is prescribed by the Civil Procedure Rules (CPR). It now includes personal service, service by post, and service by certain electronic means,[265] but the need for some formality is justified by the significant consequences of an action having been commenced. Service on a partnership is also regulated by the CPR. Legislation provides that an English company may be served at its registered office[266] (although if in liquidation on its liquidator, and then only with permission of the court[267]). An overseas company may be served by making service on the person authorized to accept service on its behalf, but if this does not work, process may be served leaving it at or posting it to any place of business within the jurisdiction.[268] In this context, a place of business denotes a fixed and definite place from which the business of the company is carried out.[269] If at this place contracts are made which bind the company, the company will probably have a place of business within the jurisdiction.[270] But the procedures for service on corporations set out in CPR Part 6 are

---

[264] Mance LJ in *Raiffeisen Zentralbank Österreich AG v Five Star Trading LLC* [2001] EWCA Civ 68, [2001] QB 825 at [33]. The case concerned the impact of the Rome Convention on common law rules on assignment of intangibles, but the point is important and general.

[265] CPR r 6.2.

[266] Companies Act 2006, s 1139(1) (not yet in force).

[267] Insolvency Act 1986, s 130(2).

[268] Companies Act 2006, s 1139(2) (not yet in force).

[269] *South India Shipping Corp Ltd v Export-Import Bank of Korea* [1985] 1 WLR 585 (CA); *Re Oriel Ltd* [1986] 1 WLR 180 (CA).

[270] cf *Adams v Cape Industries plc* [1990] Ch 433 (CA), a case on the recognition of foreign judgments.

alternatives to statutory service, and these widen and relax the methods of service on a company.[271]

3. CONTESTING JURISDICTION

A defendant who considers that as a matter of law the court has no jurisdiction over him or over the subject matter of the claim, or who contends that service was irregular, or on some other ground seeks to have service set aside, must first acknowledge service. This is a purely formal step, for he may then make an application within a short fixed period, under CPR Part 11,[272] for a declaration that the court has no jurisdiction, and for relief which follows from that: as the contention is that he should not have been served, the usual relief will be the setting aside of service. Where he has been served within the jurisdiction, the most common ground for objection is that the Regulation provides that he is not liable to be sued in the English courts; he may also plead a personal immunity from the jurisdiction of the courts or that the subject matter of the claim is something over which the court has no jurisdiction: in any such case service should be set aside. But if he acknowledges service but makes no application under Part 11, or if he takes a step in the action otherwise than to contest the jurisdiction, he will be taken thereby to have submitted to the jurisdiction, and this submission will itself become the basis for the jurisdiction of the court, no matter that a challenge could have been made successfully.[273] Everything, apart from provisional or protective measures, waits for the final resolution of the challenge to the jurisdiction. Proceedings on the merits only start after that.

4. APPLYING TO STAY THE PROCEEDINGS

A defendant who cannot argue that the court lacks jurisdiction and that he should not have been served may still apply to stay the proceedings on the ground that, although the court does have jurisdiction over him, the claimant should nevertheless sue him in the courts of another country. Confusingly, perhaps, the application is also made under CPR Part 11, and within its time frame, even though the defendant is not contesting the

---

[271] CPR rr 6.2(2), 6.5(6); CPR 6 PD, para 6.2; *Saab v Saudi American Bank* [1999] 1 WLR 1861 (CA).

[272] This procedure for contesting the jurisdiction is applicable whether the case is one to which the Regulation applies, one based on service within the jurisdiction, or one based on service out of the jurisdiction.

[273] The exception to this proposition is that where there was no subject matter jurisdiction, personal submission cannot remedy the deficiency, and jurisdiction remains non-existent.

jurisdiction of the court.[274] If his argument succeeds, the English action will not be dismissed[275] but will remain stayed: pending but held in abeyance.[276] Although he cannot be ordered to do so, the claimant will have no practical alternative to suing in a foreign court. In principle a stay may be lifted if some problem arises, or if an undertaking given to the court by the defendant is not observed: as the action remains pending throughout, there is no problem of limitation. Where service was made within the jurisdiction, two main grounds exist for seeking a stay of proceedings: that the *forum conveniens* is elsewhere, and that bringing the English action is a breach of contract which should be stopped. The relief is common to both, but the principles which lead to it are sharply distinct.

(a) *Forum* (non) *conveniens*

If the defendant can show that there is another court which is available to the claimant, and which is clearly more appropriate than England for the trial of the action, a stay will generally be ordered unless the claimant can show that it would be unjust to require him to sue there. The two limbs of the test are distinct, with individual burdens of proof, but at the end of it, a court will still ask whether the interests of justice require a stay of proceedings.

The English[277] development of this doctrine, principally by the House of Lords, has made a distinctive contribution to common law jurisdictional thinking.[278] What underpins it is the proposition that if the parties are content to have a trial in England, no-one will stand in their way;[279] but if they are not in agreement, there is no compelling reason why the claimant, rather than the defendant, should get his way and have the trial in England. Once that is accepted, all that remains is to elaborate the test which will implement the principle. In England this is done by pointing

---

[274] This represents a clear departure from the practice prior to 1999, when a challenge to the jurisdiction and an application for a stay were made by distinct mechanisms, reflecting their distinct intellectual bases. But it is undeniably convenient to have a single procedure for all objections to being sued in England.

[275] Although for the proposition that it may be dismissed if a stay would leave the claimant unable to sue in the foreign court, see *Haji-Ioannou v Frangos* [1999] 2 Lloyd's Rep 337 (CA).

[276] *Rofa Sport Management AG v DHL International (UK) Ltd* [1989] 1 WLR 902 (CA).

[277] It was developed much earlier in Scotland, and embedded in the American constitutional guarantee of due process, long before it was accepted in England.

[278] The leading authorities are *Spiliada Maritime Corp v Cansulex Ltd* [1987] AC 460, *Connelly v RTZ Corp plc* [1998] AC 854, and *Lubbe v Cape plc* [2000] 1 WLR 1545 (HL). For the steps which led to *Spiliada*, see *The Atlantic Star* [1974] AC 436, *MacShannon v Rockware Glass Ltd* [1978] AC 705, and *The Abidin Daver* [1984] AC 398.

[279] Unless there is an absence of subject matter jurisdiction, or if Art 22 of the Regulation denies the jurisdiction of the English court.

out that there is a court, clearly more appropriate than England for the trial of the action, and asking whether there would be any injustice in having the trial take place there. In Australia, the same broad principle is accepted but is applied very differently: the immediate focus is not on the comparative appropriateness of the foreign court as against the local one, but on whether the Australian court is clearly inappropriate for the trial:[280] this may be considered a more seemly question for an Australian judge to answer. Even so, it should be observed that the leading Australian cases have tended to be personal injury cases, for which the prospect of making the injured claimant go limping off to a court far away, but preferred by the wrongdoer, is unattractive. The English doctrine, by contrast, was developed in commercial disputes. The Australian approach also reflects a view that, if a court is given jurisdiction, it should require clear and convincing grounds before it declines to exercise it; and this is therefore halfway to the civilian view that if the legislator has vested the judge with jurisdiction he has told the judge to adjudicate and the judge should not think he has power to set aside the law, whether on grounds of *forum conveniens* or otherwise. But civilians do not always understand the doctrine of *forum conveniens*: even the European Court evidently believes that a stay can be ordered against the wishes of the defendant.[281] It is a necessary and subtle counterpart to rules of jurisdiction based on service, which are otherwise too broad and insensitive to be acceptable by themselves. It is confirmed by statute;[282] has been embraced by the profession; and has been taken up throughout the common law world. The distrust of judicial discretion which such criticism betrays gives no ground for objection to the common law. Lord Goff of Chieveley, the principal architect of the developed law, described the doctrine as the 'most civilised of legal principles',[283] and he is right: it allows a judge in one country to yield to the submission that the courts of another country are better placed to give the parties the adjudication they deserve. It gives effect to that judicial comity which acknowledges that where sovereignties collide, a sensitive solution is preferable to an abrupt one.

More criticism is sometimes offered by arguing that the doctrine allows parties to litigate about where to litigate, and that this is unwelcome when

---

[280] *Oceanic Sun Line Special Shipping Co v Fay* (1988) 165 CLR 197; *Voth v Manildra Flour Mills Pty Ltd* (1990) 171 CLR 538; *Henry v Henry* (1996) 185 CLR 571 (which says that it may well be inappropriate if the foreign action was started first); *Régie Nationale des Usines Renault v Zhang* (2003) 210 CLR 491.

[281] Case C–281/02 *Owusu v Jackson* [2005] ECR I–1383 at [42].

[282] Civil Jurisdiction and Judgments Act 1982, s 49.

[283] *Airbus Industrie GIE v Patel* [1999] 1 AC 119.

what they ought to be doing is to devote their resources to trying the merits of the claim. But this is far from convincing. A brisk preliminary skirmish on jurisdiction may well allow each side to gauge the strength of the other's case and the stomach each has for the fight. After the issue has been decided, the case may well settle and, if it does, settle on better informed terms than would otherwise have been the case. If this is so, the doctrine of *forum conveniens* also justifies itself as a species of alternative dispute resolution. But this is an uncovenanted-for, if also manifest, benefit.

Descending to the detail of the test, the first limb requires that the foreign court be clearly or distinctly more appropriate than England. Attention will focus on the location of the events and the witnesses to them, the law which will be applied to determine the case, general issues of trial convenience, the relative strength of connection with England and with the alternative forum, and so on. The assessment of these factors is a matter for the trial judge.[284] In order to show that the foreign court is available as well as appropriate, all that is required is that the court have jurisdiction over the defendant, which may be founded on the defendant's undertaking to submit to it, given as late as the hearing of the application for a stay.[285] The fact that the claimant lacks the resources to sue in the foreign court does not make that court unavailable, although it may well be relevant under the second limb.[286]

Once the defendant has shown the natural forum to be overseas, the claimant may oppose a stay by seeking to show that it is unjust to confine him to his rights and remedies as the foreign court will see them. Arguments that damages will be lower or civil procedure less favourable to him will be generally[287] inadmissible, for as long as the foreign court has a developed system of law, it is inappropriate for the English courts to pass judgment on it, and still less on individual rules self-servingly extracted from it. But if there is cogent[288] evidence that the claimant will not receive a fair trial, especially on racial or religious grounds, it will probably be unjust to stay the proceedings. And if funding the action in the foreign court is beyond

---

[284] A point made by Lord Templeman in *Spiliada Maritime Corp v Cansulex Ltd* [1987] AC 460 (HL), and reiterated periodically since. For a matchless appreciation of the issues as they appear from the heady atmosphere of the courthouse in Galveston, Texas, see *Smith v Colonial Penn Insurance Co* 943 F Supp 782 (1997) (US Dist Ct).

[285] Although this may bear on the issue of costs.

[286] *Lubbe v Cape plc* [2000] 1 WLR 1545 (HL).

[287] *Spiliada* at 482. Although from time to time a court fails to respect this principle, and finds an injustice in, eg, the effect of the costs rules of the foreign court (for example, *Roneleigh Ltd v MII Exports Inc* [1989] 1 WLR 619 (CA)), such cases must be wrong in principle. For a ringing statement of orthodoxy, see *The Herceg Novi* [1998] 4 All ER 238 (CA).

[288] *The Abidin Daver* [1984] AC 398: attack by innuendo is absolutely inadmissible.

the means of the claimant, whereas financial support would be available to him in England, it will be unjust to stay, at least in a case which requires substantial labour to prepare the evidence and conduct the trial: this may make a significant, but limited, inroad on the principle that critical comparison with the foreign court's procedure will not be invited.[289]

Even if the claimant will lose in the foreign court, because the claim he makes in England will not be open to him in the foreign court or because the defendant will have a good defence to the action, this should be an irrelevance: after all, strict impartiality should be the watchword. But there is some support[290] for the view that in this case it would be unjust to order a stay. Such favouring of claimant over defendant is unprincipled and wrong: the idea that the rules are different in a case where the claimant has only one court in which he can expect to win is as wrong as it would be if a defendant were to say that the foreign forum is the only court in which his defence can be successfully advanced. No account whatever ought to be taken of this fact, save perhaps where, in a contract dispute, the foreign court will disregard an express choice of law, so that to try to relocate the case to a foreign court would be for the defendant to engineer a constructive breach of the parties' contract.

If relief is granted, the case is stayed, and remains pending. The stay may well be on terms which reflect undertakings given to the court by the defendant, so that if these turn out to be ineffective the stay can be lifted and the action allowed to proceed. If, by contrast, the action were to be dismissed, it is difficult to see how these undertakings could be enforced, or the action revived.

(b) Suing in England in breach of contract

The second basis on which the defendant may seek a stay of proceedings is the existence of a contract by which the claimant bound himself to sue in a foreign court and not to sue in England.[291] Here, rather than the burden lying on the defendant to persuade the court, a stay will be ordered unless the claimant can establish strong reasons for the court not to do so.[292] Although it might have been possible to adapt the ordinary *forum non*

---

[289] *Lubbe v Cape plc* [2000] 1 WLR 1545 (HL), explaining *Connelly v RTZ Corp Ltd* [1998] AC 854. Were the common law otherwise, it probably would have fallen foul of Art 6 of the European Convention on Human Rights.

[290] *Banco Atlantico SA v British Bank of the Middle East* [1990] 2 Lloyd's Rep 504 (CA). Moreover, the spurious distinction makes a shadowy appearance in the cases on anti-suit injunctions, such as *Airbus Industrie GIE v Patel* [1999] 1 AC 119.

[291] If the argument is that there is a valid and binding arbitration agreement, the Arbitration Act 1996, s 9 makes a stay mandatory, and no element of discretion arises.

[292] *Donohue v Armco Inc* [2001] UKHL 64, [2002] 1 All ER 749.

conveniens test to cover this kind of case,[293] the courts have refused to do this, for fear that it would weaken the conclusive effect of agreements on choice of court.[294] There are two parts to the analysis. First, the agreement must be examined. It will have to be shown that the alleged agreement on choice of court is valid[295] and effective; that it applies to the particular action brought by the claimant; and that it makes the bringing of the English proceedings a breach of contract. If so, a stay will usually be the most appropriate remedy. The questions of construction and validity are undertaken by reference to the law which governs the jurisdiction agreement, which will often, but need not, be the law governing the contract of which it forms a part, and any overriding provision of the *lex fori*.[296] But as a contractual promise, the jurisdiction agreement is construed like any other term of the contract and the law which governs it will determine its effectiveness. So far as concerns its material scope, the defendant will need to show that the words were wide enough to encompass the action brought by the claimant: a term which says it applies to 'all actions under this contract', may, for example, be said not to extend to a claim alleging pre-contractual misrepresentation or claims in respect of equitable obligations. But where the law governing the contract is English, such logic-chopping will be very strongly discouraged: there is a very strong judicial instinct to construe the clause and the intentions of the parties widely and inclusively, so that the untidiness, or worse, of two courts having competence over parts of the matter will not arise.[297] As regards the exclusivity of jurisdiction, there is no breach of contract unless the parties obliged themselves and each other not to sue in the English court.[298] They do not need to have used the word 'exclusive', but it certainly helps if they

---

[293] By using the test as it applies in service out of the jurisdiction, which is examined below, and where the claimant bears the burden of proof on all points.

[294] If it were clear that it was the service out version of *Spiliada* (n 278 above) which applied here, there would be small chance of this dilution. But maybe even that is enough to demand a separate test.

[295] Invalidity may be brought about by the Unfair Terms in Consumer Contracts Regulations 1999 (SI 1999/2083).

[296] *Hoerter v Hanover Telegraph Works* (1893) 10 TLR 103 (CA). Although Art 1(2)(d) of the Rome Convention means that the Convention makes no claim to govern this question, the common law rule is that the agreement is governed by the law of the contract in which it is contained.

[297] *Harbour Assurance Co (UK) Ltd v Kansa General Insurance Co Ltd* [1993] QB 710 (CA); *The Pioneer Container* [1994] 2 AC 324 (PC); *Premium Nafta Products Ltd v Fili Shipping Co Ltd* [2007] UKHL 40, [2007] Bus LR 1719. The authorities are mainly on arbitration agreements, but the principles are common.

[298] If they did not, the principles governing a stay will be the ordinary ones examined under *forum non conveniens*, subject to the point that the claimant may not be permitted to point to the court he agreed to nominate with a view to establishing the injustice of a stay.

do: inept wording, as where 'the parties submit to the jurisdiction of the courts of X' or 'the courts of Y are to have jurisdiction over all disputes', is harder to construe with confidence,[299] and defeats the whole object of making jurisdiction a matter of certainty rather than lottery. But again, where English is the governing law, there will be a preference for finding that the agreement was exclusive.[300]

If the clause is interpreted in such a way as to make it a breach of contract for the English proceedings to have been brought, the grant of a stay is probable, although not inevitable.[301] If England is the natural forum, and if there are additional powerful reasons why the claimant should nevertheless be permitted to break his contractual promise, the action will be allowed to continue. The most compelling reason for not staying the proceedings will be if there are non-parties also implicated by the facts of the dispute but who are not privy to the particular agreement: it may be very inconvenient for the litigation to take place in international fragments.[302] After all, a court has a duty to secure the proper administration of justice, and this may mean that a private agreement on jurisdiction has to be subordinated to the broader public interest. But otherwise, the claimant should not be heard to complain about particular aspects of the legal system which he chose and may have been paid to agree to. If the action is nevertheless allowed to proceed in England despite the agreement on exclusive jurisdiction, it is unclear what, if anything, prevents the defendant counterclaiming for damages for any proven loss flowing from the breach of contract. To allow the action to continue despite a valid and binding choice of court agreement is only to refuse relief by way of specific enforcement; a remedy for damages for breach of contract is a common law right which, in principle, the defendant may assert, by counterclaim if necessary. It may be difficult to obtain proof of loss, and it is also apparent that there may be some judicial awkwardness in allowing such a claim to proceed. But damages for breach of contract remain a common law right; they have been allowed for breach of jurisdiction agreement by suing overseas;[303] and if the agreement on jurisdiction was

---

[299] Although it may still be a breach of a non-exclusive agreement on jurisdiction to sue outside the nominated court: *Sabah Shipyard (Pakistan) Ltd v Pakistan* [2002] EWCA Civ 1643, [2003] 2 Lloyd's Rep 571.

[300] *Sohio Supply Co v Gatoil (USA) Inc* [1989] 1 Lloyd's Rep 588 (CA).

[301] *The El Amria* [1981] 2 Lloyd's Rep 119 (CA); *The Pioneer Container* [1994] 2 AC 324 (PC).

[302] *Bouygues Offshore SA v Caspian Shipping Co (Nos 1, 3, 4, 5)* [1998] 2 Lloyd's Rep 461 (CA); *Donohue v Armco Inc* [2001] UKHL 64, [2002] 1 All ER 749.

[303] *Union Discount Co Ltd v Zoller* [2001] EWCA Civ 1755, [2002] 1 WLR 1517; *National Westminster Bank plc v Rabobank Nederland* [2007] EWHC 1056 (Comm), [2007] EWHC 1742 (Comm), [2008] 1 Lloyd's Rep 16.

~ould denature it to withhold the usual remedy

ΙΕ OUT WITH THE PERMISSION
OF THE COURT

not in England, so that he cannot be served as of right,
served on him overseas in order to found the jurisdiction
rder 11 of the Rules of the Supreme Court, which previ-
.ed the procedure, is now replaced by CPR Part 6, but the
on the interpretation of the earlier rules are, inevitably, still
t. The procedure is for the claimant to apply without notice to his
.ent for permission to serve in accordance with CPR Part 6. He must
the grounds on which the application is made, and must identify the
ragraphs of rule 6.20 relied on.[304] In principle he will not be allowed to
add new claims to supplement or to amend those which were advanced
when permission was sought;[305] a fresh application for permission will
be required. And he must be full and frank in drawing to the attention of
the court arguments which would be made by the defendant in opposition
to application.[306] Once permission has been granted and service has been
made, the defendant is required to acknowledge it, but may then apply
under CPR Part 11 to have the order granting permission, and the service
of process, set aside. On the hearing of this application, the claimant bears
the burden of proof on all those issues which determine whether permission should have been given in the first place: the fact that the application
is by the defendant does not mean that the burden has now shifted to
him.[307] The jurisdiction to serve out which is being invoked is an exorbitant one,[308] and the onus of persuasion lies on the party seeking the grant
of permission to do it.

The claimant is required to show three things: that each pleaded claim
falls within the letter and spirit[309] (for otherwise the paragraphs of an
exorbitant jurisdiction would have been widened still further) of one or

---

[304] CPR r 6.21(1)(a).

[305] *Parker v Schuller* (1901) 17 TLR 299 (CA).

[306] Several cases have considered whether breach of this obligation should lead automatically to the setting aside of permission, but the answers are not completely consistent. Evidently
it will be a matter of degree.

[307] *Artlev AG v Joint Stock Co Almazy Rossii-Sakha*, 8 March 1995 (CA).

[308] So said Lord Diplock in *Amin Rasheed Shipping Corp v Kuwait Insurance Co* [1984] AC
50, 65. But the High Court of Australia did not agree: *Agar v Hyde* [2000] HCA 41, (2000) 201
CLR 552. It is probably right if service out is subject to *forum conveniens*.

[309] *The Hagen* [1908] P 189 (CA); *Johnson v Taylor Bros* [1920] AC 144, 153; *Mercedes-Benz
AG v Leiduck* [1996] 1 AC 284, 289 (PC).

more of the paragraphs of rule 6.20; that England is the proper place in which to bring the claim;[310] and that he believes that his claim has a reasonable prospect of success on its merits.[311] These three elements are distinct and must be individually satisfied: a clear success in one cannot condone failure in another.

6. THE PARAGRAPHS OF RULE 6.20

The paragraphs of rule 6.20 define the claims in respect of which the court has power to grant permission to serve out. At first sight it makes sense for the law to have categories of case into which the claims must fit before permission can be given, but at second sight this proves to be an illusion. Permission will not in any event be granted unless England is the proper place to bring, or natural forum for, the claim. If this condition, which emerged as a specific and discrete requirement relatively recently,[312] is satisfied, it is difficult to see what value is added by these more primitive, pigeonhole, criteria, or why there should not be an additional, open-ended, rule for any other case in which permission should be given, such as that in the law of Ontario: 'In any case to which Rule 17.02 does not apply, the court may grant leave to serve an originating process or notice of a reference outside Ontario'.[313] The law needs to be rethought. The real question is whether, had the central role of *forum conveniens* been appreciated from the outset, the law would have devised these pigeonholes as well, and insisted on compliance with their letter and their spirit before permission to sue in the natural forum was granted. A rational answer would be negative. Nevertheless, the paragraphs of rule 6.20 are the law. If there is any uncertainty about any fact which is required to bring the claim within the paragraph relied on, the claimant is required to make out a good arguable case, which is less than satisfying a balance of probability, upon it.[314] So if he applies for permission to serve on the basis that the claim arises from a contract made within the jurisdiction but the defendant, whilst admitting that there is a contract, denies that it was made in England, the claimant must show a good arguable case that England is where it was made. These geographical elements are matters of English domestic law; the broad legal concepts are defined by English law, including its private international law. So in the case just mentioned,

---

[310] CPR r 6.21(2A).

[311] CPR r 6.21(1)(b).

[312] In *Spiliada Maritime Corp v Cansulex Ltd* [1987] AC 460, although there had been occasional trailers for it in earlier cases.

[313] Rules of Civil Procedure, RRO 1990, Rule 17.03(1).

[314] *Seaconsar Far East Ltd v Bank Markazi Jomhouri Islami Iran* [1994] 1 AC 438.

if the defendant were to concede that there was a contract as a matter of English domestic law, but deny that it was a valid contract according to its governing law, the plea is referred to the law which governs the contract. But if he puts in issue the proposition that it was made in England, this will be tested by reference to English domestic law.

Each separate claim must fall within a paragraph of rule 6.20; any which do not will be deleted.[315] In the account which follows we will deal with only those which are of practical importance. Those dealing with commercial cases are given first; then those less frequent in commercial litigation; and then the remainder.

(a) Contracts

Three paragraphs deal with contractual claims. Under paragraph 5, service out may be ordered where a claim is made in respect of a contract where that contract was made within the jurisdiction, or was made through an agent trading or residing within the jurisdiction, or is governed by English law, or contains a term to the effect that the court shall have jurisdiction to determine any claim in respect of the contract. Under paragraph 6, service may be ordered when a claim is made in respect of a breach of contract committed within the jurisdiction. Paragraph 7 provides for service where a claim is made for a declaration that no contract exists where, if the contract were found to exist, it would have fallen within paragraph 5.

As said above, if it is not admitted, there must be a good arguable case that there is a contract, valid according to rules of English private international law;[316] the place of its making is determined by English domestic law.[317] Although the paragraphs are drawn widely, the contract must be one by which the claimant and defendant are alleged to be bound: it is not enough that a contract *inter alios* forms the background to the claim.[318] For the purposes of paragraph 6, breach by a repudiatory act occurs where the act was done; breach by non-performance where the required act was to have been performed. Paragraph 7 is a newer addition to the rules, designed to make it easier to bring a claim for a declaration of non-liability under an alleged contract, a claim which fell only uncertainly

---

[315] For otherwise the scope of the rule would be extended: *Metall und Rohstoff AG v Donaldson, Lufkin & Jenrette Inc* [1990] 1 QB 391 (CA).

[316] *Amin Rasheed Shipping Corp v Kuwait Insurance Co* [1984] AC 50; *Bank of Baroda v Vysya Bank Ltd* [1994] 2 Lloyd's Rep 87.

[317] *Chevron International Oil Co v A/S Sea Team (The TS Havprins)* [1983] 2 Lloyd's Rep 356.

[318] *Finnish Marine Insurance Co v Protective National Insurance Co* [1990] 1 QB 1078.

under the predecessor of paragraph 5. It probably applies generally to claims which deny that a contractual duty is owed to the defendant, but which the defendant alleges is owed, rather than being limited to cases in which it is claimed that no contract ever existed.[319] It is also to be expected that a claim for relief which is consequential upon holding that there is no contract is also within paragraph 7. Convenience suggests that it should be. Even so, the fact that these submissions have to be made goes to reinforce the question why the jurisdiction of the court over a claim which has England as its natural forum should be limited by category.

(b) Torts

Under paragraph 8, service out may be authorized where a claim is made in tort where the damage was sustained within the jurisdiction, or where the damage sustained resulted from an act committed within the jurisdiction. Under the previous rule, which required that the claim be 'founded on *a* tort', it had been held that this required there to be an actual tort, ascertained by reference to rules of English private international law.[320] The omission of the indefinite article makes it uncertain whether paragraph 8 requires that there must be *a* tort, demonstrated (where it is not admitted) to the level of a good arguable case. If, by contrast, the paragraph requires only that the pleaded claim be properly formulated in the terminology of tort, or be characterized as tortious, there will be no need to show a good arguable case upon actual liability before service out may be authorized.[321] It is hard to say which view is to be preferred. It appears odd that because the term 'contract' does not describe a cause of action, but 'tort' does, a jurisdictional requirement of liability is imposed by paragraph 8 which is absent from paragraphs 5 to 7. No obvious policy requires this and, as a result, it may be preferable to read paragraph 8 as referring to the characterization of the claim rather than to the existence of liability. Damage is sustained in England if some significant damage is sustained in England: it need not be all, nor even most, of it.[322] It is unclear whether 'sustained' should reflect or reproduce the interpretation of where damage 'occurred' within Article 5(3) of the Regulation, but if it does, the focus will be on the place of the direct damage done to the immediate victim of

---

[319] A court will not grant leave to serve a claim for a negative declaration unless it is an appropriate case for the seeking of such relief: *Messier Dowty Ltd v Sabena SA* [2000] 1 WLR 2040 (CA).

[320] RSC Ord 11, r 1(1)(f) as interpreted in *Metall und Rohstoff AG v Donaldson, Lufkin & Jenrette Inc* [1990] QB 391 (CA). See below, ch 5.

[321] Although the requirement of CPR r 6.21(1)(b) will still need to be satisfied.

[322] *Metall und Rohstoff AG v Donaldson, Lufkin & Jenrette Inc* [1990] 1 QB 391 (CA).

it. In the case of purely economic losses or damage to reputation, the location of the damage is undeniably artificial. An act is committed within the jurisdiction if substantial and efficacious acts were committed within the jurisdiction, even if other substantial acts were committed elsewhere.[323] It must be the act of the actual defendant, but the act of one joint tortfeasor is the act of all.[324]

(c) Constructive trusteeship and restitution

Paragraph 14 allows service to be authorized where a claim is made against the defendant as constructive trustee and his alleged liability arises out of acts committed within the jurisdiction. The former rule made it explicit that the acts committed within the jurisdiction were not required to be those of the defendant; it is unlikely that their omission from paragraph 14 reflects a desire to narrow the scope of the provision. The acts must still have something to do with the defendant.[325] Only some of the acts, not necessarily the receipt of the assets, need take place within the jurisdiction.[326] So as long as a participant in fraud takes part in a scheme where one of the wrongdoers did acts in the jurisdiction, service out may probably be made on all.[327] Paragraph 15 allows service to be authorized where a claim is made for restitution where the defendant's alleged liability arises out of acts committed within the jurisdiction. This is a new provision; it probably requires that there is a link between the defendant and the acts committed in the jurisdiction, but does not require that the defendant himself do the local acts.[328]

(d) Other commercial claims

Paragraph 1 applies if the defendant is domiciled within the jurisdiction,[329] although this fact will often mean that the jurisdictional rules of the Regulation will apply, and permission to serve will not be needed. Paragraph 2 applies if the claim is made for an injunction ordering the defendant to do or to not do an act within the jurisdiction. The injunction must comprise a

---

[323] *Metall und Rohstoff.*

[324] *Unilever plc v Gillette (UK) Ltd* [1989] RPC 583 (CA).

[325] *NABB Bros International Ltd v Lloyds Bank International (Guernsey) Ltd* [2005] EWHC 405 (Ch), [2005] ILPr 506.

[326] *ISC Technologies Ltd v Guerin* [1992] 2 Lloyd's Rep 430; *Polly Peck International plc v Nadir* 17 March 1993 (CA), a case on RSC Ord 11, r 1(1)(t).

[327] If one can be served otherwise, it will also be possible to apply for permission under para 6.20(3) to serve a co-defendant as a necessary or proper party.

[328] *NABB Bros International Ltd v Lloyds Bank International (Guernsey) Ltd* [2005] EWHC 405 (Ch), [2005] ILPr 506.

[329] Within the meaning of the 1982 Act: CPR r 6.18(g).

substantial element of the relief sought,[330] and it must be an injunction in respect of substantive rights: an application for a freezing order, or other relief not predicated on the existence of substantive rights, is not within the paragraph[331] but is specifically provided for by paragraph 4 instead. Paragraph 3 applies if the defendant is a necessary or proper party to a claim against someone who has been or will be served; the paragraph is a broad one which serves the efficient disposal of claims; its wording is deliberately disjunctive.[332] Paragraph 9 applies if the proceedings seek the enforcement in England of any judgment or arbitral award.[333] And paragraph 17 applies when a party seeks an order that costs be awarded to or against a non-party to the proceedings.[334]

(e) Property, trusts, and other cases

Claims relating wholly to property in England fall under paragraph 10; this provision appears to be of substantial, but largely untapped, width.[335] Claims to execute English trusts under paragraph 11; claims in the administration of the estate of an English domiciliary under paragraph 12; and probate actions under paragraph 13. And paragraphs 16 to 18 make up a list of other causes of action, almost all statutory and where the statutory duty is reinforced by the right to seek permission to serve out.

7. ENGLAND IS THE PROPER PLACE IN WHICH TO BRING THE CLAIM

The second requirement cast on the claimant is in rule 6.21(2A), which echoes, in modified language, the earlier rule[336] that England must be shown, clearly or distinctly, to be the most appropriate forum. The factors which are relevant when a stay is sought of English proceedings apply, *mutatis mutandis*, here as well. It is unclear why the draftsman elected not to use the 'natural forum' formula which had been hallowed by judicial and professional usage, but little turns on it. However, it is possible that in an extreme case, England may be the proper place to bring a claim even

---

[330] *Rosler v Hilbery* [1925] 1 Ch 250 (CA).

[331] *Mercedes-Benz AG v Leiduck* [1996] 1 AC 284 (PC).

[332] *Petroleo Brasiliero SA v Mellitus Shipping Inc* [2001] CA Civ 418, [2001] 1 All ER (Comm) 993.

[333] The judgment or award must have been given by the time permission is sought: *Mercedes-Benz AG v Leiduck* [1996] 1 AC 284 (PC).

[334] Supreme Court Act 1981, s 51.

[335] *Re Banco Nacional de Cuba* [2001] 1 WLR 2039.

[336] But which was never so expressed in statutory form. *Spiliada Maritime Corp v Cansulex Ltd* [1987] AC 460 showed this to be a discrete component of RSC Ord 11, r 4(2), which required that the case be shown to be a proper one for service out.

though England is not the natural forum: if the alternative[337] forum is some war-torn or hopeless corner of the globe, trial in England may be in the proper place. It is less certain whether this condition would be satisfied if financial support for the claim were available only in England and not in the alternative forum. The logic of recent cases on *forum conveniens* would suggest that this is so; and if the defendant is before the court, albeit that he has not yet submitted to the jurisdiction, it would be remarkable, and arguably a breach of the European Convention on Human Rights, for a court to set aside service and leave the claimant without effective remedy.[338] On the other hand, there are manifest points of distinction if the courts do not wish to be pushed this far.

8. THE CLAIM HAS A REASONABLE PROSPECT OF SUCCESS

Service out will not be authorized unless the claimant states his belief that the claim has a reasonable prospect of success. If the defendant considers that the claim falls below this standard, he should probably challenge the obtaining of permission on the ground that the claimant could not properly have held and stated this belief; and if he succeeds on this point the court will set aside the permission and the service of process.[339] It was once required of a claimant that he show a good arguable case on the merits of his claim, which, if opaquely, required a higher standard of probability of winning; but this was deliberately relaxed in 1994.[340] It appears to be entirely justified: if England is the natural forum, why should a claimant who wishes to serve out be required to have a higher apparent chance of success than one who can serve within the jurisdiction? On the other hand, a defendant served out of the jurisdiction used to know that he could appear and defend the case on its merits, in which case any judgment against him would be likely to be internationally effective, or ignore the summons, and know that although the judgment against him was certain to be enforceable in England it was most unlikely to be enforceable in

---

[337] In this context this will probably be where the defendant is resident and can, in principle at least, otherwise be sued.

[338] cf *Lubbe v Cape plc* [2000] 1 WLR 1545 (HL).

[339] cf *Seaconsar Far East Ltd v Bank Markazi Jomhouri Islami Iran* [1994] 1 AC 438. It may be dangerous to make the argument by means of an application under CPR r 3.4(a) or CPR r 24.2(a)(i), as these are not challenges to the jurisdiction of the court and may therefore be seen as submission.

[340] *Seaconsar Far East Ltd v Bank Markazi Jomhouri Islami Iran* [1994] 1 AC 438; followed on this point by the High Court of Australia in *Agar v Hyde* [2000] HCA 41, (2000) 201 CLR 552.

any other country: there was a choice. But the scheme now consecrated by the Brussels Regulation ensures that in a civil or commercial matter, a judgment based on service out under CPR Part 6, and given in default of appearance, will not be recognized and enforceable only in England. Instead, it will be effective in all the Member States, and it has therefore greatly raised the stakes, making it much more risky for a defendant to elect not to appear and to allow judgment to be entered against him in default. To do that to a defendant at the very same time as lowering the bar on the question how convincing the claimant needs to be on the merits is to strike a double blow at the overseas defendant. The policy behind this is not easy to understand.

E. OFFENSIVE FORUM-SHOPPING

The traditional rules of jurisdiction now curtail the extent to which a claimant may forum-shop in the English courts. But there are two ways in which the common law responds to the practice of forum shopping to a foreign court: by granting injunctions to impede the foreign proceedings, and by allowing actions to be brought for declaratory relief.

I. ANTI-SUIT INJUNCTIONS

As Lord Goff of Chieveley pointed out,[341] the jurisdictional scheme put in place by the Regulation is common to the Member States, and has the Court of Justice sitting above it to ensure the proper interpretation of its rules.[342] The common law world is different. Order and fairness between states is achieved by the doctrine of *forum non conveniens*, by which a court directly limits its own jurisdiction, and by the anti-suit injunction, by which a court indirectly places limits on the jurisdiction of other courts. It is the second of these with which we are now concerned. A court with personal jurisdiction over a respondent may order him not to bring or not to continue proceedings in a foreign court, by granting an injunction against suit. The order is not addressed to the foreign judge, who is manifestly neither subject to the personal jurisdiction of the English court nor on the receiving end of its order, but to the respondent, who is ordered to exercise self-restraint or suffer the consequences prescribed by law. Even so, a foreign judge may not appreciate the subtlety of the distinction,[343] and for

---

[341] *Airbus Industrie GIE v Patel* [1999] 1 AC 119.

[342] No irony is intended.

[343] For a telling German refusal to see the point see *Re the Enforcement of an English Anti-suit Injunction* (Case 3 VA 11/95) [1997] ILPr 320 (Regional Court of Appeal, Düsseldorf). For an

this reason, a concern for comity constrains the court in the exercise of its discretion.[344] This potent remedy gives the English court an international reach by which to control what it finds to be wrongful recourse to a foreign court. Although the remedy is also found in other common law systems, it is largely unknown in civilian systems. It has been held to be incompatible with the jurisdictional scheme of the Regulation,[345] but this applies only to civil or commercial proceedings in the courts of another Member State. It is necessary to deal separately with two points: personal jurisdiction over the respondent and the exercise of the court's discretion.

(a) Personal jurisdiction over the respondent

The respondent must be served with process to be made subject to the personal jurisdiction of the court in respect of the claim for an injunction. An anti-suit injunction is an application for final[346] relief in respect of legal or equitable rights, and process must be lawfully served in accordance with the Regulation or the traditional rules, as the case may be. Where personal jurisdiction is founded on the traditional rules, it may therefore be necessary to seek permission to serve out of the jurisdiction. No paragraph of rule 6.20 is specifically dedicated to applications for an anti-suit injunction, but there is nothing to prevent the cause of action which founds the claim to relief being brought within any paragraph which will accommodate it. So if the claim for an injunction is based on the fact that there is a contract falling within rule 6.20(5), which gives a legal right not to be sued, this paragraph may be relied on in the application for permission. A respondent domiciled in another Member State may object to the personal jurisdiction of the court by pointing to the Regulation, but if the offending proceedings are in a non-Member State, there is no offence in ordering the injunction.

(b) Discretion to order an injunction

The injunction must be founded on a demonstrable legal right not to be sued in the foreign court, or on an equitable right not to be sued in the foreign court; and in the latter case, at least, it must also be shown that England is or would be the natural forum for the litigation of the

---

even more telling English refusal to see the very same point, see *Tonicstar Ltd v American Home Insurance Co* [2004] EWHC 1234 (Comm), [2005] Lloyd's Rep IR 32.

[344] *Airbus Industrie GIE v Patel* [1999] 1 AC 119.

[345] Case C–159/02 *Turner v Grovit* [2004] ECR I–3565.

[346] Although it is possible to apply for an interim anti-suit injunction to preserve the status quo until the application for a final injunction can be heard.

substantive dispute.[347] This last condition is satisfied if the respondent could and should bring any claim he has before the English courts, but it is also satisfied, in principle at least, even though the respondent would lose if he had to sue in England: the critical question is where the trial of the dispute has its natural home, not where the respondent may find a court which will allow his claim to succeed and the defence to be overcome.[348] Although it may be thought that an English court should be able to restrain wrongful behaviour committed anywhere by anyone subject to its personal jurisdiction, it has been accepted that some limitation needs to be placed on this power. It might have been done through the development of a choice of law rule,[349] to determine whether the respondent's conduct should be evaluated by reference to English or a foreign law. Instead, it was achieved by insisting on a natural forum connection which, when satisfied, makes it singularly appropriate for the English court to exercise its discretion, and to apply English law and equity in granting relief. In other words, if England is the natural forum, judicial comity is not infringed by the intervention of an English court applying English law. Subject to his satisfaction of this condition, the applicant must show that the respondent is vexatious or oppressive in bringing the foreign action.[350] The meaning of these terms retains an element of flexibility, but if the foreign action is brought in bad faith or to harass, or if it is bound to fail if defended but its defence is certain to cause trouble and expense, or if its consequences may be unjustifiably involved,[351] the party bringing it may be ordered to restrain himself. The absence of a real link between the acts complained of and the foreign court may help to indicate that there is oppression;[352] if it is otherwise unconscionable to bring the action it may be restrained. Australian equity holds the foreign action unobjectionable if it seeks relief which would not be available from a local court,[353] but this seems perverse,[354] for the more foreign the action is, the less it will be possible to

---

[347] *Société Nationale Industrielle Aérospatiale v Lee Kui Jak* [1987] AC 871 (PC); *Airbus Industrie GIE v Patel* [1999] 1 AC 119.

[348] This is the effect of *Midland Bank plc v Laker Airways Ltd* [1986] QB 689 (CA). This decision was conspicuously not approved in *Airbus Industrie GIE v Patel*, but it is right, for the law has no business in preferring the successful claim of the respondent to the successful defence of the applicant. The idea special rules apply in 'single forum' cases is unsound though still heard.

[349] cf Briggs [1997] LMCLQ 90.

[350] *Société Nationale Industrielle Aérospatiale v Lee Kui Jak* [1987] AC 871 (PC).

[351] ibid (consequential contribution proceedings would be intolerably complex).

[352] *Midland Bank plc v Laker Airways Ltd* [1986] QB 689 (CA).

[353] *CSR Ltd v Cigna Insurance Australia Ltd* (1997) 189 CLR 345.

[354] It is also contrary to *Midland Bank plc v Laker Airways Ltd* [1986] QB 689 (CA).

order restraint. According to Canadian equity,[355] before applying for the injunction, the applicant must make any jurisdictional application to the foreign court: an injunction will not be granted unless the foreign court fails to respect principles of *forum conveniens* but then, having refused to observe comity, it can expect no comity in return.[356] Although this has sometimes been said to be the general rule in England,[357] clarification of the requirement that England be shown to be the natural forum makes it an unnecessary, and possibly undesirable, requirement in England. There is something unattractive in encouraging an English court to sit as if it were hearing an appeal from a foreign court;[358] and if the application is delayed until the issue has been fought in the foreign court, it may mean that the time for an injunction has passed.

Where the claim to an injunction is founded on a contractual right not to be sued in the foreign court, it is uncertain whether England must be the natural forum for the action.[359] If England is the chosen court, there will be no difficulty,[360] but if the nominated court is in a non-Member State the answer is less clear. On one view the existence of a legal right not to be sued is enough by itself, but it may also be said that if neither the nominated court nor the action to be restrained is in England, it is none of the English court's business to say where the trial should take place, however much the respondent may appear to be at fault.[361] But where it is appropriate for the court to exercise its discretion, it is unlikely that there is a distinct need to demonstrate vexation or oppression: an injunction in support of a legal right not to be sued in the foreign court will be granted unless there is good reason not to do so.[362] To say that there is oppression or vexation whenever there is a legal right not to be sued seems unnecessary and illiterate: an injunction in equity's auxiliary jurisdiction and in support of legal rights does not need to be founded on an equitable right.

[355] *Amchem Products Inc v British Columbia (Workers' Compensation Board)* [1993] 1 SCR 897, (1993) 102 DLR (4th) 96.

[356] This may be thought of as the 'Be Done By As You Did' version of comity, in homage to Charles Kingsley, *The Water-Babies*.

[357] *Barclays Bank plc v Homan* [1993] BCLC 680, 686–7 (Hoffmann J) 703 (CA).

[358] cf *The Angelic Grace* [1995] 1 Lloyd's Rep 87, 95 (CA).

[359] The point was left open in *Airbus Industrie GIE v Patel* [1999] 1 AC 119.

[360] *Continental Bank NA v Aeakos Compania Naviera SA* [1994] 1 WLR 588 (CA).

[361] But the Bermuda Court of Appeal displayed no hesitation about it in *IPOC International Growth Fund Ltd v OAO 'CT Mobile'* [2007] Bermuda LR 43.

[362] *Donohue v Armco Inc* [2001] UKHL 64, [2002] 1 All ER 749.

2. NEGATIVE DECLARATIONS

The development of the doctrine of *forum conveniens* was the first substantial means by which a defendant could challenge the jurisdictional dominance of the claimant; and an anti-suit injunction may be seen as the second: the party sued is not obliged to sit back and wait to be sued, where and when his opponent chooses, but may try to forestall his being sued in a court whose jurisdiction he regards as uncongenial. For the sake of completeness, therefore, we should mention the third means which may be resorted to: bringing proceedings on the merits of the claim for a declaration that he, the 'natural defendant', owes no liability to the opponent. This, if successful, will either prevent the opponent bringing proceedings of his own or mean that, if he does, the principles of *res judicata* may forestall the enforcement of a foreign judgment.

The early history of such actions showed clear judicial hostility.[363] Courts would be slow to exercise jurisdictional discretion in support of them;[364] they risked being struck out as premature or abusive, or otherwise impeded. The suspicion that they were open to abuse by forum shoppers was widely held; and their potential to harass an opponent, who may not have decided whether to sue and who may not be ready for the fight, was considerable. But the sea has changed, and there is now no encouragement to disparage such actions. Three principal reasons may be given. First, it became the practice of the Commercial Court to entertain such actions, and to find them justifiable: insurers, suppliers, and others will often need to know whether they have legal obligations to an insured (so they can step in and conduct the defence if they do) or a distributor (so they can terminate supplies and retain another if they do not). The practice of the courts simply undermined the contrary view of the law. Secondly, in the context of the Regulation, it is settled that an action for a declaration of non-liability brought in a court which has jurisdiction over the defendant thereto, cannot be objected to on jurisdictional grounds: there is no wrong in suing in a court with jurisdiction under the Regulation.[365] Thirdly, the Court of Appeal has given its seal of approval to this new approach,[366] seeing the merit in such claims, rather than criticizing or obstructing them, as good and useful means of resolving disputes. It is hard to disagree: the legal certainty which can be brought about by a prompt application for a

---

[363] *Guaranty Trust Co of New York v Hannay* [1915] 2 KB 536 (CA); *The Volvox Hollandia* [1988] 2 Lloyd's Rep 361 (CA).
[364] By refusing permission to serve out of the jurisdiction.
[365] Case C–406/92 *The Tatry* [1994] ECR I–5439.
[366] *Messier Dowty Ltd v Sabena SA* [2000] 1 WLR 2040 (CA).

declaration may be far preferable to the limbo of waiting to see whether proceedings are commenced by the other party. Abusive use of the procedure can still be prevented, but there will now be no presumption of abuse; and as this new wisdom beds down in the law, the need for separate mention of proceedings for negative declaratory relief will become a thing of the past.

F. JURISDICTION TO OBTAIN INTERIM RELIEF

Interim relief, which includes provisional and protective measures, may be ordered in support of actions in the English courts, or of civil or commercial claims in the courts in another Member State (Article 31 cases), or in support of other actions in those courts or elsewhere.[367] If the respondent is present within the jurisdiction of the court he may be served with process as of right: it is irrelevant that he may be domiciled in another Member State and so not be subject to the jurisdiction of the English courts over the merits of the claim. If he is outside the territorial jurisdiction, an application for permission to serve the claim form out of the jurisdiction must be made under CPR rule 6.20(4): this is so even in relation to applications falling within Article 31 of the Regulation. But in all cases, the fact that the court may lack jurisdiction to try the case on the merits is a material factor in determining whether it is expedient to grant the relief;[368] and it will also be relevant in deciding whether the court should grant permission to serve out, as rule 6.21(2A) also applies to applications under rule 6.20(4). As regards whether it may be inexpedient to grant the relief, it has been suggested that where the court seised of the merits could have granted but decided not to grant relief, an English court should be slow to act to contradict it; but where it had no power to grant relief, an English court should be inclined to make an order to assist the foreign court. Not everyone will instantly see that it is right to think of 'assisting' a court whose legislator has, one supposes deliberately, withheld certain powers from it.[369]

---

[367] Civil Jurisdiction and Judgments Act 1982, s 25.
[368] ibid s 25(2).
[369] *Crédit Suisse Fides Trust SA* v *Cuoghi* [1998] QB 818 (CA); *Motorola Credit Corp v Uzan (No 2)* [2003] EWCA Civ 752, [2004] 1 WLR 113.

4

Recognition and Enforcement of Foreign Judgments

A. RECOGNITION, ENFORCEMENT, AND RELATED MATTERS

The judgments of foreign courts have no direct effect in England. If adjudication is thought of as an incident of state sovereignty, this will come as small surprise. But it has long been recognized that there is a countervailing general public interest. This requires that those who have had a hearing and received judgment should, for one reason or another, abide by its terms, and that the law should discourage or prevent the reopening of disputes which have already had a hearing and an adjudication. A related idea would encourage or require litigants to put forward all their issues for adjudication at once, rather than holding some back for a subsequent dispute. This broad principle is not limited to cases where the first judgment was obtained in England but, subject to conditions, applies just as much to foreign judgments. Accordingly, foreign judgments may be given effect in England according to the rules of the common law and statute under the schemes examined in this chapter. As will be seen, there are degrees of foreignness, and the schemes accordingly comprise three broad categories. The judgments most readily given effect to in England are those from other parts of the United Kingdom and from Member States of the European Union,[1] where the rules are easily satisfied and procedures for enforcement are notably brisk. In the furthest category are judgments from the whole of the rest of the world, for which the common law alone supplies both the rules for recognition and enforcement and the procedure for enforcement. Lying somewhere between the two are judgments from a number of states which are party to a bilateral treaty with the United Kingdom or are territories of the Commonwealth. For these, statutory conditions for recognition and enforcement reflect the common law, but enforcement is more direct.

---

[1] Or states party to the Lugano Convention, for which the rules are substantially the same.

An important distinction must be drawn at the outset between the re(
ognition of a judgment and its enforcement; and between these and t'
other effects which can be derived from a foreign judgment. *Recognition*
a judgment means treating the claim which was adjudicated as having b
determined once and for all. It does not matter whether it was determi
in favour of the claimant or the defendant, though judgments *in perso*
are only ever recognized as effective against particular parties, and
material question will be whether that person is bound. By contrast, j
ments *in rem*[2] are recognized generally or universally, and not just ag;
particular parties to the litigation. When the judgment is recogni
the matter is *res judicata*, and the party bound by it will be estopped from
contradicting it in subsequent proceedings in an English court.[3] For the
foreign judgment to achieve recognition, qualifying conditions have to be
met, which specify the connection between the foreign court and the parties, accommodate and limit the scope of objections to the judgment, and
define the judgments to which this status of *res judicata* will be accorded.
The principles of *res judicata* can operate in relation to entire causes of
action ('cause of action estoppel') as well as on discrete issues which arose
and were determined in the course of the trial of a cause of action ('issue
estoppel').[4] Given a *res judicata*, a party bound by the judgment who brings
proceedings in England to try and obtain a ruling which contradicts it may
be met with the plea of estoppel by *res judicata*, and stopped in his tracks.

Recognition serves two purposes. Where judgment has been given in
favour of the defendant, dismissing the claim, it operates defensively by
allowing the defendant who has won in a foreign court to rely on this to
defeat a subsequent action brought by the unsuccessful claimant. Where
the foreign judgment was in favour of the claimant, the position is more
complex, because the claimant may not have succeeded on every part of
his claim. To take the easiest case first, if the claimant[5] obtained judgment
in respect of the whole of the claim, he may wish to go further, and bring
proceedings for the *enforcement* of the judgment, for example, by collect-
ing money which the foreign court ordered to be paid and which remains
unpaid. Not every judgment entitled to recognition may be enforced in
England,[6] but to be enforced, a foreign judgment must first be recognized.

---

[2] eg, on the status of a person, or the ownership of a thing.

[3] See generally Spencer Bower, Turner, and Handley, *The Doctrine of Res Judicata*
(3rd edn, 1996).

[4] *Carl Zeiss Stiftung v Rayner & Keeler Ltd (No 2)* [1967] 1 AC 853.

[5] Which expression includes counterclaimant or party, not excluding a defendant, in whose
favour an order has been made.

[6] If the particular judgment cannot be enforced, eg because the remedy ordered by the
foreign court falls outside those which can be enforced in an English court, there is nothing

If it is to be enforced at the behest of the successful claimant, the judgment must meet further conditions; but if enforcement is ordered, the judgment may be executed as if it had been given by an English court, either because it is ordered that the judgment be registered pursuant to statute which provides for this effect or (if enforced under the common law) because an English court gives its own judgment which itself becomes the order which may be enforced.

A third possibility is that the claimant was partially successful. If, for example, he succeeds on his claim but recovers a smaller sum in damages than he had hoped for, he may seek to improve on the first result by suing on the underlying cause of action in the English courts. In this case neither recognition[7] nor enforcement will stand in his way, but the manifest unfairness of his trying to have a second bite at the cherry induced Parliament to legislate to remove the right to sue again.[8]

The tradition of English textbooks is to concentrate on the enforcement of judgments, and to treat recognition as an afterthought of limited practical importance. But the logic of the law is that recognition is the necessary primary concern, for without it the judgment can have no effect in the English legal order. In relation to the three regimes for recognition and enforcement, therefore, we will start with the criteria for recognition, and will then examine what else is required for enforcement.

We will first examine judgments in civil or commercial matters from the courts of Member States and falling within the Brussels Regulation.[9] Secondly, we look at recognition and enforcement of judgments at common law, where the rules are restricted neither by geography, nor by subject matter, nor by type of court. Finally we mention the statutory registration schemes developed to simplify procedure in relation to enforcement at common law, but which apply only to specific courts in specified countries. In this chapter the focus of attention will be on judgments *in personam*. The recognition of judgments in family law, the administration of estates, and insolvency are dealt with within the chapters which examine this subject matter.

---

to prevent the claimant seeking recognition where enforcement is not available, and using the principles of *res judicata* to short-cut his way to victory in the English action.

[7] For there will be no discrete issue on which the defendant won (but if there is, such as a refusal to award a particular head of damages, issue estoppel in the defendant's favour on this issue will be available).

[8] Civil Jurisdiction and Judgments Act 1982, s 34.

[9] Council Regulation (EC) 44/2001, [2001] OJ L12/1. There will be no systematic examination of the Brussels Convention, which the Regulation has effectively replaced, or of the Lugano Convention, which operates in parallel, but only in relation to Iceland, Norway, and Switzerland.

B. JUDGMENTS FROM MEMBER STATES: THE BRUSSELS REGULATION

The Regulation supplanted the Brussels Convention as the instrument by which judgments from the courts of Member States of the European Union take effect in the English legal order. The Lugano Convention continues to apply to judgments from Iceland, Norway, and Switzerland; but its provisions are similar, and will soon be identical, to the Brussels Regulation, which is where attention needs to be focused.

1. RECOGNITION

For a judgment to be recognized under Chapter III of the Regulation, it (i) must be an adjudication from a court in a Member State,[10] (ii) must be given in a civil or commercial matter, (iii) need not be in proceedings which were instituted after the Regulation came into effect, (iv) must not be impeachable for jurisdictional error, (v) must not be impeachable for procedural or substantive reasons, and (vi) must not be excluded from recognition by another treaty. It is often said that if it fails to meet these criteria, there is nothing to prevent an attempt to obtain recognition and enforcement of a judgment under the rules of the common law, on the footing that Chapter III of the Regulation is a permissive, not an exclusive, regime. That may be so. But in cases which fall within the domain of the Regulation, and of which Article 34 says they 'shall not be recognized', it is arguable that the Regulation imposes an obligation to withhold recognition which precludes allowing it by other means. Be that as it may, according to Article 33 it is not necessary to bring any form of action or procedure to obtain recognition of a judgment under the Regulation, beyond pleading it, so if a successful defendant wishes to rely on a judgment to which the Regulation applies, all he need do is plead it as satisfying the criteria for recognition. There is no objection to his bringing proceedings for a declaration that the judgment be recognized if this would serve a useful purpose. We will first examine the six points listed above.

2. JUDGMENTS: ARTICLE 32

For the purposes of the Regulation, a judgment is an adjudication by a court of a Member State, including an order as to costs.[11] This excludes

---

[10] For the purpose of the Regulation, Gibraltar is treated as part of the United Kingdom.

[11] Article 32. Where the claimant enters judgment in default of appearance or defence, in which circumstance the court is not called upon, and does not adjudicate at all, it remains to

judgments from a non-Member State, even after a judge in a Member
State has held them to be enforceable:[12] the Regulation applies to original
determinations by a judge in a Member State, but not to instances where a
judge validates or approves a decision taken by someone who is not. Many
Member States have treaties or other provisions dealing with judgments
from non-Member States, frequently in relation to former colonies; but
such bilateral relationships are not enough to admit such a judgment,
via the doorway of one Member State's private international law, into
Chapter III of the Regulation. Similar considerations explain why a decision declaring the enforceability of an arbitration award is not a judgment
within Chapter III of the Regulation either. Article 32 does include a provisional or interlocutory judgment, and will include the dismissal of a
case on jurisdictional grounds, such as by reference to a choice of court
agreement for another Member State: there is no requirement that the
judgment be *res judicata* in the court which pronounced it. A judgment
by consent is included, for it is still an adjudication made on the authority
of a judge.[13] A judgment which orders a periodical payment imposed as
a penalty for disobedience to a court order is included,[14] although it may
be enforced only if the sum due has been finally quantified by the court
which ordered it.[15] Settlements which have been approved by courts in the
course of proceedings[16] and authentic instruments[17] (unknown to English
law, they are documents authenticated by a public authority or a notary,
and which are enforceable under some laws without the need for legal
action) are enforceable under similar, but not identical, conditions.[18]

It is easy to see the final order of a court as a judgment. It is less clear
how this applies to a finding made by a court which is not embodied in its
final order: the question is whether 'judgment' includes a decision upon an
issue as well as the disposal of a cause of action. The answer is unclear, but
in principle if a judgment qualifies for recognition under the Regulation,

---

be decided whether the resultant order counts as a 'judgment'. But if there is doubt whether
it is a judgment at all, the claimant would be better advised to apply for summary judgment
instead.

[12] Case C–129/92 *Owens Bank Ltd v Bracco* [1994] ECR I–117.

[13] *Landhurst Leasing plc v Marcq* [1998] ILPr 822 (CA). But it does not include a settlement;
and if it is desired to make binding the terms on which a claim is compromised, a judgment
is much to be preferred to a contractual disposal: Case C–414/92 *Solo Kleinmotoren GmbH v
Boch* [1994] ECR I–2237.

[14] Article 49.

[15] Article 49.

[16] Article 58.

[17] Article 57.

[18] For the points of difference, see Case C–414/92 *Solo Kleinmotoren GmbH v Boch.*

it is then integrated into the English legal order. Once that is done, there is nothing to prevent an English court applying principles of issue estoppel to the judgment and to its parts, although as a matter of English private international law, rather than as a requirement of the Regulation which is *functus officio* once it has brought about the recognition of the judgment.

3. CIVIL OR COMMERCIAL MATTERS:
ARTICLE I

The judgment must be in a civil or commercial matter, the meaning of which was examined in Chapter 2. Although it has not been stated in clear and explicit terms, it seems certain that the recognizing court must decide for itself whether the judgment was given in a civil or commercial matter, and is not bound at this point simply to accept the view of the adjudicating court. After all, the adjudicating court may not have needed to decide the issue for itself. It may have deduced that if the matter was a civil or commercial one, the Regulation gave it jurisdiction, and if it was not, its own domestic law did instead.[19] Even so, it is to be expected that where the adjudicating court has given such a ruling, its conclusion will at least be persuasive. It follows that a judgment in respect of subject matter excluded by Article 1 from the domain of the Regulation will not be recognized under Chapter III. Where a single judgment deals with included and excluded matter it may be possible to sever it: this may happen when a judgment has provided for maintenance and has determined rights in property which arise out of a matrimonial relationship, or when a criminal court imposes a criminal penalty and orders compensation to a civil party. Where severance is not possible, the substantial presence of excluded matter in an indivisible judgment may wholly preclude recognition under the Regulation.[20] Where the judgment was obtained in breach of an agreement to arbitrate it is arguable that recognition is not demanded and may be withheld. To do otherwise would oblige a court to contradict its law on arbitration, which lies outside the domain of the Regulation.[21] But if Article 1(2)(d) merely means that no court has adjudicatory jurisdiction over the merits of what is still a civil or commercial claim,[22] and as jurisdictional error is not generally a basis for denying recognition,[23] recognition

---

[19] Case 29/76 *LTU GmbH & Co v Eurocontrol* [1976] ECR 1541; Case 145/86 *Hoffmann v Krieg* [1988] ECR 645.

[20] Case C-220/95 *Van den Boogaard v Laumen* [1997] ECR I-1147; and see Art 48.

[21] cf Case 145/86 *Hoffmann v Krieg* [1988] ECR 645.

[22] Case C-391/95 *Van Uden Maritime BV v Deco-Line* [1998] ECR I-7091.

[23] See Art 35, SB.5. below.

of the offending judgment may yet be required, and in turn be withheld as conflicting with the public policy of enforcing agreements to arbitrate.[24] Further clarification must come from the European Court.

4. DATE OF THE PROCEEDINGS AND THE DATE OF JUDGMENT: ARTICLE 66

The Regulation applies to the recognition of judgments given in proceedings instituted in the then-Member States after 1 March 2002. For judgments in proceedings instituted before that date, or before the accession date of a 2004 or 2007 state, but where judgment was given after the accession date, recognition is provided for if the adjudicating court founded itself on rules of jurisdiction which conformed to those of the Regulation.

5. JURISDICTIONAL ERRORS: ARTICLE 35

The adjudicating court may have erred in its application of the Regulation by accepting jurisdiction when it did not have it. Save in the exceptional cases mentioned below, this is irrelevant to the recognition of the judgment under Chapter III.[25] At a superficial level the reason is clear: it was the responsibility of the defendant to make this very argument to the adjudicating court, and had the chance to make it once, there is no reason to allow him to make it, for what might be a second time, to another court at the point of recognition. Indeed, there is every reason not to, for it would impede the free circulation of judgments if it were otherwise.

Now this is reasonable for defendants domiciled in Member States, whose jurisdictional exposure is defined and limited by Chapter II of the Regulation. It is jaw-droppingly unfair to those not so domiciled, who may be sued on the basis of Article 4. They have no chance to complain about the width of the jurisdictional rules asserted against them: neither at trial, because Article 4(2) says that they are expressly subject to the traditional and exorbitant jurisdictional rules set out in Annex I to the Regulation, nor at recognition, because jurisdictional points may not generally be taken at the point of recognition.[26] No European defendant is exposed to this lethal combination of unreconstructed jurisdictional rules, on the one hand, and the absence of right to be heard on the propriety of those rules or their application on the other. This was the calculated act of those

---

[24] *Phillip Alexander Securities and Futures Ltd v Bamberger* [1997] ILPr 73, 104; Art 34(1).
[25] Article 35.
[26] Article 35; and it is expressly forbidden to find the jurisdictional rules of the court to be contrary to public policy: Art 35(3).

who drafted the Convention[27] and the Regulation which adopts it,[28] and it takes the breath away, although to the European bureaucrat or apparatchik, no doubt it makes sense. By humiliating contrast, the Supreme Court of the United States has long held that the constitutional guarantees[29] of due process and equal treatment apply to foreigners as well as to American nationals.[30] But this form of legislative discrimination is a matter of deliberate policy. It is a pretty sorry state of affairs.

Exceptions apply only where the lack of jurisdiction is derived from the provisions on insurance contracts, consumer contracts, and exclusive jurisdiction regardless of domicile:[31] in these cases the original jurisdictional rules enshrine policies of such importance that they demand reinforcement by the recognizing court, although it is striking that this does not extend to the special rules on jurisdiction over employment contracts. Nor does it cover a case in which the adjudicating court has failed to give effect to a jurisdiction agreement which should have been validated by Article 23. This does show Article 23 to occupy a relatively low position in the hierarchy of jurisdictional rules;[32] it is not impossible that, if and when the European Union adopts and brings into effect the Hague Convention on Choice of Court Agreements,[33] this will be reconsidered as well. In the meantime, breach of an agreement on jurisdiction by one of the parties to it may found a claim for damages.

Those limited cases apart, the plea that the adjudicating court should have realized that it had no jurisdiction is inadmissible. The divergence from the approach of the common law at this point may seem sharp, for where the common law governs recognition, the first line of defence is a plea that the foreign court lacked jurisdiction. But this is an illusion. Under the Regulation, the defendant may actually make a submission to the adjudicating court that it does not have jurisdiction according to *English* jurisdictional rules: this is because the rules applicable in the foreign court are the same as those of English law.[34] But outside the Member States, where the Regulation does not apply, such an argument cannot usefully be made to the foreign court, which has no concern with English

[27] Jenard was open about it: [1979] OJ C59/20. He should have been ashamed of himself.
[28] Recital 10.
[29] Fifth and Fourteenth Amendments to the American Constitution.
[30] See eg *Asahi Metal Industry Co v Superior Court of California* 480 US 102, 108–9, 113–15 (1987).
[31] Article 35(1). Breach of a jurisdiction agreement is not included.
[32] Although the protection of the weak may justly be seen as enjoying a higher priority than reinforcing agreements made between equals who ought to be able to look after themselves.
[33] 30 June 2005.
[34] Apart from Art 4 cases, where such concerns of due process are irrelevant.

jurisdictional rules. The first opportunity to air it comes, therefore, at recognition. The schemes therefore converge in agreeing that *this* argument, that the foreign court did not have jurisdiction according to English rules, may be made once, and that it must be made at the earliest sensible point. They diverge only in the identification of this temporal point.

6. PROCEDURAL OR SUBSTANTIVE OBJECTIONS TO RECOGNITION: ARTICLE 34

There are four procedural or substantive objections, exhaustively listed in Article 34,[35] which may be made to the recognition of a judgment. Compared with their predecessors in the Brussels Convention, which were frequently said to be narrow in scope,[36] those in the Regulation are designed to be narrower still, so as to make the circulation of judgments from and within the Member States even more free. In the Brussels and Lugano Conventions there was and still is a fifth ground, for the case where the foreign judgment was founded on a conclusion about status which conflicted with the law of the recognizing state. But as questions of marriage and status were excluded from the Convention by Article 1, it was mildly surprising that there was provision for the non-recognition of judgments which had taken a view on an issue which lay outside the domain of the Convention and was unaffected by it. It was best regarded as inept use of belt and braces,[37] and it has not been reproduced in the Regulation. Its omission makes no broader point.

(a) Public policy: Article 34(1)

If recognition of the judgment would be manifestly contrary to public policy, recognition is precluded by Article 34(1). The content of English public policy is a matter for English law, although the general definition of it is implicit in the Regulation. Under the Brussels Convention it was held that where recognition of the judgment would infringe a law which was regarded as fundamental in the recognizing state, such as where the adjudicating court had failed to comply with the standards of the European Convention on Human Rights by refusing one party the right to be heard,[38] recognition could be considered to be contrary to public policy. By contrast, to recognize a judgment which contained a

---

[35] cf Art 27 BC.

[36] It appears that they are not supposed to overlap, at least where Art 34(1) is concerned: Case C–78/95 *Hendrickman v Magenta Druck & Verlag GmbH* [1996] ECR I–4943.

[37] Article 27(4) BC; Case 145/86 *Hoffmann v Krieg* [1988] ECR 645.

[38] Case C–7/98 *Krombach v Bamberski* [2000] ECR I–1935.

misapplication of European competition law could not be considered to be contrary to public policy, especially where the opportunity of bringing an appeal from adjudicating court could perfectly well have put it right.[39] The Regulation adds the word 'manifestly' to the corresponding provision of the Convention, which will presumably mean that the scope of Article 34(1) is intended to constrict rather than expand.

It seems that the argument that the judgment was obtained by fraud will not prevent recognition if the state of origin has its own procedures for investigating such a plea.[40] Even so, as will be shown below, to impeach a judgment for fraud before the original court is more difficult—and seeks a more radical remedy—than using fraud to prevent recognition of a foreign judgment in England. In that sense, the state of origin may not have a remedy which corresponds to the fraud doctrine of the common law; but the tide is running against the doctrine of fraud in foreign judgments, and this argument cannot really be expected to prevail. However, if a foreign court has refused to give effect to a commercial arbitration agreement, recognition of the judgment may be contrary to English public policy as this is set out in the Civil Jurisdiction and Judgments Act 1982, section 32:[41] the wording of the Act supports the argument that this is a matter of fundamental importance in English law. And recognition of a judgment obtained in defiance of an English anti-suit injunction must surely be contrary to public policy.[42] Were a court in a Member State ever to hand one down, recognition of a judgment for multiple damages, to which the Protection of Trading Interests Act 1980 applies, certainly would offend public policy.

(b) Judgments in default of appearance: Article 34(2)

There has been a narrowing of the defence to recognition for certain judgments in default of appearance, as now defined in Article 34(2). If as a matter of fact, and notwithstanding that the adjudicating court did not consider there to be such a default,[43] the judgment was in default of appearance, and either the document instituting the proceedings was not served in accordance with the law of the adjudicating state[44] or it was

---

[39] Case C–38/98 *Régie Nationale des Usines Renault SA v Maxicar* [2000] ECR I–2973.

[40] *Interdesco SA v Nullifire Ltd* [1992] 1 Lloyd's Rep 180.

[41] *Phillip Alexander Securities & Futures Ltd v Bamberger* [1997] ILPr 73, 103.

[42] *Phillip Alexander Securities & Futures Ltd v Bamberger* [1997] ILPr 104, 115 (CA). But the chances of this happening are now much reduced: Case C–159/02 *Turner v Grovit* [2004] ECR I–3565.

[43] This means that there must be an autonomous definition of the term: it essentially covers the case where the defendant was denied a proper right to be heard or represented: Case C–78/95 *Hendrickman v Magenta Druck & Verlag GmbH* [1996] ECR I–4943.

[44] If irregularity in service was cured under the law of the state of origin, this presumably ceases to be a maintainable point.

served but not, according to the assessment of the judge in the recognizing state, in sufficient time to allow the defendant to arrange for his defence,[45] recognition will in principle be denied. This provision is intended to reinforce[46] the legal protection of the defendant, by giving him the right to be properly and timeously summoned; although if the document was duly served,[47] the requirement is merely that it be in time to allow him to forestall judgment in default of appearance. Whether the time was sufficient is assessed in the light of the mode of service. Where service has been made on the defendant personally, a relatively short period is probably all one needs to interrupt judgment being given in default. But where 'pretend' service was made on, say, the local consul, or on the *parquet* for onward transmission to the defendant, or by leaving it at a post office or the last known address, the time period may properly be much longer. Likewise, orders obtained without notice to the respondent will be denied recognition,[48] so a freezing injunction obtained without notice will be denied recognition. The order may lose its original default character if a subsequent application is made to set it aside but this is dismissed.[49] The true answer should depend upon whether the respondent was disadvantaged by the fact that the order had already been made in proceedings in which he did not appear.[50] If he was, with the result that he faced an uphill struggle as a result of the default judgment, his application to set aside should not involve the loss of the shield of Article 34(2); but if his application had the effect of reimposing the original burden of proof on the applicant, any new or confirmed order will not be vitiated. Moreover, and in contrast to the corresponding provision of the Brussels Convention,[51] the Regulation provides that the shield of Article 34(2) will be lost if the defendant had the opportunity of bringing proceedings to challenge the judgment but did not do so. It is submitted that this cannot be taken at face value, but must be interpreted as meaning that the defendant had a

---

[45] Case 228/81 *Pendy Plastic Products v Pluspunkt* [1982] ECR 2723; Case 49/84 *Debaecker and Plouvier v Bouwman* [1985] ECR 1779.

[46] Article 26 will oblige the adjudicating court to check, in the case of an absent defendant, that the defendant has been served and has had time to arrange for his defence; the recognizing court must, however, make that assessment for itself.

[47] As it is the document of the adjudicating state, this is the law by which it must be served, although irregularities which may be cured by this law will obviously be curable: Case C–305/88 *Isabelle Lancray SA v Peters und Sickert KG* [1990] ECR I–2725.

[48] Case 125/79 *Denilauler v SNC Couchet Frères* [1980] ECR 1553.

[49] A proposition denied by *Orams v Apostilides* [2006] EWHC 2226 (QB), [2007] 1 WLR 214, which is wrong (now referred by the Court of Appeal and pending as Case C–420/07).

[50] cf Case C–474/93 *Hengst Import BV v Campese* [1995] ECR I–2113.

[51] Article 27(2) BC.

reasonable opportunity to bring proceedings in which he would have been under no appreciable disadvantage when compared with the defendant who did appear.[52]

(c) Irreconcilability with English judgment: Article 34(3)

If recognition of the foreign judgment produces consequences which are incompatible with an English judgment in a dispute between the same parties, whether this was handed down earlier or later than the foreign one, recognition will be refused by Article 34(3).[53] In principle, Article 27 should prevent parallel proceedings at the point when the second action is commenced, or the rules of *res judicata* should apply if the English judgment has not yet been given, so that the English court could therefore recognize the foreign judgment when handed down. If all goes according to the plan of the Regulation, there will be little work for Article 34(3) to do. But when this does not quite happen, an English court is entitled to prefer its own judgment. Irreconcilability may involve a measure of evaluation. A judgment that a contract was lawfully rescinded is certainly irreconcilable with an order that damages be paid for its breach.[54] But a decision that A is liable to B for breach of warranty of quality may not be irreconcilable with a judgment that B was liable to pay the price of goods sold and delivered by A. Again, a decision that A is liable to B for damage to B's cargo is irreconcilable with one that B owes no liability for damage to the cargo, but is not irreconcilable with a claim for damages for short delivery.

(d) Irreconcilability with prior foreign judgment: Article 34(4)

If a judgment from a non-Member State was given in proceedings between the same parties and involving the same cause of action, and satisfies the criteria for its own recognition in England, and was the first to be handed down, and is irreconcilable with a later Member State judgment, Article 34(4) provides that the later, Member State, judgment will not be recognized. The text does not say that proceedings to secure the enforcement of the non-Member State judgment should have been instituted: indeed, as that judgment may well be entitled to recognition without any such proceedings, there would be no reason to infer such a limitation.

Where there is irreconcilability between two different and foreign Member State judgments, the first one is recognized, and the second one,

---

[52] Case C-283/05 *ASML Netherlands BV v SEMIS GmbH* [2006] ECR I-12041.
[53] Case 145/86 *Hoffmann v Krieg* [1988] ECR 645.
[54] Case 144/86 *Gubisch Maschinenfabrik KG v Palumbo* [1987] ECR 4861.

if irreconcilable with it, is not. This is consistent with the view taken in English common law as well.[55]

(e) Australian and Canadian defendants: Article 72

Article 59 of the Brussels and Lugano Conventions permitted states to enter bilateral treaties with a non-Contracting State, to stipulate for the local non-recognition of judgments from other Contracting States, where these judgments were founded on the national jurisdictional rules whose use was authorized by Article 4, and which were given against nationals or domiciliaries of the non-Contracting State. The United Kingdom concluded such treaties with Australia[56] and Canada,[57] and Article 72 provides that these remain in force. But there will be no new bilateral treaties, as competence in external relations in the field of the Regulation now reposes in the European Union.[58]

(f) No other grounds for non-recognition

There is no other ground upon which it is permitted to impeach the judgment and deny it recognition. Article 35 precludes any further review of the jurisdiction of the foreign court, and explicitly provides[59] that public policy may not be invoked to launch a collateral attack on the jurisdiction of the adjudicating court. This is obviously aimed at judgments based on Article 4;[60] but it is submitted that it does not prevent the denial of recognition to judgments which disregard a valid and binding arbitration agreement, for in such a case it is not the jurisdiction, but the rejection of the arbitration defence, an excluded matter, which is the basis for objection.

Article 36 absolutely prohibits any review of the merits of the judgment, although this must be permitted to the extent required to apply the provisions of Article 34.[61] What may appear to be an exception arises when a court is called upon to recognize a provisional or protective measure which was granted on the basis of Article 31, that is, not by the court with jurisdiction over the merits of the claim. The extent of the permitted review is to ascertain that the order is, as a matter of substance, a

---

[55] *Showlag v Mansour* [1995] 1 AC 431 (PC).
[56] Reciprocal Enforcement of Foreign Judgments (Australia) Order 1994 (SI 1994/1901), Sch, Art 3.
[57] Reciprocal Enforcement of Foreign Judgments (Canada) Order 1987 (SI 1987/468), Sch, Art IX.
[58] And see Opinion C–1/03 *Lugano* [2006] ECR I–1145.
[59] Article 35(3).
[60] But also Art 5(4): Case C–7/98 *Krombach v Bamberski* [2000] ECR I–1935.
[61] Case C–78/95 *Hendrickman v Magenta Druck & Verlag GmbH* [1996] ECR I–4943.

provisional or protective one; but if it is not, it will be denied recognition. This limitation appears to be necessary to counter the inherent weakness of Article 31, which simply abnegates any jurisdictional control over such measures. Accordingly, if a foreign court has made an order for an interim payment, but does not have jurisdiction over the merits of the claim (perhaps because the parties have agreed to arbitrate, with the result that no court has merits jurisdiction), an English court, called on to recognize and enforce the order, may and must check that it is provisional or protective: that is to say, limited to assets within the territory of the court which made the order,[62] and guaranteed to be reversible in the event that the applicant does not succeed on the substantive claim.[63]

7. JUDGMENTS UNDER APPEAL: ARTICLE 37

If an 'ordinary appeal' is pending against the judgment in the state of its origin, Article 37 permits, although does not oblige, the recognizing court to stay any proceedings in which the issue of recognition will arise. All English appeals are, apparently, ordinary appeals.[64] The sense of this is clear: a court must have the power to conclude that it is inappropriate to proceed in a case in which the foreign judgment upon which issues turn may be reversed on appeal. This would appear to require some assessment of how likely it is that the judgment will be reversed, and the degree of prejudice likely to be suffered if the application is or is not stayed; but it has also been held that this is impermissible as it involves a review of the merits of the judgment.[65]

8. EFFECT OF RECOGNITION

The main consequence of recognition will usually be to pave the way for the enforcement of the judgment, the procedure for which is examined below. But this is not the only effect the recognition of the judgment may bring about. To recognize a judgment means, in principle at least, to give it the effect it has under the law of the state in which it was given.[66] So if

---

[62] If that requirement is taken seriously, it may be very rare for such an order ever to be presented for recognition in another country. But in the case of an English freezing order, not made in relation to assets as distinct from being ordered against a defendant personally, this limitation may be an irrelevance, and the order more likely to be presented for recognition in another country.

[63] Case C–99/96 *Mietz v Intership Yachting Sneek BV* [1999] ECR I–2277.

[64] Article 46(2).

[65] *Banco Nacional de Comercio Exterior SNC v Empresa de Telecomunicaciones de Cuba* [2007] EWHC 2322 (Comm).

[66] Case C–145/86 *Hoffmann v Krieg* [1988] ECR 645.

the judgment is in the nature of a provisional order, which would not be taken as binding or conclusive in subsequent proceedings in the adjudicating court, it should be given neither more nor less an effect in England. In certain cases a judgment may be regarded by the adjudicating court as impinging upon non-parties,[67] such as sureties for the defendant, or an insurer; but whether this must be respected and given effect by an English court is unclear. The problems arise at a number of levels. First, it may be argued that, so far as the non-party was concerned, the judgment must have been given in default of his appearance, and so be denied recognition against him by reason of Article 34(2). Secondly, it may be contrary to public policy, as crystallized in the European Convention on Human Rights, for a person to be bound by a judgment in respect of which he had no right to be heard. Thirdly, it may be that once the judgment has been shown to qualify for recognition as between the parties to it, it is thereafter for English private international law, and not for the Regulation, to determine what further effects it may have.

9. ENFORCEMENT

Any judgment which is entitled to recognition and is enforceable in the state in which it was given[68] may, in principle, be enforced by the procedure set out in detail in Articles 38 to 52. In England, an application is made to the High Court[69] for an order that the judgment be registered pursuant to the Regulation, by producing an authenticated copy of the judgment[70] and proof in standard form that it is enforceable under the law of the state in which it was given.[71] When registered for enforcement under the Regulation, the judgment[72] has the same force and effect for the purposes of enforcement as if it were an English judgment. This is easy to understand when dealing with a money judgment, but enforcement under the Regulation applies also to non-money judgments. In the case of a foreign order of a type close or identical to an English equivalent, there is little difficulty in giving effect to paragraph 1(3). Where the order is rather different, it is unclear exactly what an English court is to do. The practice of the German courts apparently is to transmute the order into its nearest

---

[67] cf Schlosser [1979] OJ C59/71, 127–8.
[68] Article 38.
[69] Annex II to the Regulation.
[70] Article 53(1).
[71] In the form in Annex V to the Regulation.
[72] SI 2001/3929, Sch 1, para 1(3).

German equivalent,[73] and to use this as the template for enforcement. It is difficult to see that there is a better alternative.

(a) Application without notice

The first stage of enforcement requires the applicant to produce a copy of the judgment and certain other specified documents, and applies, without notice to the respondent, for an order for registration: the respondent has no right to be heard at this stage.[74] The Regulation does not allow the court to refer to Articles 34 and 35 in order to refuse to make the order for registration.[75] This made a departure from the previous law, and was made to counter the prevarication and chauvinism which may be encountered on an application to enforce a foreign judgment against a local. Even so, in a truly egregious case there must still be a discretion to refuse to register, a conclusion which is reinforced by the fact that either side may appeal against the decision on the application.[76] But assuming that the court grants the order, it will notify the applicant and serve the order for registration on the respondent, who may learn about it for the first time.[77]

(b) First appeal against the decision on the application for registration

If the application for registration was refused, Article 43 permits the applicant to appeal.[78] If the application was granted, Article 43(5) gives the respondent one month if domiciled in the enforcing state, or two months if domiciled in a different Member State,[79] from the date of service, to launch an appeal under Article 43 against the order for registration. This marks the stage in the procedure when, in practice, the arguments touching recognition will be raised. According to Article 45(1), the order for enforceability can be refused or revoked only on the grounds specified in Articles 34 and 35, but this cannot be quite right. A court hearing the appeal may conclude that the judgment was not in a civil or commercial

---

[73] Zuckerman and Grunert [1996] *Zeitschrift für Zivilprozess International* 89.
[74] Article 41.
[75] Article 41.
[76] Article 43(1).
[77] Article 42(2).
[78] Annex III to the Regulation. The more usual English usage would be an application to set aside the *ex parte* order for registration, rather than an appeal, but the terminology is established by the Regulation.
[79] It is not said how long is allowed if he is not domiciled in a Member State, but the answer is presumably two months which can be extended.

matter,[80] or was for a periodic payment which had not been quantified,[81] or was of a measure which should not have been granted under Article 31, or in respect of which there was a bilateral treaty:[82] Article 45 appears to direct the court to ignore all such facts and matters; it cannot be taken to mean what it appears to say.

(c) Further appeal on a point of law

The order made on the hearing of the Article 43 appeal may itself be further appealed, but only once, and on a point of law. The grounds on which the court hearing the further appeal may revoke or refuse registration are again defined by the unconvincing Article 45(1).

10. PROCEDURAL MATTERS CONCERNING ENFORCEMENT: ARTICLES 46 AND 47

If an appeal has been lodged, or could still be lodged, against the judgment in the court of origin, Article 46 provides that the court hearing the appeal under Article 43 or the further appeal under Article 44[83] may, on the application of the respondent, stay the appeal proceedings; it is also, presumably as an alternative, empowered to authorize enforcement on the condition of provision of security. After the order for registration has been made, Article 47 permits the court to grant protective measures against the property of the respondent, but until the final determination of the appeal, only protective measures may be taken. The dominant principle in all these cases will be the need to strike a fair and proportionate balance between the interests of the applicant who, having won, should not be kept out of his money by a prevaricating respondent; and the respondent whose rights to appeal are prescribed by law and should not be undercut by allowing irreversible measures of enforcement to take place in advance of its determination.

11. UNCONTESTED JUDGMENTS

For all that enforcement under the Brussels Regulation is brisk, it is still possible for a judgment debtor to slow down the process of enforcement against him. It is still easier to enforce in London a judgment from Manchester than one from Munich; harder to enforce one from Latvia

---

[80] Article 1.
[81] Article 49.
[82] Article 72.
[83] Thereby reversing the effect of the decision: Case C–439/93 *SISRO v Ampersand Software BV* [1995] ECR I–2269.

than from Leeds. On the footing that this was undesirable, a Regulation was made to provide for judgments on 'uncontested' claims to be certified by the issuing court with a 'European Enforcement Order'. This will allow them to be registered in other Member States, with extremely minimal rights of opposition before the registering court.[84] So far this is permitted only for judgments in proceedings which the defendant did not contest, but one imagines that the scheme will be proclaimed a success and extended. The eventual aim is not that there be free movement of judgments, but that the Member States be understood and organized, for this purpose, as a single law district, in which Birmingham is no more (or less) foreign than Bucharest.

C. JUDGMENTS FROM OTHER EUROPEAN PLACES: 1982 ACT

1. LUGANO STATES

The Lugano Convention, which was given effect by amendment made to the Civil Jurisdiction and Judgments Act 1982, is the vehicle for the recognition and enforcement of judgments from Iceland, Norway, and Switzerland. Applications for registration of these judgments, under section 4 of the Act, will continue to be governed by the provisions of those Conventions.[85] The rules of these Conventions are similar, and will soon be the same, as those now in the Regulation. It does not merit closer examination here.

2. SCOTLAND, NORTHERN IRELAND, GIBRALTAR

As well as providing the mechanism for the recognition and enforcement of judgments under the Brussels Convention, which function is now mostly spent, the 1982 Act continues to provide for the recognition and enforcement of judgments from Scotland and Northern Ireland, and Gibraltar. Judgments from other parts of the United Kingdom, whether for money or otherwise, may be registered for enforcement subject to only minor restrictions.[86] For the purpose of the Regulation,[87] Gibraltar is treated as part of the United Kingdom. In England, however, judgments from

---

[84] Regulation (EC) 805/2004, [2004] L143/15.
[85] Recital 10; Art 71.
[86] 1982 Act, s 18; Schs 6, 7.
[87] And by contrast with the position under the Brussels Convention.

Gibraltar are recognized and enforced by reference to provisions which are modelled on the rules of the Brussels Convention.[88]

D. JUDGMENTS FROM THE REST OF THE WORLD: COMMON LAW

By contrast with the closed world of the Member States, whose judgments are recognized under the Regulation, the rules of the common law have to deal with the recognition of judgments from the courts of the rest of the world, from China to Peru.[89] The basic scheme of common law recognition is that if the foreign court is adjudged to have been competent, as a matter of *English* law, to give a judgment by which the losing party was bound, this may, and if there is no other defence to the claim for recognition will, be recognized as making the cause of action or the issue *res judicata*. If all that a party requires is for the judgment to be recognized, it is sufficient to plead the effect of it as *res judicata*, but if the judgment creditor wishes to enforce the judgment in offensive fashion, he will need to bring an action on it at common law: the claim is founded on the judgment rather than the underlying cause of action, for the judgment gives rise to a distinct legal obligation.[90] In the case of an action to enforce it, the judgment must meet further criteria which determine its enforceability by action in the English courts.

I. RECOGNITION

A judgment will be recognized at common law if it is the final and conclusive judgment of a court which, as a matter of English private international law, had 'international jurisdiction', and as long as there is no defence to its recognition. By contrast with some forms of statutory enforcement procedure, there is no requirement that the judgment be that of a superior court: any judicial tribunal will suffice for the common law. But the award of an arbitral tribunal is not sufficient,[91] nor is the decision of an administrative body. A court, and only a court, will do.

In principle, at least, only final and conclusive orders are recognized. The terminology is used more easily than it is defined, but 'final' means

---

[88] 1982 Act, s 39; Civil Jurisdiction and Judgments Act 1982 (Gibraltar) Order 1997 (SI 1997/2602).

[89] And to judgments from the Member States if and in so far as these fall outside the scope of the Regulation.

[90] *Godard v Gray* (1870–71) LR 6 QB 139.

[91] These do not give rise to issues of recognition in this sense; and their enforcement is regulated by specialist Convention and statute.

that this cannot be reopened in the court which made the ruling, even though it may be subject to appeal to a higher court; and 'conclusive' that it represents the court's settled conclusion on the merits of the point adjudicated.[92] For this reason, a foreign freezing order will not be recognized, as it is not predicated upon a final determination of the validity of the claim, nor is it usually incapable of review and revision by the court which ordered it. Likewise, recognition will not be accorded to a decision that there is, for example, a good arguable case on a disputed point, jurisdictional or otherwise: the decision may be final, in that the court will not itself reconsider the question, but is not conclusive if it would not tie the hands of the same court at a later stage when the merits are tried. By contrast, an order made on an interlocutory matter may be recognized if it represents the last word of the court on the point in issue. An example may be an order dismissing an action on the ground that it was covered by a jurisdiction agreement for a specific court: if this represents the court's final decision, it is in principle entitled to recognition.[93] A difficulty therefore arises in relation to default judgments, which will often be liable to reopening in the court in which they were entered, at least on conditions, and not usually only within a fixed time limit. It would appear to follow that these cannot be recognized as final, with the counter-intuitive result that if the defence is so hopeless that the defendant elects to allow judgment in default of appearance to be entered against him, the claimant may be left with a judgment of reduced effectiveness. The argument may be met by a contention that a default judgment is not, in the material sense, a provisional one which it expects to reconsider. It is instead the court's settled conclusion unless and until something happens which may never happen.[94] On the other hand, the claimant may do better to hurry slowly, and to apply for summary judgment on the merits of the claim.

2. INTERNATIONAL JURISDICTION

A foreign court has international jurisdiction, as this is defined and acknowledged by English private international law, if the party against whom the judgment was given submitted to the jurisdiction of the court, or was present or resident—either will suffice—within the jurisdiction of the court when the proceedings were instituted.[95] The occasional

---

[92] Which may be the whole dispute or a single point: *The Sennar (No 2)* [1985] 1 WLR 490 (HL).

[93] Ibid; cf *Desert Sun Loan Corp v Hill* [1996] 2 All ER 847 (CA).

[94] *Ainslie v Ainslie* (1927) 39 CLR 318.

[95] Which probably means when process was served on him: *Adams v Cape Industries plc* [1990] Ch 433, 518 (CA).

suggestion that the nationality of the defendant is sufficient[96] is discredited today. The grounds stated are exhaustive; at present English law does not acknowledge jurisdictional competence on the basis that the foreign court exercised a jurisdiction which mirrors that which English law would exercise itself,[97] nor that the foreign court was the natural forum for the trial of the action.

Such a step has been taken, however, by the Supreme Court of Canada, which has since embarked on a wide and radical re-examination of the law which connects the exercise of jurisdiction, the power to grant anti-suit injunctions, and the recognition of foreign judgments.[98] Recognition extends to judgments from courts having a real and substantial connection to the dispute;[99] and it will require only a short further step to refine this to denote a court which is the *forum conveniens*. The argument is clear enough: if the claimant has sued in the court which is, in Canadian eyes, the most proper and appropriate place for the claim to have been brought, why should the judgment be denied recognition? A pragmatic answer might be that it makes life awkward for a defendant, who may face real difficulty in seeking to predict whether it is safe to allow judgment to be entered in default of appearance, or prudent to appear and defend. As to this, it might be said that the interests of the defendant are not necessarily paramount; and if the claimant has played by the rules of *forum conveniens*, it may be that the balance should be held to favour him.

As a matter of English law, such a development would require legislation. And it is important to understand how radical the Canadian departure is. For the English common law enquires into whether the party to be bound to the judgment has acted in such a way as to have assumed a personal obligation to obey the judgment: his submission to the jurisdiction of the court is the commonest example, but his presence within the jurisdiction also places him in the way of obedience. The Canadian development, however, does not focus on whether the party to be bound has assumed an obligation, but on whether the Canadian court should impose one for reasons of its own. There is nothing wrong with such a development, but far from being a modernization of the details, it represents a

---

[96] *Emanuel v Symon* [1908] 1 KB 302 (CA).

[97] Traditionally this proposition is supported by *Schibsby v Westenholz* (1870) LR 6 QB 155. The analogy is not exact, for it took no account of the fact that an English court would not have exercised the jurisdiction invoked unless it was also the natural forum for the claim.

[98] See in particular *Amchem Products Inc v British Columbia (Workers' Compensation Board)* [1993] 1 SCR 897, (1993) 102 DLR (4th) 96.

[99] *Morguard Investments Ltd v De Savoye* [1990] 3 SCR 1077, (1991) 76 DLR (4th) 256; *Beals v Saldanha* [2003] 3 SCR 416, (2003) 234 DLR (4th) 1.

fundamental reorientation of the law on foreign judgments. It is not clear that the Supreme Court fully appreciated what it was doing.

(a) Submission

No injustice is done to a party who submits to the jurisdiction of a court if its adverse judgment is taken as binding him. So a defendant who voluntarily submits to the jurisdiction of a foreign court is, in principle, subject to its international jurisdiction if the decision goes against him. A claimant, or counterclaiming defendant also clearly submits to the jurisdiction for the purposes of a decision against him; but whether a claimant is taken to submit to any and every counterclaim will depend on whether the counterclaim arises out of the same facts or transaction as his claim or out of facts which are reasonably connected: a test of broad common sense applies.[100]

If a defendant appears for the purpose only of contesting the jurisdiction of the court, or to seek a stay in favour of another court or for arbitration, or to protect property which is threatened with seizure in the proceedings, the Civil Jurisdiction and Judgments Act 1982, section 33(1), provides that the appearance will not on that account be a submission. This represents a departure from the common law which had held[101]—extraordinarily, as it now seems—that to appear before a court to apply for jurisdictional relief was voluntarily to submit to its jurisdiction.[102] It appears to follow that if the defendant is required, strictly or as a matter of good practice, to plead to the merits at the same time as making his jurisdictional challenge, or finds that he is compelled to participate in other interlocutory procedures in order to keep his jurisdictional challenge alive, the statutory protection is not lost.[103] To claim the protection of the statute, it may be that the challenge has to be to the international, rather than to the local or internal, jurisdiction of the court, as the existence or non-existence of local or internal jurisdiction is generally of no

---

[100] *Murthy v Sivasjothi* [1999] 1 WLR 467 (CA).

[101] *Henry v Geoprosco International* [1976] QB 726 (CA).

[102] The reasoning being that if relief is applied for, the very making of the application involves accepting that the court has jurisdiction to grant it; and there is therefore a submission. A more sophisticated analysis would have been that to submit to the power of a court to rule on its jurisdiction is not the same thing as to submit to its power to rule on the merits: *Williams & Glyn's Bank v Astro Dinamico* [1984] 1 WLR 438 (HL).

[103] *Marc Rich & Co AG v Soc Italiana Impianti PA (No 2)* [1992] 1 Lloyd's Rep 624 (CA). In principle, if the foreign court does not characterize the defendant's participation as amounting to an appearance, an English court should not do so either: *Adams v Cape Industries plc* [1990] Ch 433, 461; *The Eastern Trader* [1996] 2 Lloyd's Rep 585.

relevance to the English law on recognition.[104] So if a defendant argues
that she should be tried in another country, this will be protected from
being counted as submission, but if she argues that she should be tried
in one city rather than another, or in the High Court rather than a lower
court, or in a state court rather than a federal court, these arguments will
be less likely to secure the protection of the statute. On the other hand, if
the defendant appears under protest, whatever that may mean, to defend
the case, her unenthusiastic appearance is nevertheless a voluntary one.

A troublesome argument, which appears to have proved more attractive than it should have, proposes that if a party has made an application to
a court for a particular form of relief, issue estoppel may arise out of the
decision of the court adverse to the applicant. It follows, so the argument
runs, that if a party applies to a foreign court for a stay or dismissal on the
ground that the court has no jurisdiction, the decision of the foreign court
that it does, and any finding made in support of this decision, may give
rise to an estoppel, and be utilized by the opposite party in an attempt to
secure recognition of the consequent judgment. If at first sight this may
appear sound—a party who has applied for an order ought to be bound by
the court's decision on it—then second thoughts are called for. A party
can only be bound if he submitted to the jurisdiction of the foreign court
in the first place, and if he appeared for the purpose of contesting the jurisdiction, section 33(1) provides him with an answer to the contention that
he submitted. It denatures section 33(1) to hold that an adverse decision
on the motion to contest the jurisdiction is itself entitled to recognition.
The conclusion must be that before any question of recognition as *res
judicata* can arise by reason of a party's submission, there must actually be
submission; and if section 33(1) provides that there is not, that is the end
of the argument.

Submission may also be made by contractual agreement. The dispute
and the particular court[105] in which the action is brought must fall within
the four corners of the contractual term. To the extent that this raises a
question of construction, the principles will be the same as those examined in relation to jurisdiction. The term itself must have remained valid

---

[104] *Pemberton v Hughes* [1899] 1 Ch 781. For a challenge to the existence of a power of
attorney to accept service of process and whether this constitutes a challenge to the jurisdiction protected by s 33, see the divergent analyses in *Desert Sun Loan Corp v Hill* [1996] 2 All
ER 847 (CA).

[105] There are cases where a court bears the same name as one contractually agreed to at an
earlier date, but where revolutionary political change means that it is no longer to be seen as the
'same' court: *Carvalho v Hull Blyth (Angola) Ltd* [1979] 1 WLR 1228 (CA).

and contractually enforceable at the date of the action.[106] It has been said that an implied agreement to submit will not suffice.[107] A better view may be that an implied agreement is possible, but will be found to have been made only in the clearest of cases.

These principles also apply to judgments *in rem*. A foreign judgment which purports to decide *in rem* upon, for example, the ownership of property, will be recognized if the property in question was within the territorial jurisdiction of the court: this closely reflects the principle that title to property is governed by the law of the place where the property was when something happened to it.[108] But if it was not, the judgment may still be given effect between the parties as creating a personal obligation, binding on each by virtue of his submission to the jurisdiction of the foreign court.[109]

(b) Presence or residence

If the defendant was present within the territorial jurisdiction of the foreign court on the date on which the proceedings were commenced, he is considered to be subject to its international jurisdiction: he places himself in the way of an obligation to obey a local judge.[110] At one time the rule was taken to require residence rather than presence, but it is now tolerably clear that either presence or residence on the material date will suffice.[111] Of course, if the defendant satisfied neither condition on the day in question, but did appear to defend the proceedings, there will be a submission in any event. It has been held that the relevant territorial jurisdiction is defined by reference to the court seised, so that a defendant sued in a state court must be within the territorial jurisdiction of the state, but if sued in a federal court all that is required is that he be within the federation; but insofar as this ascribes an international relevance to rules of local jurisdiction it is to be questioned whether it is correct.

It is still curious that this rule acknowledges in a foreign court a jurisdiction effectively wider than English law would claim for itself. On the existing state of the authorities, it is irrelevant that the foreign court was a *forum non conveniens* so that, if the roles were reversed, an English

---

[106] *SA Consortium General Textiles v Sun and Sand Agencies Ltd* [1978] QB 279 (CA).
[107] *Vogel v RA Kohnstamm Ltd* [1973] 1 QB 133, not following *Blohn v Desser* [1962] 2 QB 116.
[108] See ch 8, below.
[109] *Pattni v Ali* [2006] UKPC 51, [2007] 2 AC 85.
[110] *Adams v Cape Industries plc* [1990] Ch 433 (CA).
[111] *State Bank of India v Murjani Marketing Group Ltd*, 27 March 1991 (CA).

court would have stayed its proceedings and declined to adjudicate. It was explained above that the development of the law in the Supreme Court of Canada pointed to the widening of the grounds of recognized international jurisdiction. The Supreme Court did not use its new idea as a basis for also narrowing, in this respect, the definition of jurisdictional competence: it continues to regards 'tag' jurisdiction as sufficient.[112] Of course, if a defendant submits by voluntary appearance, there will be no question of denying recognition to the judgment, any more than there will be of staying an English action in which the defendant submits. But in cases in which the foreign court has exercised a jurisdiction which is so wide that it has not observed the kind of comity which an English court would have, it does look a little odd that its judgment will be recognized. In Canada, it would not be.[113] Such a change could not now occur in England without legislation.[114]

The presence of a natural person is easy to ascertain, but the same rule applies also to corporate defendants. Companies do their business through others: other companies, which may or may not be in common ownership; representatives; agents; and nowadays, websites. The presence rule is applied with as much common sense as possible. Where the presence of a company is concerned, the rule calls for a reasonably fixed and definite place of business, maintained by the corporation and from which its business is done.[115] So a peripatetic sales representative does not establish the presence of the company represented, even if a foreign court may regard it as sufficient for the purpose of its own jurisdictional rules. The same is true of a local representative who merely acts as a conduit for those wishing to transact business with the defendant who is otherwise out of the jurisdiction.[116] But if the local entity has been given power to make contracts which bind the defendant, it is probable that the test of corporate presence is satisfied if the entity operates from a fixed place of business.[117] Although a company may therefore be present if another entity is doing its business as well as its own, there is no broader English doctrine which allows all the members of an economic group to be treated

---

[112] That is, jurisdiction established (as people fervently suppose to be the law) by touching the defendant with the writ. It is, however, correct to observe that the decision of the Supreme Court does give effect to its view that the recognition of foreign judgments should be more frequent than it is.

[113] cf *Amchem Products Inc v British Columbia (Workers' Compensation Board)* [1993] 1 SCR 897, (1993) 102 DLR (4th) 96.

[114] cf *Owens Bank plc v Bracco* [1992] 2 AC 443.

[115] *Adams v Cape plc* [1990] Ch 433 (CA).

[116] cf *Littauer Glove Corp v Millington (FW) (1920) Ltd* (1928) 44 TLR 746.

[117] *Adams v Cape Industries plc* [1990] Ch 433, 531 (CA).

on the basis that if one is present all are present,[118] or that one member of the group is the *alter ego* of the others; and English law does not regard a foreign court as having international jurisdiction simply because the company can be said to have transacted, or to be still transacting, business within the territorial jurisdiction of the court. Only if the corporate veil can be lifted can the formal position be departed from, and this is in English law a rather rare event.

The recognition rule therefore mirrors the general jurisdictional rule of English law that if a company is present, in the sense of having a place of business, within the jurisdiction it can be sued,[119] and nothing turns on whether the claim arises out of the conduct of the company in the particular place: it is subject to the unlimited jurisdiction of the court or not at all; but there is no middle way. This contrasts with the jurisdictional rule in Article 5(5) of the Regulation and may explain why, given the dramatic consequences of finding that there is corporate presence, the common law requirements are relatively demanding.

3. DEFENCES TO RECOGNITION AT COMMON LAW

A judgment will be denied recognition as *res judicata*, and there can therefore be no question of its enforcement, if any of the defences allowed by English private international law is made out. But it needs to be said at the outset that it is no defence that the foreign court got the law or the facts, or both, wrong, or that it applied the wrong choice of law rule, or that it tried to apply English law and made a real mess of it.[120] The merits of the judgment are not reviewable, so the allegation that the foreign court erred in its reasoning is simply inadmissible, no matter how blatant its truth. Were it otherwise, almost every judgment would be re-examinable, and the advantage of the rule would be utterly lost. Even so, in a case where a court has failed to give effect to an agreement on choice of law, there may be room for a limited reconsideration of the rule. A judgment will be denied recognition at common law if the adjudicating court failed to give effect to a choice of court clause or arbitration agreement;[121] it may be wondered whether the policy which this enshrines ought not to extend this to disregard of an agreement on choice of law. The analogy lies in the

---

[118] *Adams v Cape Industries plc* [1990] Ch 433, 532–9.
[119] By being served there: Companies Act 2006, s 1139 (not yet in force).
[120] *Godard v Gray* (1870) LR 6 QB 288.
[121] Civil Jurisdiction and Judgments Act 1982, s 32 (unless the other party acquiesced in the breach).

fact that all such provisions are designed to make dispute resolution clear and predictable; and if the claimant elects to sue in a court which will pay them no heed, the view that he should not profit from his breach is not unattractive. The argument awaits authoritative approval. Subject to that, six possible defence arguments need to be mentioned.

(a) Disregard of arbitration or choice of court agreement

If the foreign court exercised jurisdiction in breach of a valid choice of court or arbitration agreement, its judgment may not be recognized at common law, even if the foreign court addressed the very issue and concluded, entirely in accordance with its own law, that there was no breach. It is otherwise if the complaining party acquiesced in the breach.[122] It follows that if the court rules against the claimant, it is not open to him to complain about the disregard of the agreement, because he brought it about.[123] The justification for this defence is the premium placed on the support of these clauses; but the rule is one which operates only where recognition is governed by the common law. Where the Regulation requires recognition, it has no application. Where the judgment comes from a court in a Member State, therefore, it is only the arbitration component of the rule which may be of relevance.

(b) Absence of local jurisdiction

It is unclear whether or to what extent the fact that the court did not have jurisdiction under its internal law may furnish a defence, for the authorities are old and inconclusive.[124] But if under the foreign law the judgment is a complete nullity, and not just voidable—presumably a rare state of affairs—it would be odd for it to be recognized in England, particularly if the defendant had been locally well advised to ignore the proceedings. If the judgment is, however, voidable, it is valid and remains so unless and until proceedings are taken to set it aside. As an English court cannot assume that this will happen, the result must be that the judgment will be recognized notwithstanding the fragility of local jurisdiction.

(c) Fraud

When it is alleged that the judgment was procured by fraud, the defences to recognition become more complicated. Although, as said above, the

---

[122] 1982 Act, s 32. And see *Marc Rich & Co AG v Soc Italiana Impianti PA* [1992] 2 Lloyd's Rep 624 (CA).
[123] *The Sennar (No 2)* [1985] 1 WLR 490 (HL).
[124] *Vanquelin v Bouard* (1863) 15 CBNS 341; *Pemberton v Hughes* [1899] 1 Ch 781.

merits of the judgment may not be re-examined by an English court, a different approach prevails if there is a credible allegation that it was procured by fraud.[125] It is an ancient principle of the common law that fraud unravels everything; that fraud is a thing apart.[126] Both the definition of fraud and its effect are controversial. Fraud has been held to encompass any misleading or duping of the foreign court. This may include advancing a claim known to be false, fabrication of evidence, intimidation of witnesses, and so on: the fraud will generally lie in the use of improper means to defeat, or pervert, the course of justice to prevail over the defendant.[127] Whether this covers the case where a claimant pleads a case to which he knows the defendant may have an answer is unclear, but it cannot realistically be expected that in adversary *inter partes* procedure the claimant has a duty to plead his opponent's case for him. On the other hand, an English claim form must contain a declaration of the truth of its contents,[128] and if the civil procedure of the foreign court was similar, this may provide the basis for characterizing a foreign pleading as fraudulent.

The matters which support the allegation may be put forward to oppose the application for summary judgment, and if credible will be investigated,[129] even though they were put before, and specifically rejected by, the foreign court. In sharp contrast to what is required to impeach an English judgment for fraud, the defendant need show no new discovery of evidence which could not have been put forward at trial: he may recycle the very evidence which failed to persuade the foreign court. But the position is not quite as stark as this may suggest. In order to have the allegation of fraud investigated, the defendant will have to make a credible case that the foreign court was the victim of, or party to, fraud. The evidence required to reach the standard of credibility will vary from court to court: it is reasonable to suppose that an English court will take much more persuading that fraud deceived an Australian or American court than where the judgment came from Burma or Guinea-Bissau, or some other place with less of an international reputation for judicial excellence. The standard which must be met to trigger a review is, on this view of

---

[125] *Abouloff v Oppenheimer* (1882) 10 QBD 295 (CA); *Vadala v Lawes* (1890) 25 QBD 310 (CA); *Syal v Heyward* [1948] 2 KB 443 (CA); *Jet Holdings Inc v Patel* [1990] 1 QB 335 (CA); *Owens Bank Ltd v Bracco* [1992] 2 AC 443.

[126] *HIH Casualty and General Insurance Ltd v Chase Manhattan Bank* [2003] UKHL 6, [2003] 2 Lloyd's Rep 61 at [15].

[127] Although the defendant may also use fraud to support a defence which defeats the claim and, if this happens, the claimant may seek to impeach the judgment which the defendant seeks to have recognized in his favour.

[128] CPR, Pt 22.

[129] *Jet Holdings Inc v Patel* [1990] 1 QB 335 (CA).

the matter, contextual. Even so, the law is controversial, for some see in it the view[130] that a foreign court is less skilled than the English court at the detection and rejection of fraud; and as a new discovery of evidence is required to impeach an English judgment for fraud,[131] it should, so the argument runs, equally be required for a foreign judgment. Although this criticism has found a measure of judicial[132] and other support, the fraud rule is soundly based and the criticism is less so. Two reasons may be given. First, it is dangerous for the law, in effect, to require a defendant to make his allegations in a court which may have been selected by the claimant *mala fide* and for reasons of his own illicit advantage: the proposition that the defendant is entitled to a hearing of a serious allegation in a court over which no suspicion may float is inherently attractive. Secondly, a finding of fraud in relation to a foreign judgment means only that the judgment may not be recognized in England, just as a finding that an arbitral award was contrary to English public policy means only that the award cannot be enforced in England. The finding of fraud does not impeach the judgment or award *in toto* and *in rem* to prevent its recognition and enforcement outside England. It is much less dramatic, and much more domestic, a measure than is the setting aside for all international purposes of an English judgment; and the justification for intervention may, for this reason, properly be rather more modest.

However, if the allegation of fraud has already had an independent hearing in, and been rejected by, a court of the defendant's own choosing, this fact may preclude its being raised *de novo* in England. Either the principles of *res judicata* will mean that the second judgment is binding on the party who brought the proceedings in which it was handed down, or it may be an abuse of the process of the English court for it to be advanced again.[133] Too vigorous use of the abuse of process doctrine has the potential to overwhelm much of the fraud defence;[134] there is need for caution before the fraud defence is altogether swept away. For even if the defendant has chosen to make the allegation of fraud before another court but in the country of the original judgment, it may be that he did so because he

---

[130] Politically incorrect, but surely, in many cases, manifestly accurate.

[131] *Hunter v Chief Constable of the West Midlands* [1980] QB 283 (CA).

[132] See, eg, *Owens Bank Ltd v Bracco* [1992] AC 443; *Owens Bank Ltd v Etoile Commerciale SA* [1995] 1 WLR 44 (PC).

[133] *House of Spring Gardens Ltd v Waite* [1991] 1 QB 241 (CA). There is no reason in principle why the findings against the judgment debtor in the second action should not give rise to an estoppel, but cf the 1982 Act, s 33(1)(c).

[134] *Owens Bank Ltd v Etoile Commerciale SA* [1995] 1 WLR 44 (PC); *Desert Sun Loan Corp v Hill* [1996] 2 All ER 847 (CA).

faced the prospect of execution against assets which he had in that country. His choice to sue in the form of an action to set aside the judgment in the courts of that country will have meant that he faced a much stiffer task[135]—in all probability, needing a fresh discovery of evidence—than he would have done if he had merely defended enforcement elsewhere; and although his choice to bring his action where he did was technically voluntary,[136] it will have been very much constrained by the prospect of execution. Against this background, to find that there is no right to raise the defence anew, will require considerable care.

(d) Want of natural or substantial justice

If the proceedings in the foreign court fell short of the standards set by the rules of natural justice such as the right to be notified, represented, and heard;[137] or if the procedure violated substantial justice such as by adopting a global and non-judicial assessment of damages,[138] it may be possible to deny recognition to the judgment. Such cases are historically rare. The enactment of the Human Rights Act 1998 has raised the profile of this defence, and it has been applied in the context of recognition of judgments under the Brussels Regulation.[139] However, in the context of a judgment from the United States, obtained in proceedings which fell short of what was required by the European Convention on Human Rights, the House of Lords refused to see the 'violation' of Article 6 of the Convention by the American court as reason to refuse recognition of its judgment, which is very odd, and looked even odder when the court made an order confiscating the defendant's English property.[140]

It is unclear whether the argument may be advanced in a case in which it has already been advanced in the foreign jurisdiction. The analogy from international arbitration suggests that it should not,[141] but it has been judicially suggested that, as with fraud, the view of the foreign court does not preclude the English court from making its own assessment.[142] But even if

---

[135] Which may also mean that it was a different cause of action, or issue, from that which arises before the English court in an enforcement context, and that *res judicata* is not applicable.

[136] p 139 above.

[137] cf, from the context of judgments falling within the Regulation, Case C–7/98 *Krombach v Bamberski* [2000] ECR I–1935.

[138] *Adams v Cape Industries plc* [1990] Ch 433 (CA).

[139] *Maronier v Larmer* [2002] EWCA Civ 774, [2003] QB 620.

[140] *Barnette v United States* [2004] UKHL 37, [2004] 1 WLR 2241; cf *Pellegrini v Italy* (2002) 35 EHRR 2 (ECtHR).

[141] *Minmetals Germany GmbH v Fercosteel Ltd* [1999] CLC 647.

[142] *Jet Holdings Inc v Patel* [1990] 1 QB 335 (CA).

this is correct, one supposes that the court will not allow an argument to be advanced past the point where it becomes an abuse of process.

(e) Public policy

If recognition of the judgment would offend English public policy, it is obvious that it will not be recognized. Judgments based on laws repellent to human rights, or producing a result which is equally repellent, for example, will be denied recognition, either on this basis or as a result of the application of the Human Rights Act 1998. A judgment obtained in defiance of an English anti-suit injunction will be denied recognition on this ground;[143] it is much less likely that a judgment obtained in defiance of a foreign anti-suit injunction could be so stigmatized.

(f) Prior English judgment

If the judgment is inconsistent with an English judgment, or with a foreign one handed down earlier in time, which is entitled to recognition in England, it cannot be recognized, for there will have remained no issues to adjudicate.[144]

4. THE EFFECT OF RECOGNITION AT COMMON LAW

The most usual reason to seek the recognition of a foreign judgment at common law will be to pave the way for an action by the judgment creditor to enforce it against the judgment debtor. If the party in whose favour it was given wishes to enforce it, he may bring an action to enforce the judgment, subject to the further limitations examined below. However, there are two further consequences of recognition which may be of importance. First, if the party against whom the judgment was given was subject to the international jurisdiction of the foreign court—the claimant will necessarily[145] have been, the defendant may have been—and no defence applies, the cause of action or the issue, as the case may be, will be regarded as against him[146] as *res judicata*. This means that he may not contradict it in or by later English proceedings unless some exception to the application

---

[143] *Phillip Alexander Securities and Futures Ltd v Bamberger* [1997] ILPr 73, aff'd 104 (CA).
[144] *Showlag v Mansour* [1995] 1 AC 431 (PC).
[145] Except in his capacity as defendant to a counterclaim which was not sufficiently within the penumbra of the claim he advanced.
[146] And against his privies: those with the same interest or title in the matter, especially if they have stood by, hoping to be regarded as strangers, while one with the same interest as them fights the case: *House of Spring Gardens Ltd v Waite* [1991] 1 QB 241 (CA).

of the doctrine of *res judicata* applies.[147] But secondly, if the party in whose favour the judgment was given, and *against whom* there is no *res judicata*, had been hoping for a better outcome, or seeks to rely on a claim which was not put forward the first time around, he may fail: Civil Jurisdiction and Judgments Act 1982, section 34, now generally prevents suing for a second time on the same underlying cause of action in the hope of improving on the result obtained first time round.[148] In the interpretation of the 'same cause of action' it has been held that any claim which arises out of a single contract constitutes the same cause of action as any other, so that a failure to deliver part of a consignment of goods has the same cause of action as the failure to deliver the balance of the cargo. But a claim for damages for one's own injury is not the same cause of action as a claim for damages for a child's loss of dependency;[149] and it is debatable whether a claim for damages for pecuniary loss resulting from personal injury has the same cause of action as a claim in respect of pain and suffering caused by the same injury, for in a tort claim there is no liability without damage, and the two types of damage may indicate two causes of action. Even so, a claimant who manages to steer a careful course around section 34 may well find that his claim is considered to abuse the process of the court if it raises a matter which could and should have been advanced in the first action.[150]

5. ENFORCEMENT

As a matter of theory, a foreign judgment which satisfies the criteria for its recognition creates an obligation which the judgment creditor may sue to enforce in an action, founded on the foreign judgment, at common law. The action is brought as one for debt; it follows that only final judgments for fixed sums of money can be enforced by such proceedings.[151] As for its being final and conclusive, a judgment which may be reviewed or revised by the court which gave it is not final,[152] but its being subject to appeal to a higher court is irrelevant. This is in fact much the same requirement as will already have applied to its recognition in the first place, and although

---

[147] *Carl Zeiss Stiftung v Rayner & Keeler Ltd (No 2)* [1967] 1 AC 853.

[148] *Republic of India v India Steamship Co Ltd (The Indian Grace)* [1993] AC 410; *Republic of India v India Steamship Co Ltd (The Indian Grace) (No 2)* [1998] AC 878.

[149] *Black v Yates* [1992] QB 526.

[150] *Henderson v Henderson* (1843) 3 Hare 100.

[151] The tail may be wagging the dog. The Supreme Court of Canada has taken the view that a non-money judgment may in principle be enforced: *Pro-Swing Inc v Elta Inc* [2006] 2 SCR 612, (2006) 273 DLR (4th) 663, although in that case it did not do so.

[152] *Nouvion v Freeman* (1889) 15 App Cas 1.

the requirement is always stated as an enforcement condition, this reflects only the tradition of seeing the law on foreign judgments as concerned with their enforcement rather than with recognition. As a debt claim must be based on a judgment for the payment of a fixed sum in money, if the sum is open to variation by the court which awarded it, it is not final and cannot be enforced.[153] If the judgment was final as regards liability but reviewable as regards damages, or led to the making of a non-money order, the finding of liability may be recognized as *res judicata* if and when an action is brought on the basis of the underlying cause of action.

But there is no jurisdiction to enforce a foreign penal, revenue, or analogous law; and if the action to enforce the judgment would have this effect it will be dismissed. So if a foreign taxing authority has obtained a judgment in its favour, enforcement of the judgment by action in England will necessarily fail.[154] Nor, by reason of the Protection of Trading Interests Act 1980, section 5, may an action be brought to recover any part of a foreign judgment for multiple damages, even—perhaps unexpectedly—for the unmultiplied compensatory element. By curious contrast, it appears that judgments for exemplary damages, unless truly extreme and on that account contrary to public policy, are not covered by the Act, and prevented from enforcement by the rule, as long as the judgment debt has not been calculated by 'doubling, trebling or otherwise multiplying' the sum fixed as compensation.[155] The logic of this is elusive, not only because the difference between multiplication and addition has not been generally thought of as being legally, as opposed to mathematically, significant, but also because the award of such damages is often in partial compensation for the fact that costs are not recoverable.[156]

The claimant will plead that the judgment debt is due and owing, and will usually apply[157] for summary judgment on the ground that the defendant has no real prospect of successfully defending the claim. If the application succeeds judgment will be entered forthwith. But if it is shown on the hearing of the application for summary judgment that the defendant has a real prospect of defending the claim, the court will dismiss the application and the matter will proceed to trial in the usual way.

---

[153] Although if, for example, instalments already due are now fixed and beyond review, enforcement of these by debt action is possible.
[154] *United States of America v Harden* (1963) 41 DLR (2d) 721 (Can SC).
[155] Protection of Trading Interests Act 1980, s 5.
[156] And see, for the same proposition in the European context, *SA Consortium General Textiles SA v Sun & Sand Agencies Ltd* [1978] QB 279 (CA).
[157] CPR r 24.2.

E. JUDGMENTS FROM SOME OF THE REST OF THE WORLD: THE 1920 AND 1933 ACTS

As explained at the outset, there are some countries whose judgments are registered for enforcement pursuant to the provisions of one of two statutes. The terms of the statutes are very close to the common law as this was understood at the date of enactment, so in substance, although not in form, recognition will be according to the rules of the common law. As regards enforcement, the few further conditions are much the same as those of the common law. But instead of it being necessary to commence original proceedings by service of a claim form, proceeding from there to an application for summary judgment, these two statutes allow the applicant to register the judgment for enforcement, it being then of the same force and effect for enforcement as if it had been an English judgment. The respondent may apply to set aside the registration and the order for registration; and it is on the hearing of this application that the principal issues will emerge. The substantive grounds on which registration may be obtained or set aside closely reflect the common law.

I. ADMINISTRATION OF JUSTICE ACT 1920

Part II of the 1920 Act applies to many, but mainly smaller, colonial and Commonwealth, territories: of the larger jurisdictions the Act applies to Malaysia, Singapore, Nigeria, and New Zealand.[158] It does not depend on any treaty with the foreign state; it applies to judgments from 'superior courts', which may be registered under the Act within twelve months of their being delivered.[159] Upon an application to set aside the registration, the grounds which satisfy the requirement of international jurisdiction, and the permitted defences to recognition, differ from those of the common law only in minor detail; although if the judgment is still subject to appeal it may not be registered.[160]

---

[158] Reciprocal Enforcement of Judgments (Administration of Justice Act 1920, Part II) (Consolidation) Order 1984 (SI 1984/129), as amended by SI 1985/1994, SI 1994/1901, and SI 1997/2601. It no longer applies to Hong Kong. The Act has never applied to South Africa.

[159] Section 9.

[160] Section 9(2)(e).

2. FOREIGN JUDGMENTS (RECIPROCAL ENFORCEMENT) ACT 1933

The 1933 Act allows for enforcement of judgments from countries with which there is in force a bilateral treaty. It applies to judgments from Australia[161] and Canada;[162] also from Guernsey, Jersey, India, the Isle of Man, Israel, Pakistan, Surinam, and Tonga, but it applies only to courts identified by name in the order which implements the bilateral treaty: judgments from other courts in these countries may still be enforced by action at common law. The grounds of international jurisdiction and the defences to recognition[163] differ from those of the common law only in minor detail; if the judgment is subject to appeal the application for registration may be stayed.[164]

---

[161] SI 1994/1901.
[162] SI 1987/468, 2211; SI 1988/1304, 1853; SI 1989/987; SI 1991/1724; SI 1992/1731; SI 1995/2708. Québec is not included.
[163] Section 4.
[164] Section 5.

5

Contracts

A. INTRODUCTION

From the beginning of time until 1991, the rules for choice of law in respect of contractual obligations were established by the common law. Since then the question has been mostly governed by the Rome Convention on the law applicable to contractual obligations 1980, as enacted by the Contracts (Applicable Law) Act 1990.[1] The Rome Convention harmonized the choice of law rules for contractual obligations for the then Member States of the European Union,[2] in which it applies to contracts made after 1 April 1991.[3] If[4] there was a justification for the new law, it was that if choice of law rules were certain, predictable, and uniform, this would make a contribution to the free movement of persons, goods, and services throughout the Member States. There is still no sign of the empirical research which justified this alleged truth, however. The Rome Convention was the first stage in the larger project of harmonization of choice of law rules across the Member States. A European Regulation for choice of law in tort and unjust enrichment has now been adopted: it will be known as 'Rome II'. Negotiations to convert the Rome Convention into a Regulation, which will apply in all Member States, made rather slow progress.[5] This was attributable, at least in part, to an ambition to expand the Regulation to include several issues, some of considerable complexity, which were not covered by the Rome Convention clearly or at all. More or less final agreement on a text was reached late in 2007; most of the complex or radical suggestions were not adopted. Nevertheless, as 'Rome I' is closely modelled on the Convention, and as its status in the United Kingdom remains uncertain, it is dealt with at the end of this chapter.

---

[1] Hereinafter 'the 1990 Act'. A consolidated version of the text of the Convention is printed at [1998] OJ C27/34.

[2] This included Denmark, but not those states which acceded in 2004 and 2007. Iceland, Norway, and Switzerland are not party to the Rome Convention.

[3] Article 17; SI 1991/707.

[4] The proposition is controversial.

[5] More is planned by the European Union, in the fields of property and family law.

Some say that the Rome Convention is inspired by the common law's choice of law rules for contracts, but it would be unwise to place much weight on that assertion or to interpret the Convention by the fading light of authorities on the common law. And the status of the Convention as an international text means that the need for it to have as uniform an inter-pretation as possible[6] must draw it away from any common law ancestry which some say it had. The report of Professors Giuliano and Lagarde[7] is the authorized[8] aid to its interpretation. Although matters excluded from the Convention continue to be governed by the common law, these are relatively few and generally rather minor, and mostly non-contractual in any event, the contract choice of law rules of the common law now occupy only this residual role.[9] Even so, occasional comparison of a rule in the Convention with its common law counterpart may offer a vantage point to assess the benefits and shortcomings of each. We will therefore examine the common law rules for choice of law only within the framework of the Rome Convention.

So far as the operation of the Convention is concerned, it is irrelevant that none of the parties has any connection with England or even with the European Union, or that the law which the Convention makes applicable is that of a country which is not a signatory to the Convention,[10] or that the choice of law lies only as between the parts of the United Kingdom.[11]

1. JURISDICTION OVER CONTRACT MATTERS

The majority of contractual claims will arise as civil or commercial mat-ters, and jurisdiction over defendants in respect of them will therefore fall within the domain of the Brussels Regulation.[12] It is reasonable to suppose that the definition of 'contract' in the Rome Convention and the Regulation will be substantially the same, and it is probable that these two European instruments, as well as the Rome II Regulation,[13] may be considered side-by-side in determining whether a particular cause of action (say for a payment of an agreed sum of money on the unilateral ter-mination of a distribution agency) is contractual.[14] But it seems probable

---

[6] Article 18.
[7] [1980] OJ C282/1.
[8] 1990 Act, s 3(3).
[9] The rules of the common law were set out in detail in Dicey & Morris, *The Conflict of Laws* (11th edn, 1987).
[10] Article 2.
[11] Article 19; 1990 Act, s 2(3).
[12] Regulation (EC) 44/2001, [2001] OJ L12/1, ch 2, above.
[13] Regulation (EC) 864/2007, [2007] OJ L199/40; see ch 6 below.
[14] Case 9/87 *SPRL Arcado v SA Haviland* [1988] ECR 1539.

that the interpretation of the term 'contract' in CPR Rule 6.20 will be different, and will continue to be defined by the common law conflict of laws.[15] Accordingly, a claim founded on the principle that a person who gives professional advice to one who relies on it may incur liability if he is negligent,[16] may yet[17] be held to be contractual if the question arises in the jurisdictional context of the Regulation, but will be a claim in tort if it arises in the context of an application for permission to serve out under Rule 6.20.

2. THE PROBLEMS OF AUTONOMY AND CHOICE OF LAW

As will be seen, the general principle which underpins the choice of law, at common law and under the Rome Convention, is that parties have very substantial autonomy,[18] and that if they can choose to make any contract they wish, it follows that they can choose any law they wish to govern it./But this deceptively clear proposition almost immediately leads into a logical thicket. For whether they made an effective choice must be, if it is disputed, determined by reference to a law: but which one? Will that law which makes that assessment do so finally or only provisionally? Can the law whose significance derives from the fact or allegation that it was chosen also be the law which determines whether a permissible choice was made? If the parties purport to alter the law they have chosen, which of the various available laws determines whether they have made that choice lawfully and effectively? If the parties dispute whether a contract has been made, can the law which would govern it if it were assumed to be valid properly answer the question whether it *is* valid, or whether an alleged choice of law is effective? If the identification of a governing law depends on the terms of the contract, but the terms of the contract depend on the governing law, where does the analysis begin? The principle of party autonomy cannot be self-justifying: some external point of reference is required to explain why and when recourse to autonomy is justified. The theoretical difficulties which can be spun out of such self-absorbing navel-gazing can obscure the fact that the rules work satisfactorily, at least where there is common ground that the parties are contractually bound,

---

[15] For the view that statutory reform of choice of law does not affect issues which are procedural (which service out must surely be) see *Harding v Wealands* [2006] HKHL 32, [2007] 2 AC 1.

[16] *Hedley Byrne & Co Ltd v Heller & Partners Ltd* [1964] AC 465.

[17] No case has yet held this to be so.

[18] Nygh, *Autonomy in International Contracts* (1999).

and the only issue concerns the performance of their agreement. But, as will be seen, there are other places, especially where the very existence of the contract is a matter of dispute, in which the theoretical underpinnings of the law are not as firm as they might be.

B. THE ROME CONVENTION

The Rome Convention applies to contractual obligations entered into after 1 April 1991, except for the matters specifically excluded from its scope by Article 1: Article 1 therefore identifies the material scope of the Convention as an instrument which defines its own domain. But even in the areas which are outside the legislative grasp of the Convention, there is no reason why the common law rules for choice of law, operating on their own authority, may not refer some or all of the excluded issues to the governing law as this is identified by the Rome Convention for issues which do fall within its scope. So, for example, arbitration agreements are excluded from the Convention by Article 1(2)(d); the Rome Convention therefore makes no claim to apply its rules for choice of law to them. Nevertheless, the common law is free to decide that the law which governs an arbitration agreement will often be the law which governs the contract of which it is a term, and that this may be identified by the Rome Convention. The process may be regarded as the inverse of what is done by Article 4 of the Brussels Regulation on jurisdiction.[19] That provision coopts the jurisdictional rules of the common law for a certain portion of the Regulation's determination of jurisdiction. In the context of the Rome Convention, the common law may be seen to incorporate the Convention for purposes which are, and remain, its own. There is a dynamic equilibrium at work.

The Rome Convention applies to all such cases litigated before an English court and involving a choice between the laws of different countries.[20] It is in force throughout much of the European Union,[21] and it is required to be construed with a view to securing uniformity of interpretation and application.[22] It follows that most of its definitional terms should receive an independent or autonomous interpretation, rather than being read as though they were contained in domestic English legislation. Protocols give the European Court competence to give preliminary rulings

---

[19] Regulation (EC) 44/2001.
[20] Article 1(1). For this purpose the separate parts of the United Kingdom are treated as separate countries: Art 19 provides that a state may do this, and by the Contracts (Applicable Law) Act 1990, s 2(3), the United Kingdom did so.
[21] Although not the states which acceded in 2004 and 2007.
[22] Article 18.

on interpretation,[23] but references under it are permissive, and none has been made to date. But if and when the Convention is transformed into a Regulation, the common reference procedure under Articles 234 and 68 EC will apply instead.

The material scope of the Convention is defined inclusively and exclusively: to determine whether an issue is subject to the choice of law rules of the Convention, it must be within the general scope of the Convention, and not specifically excluded from it. It is to this that we first turn.

I. DOMAIN OF THE CONVENTION

The Convention applies to identify the law applicable to 'contractual obligations' in agreements made after 1 April 1991. The starting point is to ask whether the meaning of this expression is taken from national law, so that the definition of contractual obligation is, for an English court, exactly the same as in English private international law or whether, on the other hand, it has an autonomous meaning, which will largely overlap, but which will not be congruent, with the meaning of the expression in English law. If examined in the detail which it really needs the question is of great complexity, for as soon as one lets go of the characterization categories of English law, and the relationship between them, it becomes necessary to define the outline of the new category, and to explain whether it overlaps with, or overrides, those it cuts across. It would be so much easier to treat the Convention's expression 'contractual obligations' as if it operated only within the territory which English private international law would define as contractual; and it is doubtless true that in the majority of cases no difference would emerge between the various possible approaches. The reader who wants an easier life should consider skipping the remainder of this section. But categories have edges, and in the delineation of these it is unlikely that the simple solution is right. The fact that the Convention is meant to be interpreted with regard to its uniform character, and that it will be less likely to achieve its aim if it is interpreted within the framework of national laws, must result in its being given an autonomous meaning. As a result, it is a delusion to think of the rules of the Rome Convention as being neatly slotted into the space defined, but now vacated, by the common law rules for choice of law. It is necessary to define contractual obligations for the purpose of defining the scope of the Rome Convention, without looking backward to the common law, whose detail but also whose definitions it has supplanted. The definition is an autonomous one, drawn out on squared, not foolscap, paper.

---

[23] Brussels Protocol, which is in the 1990 Act, Sch 3; Second Protocol [1989] OJ L48/17.

(a) 'Contractual'

The autonomous definition of contractual obligations will encompass most obligations regarded as contractual in English law, and will exclude most which are not. If, as said earlier in this section, the definition of contractual obligations follows that used for special jurisdiction under Council Regulation (EC) 44/2001, the defining characteristic of a contractual obligation will be one that was freely entered into with regard to another, identified, person. On the basis of the jurisprudence of the Court of Justice, the obligations of a member to his trade association or of a shareholder to his company will be contractual even if national law categorizes them differently, because the relationship between the parties is one in which the obligations were freely undertaken in relation to identified others. Conversely, the claim of a sub-buyer to enforce the manufacturer's warranties of quality will not be contractual, even where so understood in national law, and even though the manufacturer's obligations were undertaken by him freely and voluntarily, because the sub-buyer seeking to enforce them was not identifiable by the manufacturer. It seems probable that any obligation said to be contractual must be tested by reference to both components of this definition; whether it must always satisfy them is less easy to say.

That the obligation be freely and voluntarily assumed cannot mean that it must be one which was expressly agreed to, or one which could have been excluded by the choice of the parties. Were it otherwise, the obligations of a supplier in a consumer contract, which are often incapable of being excluded by contractual term, would not be contractual, nor would some of the terms and conditions implied by law into a contract for the sale of goods. Instead, it appears that the relationship created, as distinct from the individual terms found within it, is probed to see whether it was voluntary. And subject to one point, it is probable that the relationship is still contractual, regulated by the Rome Convention, even if it is alleged that the agreement was vitiated from the outset,[24] or even void *ab initio.*[25] It is a common usage in domestic law to talk of a void contract, even though it is, from one point of view, a nonsense. And the Rome Convention, as we shall see, indicates which law is to be applied when it is alleged that a party did not consent,[26] and when dealing with the consequences of nullity.[27] It

---

[24] cf *Agnew v Länsförsäkringsbolagens AB* [2001] 1 AC 223.
[25] But cf *Kleinwort Benson Ltd v Glasgow City Council* [1999] 1 AC 153.
[26] Article 8.
[27] Although the provision which secures this—Art 10(1)(e)—is not in force in England (1990 Act, s 2(2)), this fact does not alter the scope of the Convention, just its effect in England.

follows that a 'void contract' is still within the scope of the Convention. The one point of qualification is that according to the Rome II Regulation,[28] the choice of law rules which it lays down will apply to 'any consequence arising out of ... *culpa in contrahendo*'.[29] This is usually understood as pre-contractual fault; but as Article 12 refers such issues to the law which applies to the contract, or which would have applied to it if it had been entered into, the practical effect is to subject such issues to the choice of law framework of the Rome Convention. As a result, the Convention will apply to obligations which were not created by the contract, but which arise before its creation as well as after its termination. So whether there is an obligation to negotiate in good faith, or to make disclosure of matters material to the agreement, or to refrain from taking advantage of a dominating position are all tested by reference to the Convention, for all go to the question whether there was an obligation, freely entered into, or the material validity of that obligation.[30] Likewise, questions which arise after termination or rescission are within the scope of the Convention, so remedies consequent upon breach, or on rescission, of a contract will be dealt with by the choice of law rules of the Convention.[31] The obligations which arise from the nullity of a contract are also within the framework of the Convention, although, as will be seen, with slight qualifications.

But obligations can be freely assumed outside the domestic law of contract, and these are problematic. Liability for statements negligently made to someone who was expected to rely on them is sometimes explained as resting on a voluntary assumption of liability,[32] which comes close to replicating the autonomous definition of contracts. Moreover, if liability under this principle of domestic law is said to arise from a relationship 'equivalent to contract', which is not contractual only by reason of the absence of consideration,[33] it is plausible that these will be contractual obligations for the purpose of the Rome Convention. After all, English private international law long acknowledged that a promise unsupported by consideration counted as a contract,[34] and it may follow, for example, that the question whether the person who has agreed to provide a reference to another owes liability to the recipient will be a matter for the Rome Convention. Similarly, the obligations of someone who volunteers

---

[28] Regulation (EC) 864/2007.

[29] Article 2.

[30] Article 8(1).

[31] Even if some of them do not, technically, fall within its material scope.

[32] *Henderson v Merrett Syndicates Ltd* [1995] 2 AC 145.

[33] *Hedley Byrne & Co Ltd v Heller & Partners Ltd* [1964] AC 465.

[34] *Re Bonacina* [1912] 2 Ch 394.

to assume fiduciary duties in relation to another may be seen as obligations freely entered into, and the existence of these duties, their extent,
and their consequences will be subject to the Rome Convention. After
all, the fact that such obligations are treated as equitable in domestic law
is a historical and doctrinal accident which is unlikely to be echoed in
the Rome Convention. The eventual answer in relation to the first part
of the autonomous definition will be to ask whether the relationship out
of which the liability is said to arise can be described as one in which the
defendant freely assumed obligations in relation to another and, if he did,
the law which governs the relationship will be that specified by the Rome
Convention.

The second aspect of the definition of 'contractual' appears to require
that the obligation be assumed in relation to another who can be identified,
so that if the defendant has no idea who the other party is, the relationship is not contractual.[35] But this cannot be correct, and cannot comprise
part of the basis of a workable definition. Were it taken at face value Mrs
Carlill, through whose legendary purchase of the carbolic smoke ball
every first year law student discovers the law of contract,[36] would not be
party to a contractual obligation. The Carbolic Smoke Ball Company neither knew nor cared who its customers were, any more than does anyone
who advertises a reward, or the fire brigade which responds to a call for
help, or the transport company which sells more than one ticket at once.
Nor would an assignee ever have a contractual claim to enforce against
the original obliged party. In none of these cases is the identity of the
other party known to, or probably even discoverable by, the supplier or
advertiser or debtor; and that would appear to carry the obligations of
the relationship outside the Rome Convention. The trouble is that these
cases must be contractual, for the law has no other category into which it
would be even remotely realistic to accommodate them. The supposed
requirement that there be an identified or identifiable 'other' is unsound.
An obligation is contractual if the defendant freely assumes a promissory
obligation to another or to others, but that if the promisor does not know,
or wish to know,[37] the identity of the other this is immaterial to its characterization. But it does entail the conclusion that the claim of the sub-buyer
to enforce the original seller's obligations may sometimes be contractual.

---

[35] Case C–26/91 *Soc Jakob Handte v Soc Traîtements Mécano-chimiques des Surfaces* [1992]
ECR I–3967.
[36] *Carlill v Carbolic Smoke Ball Co* [1893] 1 QB 256 (CA).
[37] Such as where an offer is made to the world for acceptance without the need for communication, or where the offer is made to a single promisee, but without restraint on assignment.

So also will be an obligation undertaken with the deliberate intention that it be enforceable by a non-party: there is no reason to suppose that after the partial abolition of the English doctrine of privity of contract,[38] consensual obligations enforceable by non-parties will be excluded.

(b) 'Obligations'

The Giuliano–Lagarde report states that gifts are included within the scope of the Convention where these are seen as contractual: a curious proposition for an English lawyer,[39] but one which underlines the different contours of the autonomous conception of contract. The sense in which they give rise to enforceable obligations is obscure, especially as the Convention does not apply to the constitution of trusts.[40] There may be requirements of formal validity; if there is a right to revoke a gift on account of ingratitude,[41] perhaps this right (or the obligation to be grateful) is contractual.

Property rights are excluded. So intangible property, such as intellectual property rights, in principle lies outside the scope of the Convention, although contracts to create or transfer such rights will be within it, just as are contracts to transfer tangible movable or immovable property. A more troublesome question arises in connection with the assignment of intangible movable property in general, such as shares, policies of insurance, contractual debts, and so forth. There is a view, respectable and ancient, that all these are property, and that their status as property is separate and distinct from the contract which created them: a contract may well be needed to give birth to the right, but once this act of creation has taken place what results is a right of property which can be bought, sold, mortgaged, pledged, assigned, alienated, bequeathed, confiscated, and obtained by deception. From this it follows, so the argument runs, that the legal relationships thus created, at least between donor and donee, are proprietary and are not contractual, and that the issue of what law governs dealings with these rights is therefore not governed by the Rome Convention.

The difficulties presented by this argument arise on two levels. True, transfers or assignments of some forms of intangibles, such as shares and intellectual property rights, are undeniably proprietary and are distinct from any contract which created them. And in English law, and perhaps

---

[38] Contracts (Rights of Third Parties) Act 1999.
[39] [1980] OJ C282/1, 10.
[40] Article 1(2)(g).
[41] A rule which would greatly contribute to the civilization of teenagers.

in others, there are many contexts, of which insolvency is certainly one, where it is convenient for contractual debts to be regarded as property rights. But the view that there is a difference between owning a debt (which is a statement made in proprietary language) and being owed a debt (which is in contractual language) requires the fiery certainty of faith, for it looks awfully like an illusion: the question of who owns a debt is coterminous with the question to whom the debt is owed, and there is no easy way in which the two can be separated so as to make a distinction between them. At a more general level, it is easy to see the distinction between contract and property where, in the real world, the conclusion of a contract will be followed by delivery or conveyance; but when dealing with simple contractual obligations there is no clearly separate item to regard as 'intangible property': the whole of the question is contractual, there being neither need nor room for a separate property: after the contract has been executed, nothing remains to be done.[42] There is difficulty in accepting the argument that these are things rather than obligations when the property is a simple contractual debt. But even if that were not so, Article 12 of the Rome Convention contains a rule to deal with choice of law for the voluntary assignment of contractual obligations. Although it extends only to the single question of which law governs the assignment of such rights, it overrides any objection that a contractual choice of law rule is inapplicable to an issue which the Rome Convention (as opposed to anything else) considers as contractual. There is therefore no basis for excluding the assignment of contractual rights from the scope of the Rome Convention; the law which governs their assignment is that specified by Article 12 of the Convention.[43]

(c) Concurrent liabilities

In some contexts—in the field of employment law[44] and in the provision of professional services,[45] for example—English domestic law permits a claimant to frame his claim concurrently in contract and in tort, or electively between them; and English private international law has been understood to allow this as well. Despite the view of the Court of Appeal

---

[42] *Raiffeisen Zentralbank Österreich AG v Five Star Trading LLC* [2001] EWCA Civ 68, [2001] QB 825. See also below, p 227.

[43] The content of the rule is examined in ch 8. An intense debate, which began in 2005 and which is continuing, took place within the negotiations to settle the terms of the Rome I Regulation.

[44] cf *Coupland v Arabian Gulf Oil Co* [1983] 1 WLR 1151 (CA).

[45] *Henderson v Merrett Syndicates Ltd* [1995] 2 AC 145.

that this approach would be consistent with the Convention,[46] it is not clear that it really is. For if the claimant formulates in tort a claim which would otherwise fall within the four corners of the Convention—he alleges that his employer breached the common duty of care, rather than pleading a broken contractual promise to take care; he alleges negligent misstatement on the part of his investment adviser, rather than a breach of a contractual promise to use reasonable care and skill—it means that a claim between two contracting parties, falling within the material scope of the Convention, will be subjected to a law other than that specified by the Convention, and the apparently mandatory words of Article 1 will have been overcome. A similar argument could be advanced if a claimant were to elect to enforce fiduciary duties owed by his opponent, rather than the contract between them.[47] The traditional[48] English view is that the freedom of a claimant to elect how to frame the claim continues in full force and effect, and until abrogated by judicial decision, this procedural right represents the law.[49] Yet if judged by result, it is undeniable that the Convention will have failed, in this respect, to do what it set out to do; and this cannot be accepted without substantial reservation.[50]

(d) Excluded issues

The Convention eschews any claim to govern the matters set out in Article 1(2), and to these the appropriate choice of law rule is a matter for the common law conflict of laws. Many of these would not be seen as contractual in any event, so Article 1(2) mainly confirms what was already known. They are: status and the capacity of natural persons;[51] contractual rights relating to wills and succession and matrimonial property rights; and rights and duties arising out of a family relationship;[52] obligations arising from bills of exchange and promissory notes and other negotiable instruments

---

[46] *Base Metal Trading Ltd v Shamurin* [2004] EWCA Civ 1316, [2005] 1 WLR 1157.

[47] Assuming for present purposes (but see ch 7, below) that there is a different choice of law rule for claims based on fiduciary duties. For the conclusion that there is not, reference should be made to the actual result, as distinct from the reasoning, in *Base Metal Trading Ltd v Shamurin*.

[48] Although this is not exactly what it seems, for there is also a general view that concurrency as between the principles of common law and equity is not conducive to the rational development of the law: see Burrows (2002) 22 OxJLS 1.

[49] If it were a procedural matter, but which it surely cannot be, it would be unaffected by the Rome Convention: Art 1(2)(h). See further Briggs [2003] LMCLQ 12.

[50] Of course, if the non-contractual claim is found to be governed by *lex contractus*, any objection is sharply reduced. See further on this Briggs (2007) 123 LQR 18.

[51] Article 1(2)(a); though this is subject to Art 11; see below.

[52] Article 1(2)(b).

where these arise from their negotiable character;[53] questions governed by the law of companies, such as creation, capacity, and winding-up;[54] the power of an agent to bind a principal, or organ of a company to bind the company, to a third party;[55] the constitution and internal relationships of trusts;[56] evidence and procedure.[57] Also excluded is insurance where the risk is situated in the territory of the European Union: in relation to insurance a separate, and highly complex, system of rules deals with choice of law.[58] Where any of these issues arises for decision in an English court, common law conflict of law rules will continue to apply until these are, in their turn, displaced by European Regulations. As explained in the chapters where they arise for examination, the *lex domicilii* has a dominant role in relation to wills, succession, and family matters; the *lex situs* in relation to negotiable instruments; the *lex incorporationis* in relation to companies; the proper law of the trust in relation to trusts; and the *lex fori* over issues of evidence and procedure: none of these was traditionally seen as a contractual issue, and that has not changed. In relation to the power of an agent to bind a principal to a third party, the exclusion was probably brought about by the complexity of the issue and the irreconcilable differences between the common law and civilian analyses of agency; but it will remain open to the common law conflict of law rules to decide that this issue is governed by the law which governs the contract of agency, which will in turn be identified by the Rome Convention. Although the Convention makes no claim to govern this issue, it does not prevent a national law taking that step in the exercise of its own legal authority.

In the same way, although Article 1(2)(d) excludes agreements on arbitration and choice of court from the domain of the Convention,[59] which is contrary to the view of English law that the validity of these is usually a matter for the law of the contract in which they were contained, which may be regarded as the 'proper law' of the agreement.[60] An agreement

---

[53] Article 1(2)(c). But contracts pursuant to which these instruments are issued are not excluded: [1980] OJ C282/1, 10.

[54] Article 1(2)(e).

[55] Article 1(2)(f). But in so far as they are contractual, relations between principal and agent and agent and third party are not excluded: [1980] OJ C282/1, 13.

[56] Article 1(2)(g).

[57] Article 1(2)(h).

[58] Article 1(3). But the exclusion does not apply (so the Convention does apply) to reinsurance: Art 1(4).

[59] Although they may be taken into account in the determination of the governing law.

[60] See *Egon Oldendorff v Libera Corp* [1995] 2 Lloyd's Rep 64. The 'proper law' is the term which was used at common law to signify the law by which the validity of the contract was tested, and is used in this context to acknowledge that the identification of the law which

on jurisdiction or arbitration will generally be valid if effective under its proper law, and not if not. But the *lex fori* can in certain cases override this answer: by denying effect to an agreement valid under its proper law[61] or by regarding as valid an agreement invalid and ineffective under its proper law.[62] Indeed, the reason for this exclusion from the scope of the Convention is that under the laws of many countries, the validity of such agreements is seen as a procedural matter, concerned with jurisdiction as a matter of public law, rather than a private contractual one. But again, the Convention presents no obstacle to English private international law deciding on its own authority to treat jurisdiction and arbitration agreements as being governed by the law which applies to the contract of which they are a part, and this therefore remains the position in England.

The status of a person is predominantly the concern of the law of the domicile, as is that person's capacity. Contractual capacity is governed by the common law conflict of laws, according to which an individual would be capable if she had capacity either by the law of the country with which the contract was most closely connected or by the law of her domicile.[63] But the Convention intrudes on this in one respect. Article 11 provides that where two individuals make a contract in the same country, and one later relies on a personal incapacity according to some other law to plead the invalidity of that contract, she may do so only if the other party was, or should have been, aware of it. For corporations, the existence and extent of contractual capacity is a matter for the *lex incorporationis*. But the legal effect of a contract made by a corporation without capacity to do so is a matter for the *lex contractus*.

2. EXPRESS CHOICE OF GOVERNING LAW

Article 3 of the Convention provides that a contract is governed by the law chosen by the parties, provided that this choice is express or may be demonstrated with reasonable certainty by the terms of the contract or the circumstances of the case. The parties are free to choose a law having no other connection to the facts of the contract. They may choose different

---

governs a jurisdiction or arbitration agreement is a matter for the common law rules of the conflict of laws.

[61] See *The Hollandia* [1983] 1 AC 565 (which would be decided differently today) on the Carriage of Goods by Sea Act 1971; and the provisions of the Brussels Regulation controlling jurisdiction agreements in insurance, consumer, and employment contracts.

[62] cf Case 25/79 *Sanicentral GmbH v Collin* [1979] ECR 3423, where Art 17 BC, substantially re-enacted as Art 23 of the Brussels Regulation, overrode a rule of the proper law which denied that a jurisdiction agreement could oust the jurisdiction of the employment tribunals.

[63] *Charron v Montreal Trust Co* (1958) 15 DLR (2d) 240 (Ont CA).

laws for separate parts of the contract and, so far as the Convention is concerned, may alter the governing law at any time. The Convention broadly adopts the principle of party autonomy, and draws certain conclusions from it, allowing a choice to be decisive except only in relation to limited and clearly specified matters; but it requires two things: the choice to be made, and that choice to be expressed or demonstrable. This will preclude the argument that the parties, as reasonable people, must have made a choice but which they did not trouble to express.

A choice expressed in the form 'this contract shall be governed by the law of France' will therefore be effective to make French law the governing law; and a less artful choice, such as 'this contract shall be construed in accordance with French law', will probably be taken the same way. Life is easier when parties take advantage of the freedom to choose and express that choice clearly: Article 3 helps those who help themselves. But one could be forgiven for thinking that some draftsmen regard a clear expression of choice as being too easy, rejecting it for something more likely to generate work for the litigation department. A choice of the law of the United Kingdom, or of British law, for example, cannot be given literal effect, because there is no such law to be chosen; and to interpret this as an express choice of English law is to make an assumption which is probably factually correct[64] but politically incorrect. Certain items are not on the menu. The Convention limits the choice which may be made to the law of a country,[65] which excludes the possibility of choosing the *lex mercatoria*, or the principles of a religion or other cult to govern a contract: whatever these are, they do not constitute the law of a country, and they cannot govern a contract.[66]

Nor is it clear that Article 3 will always validate a purported choice which is expressed formulaically, such as where the contract is expressed to be governed 'by the law of the place where the carrier has its principal place of business'. If there is no dispute about these identifiers, the expression of choice will be effective. But what if there is genuine disagreement about who (shipowner, charterer) is the carrier, or which is the principal place (of day-to-day decision-taking, of supervisory direction) of business?[67] In principle, the governing law will be charged with answering these questions, for they go to the construction of a term of the contract. The trouble arises where answers to these questions are required in

---

[64] cf *The Komninos S* [1991] 1 Lloyd's Rep 370 (CA).
[65] Article 2.
[66] *Halpern v Halpern* [2007] EWCA Civ 291, [2007] 2 Lloyd's Rep 56.
[67] *The Rewia* [1991] 2 Lloyd's Rep 325 (CA).

order to identify the governing law in the first place. Although the Court of Justice has held, in the jurisdictional context, that a provision in such terms may be effective as an agreement on jurisdiction,[68] this presupposes that the choice of law rules of the court seised have served to identify the geographical place which is referred to. But if one asks the simple question whether these words choose a law, expressly or as may be identified with reasonable certainty from the terms of the contract or the circumstances of the case, the answer is no. It is no help to say that, as a matter of English law, the carrier will be regarded as the charterer, or the principal place of business that from which day-to-day control is exercised: the Rome Convention is meant to operate independently of English law, and to be a full, complete, and sufficient code for the identification of the governing law. From that point of view, some forms of words, although superficially intelligible, do not achieve it.

As a matter of common law, if the parties did not choose a law but selected English jurisdiction, this was not taken as an unequivocal and express choice of English law to govern the contract, but would be taken to have that effect unless substantially all the other factors came together in pointing to another law.[69] Under the Rome Convention this will not be taken to fall within Article 3 as an express choice of English law, or, at least not certainly, as a case where the choice of English law can be deduced with reasonable certainty from the contract; but it will certainly be effective within the framework of Article 4, in default of an Article 3 choice. But if the parties contract on the basis of a standard form, which is known in the trade as being founded on English law, this may be a case in which the parties' actual choice may be deduced from the terms of the contract or the circumstances of the case.[70]

(a) Split choice, deferred choice, altered choice

Although it allowed for freedom to choose the proper law of a contract, the common law was reluctant to permit two laws to govern different parts of the contract, no doubt to avoid the risk of contradiction which might well arise from allowing it. And it denied the validity of an agreement to defer making the actual choice of law to a date in the future: it was not open to the parties to specify that no choice of law was to be made until, at

---

[68] Case C–387/98 *Coreck Maritime GmbH v Handelsveem BV* [2000] ECR I–9337.
[69] *Compagnie Tunisienne de Navigation SA v Compagnie d'Armement Maritime SA* [1971] AC 572.
[70] Giuliano-Lagarde Report [1980] OJ C282/1, 17.

some point after the formation of the contract, one party nominated it.[71] Such a 'floating' choice of law was axiomatically precluded, on the footing that a contract must be a source of obligation from its inception, and in the absence of a governing law it would contain no mechanism to impose any obligations. But there appeared to be no obstacle to prevent the parties changing the proper law: if it was open to them to vary the contract, it must also have been open to vary this provision as well.[72] As a matter of logic, if not clear authority, however, the alteration to the proper law would need to comply with, or be licensed by, the original proper law as well as being permitted by English law: the contract would be and remain a source of obligations governed by its original proper law unless and until this proper law recognized the validity and effectiveness of a change.

The position under the Convention is simpler and more complex. Proceeding from the view that the parties are permitted to exercise freedom of choice, it is provided that they may agree to have separate parts of the contract governed by different laws.[73] They may agree to alter the governing law at any time,[74] but it is not made clear whether the question of whether a purported variation was effective is referred to anything other than the Rome Convention itself, or is subject to any conditions which the parties may have imposed on the exercise of this power. As a matter of logic, if the parties expressly choose the law of Ruritania to govern the contract, according to which law no subsequent variation of governing law is permitted, it is hard to see why the Rome Convention should authorize the making of a change which the parties have bound themselves not to make: if this is correct, a rule of double reference would be applicable here: the Rome Convention will allow the change as a matter of private international law, but to avoid being a breach of contract, the change of law must be permitted by the law which governed the contract as the source of the parties' rights and duties.[75] Any other solution appears to degrade the law chosen by the parties to define the obligations of the contract they agreed to make.

It is not clear from the Convention whether the parties may choose not to have a law at the outset. Logic suggests a negative answer, for a contract without a law makes no more sense under the Convention than it did

---

[71] *Armar Shipping Co Ltd v Caisse Algérienne d'Assurance* [1981] 1 WLR 207 (CA).
[72] *Whitworth Street Estates (Manchester) Ltd v James Miller & Partners Ltd* [1970] AC 583.
[73] Article 3(1).
[74] Article 3(2).
[75] But in *Aeolian Shipping SA v ISS Machinery Services Ltd* [2001] EWCA Civ 1162, [2002] 2 Lloyd's Rep 641, the court appeared to treat the question as one of simple fact, not dependent upon satisfaction of any additional condition.

under the common law;[76] but if the law is initially supplied by Article 4, it is arguable that this law plays a part in determining whether the making of a later choice is effective. Here again, it is one thing to provide that the parties may agree to, or choose to, alter the governing law, but it is quite another to deduce precisely how this works in an individual case.

(b) The meaning of 'law'

According to the Convention, 'law' means the domestic law of the country chosen by the rules of the Convention: the possibility of *renvoi* to another law is excluded by Article 15. The general justification for this lies in the pragmatic argument that if the parties went to the trouble of choosing a law it would be unlikely to the point of perversity for them to have chosen anything other than the domestic law of the nominated country. Where they have not chosen, they may have been perfectly content to accept a default option; but for this version of the governing law to mean something different would be unacceptable. One might question the wisdom of the exclusion of *renvoi* for the case where the parties have not chosen a law but have chosen a forum for adjudication. The common law orthodoxy, which carried into the Convention,[77] that this is a pretty powerful indicator of choice for the domestic law of the court chosen, looks odd. For it is a clear and unambiguous choice for whatever law the court at the place of trial would itself have applied. But this pattern of reasoning is apparently precluded by Article 15, so indirect and unreliable means will have to be used to achieve what cannot be done directly.

3. NO EXPRESS CHOICE OF GOVERNING LAW

Save for the case of consumer contracts, Article 4 provides that, if not chosen in accordance with Article 3, the governing law is that of the country with which the contract is most closely connected. The looked-for connection is therefore to a country, rather than to a legal system; once the connection to a country has been ascertained, the law of that country applies to govern the contract.[78] This may mean that although a contract is most closely connected to English *law*, it may still be more closely connected to another *country*, and it will be the latter which identifies the governing law. This would be, or is, unfortunate. For example, there may be a set of connected contracts: a bill of lading and contracts made in

---

[76] *Amin Rasheed Shipping Corp v Kuwait Insurance Co* [1984] AC 50.
[77] Giuliano-Lagarde Report [1980] OJ C282/1, 17.
[78] *Crédit Lyonnais v New Hampshire Insurance Co* [1997] 2 Lloyd's Rep 1 (CA).

accordance with it,[79] or letters of credit or of comfort, issued as part of a larger financial transaction,[80] or contracts of reinsurance made back-to-back with contracts of insurance,[81] in which an express choice of law is made in some but not all contracts. Common sense would say that all were probably intended to be governed by the same law, to prevent the dislocation which would otherwise be risked. But in the absence of an express choice of law, recourse to Article 4 makes it difficult to give effect to what may be seen to have been the implied intention as regards governing *law* if the balance of factual connections points to a different *country*.

It is not clear how the degrees of connection are to be assessed. Under the common law there had been an informal hierarchy of connection, so that the place of arbitration was seen as a strong connection, the place of domicile of the parties as a weak one, and the others ranged between the two. This was probably based on an unarticulated reflection of how far, if at all, each allowed the court to read the parties' minds as regards intended proper law. If this is correct, it will be inapplicable in the context of Article 4, where the search is not for clues to intention as to law, but for connections to a country, where intention is not relevant.

Presumptions,[82] of uncertain utility, provide that the country most closely connected to the contract is that of the habitual residence (but for a corporation, its central administration) of the party whose performance is characteristic of the contract, unless the contract is made in the course of that party's trade or profession, in which case the country presumed is that of the principal place of business. For contracts concerning an immovable it is the country where the immovable is situated; different and complex presumptions apply to contracts for the carriage of goods. The technique of providing presumptions[83] was not part of the common law, and it will take a while to discover how useful these presumptions really are. But it is important to observe that the focus is not on the place of characteristic performance, rather on the residence of the party who is to make it.[84] The characteristic performance referred to is usually taken to be the performance for which the payment is made by the counter-party; but if a contract does not conform to the model of sale and purchase (ironically,

---

[79]   *The Mahkutai* [1996] AC 650 (PC).

[80]   *Bank of Baroda v Vysya Bank Ltd* [1994] 2 Lloyd's Rep 87.

[81]   cf *Forsikringsaktieselskapet Vesta v Butcher* [1989] AC 852, where the contracts were governed by different laws.

[82]   Article 4(2)–(4).

[83]   Apart from that applicable to a choice of jurisdiction or arbitration.

[84]   Presumably he will be the dominant party, most likely to have dictated the terms of the contract, and most likely to have wanted his own law to be applied.

the mutual exchange of money or of options on money, the basis of the economy of the western world, will not easily fit the template), Article 4(5) concedes that the presumptions may be inapplicable, and that the question is simply one of looking for the country of closest connection, the law of which will govern. That said, however, the seller or supplier or reinsurer who undertakes performance for payment, will tend to be seen as the characteristic performer; in the case of an agreement for supply and distribution, it is the supplier, rather than the distributor, whose performance has been held to be characteristic.[85] Moreover, if the contract appears to be more closely connected to another country, Article 4(5) also provides that that country's law will apply in any event.[86]

Article 4(5) has the potential to scupper the system of presumptions: either the country identified by the presumption has the closest connection, in which case the presumption will add nothing, or it does not and another country does, in which case the presumption will not apply. Either way, the answer would be found by the direct application of the Article 4(5) test, but without the hoop-jumping which will have preceded it. In the absence of a ruling from the European Court, practice may vary from court to national court, but the English approach can best be summarized as being to apply the presumption unless there is good reason not to, an answer which actually says nothing at all.[87]

At common law it was occasionally said that a presumption of validity meant that where the issues were finely balanced, a contract should be governed by a law under which it would be valid.[88] The legitimacy of such a presumption was debatable, but could be defended as reflecting the presumed intention of the parties. There is therefore no obvious basis for including such a presumption where Article 4 of the Convention identifies the governing law, and party intention has no formal role.

4. MODIFICATION OF CHOICE OF LAW

Although choice of law made by the parties which complies with Article 3 cannot be denied, there are certain contracts, and other issues, for which the

---

[85] *Print Concept GmbH v GEW (EC) Ltd* [2002] CLC 382. The French cour de cassation has reached the same conclusion: *Optelec SA v Soc Midtronics BV* Cass Civ 1ère, 15 May 2001, [2002] RCDIP 86.

[86] See generally *Bank of Baroda v Vysya Bank Ltd* [1994] 2 Lloyd's Rep 87.

[87] *Samcrete Egypt Engineers and Contractors SAE v Land Rover Exports Ltd* [2001] EWCA Civ 2019, [2002] CLC 533; *Ennstone Building Products Ltd v Stanger Ltd* [2002] EWCA Civ 916, [2002] 1 WLR 3059; *Ophthalmic Innovations International Ltd v Ophthalmic Innovations International Inc* [2004] EWHC 2948 (Ch), [2005] ILPr 109. A stricter approach is favoured in Scotland: *Caledonia Subsea Ltd v Microperi Srl* 2003 SC 70.

[88] eg *Coast Lines Ltd v Hudig and Veder Chartering NV* [1972] 2 QB 34, 44, 48 (CA).

rules of another law, may be superimposed to limit the hegemony of the *lex contractus*. Likewise, there are certain contracts where, if the parties do not make an express choice of law, Article 4 does not supply the governing law.

(a) Certain consumer contracts

Article 5 modifies the general provisions of Articles 3 and 4 in respect of certain consumer contracts. Article 5 applies where the contract is for sale or supply (or for credit for the purpose) to a person for a purpose outside his trade or profession;[89] and does apply to a package holiday. It does not apply to a contract of carriage, or where the services are to be supplied wholly outside the country of the consumer's habitual residence. But where the contract falls within this definition, an express choice of law under Article 3 cannot deprive the consumer of the protection afforded by mandatory rules[90] of law of the country of his habitual residence if either (1) in that country the conclusion of the contract was preceded by a specific invitation addressed to him, or by advertising, and he had taken in that country all the necessary steps for his conclusion of the contract, or (2) the supplier or his agent received the consumer's order in that country, or (3) the contract was for the sale of goods and the consumer travelled from that country to another and there placed his order, the journey having been arranged by the seller for the purpose of inducing the consumer to buy. In the absence of express choice under Article 3, Article 4 does not apply. Instead, a consumer contract is governed by the law of the country of the consumer's habitual residence.[91] The fragmented state of Article 5 is presumably attributable to the history of its negotiation, but its protective intent is clear. Its application to contracts made by computer is yet to be properly explored.

(b) Individual employment contracts

Article 6 modifies the applicable law for contracts of employment. An express choice of law is effective, but only subject to the mandatory, employee-protecting laws of the country whose law would have applied in the absence of an express choice. If there is no express choice of law

---

[89] It is not specified whether the supplier must be acting in the course of his trade or profession. Cases of contracts for a mixed purpose raise problems, but if the Brussels Regulation is a guide, they will not count as consumer contracts: Case C-464/01 *Gruber v Bay Wa AG* [2005] ECR I-439.

[90] As regards this expression, see under section B.4. (c) below.

[91] Article 5(4).

under Article 3, Article 4 does not apply. Instead, the contract will be governed by the law of the country where the employee habitually carried out his work[92] or, if there is no such single country, by the law of the country where is situated the place of business which engaged him, unless (in either case) the contract appears to be more closely connected to another country.[93]

(c) Mandatory rules

Apart from the special contracts just mentioned, there are four further, general, instances in which the hegemony of the governing law is limited. The Convention identifies the first three of these as 'mandatory laws': a rather unhelpful expression whose meaning varies according to the context in which it appears. In these cases, choice of the governing law is not set aside, but its operation is in certain respects overridden and subordinated to the rules of another system of law; the same applies to a governing law identified by Article 4. It may be appropriate to picture 'mandatory laws' as directions given by the legislator to the judge, as distinct from laws which are relevant because of the way a party puts its case.

First, Article 3(3) provides that an express choice of law is still subject to the laws of another country which may not be derogated from by contractual agreement, but only if all the relevant elements at the time of choice are connected with that country. The intent is that where a contract is entirely connected only to one country, freedom of choice of law should not extend to those issues which that law regards as applicable regardless of choice. In England, an example is the requirement of consideration, so that if a contract is wholly connected to England, a choice of Scots law will be effective, but consideration will still be required for the promise to be enforceable, even though this is not required under Scots law. There is obvious room for disagreement about which elements are 'relevant' for the purpose of this rule.

Secondly, Article 7(2) provides that laws of the forum which are mandatory and must be applied by a judge regardless of choice of law will continue to be applicable. The operation of this provision is therefore entirely determined by the court in which the trial takes place, and provides, notwithstanding the uniformity in choice of law created by the Convention,

---

[92] Where the duties of the employment are carried out in more than one country, see Case C–125/92 *Mulox IBC v Geels* [1993] ECR I–4075; Case C–383/95 *Rutten v Cross Medical Ltd* [1997] ECR I–51.

[93] For cases in which the duties are carried on outside the territorial jurisdiction of any state (such as on an oil rig) see [1980] OJ C282/1, 26.

an incentive to forum-shop. In the context of a trial in England, examples may include legislation controlling contract terms which purport to limit or exclude liability,[94] the Carriage of Goods by Sea Act 1971, giving the force of law to the Hague–Visby Rules,[95] or those provisions of the Financial Services and Markets Act 2000 which make unenforceable an investment agreement made through an unauthorized person,[96] and which are not to be sidelined by the simple expedient of choosing a law other than English to govern the contract.

Thirdly, Article 7(1) of the Convention[97] would have permitted the application by a court of the mandatory laws of a third country (that is, neither the country whose law is the applicable law, nor the law of the country whose courts are hearing the case) which had a close connection with the contract. But as this would have been a dangerous novelty for judges, and a source of uncertainty for litigants, the provision was deleted from the Convention as enacted in England.[98] The legislative technique involved may bear upon the analysis of contracts which are illegal under the law of the place of performance when this is neither the governing law nor the law of the forum. It appears from the structure of Article 7 in general that the manner in which the law in question must be mandatory is that which applies under Article 7(2), but as there is no possibility of an English court being called on to apply such a rule, it need not be examined any further.

Fourthly, a rule of the governing law will not apply where its application would be manifestly contrary to public policy.[99] The relationship between this and Article 7 may not be immediately clear, but whereas Article 7 provides for the governing law to be overlaid by a rule from the domestic law of the forum, Article 16 proceeds by the blanking out of a rule of the governing law, with the result that the answer appears by default. So if the governing law allows damages to be claimed for breach of a contract to sell slaves or narcotics, Article 16 will prevent its application in English proceedings; such a case would fit less easily into Article 7(2), for no substantive rule of English law—as opposed to the principles of English public policy—demands application in such a case.

---

[94] Unfair Contract Terms Act 1977, s 27(2); Unfair Terms in Consumer Contract Regulations 1999 (SI 1999/2083) (although Art 20 expressly provides for the application of such rules as those which derive from Directive 93/13/EC [1993] OJ L95/29).

[95] cf *The Hollandia* [1983] 1 AC 565.

[96] Financial Services and Markets Act 2000, ss 26, 27.

[97] cf *The Torni* [1932] P 78 (CA).

[98] Contracts (Applicable Law) Act 1990, s 2(2).

[99] Article 16.

5. DOMAIN OF THE GOVERNING LAW

Subject to those reservations, the Convention variously provides that the governing law, ascertained as above, applies to the interpretation and performance of the contract; also to the consequences of its breach and the extinction of its obligations.[100] In relation to formal validity, compliance with the governing law is sufficient; otherwise compliance with the law or laws of the place where the parties were when they made the contract will also suffice.[101] The effect is that, subject to what follows, almost all points of construction, interpretation, and discharge (by performance, frustration, and breach) are within the domain of the governing law as, in principle,[102] is the availability of remedies for breach. The Convention provides that the consequences of nullity are governed by the governing law, but it does not insist on this; and the United Kingdom did not enact Article 10(1)(e).[103] This contractual issue is therefore examined under choice of law for restitutionary obligations but, as indicated above, many cases of nullity should be regarded as contractual and resolved in accordance with the governing law.

(a) Disputes about contractual validity

Subject to the fact that the formal validity of a contract is, by Article 9, assessed by a rule of alternative validating reference, the governing law as the Rome Convention identifies it will, in general, determine whether the contract is valid. But the concept of 'validity' covers a range of possible objections, ranging from breakdowns in formation to the effect of a change in the law making performance illegal. Nevertheless, the point of departure is that the contention that there was, or is now, no binding contract is one which will be resolved by the law which would govern the contract if it were taken to be valid. This is the effect of Articles 3(4) and 8(1),[104] and is broadly in line with what some[105] took to be the solution given by the common law. References to the putative governing law (or the governing law of the putative contract) are to this law. But the

---

[100] Article 10.

[101] Article 9.

[102] Remedies not known to English law cannot be granted: Art 1(2)(h). It is uncertain whether specific performance must be ordered in a case in which it would be available under the *lex contractus* but not, in these circumstances, under English domestic law.

[103] 1990 Act, s 2(2).

[104] Which also provides that whether a particular term is valid is determined by the law which would govern it on the footing that it was valid: a proposition which is particularly unrealistic where each party has proposed a contract term, including a choice of law, which contradicts that of the opposite party.

[105] Although not all: Briggs [1990] LMCLQ 192.

methodology involved in this approach is obviously flawed. If we suppose that one party will be contending that there was a valid and binding contract, while the opposite party argues that there never was any such thing, it is hard to see why one would proceed by assuming, conditionally but still significantly, that the first party's submission is correct and that the appropriate tool of decision is the law which would have governed the contract if it were valid. The reverse proposition, which respects another aspect of the parties' autonomy, appears equally convincing. The opposite party will say that the remedies lie in the law of restitution or not at all, so one should assume the contract to be invalid, and look to the law which would govern the restitutionary claim. If that law considers that there was indeed no valid contract, and that the claim is for restitution, the choice of law will be the restitutionary one. If instead it considers that there was a contract, and no cause for restitution, the *lex causae* will be the contractual one. Why should one of these be preferred to the other? If this is an intelligible question, the answer will be that there is no reason, and the solution must lie elsewhere.

But alternative solutions are not immediately attractive, either. One possibility might be to characterize the facts to see whether they disclose an issue falling within a broad conception of contract; but this is liable to be uncertain in the way it works. Another might be to apply the *lex fori* to decide whether there is a contract and, if there is, to use the proper law which it must necessarily[106] have to decide whether there was a valid contract. That would mean that if according to the *lex fori* there is no contract, that would be an end of it. Yet another might be to apply the putative governing law, but with a saving provision for people whose own laws would have reassured them that there was no contract and that they were not bound.[107] In effect, this is the solution adopted by the Convention. Article 8(2) qualifies the approach in Article 8(1) by allowing the party who contends that he should not be bound to rely on the law of his habitual residence 'to establish that he did not consent' if it would be unreasonable to apply the governing law to the question.[108] But if he has dealt by reference to the foreign law before, or maybe simply because he was prepared to make an international contract, he may be found to have forfeited a protection designed for the innocent abroad.[109] What precisely

---

[106] *Amin Rasheed Shipping Corp v Kuwait Insurance Co* [1984] AC 50.

[107] Foreshadowed by Jaffey (1975) 24 ICLQ 603.

[108] It is unclear whether this reference to habitual residence excludes parties who are not natural persons, for whom the corresponding point of reference is the place of business.

[109] cf *Egon Oldendorff v Libera Corp* [1995] 2 Lloyd's Rep 64.

is encompassed by the argument that 'he did not consent' is uncertain. As a matter of first impression, an argument which has at its root the proposition that X did not in law consent to bind himself to Y seems to be comprehended, and therefore any assault on the legal effectiveness of the alleged consent is within the material scope of Article 8(2). Giuliano-Lagarde expresses a different view,[110] claiming that the scope of Article 8(2) is narrower than this, and is confined to the existence, as distinct from the validity, of consent: that is, to offer and acceptance and mistake, but not to factors which render the contract voidable and the consent vitiated. It is unclear whether this is tenable; it remains to be seen whether Article 8(2) will be confined to the limited role proposed by Giuliano-Lagarde.

6. THE ROME CONVENTION IN CONTRACTUAL LITIGATION

One of the curious things about the private international law of contract is that whilst the domestic law of contract divides its subject up into familiar and everyday pieces—offer and acceptance, consideration, mistake, misrepresentation, and so on—the rules of private international law use categories and address concerns which cut across these more practical issues, or make disproportionate provision for issues (such as formal validity) which are of only occasional practical importance. As a result, it is instructive to look at the issues which might be raised in a simple contract action in an English court, and to examine how and where these points are accommodated by the Rome Convention. We will proceed on the assumption that C is suing D, a defendant habitually resident in England, for breach of contract, and examine the elements of the law of contract as if raised by D as a defence to the claim. We will also assume that by the governing law, which will be ascertained on the basis that the contract is, for this purpose at least, assumed to be valid, the contract would be valid and enforceable, and all the defences raised by D would fail; but that as a matter of English domestic law, the several defences raised by D would be well founded and that, also on the facts, D would satisfy the requirement of its being reasonable for him to rely on his own law.

If D argues that he is not bound and cannot be liable because there was no *offer and acceptance*, this plea is a matter for the governing law, for it goes to the validity of the contract; but D may rely on his own, English, law to demonstrate that he did not consent, by reason of Article 8(2). If D argues that there was no *intention to create legal relations*, the effect of

---

[110] [1980] OJ C282/1, 28.

this plea will be a matter for the governing law. But if D formulates the argument to say he did not consent to, nor had any reason to suppose that he was, entering into legal relations at all, because under English law such an agreement would not be legally enforceable, Article 8(2) may avail him. If D argues that the alleged contract cannot be enforced because the price was never agreed, and there was therefore no *certainty of contractual terms*, the governing law may again be displaced by the argument that D cannot be held to have consented to something which, as a matter of his own law, he could never have been bound by; and if this is so, Article 8(2) is in principle available to him. All these issues go to the existence of consent to bind oneself to enforceable obligations.

If D argues that he is not bound because there was no *consideration* for the promise, and that he knew that if he asked for nothing of value in return for C's promise, then he could not be said to have given his consent to be legally bound to C, it seems arguable that Article 8(2) will apply here also, even though the governing law would not regard this as a necessity for the formation of a contract. If C argues that he contracted to benefit C2, who was not a party to the contract, nor known about by D, and that under the governing law C2 may sue in his own name, D may say that under the English doctrine of *privity*[111] he would not be bound to, and did not consent to be bound by, C2. Likewise, if C argues that he contracted with D2 and the effect of their contract under its governing law was that D was bound by an obligation in it, D may argue that under the English doctrine of privity he is not taken to consent to be bound to an obligation in a contract to which he was a stranger. Article 8(2) may preserve his right to argue that he did not consent to be bound by the obligation created by the contract. These issues may not go to the question whether D agreed something with somebody, but if D submits that he did not consent to an agreement which would have legal effect or that he never consented to be bound to C2 or by D2, it is arguable, despite the apparent view of Giuliano-Lagarde, that these arguments go to the existence of the consent which C asserts and D denies.

If C argues that D is bound despite the fact that there was a *limitation or exclusion clause* in the contract, the validity of this defence will be a matter for the governing law to assess. But if the governing law would regard the limitation clause as valid, it may still be struck down as a matter of English law by reference to Article 7(2), assuming that the provision of

---

[111] But cf the Contracts (Rights of Third Parties) Act 1999 for modification of English common law.

English law relied on is one which must be applied by a judge whatever the governing law.

If D argues that his agreement was procured by *fraud*, or *negligent or innocent misstatement*, or by *material non-disclosure*, or by *duress*, or by the exercise of *undue influence*, the legal effect of his plea is that his consent was vitiated and, subject to conditions, is capable of being wiped away. If the governing law would nevertheless regard these pleas as insufficient to ground relief, may D rely on Article 8(2) to establish that he did not consent? Perhaps not: unlike issues relating to offer and acceptance, these are not factors where D will have known or believed at the time, or if asked at the time would have said that his own law provided that he was not bound to the other; to put it another way, he cannot deny that he did, albeit as a result of fraud, originally consent. Yet D may know that he has been the victim of what may be duress or undue influence; he may know that as a matter of English law he has no need to check the accuracy of representations made by another, or that he was entitled to rely on C to make disclosure in a contract made in the utmost good faith, so that he will not be bound if he relies on misrepresentations; and he may rely on the security of his own law accordingly, just as he does when he throws away an offer letter, knowing that he cannot be bound by it. Seen in those terms it is plausible that Article 8(2) should be relevant here too, for an alleged consent which does not bind D, and which D is right to assume does not bind D, is no consent at all. If D argues that the alleged contract was void on the basis of a mutual *mistake*, or his own unilateral mistake, this is, in effect, a confusion which prevents the parties coming to an agreement, and Article 8(2) is applicable in principle. If he argues that the alleged contract was void on the basis of fundamental common mistake or should be set aside on the basis of less fundamental common mistake, D is arguing that he did not consent to the terms of the contract alleged by C, because there was nothing to consent about.

If D argues that he cannot be made to perform because the contract was one which required him to perform an act which would be *illegal* under the law of the place where performance was called for, the validity of the contract is in principle a matter for the governing law, and if under that law the illegality renders the contract unenforceable there is no more to be said.[112] But the governing law may not accept this as an excuse for non-performance and, on that basis, would stand at odds with the common law, which probably held that a sufficient degree of illegality under the law of

---

[112] Article 10.

the place where the contract was to be performed rendered the contract unenforceable, whatever its proper law: an English court could hardly make an order on the basis that D was required to commit a crime in the place of performance. It is correct to point out that it was never completely clear whether this was a rule of private international law, or just the application of English domestic law: the reported cases all concerned contracts whose proper law was English, although the width of the language used did not give the impression of its being restricted to English contracts,[113] and it may be suggested that the answer depends on the magnitude of the illegality, and on the awareness of the party prepared to commit it.[114] Had it been possible to have recourse to Article 7(1), an English court might have been permitted to apply the law of the place of performance, but this provision is not part of English law, and it may be that its exclusion has killed off a rule about illegality under the law of the place of performance. But there are two alternatives. First, to apply the provision of the governing law which required performance of a criminal act, or an act tainted with illegality, may be manifestly contrary to public policy, and therefore precluded by Article 16. Secondly, however, the rule of the common law, whatever it was, may still shine through the gap in the fabric of the Convention created by the excision of Article 7(1). In other words, the question whether and when the mandatory rules of a third country (neither that whose law governs the contract nor that of the courts hearing the case) may be applied is a matter for the common law to answer as the Convention does not; and according to the common law, it is only laws of the place of performance, rendering performance illegal, which can be picked up and applied by the English court.

If D argues that he cannot be sued because C's action is barred by *limitation* or prescription, this plea will be determined by the governing law. Article 10(1)(d) so provides, but the Foreign Limitation Periods Act 1984 had already brought English private international law into line with this.

If D argues that the contract was *discharged by performance* or by C's *breach*, or by *frustration*, the plea will be dealt with by the governing law, according to Article 10. If D denies that C is entitled to the particular *remedy* claimed, the answer will come from the governing law. The extent to which an English court is required to grant remedies available under the governing law but which an English court would not grant is

---

[113] *Ralli Bros v Compania Naviera Sota y Aznar* [1920] 2 KB 287 (CA); *Foster v Driscoll* [1929] 1 KB 470 (CA); *Regazzoni v KC Sethia (1944) Ltd* [1958] AC 301; *Lemenda Trading Co Ltd v African Middle East Petroleum Co Ltd* [1989] QB 728; *Euro-Diam Ltd v Bathurst* [1990] 1 QB 30 (CA); *Soleimany v Soleimany* [1999] QB 785, 803 (CA).

[114] cf *Royal Boskalis Westminster NV v Mountain* [1999] QB 674 (CA).

uncertain, but an English court will probably be expected to follow and apply the remedial provisions of the governing law unless this is too inconvenient to be practicable, or would contravene some fundamental policy of English law.

7. THE ROME I REGULATION

A new Regulation, 'Rome I', superseding the Rome Convention, will be adopted in 2008. It will not be considered by the courts for several years: even in the Member States bound by it, it will not apply to contracts made before late 2009; and the United Kingdom exercised its right (it may change its mind, but has not done so yet) not to be bound by it in any event. A brief review is still appropriate. The basic shape of the Regulation will be that of the Rome Convention; the general issues of structure and interpretation are unchanged. So also will the substance of many of the Articles. Perhaps the most striking change is the spelling out of presumptions as to governing law, where this has not been chosen under Article 3, listed in Article 4 by reference to type of contract. In addition, there will no opting out of what was Articles 7(1) and 10(1)(e) of the Convention. However, the scope of the former provision, which allows for the application of mandatory laws of third countries, has been severely cut back, to permit only the application of rules of the law of the place of performance which render performance illegal: a formulation uncannily close to the common law. Though many adjustments are made to the detail of the Convention, and to the numbering of its provisions, none is structural. Few are of real significance, and none is for the worse. If the United Kingdom were to change its mind and to propose to be bound by the Regulation, the basic outline of its law would not be significantly altered.

The Rome I Regulation will not apply to obligations arising from dealings prior to the conclusion of a contract,[115] but as the effect of the Rome II Regulation is to subject these to the law which would have governed the contract, the exclusion from Rome I is more apparent than real.[116] A new Article 5 makes provision for choice of law in contracts of carriage of goods and persons: for the latter, the laws which may be chosen to govern are restricted. The consumer contract provisions have been refined and made more complex, but the alterations are more cosmetic than anything else. A new Article 7, dealing with insurance, gathers together and organizes the rules currently found in several European Directives: this can only be a welcome development. Though many more radical alterations were debated in the course of the lengthy negotiations, very few survived to appear in the final draft of the Regulation.

[115] Art 1(2)(j).
[116] See p 201, below.

6

Torts

A. GENERAL

After its century of tranquil slumber, during which hardly any cases were reported and everyone knew where they stood, the rules for choice of law in tort now seem to be in a state of continual revolution.[1] In 1971 the House of Lords charted a new course for the private international law of torts, and subsequent decisions refined and polished it up. In the 1990s the Law Commission, and then Parliament, persuaded themselves that they could do better; and the Private International Law (Miscellaneous Provisions) Act 1995[2] was enacted to cover some of the field. It is still in force, but it will be superseded when, in January 2009, Regulation (EC) 864/2007, which will be referred to as Rome II,[3] becomes applicable in courts across the European Union. The excuse for this last, that the completion of the internal market cannot be achieved without uniform choice of law rules for torts, is so audacious that there is really no point in spending time on it; but the result is that as matters stand in 2008, there are three schemes for choice of law which need to be dealt with.

It works this way. The common law applies to all torts which occurred before 1 May 1996. For defamation, malicious falsehood, and similar complaints, the choice of rules of the common law remains in force: the 1995 Act does not apply to it.[4] For all other tort claims, the 1995 Act imposes new choice of law rules. These were rather odd; we will see just how odd in due course. Rome II will apply from 11 January 2009, but when it does it will govern choice of law for events giving rise to damage which occurred

---

[1] See Dicey, ch 35. For the background to the 1995 Act see Law Commission Report 193: *Private International Law: Choice of Law in Tort and Delict* (1990); *Proceedings of the Special Public Bill Committee* (HL Paper (1995) no 36). For comment on the 1995 Act, see Briggs [1995] LMCLQ 519. For the detail of Rome II, see the First Cumulative Supplement to Dicey, ch 35.

[2] In this chapter referred to as 'the 1995 Act'.

[3] The Regulation is published at [2007] OJ L199/40 (31 July 2007). It is called 'Rome II' in deference to the Rome Convention on choice of law for contract, which will be reborn as 'Rome I'.

[4] Section 13.

on or after 20 August 2007,[5] although excluding defamation (which will be governed by the common law) and privacy (which may fall under the 1995 Act).[6] The scheme of this chapter is therefore to examine the rules of the common law, then the 1995 Act, then Rome II. If there is a third edition of this book, this part of it will certainly be easier to write; but when that happens, as a result of Rome II, Chapter 6 will be entitled 'non-contractual obligations' and its scope will be wider than the present chapter is. And Chapter 7 will disappear altogether. This will be symbolic, and entirely accurately so, of the manner in which the common law of private international law is simply disappearing.

1. JURISDICTION OVER TORT CLAIMS

Tort claims will usually arise as civil or commercial matters, and jurisdiction over defendants alleged to have committed them will fall within the domain of the Brussels Regulation.[7] If a tort raises an issue of title to foreign land, or requires a court to adjudicate the validity of foreign intellectual property rights, there is, as a matter of common law, no subject matter jurisdiction. In relation to foreign land, the common law rule was modified by the Civil Jurisdiction and Judgments Act 1982, section 30, with the result that the court will not lack jurisdiction to adjudicate unless the tort claim is *principally* concerned with title to foreign land;[8] it has been said,[9] if unconvincingly,[10] that the rule was never well founded so far as intellectual property was concerned. In any event, where personal jurisdiction over the defendant can be derived from the Regulation, these common law limitations are held by many to be inapplicable, even though they are concerned with subject matter jurisdiction, rather than personal jurisdiction over defendants. Where jurisdiction is to be established by service out of the jurisdiction with the permission of the court, CPR rule 6.20(8) is the main paragraph.

2. HISTORICAL AND JUDICIAL DEVELOPMENT OF CHOICE OF LAW

Despite the fact that it appeared to generate little judicial interest in England until the end of the 20th century, choice of law in tort claims

---

[5] Articles 32 and 31.
[6] Article 1(2)(g).
[7] [2001] OJ L12/1; ch 2, above.
[8] As to which see *Re Polly Peck International plc (No 2)* [1998] 3 All ER 812 (CA).
[9] *Pearce v Ove Arup Partnership Ltd* [2000] Ch 403 (CA).
[10] Because the authorities on the common law position, though predominantly Australian, left little room for doubt.

produced an enormous amount of academic examination and, particularly in the lush litigational grasslands of the United States, a considerable amount of creative judicial thinking. A contract is an agreement, and if the law which will be applied is not one which the parties chose, it will be deduced from points of connection which the parties knew about from the start. Torts, by contrast, are the law's accidents: essentially messy and unplanned, and covering a much more diverse set of interests and duties. It could be argued that a single choice of law rule is being stretched beyond its proper limits when it has to encompass claims which may include personal injury, liability for animals, defamation, nuisance, unfair competition, and conspiracy; but when causes of action arising under foreign laws of tort and delict are added in, a single and reliable choice of law rule, whether very flexible or very inflexible, will be difficult to devise.[11] Not only that, but the parties to a contract know of each other, and the range of persons with a potential claim will therefore be limited and predictable; the parties to a tort claim, often flung together or strewn about by the tort, are only sometimes knowable in advance. In devising choice of law rules this has to be borne in mind.

As a matter of history, choice of law rules in tort tended to rigidity, and to centre on the *lex fori* or the *lex loci delicti commissi*. The justification for the *lex fori* was sometimes said to lie in the similarity between torts and crimes, but this was never really convincing, and a better view was that the imposition of legal duties and civil obligations without regard to the will of the parties was a matter on which each court was entitled to prefer the standards of its own law. The justification for the *lex loci delicti commissi* was the homely advice that when in Rome, one should do as Romans do. Even at this level of generality each has an attraction, and maybe this was the reason English law blended the two into a rule of double actionability. But the objection that either could result in the application of a law which had little genuine or durable connection with the parties or the facts of the claim does not need illustration. This led to suggestions that, in the same way that a contract was governed by a proper law, so should a tort be.[12] The objection that it was one thing to subject a consensual, pre-litigation, relationship to a proper law, but quite another to subject an unplanned or non-relationship to the same process was obvious, but the sense that only the proper law could guarantee that the law eventually

---

[11] The Rome II Regulation reflects this truth in its enactment of general rule, general exceptions, and particular rules for certain kinds of tort (not counting privacy and defamation, which are excluded from its scope altogether).

[12] Originating in Morris, 'The Proper Law of a Tort' (1951) 64 Harv LR 881.

applied was the 'right' law was also strong. This sense manifested itself in different ways. In England, it led to the development of a flexible exception to the erstwhile rigid rule of double actionability, thus resulting in a high degree of predictability which could nevertheless yield in the face of unusual facts. In the United States it led to a more fundamental re-casting of the choice of law rule, where the hegemony of the *lex loci delicti commissi* was abandoned for a variety of alternative techniques. These alternative approaches to choice of law flourished in the United States, mainly because it was considered that the application of the law of the place of the tort is less attractive within a federation in which each of the states is legally foreign but not noticeably geographically so: whereas it may be plain within Europe that one is in Rome, it may not be so obvious in the United States that one is not in Kansas any more. Inter-state trade and traffic are such that a rigid preference for the law of the place where the tort occurred has an appreciable chance of choosing a law which was accidental in both senses. So a variety of alternatives was developed to seek the elusive goal of an intuitively right answer derived nevertheless from scientific theory. In the first case to breach the dam,[13] the New York Court of Appeals experimented with a test of closest connection, and with a more complex approach which asked (and sought to answer) which state or states had laws which were intended, or interested, to apply to the particular issue before the court for decision: a method oddly entitled 'governmental interest analysis'.[14] The debate later extended to inquire which state's law would be the most impaired if not applied;[15] to the use of a 'better law' approach,[16] a technique liable to make it difficult for a court not to apply its own domestic law; and the result cannot be said to promote the goal of legal certainty, whatever else it may do.[17]

An English lawyer may recoil from the thought that a clear rule, with provision for an exception to serve as a pressure valve, should be abandoned in favour of a more individual approach. After all, although torts may be accidental and unplanned, the taking of insurance against liability for torts is a public good; and an approach which makes it uncertain which law will govern a claim makes the risk one which is difficult to insure against. But if the American jurisprudence demonstrates that one size of choice of law rule does not fit all, it has done a valuable job.

---

[13] *Babcock v Jackson* 191 NE 2d 279 (1963), [1963] 2 Lloyd's Rep 286 (NY CA).
[14] Currie, *Selected Essays on the Conflict of Laws* (1963).
[15] *Bernard v Harrah's Club* 546 P 2d 719 (1976).
[16] *Cipolla v Shaposka* 262 A 2d 854 (1970); *Clark v Clark* 222 A 2d 205 (1966).
[17] For an annual survey of choice of law in the American courts see Symeonides in the American Journal of Comparative Law from vol 36 (1988) to the present.

In Canada and Australia, by contrast, the fact that many torts take place elsewhere within the federation moved the courts in precisely the opposite direction from that which drew support in the United States. Faced with the need to fashion a choice of law rule for torts committed in another Canadian province, the Supreme Court of Canada opted for a rigid *lex loci delicti* rule,[18] on the footing that this was both correct and in step with Canada's sense and understanding of its own sovereignty. Faced with similar facts in relation to intra-Australian torts, the High Court of Australia also opted for a rigid and inflexible *lex loci delicti* rule,[19] also spurning the path taken in the United States, and going out of its way to express disapproval of the pragmatic English common law amalgam of rules and exceptions. Even so, experience shows that the need to make an exception in the interests of flexibility becomes irresistible when the facts are sufficiently unusual; and the courts in Canada and Australia may yet have to eat some of their words.[20] Quite apart from that, all this modern questioning of received choice of law rules does make one wonder whether there are, in the conflict of laws in general but in tort in particular, differing degrees of foreignness, which in turn suggest that the law should develop choice of law rules which vary according to their context. After all, it was striking to see an English court treating a tort committed in Scotland or Ireland in precisely the same way as it would one committed in China or Peru, and it could have been argued that a tort committed within the territory of the European Union is less foreign than one committed outside, so that the approaches to choice of law might rationally differ. The American, Canadian, and Australian re-examinations of choice of law may in fact be symptoms of that emerging distinction; Rome II does not, however, lend it any support.

Be that as it may, the outcome is that the private international law of tort has been the testing ground for the development of alternatives to the traditional view of a single choice of law rule which can be applied to all causes of action within a single and broad characterization category. But any intellectual development is now likely to take place offshore as

[18] *Tolofson v Jensen* [1994] 3 SCR 1022, (1994) 120 DLR (4th) 299.

[19] *John Pfeiffer Pty Ltd v Rogerson* (2000) 203 CLR 503; *Régie Nationale des Usines Renault v Zhang* (2003) 210 CLR 491.

[20] It can be argued, although it is not convincing to do so, that the adoption of the principle of *renvoi* into the Australian *lex loci* rule, in *Neilson v Overseas Projects Corp of Victoria* (2005) 233 CLR 331, was a surrogate for the flexibility which the court was at pains to reject. This does not appear to be based on a fair or accurate reading of the analysis contained in the judgments.

legislation, foisted on the law by lawmakers in London and Brussels, means that common law sophistication is no longer at home in England.

B. COMMON LAW CHOICE OF LAW

The choice of law rules of the common law drew (for torts committed before 1 May 1996) and draw (for defamation whenever committed)[21] a distinction according to where the tort was committed, and locating the tort was therefore the starting point for analysis of choice of law.

1. THE PLACE OF THE TORT

The location of a tort is not problematic where all the elements making up the claim are concentrated in one place. But where this is not so, a test of location must be imperfect. Some courts preferred the view that it was the place of the damage, for until there is damage there is no tort; but the illogic[22] and arbitrariness of this were easy to see, and it was soon abandoned. The test which came to prevail, and which still prevails in Australia, asks where in substance the cause of action arose.[23] For example, if a dangerous pharmaceutical product was sold and ingested in one place, this place was where the cause of action arose, at least if the damage manifested itself in the same place, even though it had been designed and manufactured elsewhere.[24] If negligent professional advice was received and acted on in one place, this was where the cause of action arose, even though the information was given on the basis of work done elsewhere or the economic consequences were felt elsewhere.[25] If a defamatory statement was transmitted into a place where it was received and the reputation of the victim lowered in the mind of the reader, this was where the cause of action arose, even though the statement originated elsewhere.[26] Although occasionally rough and ready, and open to some manipulation by a claimant choosing to plead the facts and matters relied on in a self-serving way, the test was hallowed by usage. And even though it leaves a margin of appreciation to the judge, it is as workable as any 'place' rule could be.

---

[21] 1995 Act, s 13 (defamation), s 14(1) (date).

[22] After all, there is no tort without a tortfeasor.

[23] *Metall und Rohstoff AG v Donaldson, Lufkin & Jenrette Inc* [1990] 1 QB 391 (CA).

[24] *Distillers & Co Ltd v Thompson* [1971] AC 458 (PC).

[25] *Diamond v Bank of London and Montreal* [1979] QB 333 (CA). But for a different view in relation to negligent advice from an accountant see *Voth v Manildra Flour Mills Pty Ltd* (1990) 171 CLR 538, 568–9.

[26] *Bata v Bata* [1948] WN 366 (CA); *Gutnick v Dow Jones & Co Inc* [2002] HCA 56, (2003) CLR 575.

This is especially true when, as was found in almost every instance, the court was able to assemble the facts so that damage and the act complained of were located in a single place. In one case where this alignment was not possible, the acts (a conspiracy) could have taken place anywhere, but the intended damage could have happened only in England: the place of the damage was taken as the indicative element.[27]

The 1995 Act, reflecting Parliament's wish to protect free speech by reference to English standards, preserves the common law rules and defences for defamation, malicious falsehood, and torts, which must arise under foreign law, of a similar nature,[28] and so for these it will be necessary to determine where the cause of action arose. But it is the privilege of the claimant to plead only the facts and matters upon which he relies: if, as became increasingly common as information was accessible on the internet, he chooses to sue only in respect of reception of the statement in England, England will be where the cause of action arose.[29] The growth in libel tourism was spectacular.[30] By contrast, when the complaint extends to multinational publication of defamatory material, it appears to follow that each substantial national publication must be taken, and the law chosen for it, separately. The reason for this inconvenient result is that as a matter of English law, and in fact, each publication is a separate and distinct tort, a fresh blow to a reputation; and this principle has been relied on in the context of international defamation.[31] Even so, as the common law governs choice of law rule for defamation, its flexible exception may yet permit a marshalling of international publications into a single choice of law; and in the most egregious cases, a court may find that the English publication was so minuscule that it is an abuse of process to plead a claim which relies on English publication alone.[32]

2. CHOICE OF LAW FOR ENGLISH TORTS

Where the cause of action arose in England, English domestic law applies, alone and exclusively, and without any exception to reflect the fact that neither the parties nor the facts may have any other connection

---

[27] *Metall & Rohstoff AG v Donaldson Lufkin & Jenrette Inc* [1990] 1 QB 391 (CA).

[28] 1995 Act, s 13.

[29] *Berezovsky v Michaels* [2000] 1 WLR 1004 (HL).

[30] And pretty shameless it was too, though the antics of those involved certainly added to the gaiety of life: *King v Lewis* [2004] EWCA Civ 1329, [2005] ILPr 185; *Richardson v Schwarzenegger* [2004] EWHC 2422 (QB), on which see (2004) 75 BYIL 565.

[31] *Berezovsky v Michaels* [2000] 1 WLR 1004 (HL).

[32] *Jameel v Dow Jones & Co Inc* [2005] EWCA Civ 75, [2005] QB 946.

with England, but are wholly associated with another country.[33] True, the resultant application of English law could have been produced by the application of the double-actionability choice of law rule for foreign torts, but woven into that rule is a flexible exception, and it is this which is therefore specifically excluded from application to English torts. One can see how this is inconvenient: a defamatory statement made, for example, entirely within a delegation of foreign visitors will have no discernible impact on the English legal order, but may be enormously significant in the country of origin. If the trial nevertheless takes place in England,[34] the case for the non-application of English domestic law could hardly be higher, but on the authorities it will not succeed. A defendant applying in such a case for a stay of proceedings on the ground of *forum non conveniens* may be thought to have some chance of success, but the natural forum for an English tort is unlikely to be overseas;[35] and the defendant may have little to gain from, or little chance of,[36] giving up the right to defend in England.

3. CHOICE OF LAW FOR OVERSEAS TORTS

Where the cause of action arose in a foreign country, the rule required a claimant to show two things: that the facts would give rise to liability as a tort as a matter of English domestic law as *lex fori*, and also give[37] rise to civil[38] liability, although not necessarily in tort, under the domestic *lex loci delicti*, the law of the place where the tort occurred. This formed a rule of 'double actionability'.[39] It follows from the *lex fori* limb[40] that the only claims which can succeed are those in respect of torts known to English domestic law. Though this rule came in for criticism, and was latterly modified by the incorporation of a flexible exception,[41] it achieved two significant advantages. First, it ensured that there was a limit to the claims which could be brought before an English court. The law of tort generally

---

[33] *Metall und Rohstoff AG v Donaldson, Lufkin & Jenrette Inc* [1990] 1 QB 391 (CA).

[34] This may seem implausible, but *Berezovsky v Michaels* [2000] 1 WLR 1004 (HL) suggests that England may be an attractive place for a claimant to sue.

[35] cf ibid.

[36] The plea is inadmissible where jurisdiction is founded on a provision of the Brussels Regulation other than Art 4: Case C–281/02 *Owusu v Jackson* [2005] ECR I–1383.

[37] Not 'gave': limitation under the *lex loci delicti commissi* will bar the claim: Foreign Limitation Periods Act 1984, s 1(2).

[38] So established by *Boys v Chaplin* [1971] AC 356, and on this point overruling *Machado v Fontes* [1897] 2 QB 231 (CA), which had accepted criminal liability as sufficient to allow the action to proceed.

[39] *Boys v Chaplin* [1971] AC 356.

[40] *The Halley* (1868) LR 2 PC 193.

[41] *Red Sea Insurance Co Ltd v Bouygues SA* [1995] 1 AC 190 (PC).

imposes liability without regard to the will or intentions of the defendant, and is in this respect the dark side of the law of civil liberties. It is not
altogether unreasonable to regard English civil liberties as the benchmark
for the reception of claims otherwise arising under foreign law, especially
where there is room for flexibility.[42] Secondly, the use of English tort law
gave a foundation for the question where the tort occurred: 'the' tort must
have meant the cause of action as understood and defined by English
domestic law. The *lex loci delicti commissi* limb was originally stated in
terms of the acts not being justifiable[43] under the foreign law; this came to
be understood as asking whether the facts gave rise to civil liability under
the foreign law.[44] Taken in its two parts, the rule serves to identify which
defendant is liable, to establish which defences are available, and to limit
heads of damage recoverable, to the more restrictive of English tort law
and the civil law of the *locus delicti*. Unless the claimant can show that he
is entitled to recover under both systems he will lose. So in a defamation
claim, a defence of truth or privilege or fair comment, made out under
English law, will answer a claim even though it would not do so under the
civil law of the place where the cause of action arose; a defence under the
foreign law, say of honest belief, though unknown as such to English law,
will similarly prevail to defeat the claim.

By way of exception, if the law of some other country is more closely
connected to an issue, or even to the whole dispute, than is the *lex loci
delicti*, that law may displace the reference made to the *lex loci delicti*. It is
not clear whether this is exactly the same thing as saying that the particular law will not be applied if it has no interest in being applied to the particular facts, but both propositions have been advanced, without apparent
recognition of their difference.[45] So where two English servicemen were
involved in a traffic accident in Malta, English law displaced Maltese law
for defining the heads of recoverable damage;[46] where an English employment agency sent a labourer to work on a German construction site,
English law displaced German law on the nature and extent of the duty
of care owed by the agency.[47] Building on this principle, it was later held

---

[42] Although free recourse to public policy might have been a sufficient alternative role for
the *lex fori*.

[43] *Phillips v Eyre* (1870) LR 6 QB 1.

[44] *Boys v Chaplin* [1971] AC 356.

[45] ibid: the 'closest connection' test may point to the application of the law of a third state,
that is, neither the country of the forum nor of the place of the tort; the 'no interest in being
applied' test will simply disconnect the foreign law, leaving English law to apply by default.

[46] *Boys v Chaplin*.

[47] *Johnson v Coventry Churchill International Ltd* [1992] 3 All ER 14.

that in an appropriate case, the reference to English law as *lex fori* may be displaced in favour of a law having a much closer connection to the dispute than the *lex fori*.[48] As a result the choice of law rule may be summarized as 'double actionability with double flexibility'. But the curious thing about the exception, especially in the formulation which asks whether the foreign law has any interest in being applied to the facts, is that it is asked at all. In the Maltese case just mentioned, the view was[49] that the Maltese legislature had not intended its law to apply to the facts of such a case, and it was disapplied. The imprecise science involved in coming to any such conclusion, however, would have been unnecessary if the *lex* of the *locus delicti* were interpreted as meaning the law *including its conflicts rules*. On that basis, it would be perfectly clear whether the Maltese rule was intended to apply: one would simply ask whether the Maltese judge would have applied it had he been trying the case. The inclusion of *renvoi* in the *lex loci delicti commissi* would have achieved, at a stroke, what the exception sought to do by unreliable means. Not for the last time, an opportunity was lost.[50]

C. STATUTORY CHOICE OF LAW: PART III OF THE 1995 ACT

Part III of the 1995 Act established a new choice of law rule which applied, and until Rome II takes hold, still applies, to all other torts. The Act is expressed to apply to all issues which were, prior to 1 May 1996, governed by the common law rule of double actionability with exceptions.[51] It is necessary to identify the material scope of the 1995 Act, and then consider its choice of law rule.

I. MATERIAL SCOPE

The 1995 Act applies to torts, but without saying what it means by this.[52] It cannot be restricted to causes of action which are regarded as torts under English domestic law, for this is one half of the very rule which section 10 of the Act was enacted to abolish, so it must extend to causes of action which are in some more general sense characterized as torts. This is easier to state than to accomplish. One effect of the rule of double

---

[48] *Red Sea Insurance Co Ltd v Bouygues SA* [1995] 1 AC 190 (PC).
[49] *Boys v Chaplin* at 391–2 (Lord Wilberforce).
[50] See Briggs (1998) 47 ICLQ 877.
[51] 1995 Act, s 10.
[52] ibid s 9.

actionability was that the common law conflict of laws was never called upon to characterize a claim which was not a tort as a matter of English domestic law, for the double actionability rule ensured that every such claim simply failed. But with that benchmark gone, it is necessary to draw some lines. Claims based on the violation of privacy, or insult, unless seen as akin to defamation,[53] claims for pure economic loss resulting from negligence, or alleging the wrongful infliction of economic loss, or based on a general *actio injuriarum* and so on, all fall within the scope of the Act, on the ground that they were technically covered (not that it did the claimant any good) by the rule on double actionability. But claims for damages as a result of the breach of a statutory duty, and especially those which lie closer to public or regulatory law, may fall outside the category of torts by reason of their public law character. So claims founded on the violation of competition law, or for payments in respect of damage caused by environmental pollution, will lie closer to the edge of the rule. On the other hand, claims for treble damages under the Racketeer Influenced and Corrupt Organizations Act, and the Clayton and Sherman Acts, of United States law are considered to be torts, and subject to the argument that their application is contrary to English public policy, such claims will be possible in the English courts. It is debatable whether this is a change for the benefit of the law and litigants, for the reliable assessment of some of these foreign rights may be difficult for an English court.

But if the Act is taken seriously, problems abound, for the dismantling of the common law was not as simple as it appeared. In seeking to ascertain the scope of the Act, three particular difficulties may be observed. First, section 10 states that the Act repeals the rules on double actionability plus exceptions; and section 14(2) provides in express terms that the Act does not affect any matter which was not previously governed by the rules set out in section 10. It follows from this form of words that the Act has no application to torts committed in England. This would be an odd, and probably unintended, result, but it will take some rather muscular statutory construction, or a heroically blind eye,[54] to circumvent the plain language of the Act. True, section 9(6) provides that the Act will still apply even though events took place in England, but that is very different from establishing that the tort was committed in England; and it is in any event expressed to be subject to section 14. If the authority which established the irrelevance of double actionability to English torts were to be overruled, section 9(6) might be given the wider effect which would allow

---

[53] 1995 Act, s 13. Privacy and defamation are excluded from Rome II: Art 1(2)(g).
[54] *Roerig v Valiant Trawlers Ltd* [2002] EWCA 21, [2002] 1 WLR 2304.

the Act to apply to English torts. The legislative methodology is inept; it would have required little ingenuity to state that the Act applies to torts wherever committed if that really was what had been intended.

Secondly, as will be seen, the Act[55] directs attention to, and selects, the law of the place where the events constituting the tort occurred. This is not as easy as it seems. Read as it is written, the Act is unworkable, for until it has been decided which law, and hence which law's identification of the elements makes up the tort, no-one can say identify the elements making up the tort in the first place: one might say at this point that the chicken and the egg have come home to roost. The point is best made by illustration. Suppose an Italian claimant, in possession of promissory notes, has these impounded by an English bank on suspicion of impropriety, the notes not being returned despite its being accepted that the seizure was unwarranted.[56] If this were looked at from the standpoint of English law, there would be a claim against the bank for conversion, most of the elements of which took place in England. But from the standpoint of Italian law, the elements of the delict of *injuria* committed by the bank, by which the patrimonial estate of the claimant was diminished, were mostly located in Italy. The two torts are constructed differently, and to choose the law of the place where the elements of 'the' tort occurred is irrational. It cannot be right to frame the answer in terms of the English tort, for when there is none, the claimant would necessarily lose, and it would be found that the first limb of the double actionability rule had risen from the deep. Equally, there is no particular reason to prefer the Italian over the English analysis, because Italy may not be the place where the elements of 'the' tort occurred. This may not be crucial if both ways of formulating the claim would lead to recovery in the same measure, but if the claimant would win in one but not the other, what is the outcome to be? Is the claimant entitled to cast around for whichever of the possible formulations would benefit him, and rely on that law alone? There is some authority for the view that he may: that the court looks as the facts and matters pleaded as establishing the claimant's cause of action, and asks where these had their centre of gravity.[57] It is hard to see the wisdom in that.

Thirdly, it is unclear if the Act applies to claims which may be tortious under some systems of law, but which have been characterized differently

[55] 1995 Act, s 11.
[56] cf Case C–364/93 *Marinari v Lloyd's Bank plc* [1995] ECR I–2719.
[57] *Trafigura Beheer BV v Kookmin Bank Co* [2006] EWHC 1450 (Comm), [2006] 2 Lloyd's Rep 455.

in English private international law. There is authority for the view that claims alleging the wrongs of breach of confidence or dishonest assistance in another's breach of trust, and other breaches of equitable duty were not governed by the rule of double actionability,[58] even though they resembled torts; nor were claims for contribution, nor restitutionary claims, such as for knowing receipt of trust property, which did not look like torts.[59] If these may nevertheless be torts under a potentially-applicable foreign law, it is uncertain whether their prior or potential non-tortious characterization under common law makes the 1995 Act inapplicable to them, leaving them governed by other law choice of law rules. In the brightening light of Rome II, it is probable that the question will be able to remain unanswered; but for all that, it is an odd way to have gone about law reform.

2. CHOICE OF LAW: GENERAL RULE

According to section 11, if all the events constituting the tort occur in one country, the law of that country applies to the claim. But if the events are less conveniently grouped, a claim in respect of death or personal injury (including disease, or impairment of physical or mental condition) is in the first instance governed by the law of the place where the victim was when killed or injured;[60] a claim in respect of property damage by the law of the place where the property was when damaged;[61] and any other case by the law of the country in which the most significant element or elements of the events constituting the tort occurred.[62]

Personal injury includes psychiatric trauma or nervous shock; but a cause of action for bereavement on death appears to be governed by the law of the place where the deceased was killed, rather than the place where the claimant was when bereaved. Where the damage manifests itself long after and far away from the place where the rot set in, such as where asbestosis is diagnosed decades after the inhalation of fibres, it appears that a claim for personal injury will generally be governed by the law of the place of inhalation, but a claim brought in respect of death will be governed by the law of the place where the victim died. If either of these leads to an

---

[58] In so far as they were characterized as equitable or restitutionary obligations they had their own choice of law rule: and see, ch 7 below.

[59] For example, *Arab Monetary Fund v Hashim (No 9)* [1994] TLR 502 made some use of the rule of double actionability in relation to a claim for dishonestly assisting a breach of trust, this was not on the basis that the claim was one in tort.

[60] 1995 Act, s 11(2)(a).

[61] ibid s 11(2)(b).

[62] ibid s 11(2)(c).

arbitrary or unsatisfactory result, the rule of displacement in section 12 will be available as a corrective. Damage to property appears to exclude the loss of property, for example by theft or conversion; it works well for tangible property, but less clearly for intangibles. It does not appear to extend to cases of pure economic loss, unless this can be seen as damage to intangible property, which does not seem likely; although if a foreign law takes the view that the gist of the tort is one of damage to the patrimony of the claimant, the position is less clear. The infringement of intellectual property rights, although regarded as a tort, is not usually thought of as resulting in property damage, though it may be argued that this is exactly what an infringer does to the intellectual property of the claimant. And it is outside the cases of personal injury and property damage that the problems of definition of 'tort', examined above, will most usually arise, where the analysis for choice of law requires the elements of the events constituting the tort to be identified before it is possible to identify the applicable law by which they will be defined.

Some say that section 11 enacts a *lex loci delicti* choice of law rule.[63] It does no such thing. Had the Act sought to apply the *lex loci delicti commissi* as the choice of law rule, the point of departure would have asked where in substance the cause of action arose. Whatever section 11 does do, it does not do this. Where all elements of the tort are grouped in the one place, any rational test for the general choice of law will give the same answer; it is no more a *lex loci delicti* rule than it is a place of damage rule, or a place of the act rule, or even a proper law of the tort rule. But where the events are not concentrated in that one place, it is neither necessary nor helpful to inquire into the place of the tort. The Law Commission, whose report and draft bill provided the basis for the 1995 Act, was explicit in its view that the *locus delicti* is too often artificial, a legal fiction, to be defended as the basis for a choice of law rule.[64] Instead, the methodology adopted by the Act was to provide a simple, although sometimes arbitrary, rule, and to allow its displacement whenever necessary. Old authorities which seek to define the place of the tort should really be of no assistance in the application of the general rule provided by the 1995 Act; and the result is that the 1995 Act departed from the choice of law rule which operates throughout almost the whole of the world.

---

[63] Dicey, para 35–014.
[64] Law Commission Report No 193, *Private International Law: Choice of Law in Tort and Delict* (1990), paras 3.6, 3.10.

3. CHOICE OF LAW: DISPLACEMENT OF THE
GENERAL RULE

Following the tradition of the common law, section 12 invites the making of a comparison between the factors which connect the tort with the country whose law was ascertained by the general rule in section 11 and the factors which connect it with another country. If it is substantially more appropriate to apply the law of the latter, this will displace the former law in relation to the claim or in relation to any individual issue, as the case may be: the points of connection are to countries, but the question of appropriateness is answered in terms of a law. So in a case like *Boys v Chaplin*[65] it would be substantially more appropriate to apply English law, and not Maltese law, to the issue of general damages, for this issue is closely connected to England, where the injured party will be living and the defendant paying, and it has no impact at all on the state of Malta. It would be different if the defendant were Maltese, not least because any insurance which he may have taken out will presumably have been undertaken with an eye to Maltese law and levels of liability. More problematic is the case in which the facts are just as unconnected to Malta, but the parties are from different countries, the law of each differing from Maltese law and allowing the recovery of damages for pain and suffering. On the face of it, section 12 works on the basis of a bipolar comparison only, and does not allow a more complex analysis to indicate the irrelevance of the law applicable by virtue of the general rule; in this respect it follows the pattern of the geographical 'centre of gravity' exception of the common law, and does not apparently support the interest analysis reasoning.

Section 12 does not appear to permit displacement in favour of the law which governs a contract by which the parties were bound, and in relation to which the tort arose, for it looks at connections to a country rather than a law.[66] But this would be impossible to defend, and the courts have taken the robust view that, especially where the parties have chosen a law to govern their contractual relationship a concurrent tort, in all probability, will be governed by the *lex contractus*. The result is entirely sound, but the reasoning, that a connection to the *lex contractus* is a connection to the country whose law that is, has to be taken with a pinch of salt.[67]

---

[65] [1971] AC 356; *Edmunds v Simmonds* [2001] 1 WLR 1003 (two English friends, accident in Spain in a hired car; English displaced Spanish as the applicable law).

[66] Dr North, Law Commissioner responsible for the first part of the project, was in no doubt that this was the effect of s 12, and he was not impressed.

[67] *Morin v Bonhams & Brooks Ltd* [2003] EWCA Civ 1802, [2004] 1 Lloyd's Rep 702; *Trafigura Beheer BV v Kookmin Bank Co* [2006] EWHC 1450 (Comm), [2006] 2 Lloyd's Rep 455.

4. CHOICE OF LAW: EXCLUSION OF CERTAIN LAWS

Section 14 makes clear that the Act does not authorize the enforcement of foreign penal or revenue or other public laws, nor of any foreign law whose enforcement would conflict with public policy, nor of any foreign law which would prevent a matter of procedure being governed by English law; and it does not override the application of a rule of English law which is otherwise mandatory. In this respect it enacts what the common law had always provided, but the reference to other public laws is a novelty, and if at some later stage it is held that there is no such category of exclusion at common law, the legislation will to that extent be ineffective.

Section 14 was read by the House of Lords as meaning that the quantification of damages remained unaffected by the legislative changes to choice of law, on the ground that it was a matter of procedure.[68] This was accurate enough; but it also went on to say that the classification as procedural was established and set in stone by the Act, which seems to be a fundamental misreading of the statute and the intention of Parliament. The statute does say that nothing in it shall affect a question of procedure; it is astounding to read this as saying that the statute affects all questions of procedure by eliminating the possibility of their future judicial development. There was no need for such a decision, unless one attributes it to the fact that English law assessed the damages recoverable by the claimant for his quadriplegia at something in excess of ten times the sum recoverable under the law of the place where he was when injured. Hard cases do sometimes make bad law; but when this scheme for choice of law is displaced by the Rome II Regulation, the *lex delicti* will apply to the assessment of damages.[69]

5. CONTRACTUAL DEFENCES TO CLAIMS FRAMED AS TORTS

Where a defendant relies on a contractual promise that the claimant will not bring the action, a preliminary distinction must be drawn.[70] The question whether a valid contractual promise may be admitted as a defence to a claim in tort will be governed by the *lex delicti*. After all, a defence of *volenti* is governed by the *lex delicti*, and *volenti* and a contractual promise

---

[68] *Harding v Wealands* [2006] UKHL 32, [2007] 2 AC 1.
[69] Subject to the application of English public policy if the rule of the *lex delicti* is manifestly incompatible with it: Art 26.
[70] For common law, see *Sayers v International Drilling Co NV* [1971] 1 WLR 1176 (CA).

not to sue are two species of the same genus. But whether a binding contractual promise was made, as distinct from whether it serves as a defence if intrinsically valid, is a matter for the *lex contractus*. Quite apart from the common law logic of this, the answer is dictated by the 1995 Act: the validity of a contract has its own choice of law rule and was not, on the coming into force of the 1995 Act, governed by the rule of double actionability.[71] Take the example of a workplace injury, the contract of employment containing an undertaking not to sue the employer but to participate in a scheme of insurance. Suppose the contract was governed by Saudi law, and that both the contract in general and the insurance provision in particular were valid and enforceable under Saudi law. This, subject to one proviso, establishes the intrinsic validity of the contractual defence (if it is not valid by its governing law, it will be disregarded). The proviso is that if a mandatory rule of English law strikes down such a term even in a foreign contract, this will be applied by virtue of the Rome Convention, Article 7(2).

But assuming the promise is validated by the contract choice of law rules, whether it will be admitted as a defence to the claim in tort is a matter for the law governing the tort. This will mean the law identified by section 11, subject to the possibility that the admissibility of a contractual promise not to sue may be more appropriately referred by section 12 to the law governing the contract. On the other hand, it may be contended that where the claim is brought between parties to a contract (say) of employment, the entire issue of liability and defence to liability may be contractual, with the result that the defence is one to a contractual action. The reasoning to support this would be that the entire claim is within the scope of the Rome Convention, as it seeks to enforce obligations freely entered into in relation to another, and the Convention provides that the *lex contractus* shall apply to all such obligations. In an unexpected way, this echoes a view of Lord Denning MR, to the effect that it was not appropriate to have a choice of law rule for claim and another for defence; it was preferable to have a unitary choice of law rule for such cases.[72] It is not yet supported by authority.[73] Alternatively, section 12 of the 1995 Act could produce this result, on the footing that where a tort is committed within the context of a contractual relationship, it is substantially more appropriate—not least because this may be what the parties would have

---

[71] 1995 Act, s 14(2).

[72] *Sayers v International Drilling Co NV* [1971] 1 WLR 1176 (CA).

[73] In particular, *Base Metal Trading Co v Shamurin* [2004] EWCA Civ 1316, [2005] 1 WLR 1157 does not support it.

intended,[74] and may have insured against—to apply the law governing the contract to the entire question of liability.

D. CHOICE OF LAW: REGULATION (EC) 864/2007

The Rome II Regulation represents the future of choice of law across the courts of Europe. The scheme of the Regulation is to define its material and temporal scope; to establish a general rule to which a general exception may be made. It then makes specific provision for choice of law in relation to a number of specific torts or kinds of tort. It then extends its scope to certain issues not usually seen as torts, at least in the common law, but for which the Regulation provides the statutory choice of law rule. It respects the general rule of freedom to choose the law to govern the relationship or claim. It then deals with a number of minor and consequential issues; and then it excludes *renvoi*.[75]

I. SCOPE OF THE REGULATION

The Regulation defines its own scope in material and temporal terms. As to the former, it applies to what it defines as non-contractual obligations in civil and commercial matters,[76] whether they have arisen or are likely to arise.[77] Excluded from this general statement of material scope are revenue, customs and administrative matters, and the liability of the state for acts *iure imperii*.[78] Also excluded are obligations arising out of family and comparable relationships; matrimonial property regimes, bills of exchange, cheques and promissory notes; aspects of the law of companies; the relationships created by a trust; nuclear damage; and 'violations of privacy and rights relating to personality, including defamation'.[79] Nor does the Regulation apply to evidence and procedure.[80] It defines damage, a term which is central to the general rule on choice of law, as 'any

---

[74] Especially where the choice of law has been expressed. *Morin v Bonhams & Brooks Ltd* [2003] EWCA Civ 1802, [2004] 1 Lloyd's Rep 702; *Trafigura Beheer BV v Kookmin Bank Co* [2006] EWHC 1450 (Comm), [2006] 2 Lloyd's Rep 455.

[75] Article 24; presumably the single market simply could not cope with such sophistication.

[76] Article 1(1).

[77] Article 2(2).

[78] Article 1(1).

[79] All by Art 1(2). The list treads in the footsteps of Rome Convention, Art 1(2).

[80] Article 1(3). This will include rules about the proof of foreign law, although a review of this aspect of the Regulation will be conducted and presented by 20 August 2011: Art 30(1)(i), and Commission Statement accompanying the Regulation.

consequence arising out of tort/delict, unjust enrichment, *negotiorum gestio* or *culpa in contrahendo*, whether that damage has occurred or is likely to occur'.[81] And the law which is identified by the Regulation is to be applied whether or not it is the law of a Member State.[82]

The definition non-contractual obligations will, no doubt, be understood autonomously, but a plausible starting point will be to include all obligations which bind a defendant and which are not contractual in the sense in which that expression is used in the Brussels Regulation. No question will arise of identifying a category of obligation which is neither contractual nor tortious, for the material scope of Rome II only asks whether the obligation is contractual or non-contractual; equitable obligations will be contractual or non-contractual; there is no *tertium quid*. There will, however, be room for disagreement where obligations slide into the law of property. For example, in English domestic law, a defendant who has purloined another's tangible property is sued in tort, even if the remedy sought is delivery up. The circumstances in which equity deals with someone it finds to be a wrongdoer by charging his property, or subjecting it to a trust, defy trouble-free allocation to mutually exclusive categories of obligation claim or property claim. None of that, however, calls into the question the rightness of the definition of the scope of the Rome II Regulation. There is obviously no textual warrant for confining Rome II to obligations which lead to damage, or which are based in some narrower sense on wrongdoing.[83] It is not clear whether this will lead to a reinterpretation of the relationship between Article 5(1) and (3) of the Brussels Regulation, but a sense of coherence within the developing pan-European scheme of private international law would justify it, even if there is something ahistorical about doing so.

The Regulation applies to a number of specific types of obligation which, to an English mind, are not thought of as torts. Claims based on the principle of unjust enrichment,[84] and *negotiorum gestio*[85] (beneficial intervention in the affairs of another) are dealt with in the following chapter, on the basis that until the Rome II Regulation has wholly displaced the common law principles of choice of law, equitable and unjust enrichment claims are better studied separately from the choice of law regimes for contractual and tort clams. But this will be the last edition of this book for which this is appropriate: for the next edition of this book, Chapter 6 will deal with non-contractual obligations, and Chapter 7 will lose its

---

[81] Article 2.
[82] Article 3.
[83] cf p 81, above.
[84] Article 10.
[85] Article 11.

separate identity. Rome II also applies to *culpa in contrahendo*, that is, non-contractual obligations arising out of dealings prior to the conclusion of a contract, regardless of whether the contract is actually concluded.[86] This had the potential to make the law very difficult indeed, for pre-contractual misrepresentation, non-disclosure, duress, undue influence, etc, which may justify the rescission or avoidance of a contract, were usually thought of as contractual. But as the Regulation provides that all such matters shall be governed by the law which applies to the contract, or which would have done if the contract had been concluded, little or nothing will turn on whether the issue is dealt with by the Rome Convention or by Rome II.

The applicable law applies very broadly, and certainly more broadly than the substantive law identified by the 1995 Act does. According to Article 15, it extends to the nature and extent of liability, including vicarious liability; the grounds of exemption from liability and limitation and division of liability; existence, nature and assessment of damages,[87] the transfer of a right to damages, the question of who may obtain damages for loss sustained personally; liability for the acts of another;[88] and limitation and prescription.[89] It also applies to presumptions and the burden of proof.[90]

The material dates which define the scope of the Regulation are puzzling at first sight, but clear enough to understand. Although the Regulation shall apply (*sc.* to a court hearing a case) on and after 11 January 2009, its provisions apply (ie as the rule for choice of law) to events taking place on and after 20 August 2007, that is, on the twentieth day following the date of publication in the *Official Journal*.[91]

2. GENERAL RULE FOR CHOICE OF LAW, GENERAL EXCEPTIONS, AND CHOICE OF LAW

The general rule for choice of law is to apply the law of the country in which the damage occurs. No attention is paid to the place of the event giving rise to it, or to the place where the indirect consequences of that

---

[86] Article 12.

[87] This must see off the proposition that the assessment of damages is a procedural matter (*Harding v Wealands* [2006] UKHL 32, [2007] 2 AC 1), notwithstanding Art 1(3).

[88] Although the exclusion of certain aspects of the law of companies will diminish the scope of this.

[89] Article 15.

[90] Article 22.

[91] Articles 32 and 31, respectively: see Art 254(1) EC.

damage occur. In this respect, the choice of law rule reflects an aspect of the choice of law rule in the 1995 Act, in focusing on the geography of the damage and eschewing any concern to ascribe a place to the tort. It also reflects the approach taken by the Brussels Regulation to special jurisdiction under Article 5(3), where the place where the damage *occurs*, as distinct from the place where it *is suffered or ramifies*, is the material place. Article 4(1) of Rome II does not expressly state that the damage is that which arises directly from the tort, but will be read as though it did do so.

The law identified by Article 4(1) may be displaced by Articles 4 and 14. According to Article 4(2), where both parties are habitually resident in the same country when the damage occurs, the law of that country shall apply. According to Article 4(3), when it is clear from the circumstances of the case that the tort is manifestly more closely connected with a country other than that identified by Article 4(1) or (2), the law of that country shall apply instead. A manifestly closer connection may be based on a prior relationship, such as a contract that is closely connected to the tort in question. This provision reflects the truth that exceptions are appropriate where there is a manifestly closer relationship to something other than the answer given by the general rule. Indeed, the mystery of the position to which Canada and Australia have allowed themselves to be drawn is that where there is a manifestly closer connection, the courts of those countries are required to ignore it, an outcome which seems implausible and undesirable. The effect of Rome II ought to be that there is little scope for a party to a contract to choose to frame a claim in tort and hope by doing so to evade the choice of law rule which the Rome Convention prescribes for the contractual relationship. There may be odd cases in which Article 4(3) will not apply the *lex contractus* to the associated tort claim, but they will be few. The problem created by a claimant's right to choose the choice of law is receding fast.

Quite apart from that, Article 14 allows the parties to choose the law to govern the non-contractual obligation if either they are commercial actors who negotiate such an agreement freely, or they do so after the occurrence of the event giving rise to the damage.[92] Although there is probably room for argument about how unconstrained negotiation has to be to qualify as free, this is an eminently sensible development. The only mystery is why Parliament was so resistant to the idea in 1995, and we shall probably never know. The power to make such an agreement on choice of law comes with mild anti-avoidance provisions; but the general principle for

---

[92] Article 14.

which Article 14 stands will prevent the argument of a party who admits that the *lex contractus* is thus-and-so, but that it is inapplicable to a claim formulated as one in tort, which is just as it should be.

3. PARTICULAR KINDS OF CLAIM

The Regulation sets out, in Articles 5–9, specific choice of law rules, or specific partial choice of law rules for certain kinds of tort claim: for product liability, unfair competition, environmental damage, infringement of intellectual property rights, and industrial action. The rules are detailed and, so far as their subject matter is concerned, are something of a novelty for English private international law. They do reflect the view, considered at the start of this chapter, that the range of claims making up the private international law of tort is just too diverse for a monolithic choice of law rule to be sensible.

4. MANDATORY LAWS AND PUBLIC POLICY

In three instances, the law otherwise applicable is subjected to mandatory laws of a different system. Mandatory laws of the forum will apply. Provisions of European law, which may have been translated into domestic law will not be prevented from applying by choice of law of a non-Member State if all the elements relevant to the situation were located in Member States. And where all the elements of a situation were located in a single Member State, a choice of law by the parties shall not prejudice the application of the mandatory laws of that Member State. It is hard to find fault with that.

The application of any law identified by the Regulation may be refused if the application would be manifestly contrary to the public policy of the forum.[93]

---

[93] Article 26.

7

Other Obligations

A. GENERAL

If one were unsentimental about it, this chapter would not be here at all. There are two reasons for that. The first is that the material with which it deals, restitution and unjust enrichment, and equitable obligations, are at best doubtful tools with which to make sense of private international law. If they are given a role as characterization categories, with choice of law rule attached, they add complication, and suggest that there are even more dividing lines to be drawn than there already are. This is justifiable only if it is necessary; Occam's razor is an important part of the private international lawyer's toolkit, and this is where it comes into its own. Even so, recent case-law has thrown up a significant number of cases which, if the facts were wholly domestic, would be about unjust enrichment or concerned with equitable doctrines and remedies, and the proper analysis of such matters when the facts and are not wholly domestic needs to be explained to be understood. Even if the conclusion is that there is no distinct choice of law rule, tailor-made for these issues, the way in which that conclusion is arrived at is important in understanding the working of common law private international law. The second reason is that when the conflict of laws is finally overtaken by the Rome II Regulation,[1] choice of law for obligations will divide into contractual[2] and non-contractual and very little indeed will remain outside it.[3] The proper autonomous definition of these two categories will take no account of the peculiar sources and divisions of the common law, the terms of which will have no practical significance for choice of law. Even so, we are not there yet; and it remains important to understand how the law dealt, and should have dealt, with issues of unjust enrichment, restitution, and equitable doctrine when the facts have a foreign element to them.

---

[1] Regulation (EC) 864/2007.
[2] Governed by the Rome Convention.
[3] Only those matters excluded by Art 1(2) from the Rome Convention and from the Rome II Regulation.

As a matter of English domestic law, contracts and torts are not the only sources of enforceable right and duty, or obligation. Restitutionary obligations are now generally acknowledged to have an independent juridical basis, resting on the slightly shaky foundation of the principle against getting away with unjust enrichment.[4] Although there is considerable uncertainty about what falls within it, there is authority for the view that there is a choice of law rule, or rules, for restitutionary claims or, which is to say the same thing, that there is a characterization category with the label 'restitution' or 'unjust enrichment' stuck to it.[5] As a matter of domestic law, equitable obligations spring from a distinct historical origin, and remnants of this ancestry cast a flickering shadow on the plane of private international law. But it is unclear whether this distinctiveness—domestic, jurisdictional, and historical—really ought to be reflected in English private international law. Moreover, there is doubt about the methodology employed when equity collides with the conflict of laws. For rather than characterizing issues and choosing a law, in the ordinary way, some cases simply allow a claimant to rely on domestic English equity, albeit that this will be tweaked to make some allowance for the presence of foreign connections in the matrix. If this is indeed the way to proceed, there would appear to be little opportunity to rely on a foreign cause of action framed along similar lines. Despite the pervasive character of equity, and despite the fact that the Chancery Division and Commercial Court appear to spend a fair amount of their time handling litigation against international frauds and fraudsters, the law is in a state of arrested or retarded development; and where it exists at all, it can be very difficult to comprehend.

The difficulty is compounded by the fact that courts and scholars have failed to reach a consensus on the fundamental nature of these two areas of English domestic law. Within restitution, a state of continual intellectual uproar prevails, and domestic law causes of action are regarded and disregarded as restitutionary with unsettling rapidity.[6] There appears to be some overlap with the domains of contract and tort, which is not itself unprecedented in the common law.[7] This will tend only to increase, as

[4] This book does not seek to explain the theology of the relationship between restitution and unjust enrichment which, if it has any content, is material only within domestic law.

[5] As a matter of fact, stuck over the original label which said 'Quasi-contract', see p 210, below.

[6] The manner in which and ferocity with which the various schools of thought denounce each other's heresies is reminiscent of extreme-left politics in the 1970s. It has a nostalgia value all its own.

[7] The existence of overlapping causes of action in contract and tort is permissible and not uncommon: see eg *Henderson v Merrett Syndicates Ltd* [1995] 2 AC 145; and it is contrary to

remedies for breach of contract stray further from the limiting principle of compensation for loss, and share with the law of restitution the task of separating ill-gotten gains from the person who obtained them.[8] But there is also unease in the relationship with the law of property, as the development and use of the constructive trust continue to blur the line of demarcation which separates, or ought to separate, vindication of one's property from remedial awards against another's property. This domestic instability is reflected in the emerging rules of private international law. The fault is not entirely that of the domestic law, though: a clear and principled approach to characterization is a prerequisite to getting the ground rules straight, and characterization is not something on which the English conflict of laws has tended to spend as much time as it should.[9]

When one turns to equity, the problems are similar but worse. For whereas restitution may overlap a little with contract and tort and property, equity pervades all three. Equity does provide distinctive remedies in aid of other causes of action when acting in its 'auxiliary jurisdiction', that is, when it acts in aid of legal rights. But it also fashions causes of action in its 'exclusive jurisdiction', where no legal right is involved, but by using material and scientific concepts which are also used, if not in identical ways, by the common law. Now if all equity could be regarded as being no more than remedial law, or as procedural law, it could be fitted, *holus bolus*, into an existing (if somewhat unsatisfactory[10]) characterization category. But this is not possible, for most of equity is substantive and is not remedial. A variant upon this would be to develop a new characterization category for equitable issues. But it would need to be internally coherent, and to have a rational choice of law rule attached to it. It is very doubtful indeed that the bare fact of a common and ancient origin in the Court of Chancery[11] makes modern equity a coherent characterization category to which private international law can properly attach a uniform choice of law rule. A different view might be that 'equity' should be regarded as a meaningless expression within the conflict of laws (rather as is the arcane domestic law distinction between realty and personalty[12]), and the issues

common law principle to suppose that this is not also reflected in the relationship between restitution and other common law causes of action.

[8] *AG v Blake* [2001] 1 AC 268.

[9] See Dicey, para 2–006. *Raiffeisien Zentralbank Österreich AG v Five Star Trading LLC* [2001] EWCA Civ 68, [2001] Ch 826 is, however, a step in the right direction.

[10] cf *Harding v Wealands* [2006] UKHL 32, [2007] 2 AC 1.

[11] Or reverential statement in a doctrinal work such as Snell's *Equity* (31st edn, 2000), or Meagher Gummow & Lehane, *Equity: Doctrines and Remedies* (4th edn, 2002).

[12] *Re Berchtold* [1923] 1 Ch 112; *Re Cutcliffe* [1940] Ch 565.

which make up an equity textbook be split up and parcelled out between existing characterization categories. This would be a manageable solution, but save for one major academic study,[13] it has not really happened yet. The analysis which is put forward here is therefore one which will try to make sense of such sparse material as exists, and which attempts to propose a simple and pragmatic framework for the development of private international law. But it is not the only view which may legitimately be held. And in 2009 it will be, so far as England is concerned, little more than history.

1. JURISDICTION OVER UNJUST ENRICHMENT AND EQUITABLE CLAIMS

The difficulty which accompanies the choice of law issues makes it appropriate to mention jurisdictional issues only briefly. For restitutionary claims, those which arise in civil or commercial matters and fall within the domain of the Brussels Regulation,[14] the main question is whether any basis for special jurisdiction is provided by Article 5, for if not, a claimant may well be confined to suing where the defendant is domiciled. If the restitutionary claim arises out of a contract, that is to say, there was, or is alleged to be, an obligation freely entered into with regard to another, the fact that the court finds the alleged contract to be ineffective will not mean that the consequential restitutionary claim falls outside Article 5(1).[15] But if at the outset the parties agree that there was no enforceable agreement of any kind, and that this is why the claim now arises, it may not fall within Article 5(1).[16] If the claim arises out of a wrong, it will fall within Article 5(3), and it should not matter whether the relief sought is assessed by reference to losses or gains as long as the legal basis for liability is, in some sense of the word, wrongdoing. If this served as a limitation on the scope of Article 5(3), it is arguable that the coming into force of the Rome II Regulation will lead to a reinterpretation of Article 5(3) to cover non-contractual obligations within the material scope of that instrument, whether or not seen as based on wrongdoing. Cases which do not fall within these loose definitions will not be eligible for special jurisdiction under Article 5. The same principles will apply to equitable claims. In cases which fall to be dealt with under traditional jurisdictional rules, CPR Part 6 makes particular provision for some forms of restitutionary

---

[13] Yeo, *Choice of Law for Equitable Doctrines* (2004).
[14] Regulation (EC) 44/2001, [2001] OJ L12/1.
[15] *Agnew v Länsförsäkringsbolagens AB* [2001] 1 AC 223.
[16] *Kleinwort Benson plc v Glasgow City Council* [1999] 1 AC 153.

claim, but otherwise such actions may be accommodated within a paragraph which is not specifically dedicated to them.

B. RESTITUTIONARY CLAIMS

1. CHOICE OF LAW ACCORDING TO
THE COMMON LAW

On the footing that there is a characterization category for restitutionary claims, which may overlap with contract or tort,[17] it has to be mapped by using positive and negative indicators. As with all characterization categories, the point of departure is that of restitution as a term of art in English domestic law. Despite the judicial observation[18] that 'the receipt-based restitutionary claim' may not be appropriate for use in the construction of a characterization category, Dicey has long stated a choice of law rule for claims which are based on unjust or unjustified enrichment, *enrichissement sans cause*, and so on. If the cause of action in English domestic law is not precisely the same as its foreign law counterparts, that is not significant, for our task is to define a characterization category, not to elevate domestic law, entire and intact, onto the celestial plane of private international law. We may take as our point of departure that restitution is identified by a receipt which unjustly enriches the defendant at the expense of the claimant. The cause of action focuses on the enrichment or gain rather than on any distinct assessment of loss; and if the enrichment is justified by the laws of contract or of property, there is no basis for advancing a claim. In other words, it is enrichment *sine justa causa* which provides the basis for recovery.

Assuming the existence of a distinct category of issues, an attempt to describe the relationship to other causes of action can now be made. There may well be points of overlap. The pragmatic response to this is not to seek to define those characterization categories with such intricate precision that there is no overlap between them, but to develop choice of law rules which ensure that a single choice of law applies in the area of overlap, no matter how the claim is characterized. As regards contract, if the contract rules lead to the conclusion that a supposed contract was void or otherwise ineffective, any recovery action brought as a consequence cannot be derived from the contract and must therefore be restitutionary. As regards tort, if the victim of a tort elects not to sue for damages on account of the

---

[17] Whether it overlaps with equity is best left until choice of law for equitable claims has been examined.

[18] Auld LJ in *Macmillan Inc v Bishopsgate Investment Trust plc (No 3)* [1996] 1 WLR 387 (CA).

loss he sustained, but 'waives the tort' and pursues the profit made by the tortfeasor, the claim is restitutionary, because it is gain-based, not loss-based.[19] As regards trusts, if the claimant is a beneficiary of a completely constituted trust, a claim to enforce his rights will be governed by the rules on trusts. But a claim to have the defendant placed under fiduciary obligations as a response to her unjust enrichment is restitutionary. As regards property, a claim to vindicate that which one owns is governed by the choice of law rules for the particular type of property. But if the claimant seeks to have the defendant dealt with as though she were holding the property of the claimant, the claim may be restitutionary. And in general, if the claim is founded on an obligation owed to the claimant which is neither contractual nor tortious, in the conflicts sense, nor is founded on an existing proprietary right—always bearing in mind that these terms are given a broad construction for the purposes of characterization—it should, *faute de mieux* if not otherwise, be regarded as restitutionary. So a claim for reimbursement for intervening in another's affairs, or *negotiorum gestio*, say by putting out a fire on your neighbour's land or for discharging another's debt by paying off her creditor who was threatening to seize her goods, would be regarded as restitutionary. This may not be the most intellectually satisfying of definitions (indeed, it may not even be a definition at all), but it appears to describe much of the territory which could be considered to fall within the scope of the characterization category and rule.

Many proposals have been made for the choice of law rule to govern restitutionary claims, but none has been found to be particularly convincing. All agree that the starting point is to look to the proper law of the obligation to make restitution, but there is less agreement whether one can go further than this.[20] The balance of academic authority[21] suggests that where there was a contract between the parties, its law should govern any obligation to make restitution, but that outside this context[22] the most frequent contender is the law of the place where the enrichment[23] occurred. As an alternative, it can be suggested that the issue should be

---

[19] This view focuses on the remedy rather than on the absence of fault, for tort claims founded on strict liability are also independent of fault.

[20] See generally Bird, 'Choice of Law' in Rose (ed), *Restitution and the Conflict of Laws* (1995).

[21] Dicey, Rule 230.

[22] And disregarding restitution in relation to land, which will be governed by the *lex situs* of the land.

[23] There is also some academic support for the place of the impoverishment, presumably on the basis that this is even closer to the law which applies in the case of torts. But it has not been promoted in England, and may well be very hard to apply in practice.

governed by the law which established that the enrichment was unjust; the law under which the contract was shown to be invalid; the law which established that there was a tort; the law which established that the defendant had behaved unconscionably; and so on. This is more promising, for it accepts that there may be different laws to be applied in different types of case, and does not pretend that one rule will necessarily fit all claims. But this too can be criticized: the law which killed the contract may be that of the defendant's habitual residence,[24] or the law of the place where it was made,[25] which may have a small connection to the facts of the case; or there may be several laws which invalidate the contract, such as where there is a failure to comply with the formalities required by any of the available laws,[26] or a combination of laws which determined that there was a tort.[27] The law which establishes that the defendant has behaved unconscionably may be the *lex fori*, and there is little reason to make a bad choice of law rule bigger.

As indicated at the beginning of this section above, the answer supported by academic authority is to choose the proper law of the obligation to make restitution.[28] It is faithful to the tradition of English private international law to accept that the right to reverse an unjust enrichment is governed by the law with which the obligation has its closest and most real connection: so loose and general a formulation can hardly ever generate a solution which is wrong in principle.[29] Dicey's original statement of the rule was by importing the rule for quasi-contractual claims which had been stated in the Restatement of the Conflict of Laws.[30] This explains why the 'proper law' formulation made sense: the basic model for quasi-contractual claims was the model for contractual claims. It is less clear that it remains as helpful when one moves away from contractual-ish relationships into the other territory of the principle against unjust enrichment,[31]

---

[24] Contracts (Applicable Law) Act 1990, Sch 1, Art 11.

[25] ibid Art 9.

[26] ibid.

[27] The *lex deliciti*, and the governing law of the contract in which it was alleged that there was a promise not to sue, will be a frequent pairing.

[28] Dicey, Rule 230.

[29] The analogy is therefore with the approach taken to contracts, transfers of intangibles, where the proper law was dominant. If an analogy were sought with the law of tort it would be more oriented towards the law of the place where the obligation to make restitution arose and this, perhaps, supports the case for the law of the place where the enrichment occurred, and (presumably) should have been reversed.

[30] American Law Institute (1934). For this history, see *Barros Mattos Jr v Macdaniels* [2005] EWHC 1323 (Ch), [2005] ILPr 630.

[31] *Arab Monetary Fund v Hashim* [1996] 1 Lloyd's Rep 589 (CA); *Macmillan Inc v Bishopsgate Investment Trust plc (No 3)* [1996] 1 WLR 387 (CA).

for the notion of a proper law is then harder to explain. There is some support for a tripartite sub-division, into cases connected to a contract (the *lex contractus*), cases connected with land (the *lex situs*), and all others (the law of the place of the enrichment).[32] The first two are obvious enough. The last of these may be justified on the footing that the event which gives rise to the obligation to make restitution is the receipt or the enrichment, and the law of the place where this happened is best placed to determine whether and on what terms it should be reversed. But there are formidable drawbacks to adopting a rule drawn in such terms. The private international law of contract abandoned a 'law of the place where...' rule over a century ago,[33] presumably on the basis that it did not produce a rational solution. The law of the place of an event is prominent in the tort choice of law rule, but the facts which make up the commission of a tort will have more of a physical connection to the place of its occurrence than the facts making up the enrichment ever have to its. This is all the more true when enrichment may take the form of electronic debiting and crediting of bank accounts, which process lacks any intelligible location; it happens, but it does not happen anywhere in particular. The law of the place of enrichment is, in truth, insupportable. It would make more sense to sub-divide within the general principle of the proper law rule, but along different lines. This would separate cases where there was between the parties a prior legal relationship having its own choice of law rule from cases where there was not. The rightness of this cannot be derived from the few decided cases, but it is not contradicted by them either and, as it is hoped, may be shown to have inherent advantages over a rule expressed in more general or abstract terms. It is also inevitable, in the present stage of the law's development, that it should be expressed as a general rule, and not as a rigid one.

(a) Unjust enrichment within prior relationships

Where there was or is a prior relationship between claimant and defendant, which has its own choice of law rule, and from or in connection with which the claim arose, the law governing the restitutionary obligation (relational restitution) to restore the benefit will be overshadowed, and will usually[34] be governed, by the law which applied to this prior relationship. So if the restitutionary obligation arises upon the failure of a real

[32] Dicey, Rule 230(2).

[33] *P&O Steam Navigation Co v Shand* (1865) 12 LT 808.

[34] It seems right in principle that the rule which is primarily pragmatic should make implicit provision for exceptions on the same basis.

or supposed contract, or from the commission of a tort, the law which governed the contract or the tort will have a powerful and rational claim also to be applied to the restitutionary claim.[35] This is not because the restitutionary obligation is itself contractual or tortious—it is neither—but because it arises from and by reason of a prior relationship which is the *causa sine qua non* of the claim, and because it is simply unreal to regard the consequential obligation as free-floating, independent of, and uncoloured by its history. Quite apart from that, consistency of result will be enhanced by a choice of law rule according to which the laws applicable to history, claim, and remedy dovetail one with another. So the law governing the alleged obligation to repay sums paid over under a contract found to be void should be the same as that which applied to the supposed contract, and if the parties' supposed contract had an expressly chosen governing law, this law should certainly govern the restitutionary obligation;[36] the law governing the alleged obligation to account to one's employer for a bribe corruptly received from another should be the law of the contract of employment;[37] the law governing the obligation to account for profits made from the commission of a tort should be the law applicable to the tort.[38] In other words, a separate choice of law rule is not required.

If this is not accepted, there will be problems for which a workable solution will still have to be found. If the *lex contractus* provides that the supposed contract was void, a claim for the repayment of money or reimbursement for services or other benefits conferred will be restitutionary. If this is not governed by the *lex contractus* but by another law, that law may independently conclude that restitution is not available because it sees no unjust enrichment, on the ground that, as far as it is concerned, there is a valid contract which insulates the enrichment from the allegation of injustice. This combination of answer may be possible in theory, but it has nothing to recommend it to a court. Again, the *lex delicti* may show that there was a tort, but the claimant eschews compensation in favour of a claim against the tortfeasor for the profit generated by his wrongdoing. But if that restitutionary claim is governed by something other than the *lex delicti*, it may be that under this other law recovery is denied on the

---

[35] cf *Baring Bros & Co v Cunninghame DC* [1997] CLC 108 (Outer House).

[36] In *Dimskal Shipping Co SA v International Transport Workers' Federation (The Evia Luck)* [1992] 2 AC 152 a contract was avoided for duress by reference to its English proper law, and it appears to have been accepted without argument that restitution of money paid would be governed by English law.

[37] *Arab Monetary Fund v Hashim* [1996] 1 Lloyd's Rep 589 (CA).

[38] If the issue is characterized as one in tort under the Private International Law (Miscellaneous Provisions) Act 1995, s 9(2), the statutory choice of law rule will in any event apply.

ground that, according to it, there is no wrong. At some point it has to be recognized that the law needs to provide a reasonable solution to litigants' claims, not construct theories of unimpeachable philosophical perfection: a wholly abstract approach to law has no place in the world of men. The claim of pragmatism is that if the application of the *lex contractus* or the *lex delicti*, or analogous rules in the case of other prior-relationships, paves the way for a restitutionary claim, the choice of law rule for that restitutionary claim should be co-ordinated with one which was applied at the earlier stage, and should not contradict it. And no better solution is apparent.

(b) Unjust enrichment outside prior relationships

Where there was no prior relationship between claimant and defendant (non-relational restitution), Dicey suggests that the proper law of the obligation to make restitution is the law of the place where the enrichment occurred.[39] If there is no better connected a law, there is some justification for the place of enrichment, as providing a fixed point of sorts in a rootless set of facts; but it is submitted that it should not be accepted, even as a presumption. Several reasons may be given. For one, in cases where there has been a passing of funds, or of electronic data notionally representing funds, through sundry hands (both clean and unclean), accounts, and jurisdictions, there may be several places which could be regarded as that of the enrichment, all artificial or casual.[40] For another, it should not be possible for a calculating defendant to protect himself by arranging receipt of his enrichment in a country whose law is favourable to him. For a third, it will often be debatable whether it is the ultimate receipt or the first unjustified receipt which is critical: a rule which is based on this matter of happenstance is hard to promote. In these cases, therefore, a flexible proper law rule is inevitable and correct, and the answer should be the law which has the closest and most real connection with the alleged obligation to make restitution, without embellishment. Any attempt to specify in advance what this means does not seem sensible.

(c) Disappearance of the choice of law rule for unjust enrichment

One conclusion which may follow from this is that there is no need for a separate characterization, and separate choice of law rule, for unjust

---

[39] Dicey, Rule 230(2)(c); cf the arguable distinction between where enrichment occurs and where it is sustained.

[40] cf *Hong Kong and Shanghai Banking Corp Ltd v United Overseas Bank Ltd* [1992] Sing LR 495 (Sing HC); *Thahir v Pertamina* [1994] 3 Sing LR 257 (Sing CA).

enrichment. Where the dispute takes the form of competition for a credit balance on the books of a bank, the rules which deal with priority of claims to a contractual right, or intangible property, will suffice.[41] Where it is based on a claim for breach of an obligation, that obligation will have its own choice of law rule. Even for those claims which are said, when viewed from a particular angle, not to be based on wrongdoing (such as unjust enrichment by retention of money paid by mistake), the choice of law rule for wrongs, torts, is a perfect fit. After all, the proposition that it is not wrong to hang onto a payment made by mistake is surprising. Decently-brought-up people know it is a wrong, even though various national laws diverge in their analyses of what makes it a wrong and when it becomes one. The law may give a more complicated answer, but the claim falls within the general territory of the private international law of wrongs. It should be governed by the choice of law rule for wrongs. If the choice of law rule for unjust enrichment were to disappear—as it is about to do[42]—it would leave no trace, and none would weep over its demise.

(d) Contribution claims as restitutionary issues

Contribution claims may be brought between parties pursuant to a contract or between wrongdoers, and, in a broader context, the same issue may extend to all cases in which A has made a payment or performed a service which benefits him and B, and now seeks an *ex post facto* adjustment of their responsibilities. Where such a claim for contribution or indemnity from another is advanced on the ground that he has, by paying a claimant,[43] discharged a liability[44] owed by both, the claim can be seen as being restitutionary in nature.[45] If this analysis were correct, it would follow that the choice of law would be derived from the principles outlined above. Where there was a prior relationship—a contractual obligation to indemnify or contribute, for example—between the two, the law governing this prior relationship would in those cases deal with the claim;[46] if not—in England, where statute[47] or equity[48] undertakes the

---

[41] Chapter 8, below.

[42] When Rome II Regulation becomes applicable by courts, on 11 January 2009.

[43] Actual or potential.

[44] Actual or potential.

[45] eg, Law Commission, *Private International Law: Choice of Law in Tort and Delict* (Law Com No 193, 1990) paras 3.47–3.48.

[46] It would not matter whether the claim were seen as restitutionary but most closely connected to the *lex contractus*, or contractual and governed by the *lex contractus*.

[47] Most prominently the Civil Liability (Contribution) Act 1978.

[48] Via the principles on subrogation, although as regards these Art 13 of the Rome Convention (Contracts (Applicable Law) Act 1990, Sch 1), provides a partial statutory choice of law rule.

task—the law of closest connection would apply. There is some judicial support for this, at least to the extent of seeing the claim as restitutionary. But it has also been held that where the claim for contribution falls within the statutory wording of the Civil Liability (Contribution) Act 1978, this regime applies without regard to choice of law.[49] As a matter of statutory construction this is questionable, for there is no particular reason—either deduced from the wording of the Act or from the policy involved—to consider that Parliament intended English contribution rules to be applied to each and every respondent brought before the English courts, any more than it intended English rules on contributory negligence to be applied with equally indiscriminate effect. The correct analysis ought to be that such a claim is restitutionary, and that choice of law is well within the framework of that for restitutionary claims.

2. CHOICE OF LAW UNDER REGULATION (EC) 864/2007

When Rome II is applicable by a court seised of a claim, claims based on unjust enrichment and *negotiorum gestio* will fall within its material scope. The choice of law will be the law governing the prior relationship if there was one; if none, the law of the country in which they both had their habitual residence; if none, the law of the country in which the unjust enrichment took place or the act of intervention was performed.[50] And in any event, if there is manifestly closer connection to another country, the law of that country shall apply;[51] and general right to choose the law to govern the obligation will also apply as it applies to other non-contractual obligations.[52] The result is a sensible and rational scheme for choice of law, which draws a distinction between relationship and non-relationship cases, and which disposes of the latter by looking for the law which has the best connection to the obligation. It will, one imagines, still give rise to puzzles where, for example, the asset over which the battle is fought is a credit balance in a bank account, or where the claim could plausibly be seen as raising a question of title to property. But although it means that there is a choice of law rule for unjust enrichment and *negotiorum*

---

[49] *Arab Monetary Fund v Hashim (No 9)* [1994] TLR 502. The judge admitted that in a case falling outside the statutory scheme, the proper law of the obligation to contribute would probably be applicable. A similar conclusion appears to follow from *Sweedman v Transport Accident Commission* [2006] HCA 8, (2006) 226 CLR 362, although the essence of the reasoning is rather difficult to capture in words.

[50] Article 10 (for unjust enrichment) and Article 11 (*negotiorum gestio*), respectively.

[51] Articles 10(4) and 11(4).

[52] Article 14.

gestio, which in the present submission is not necessary, the outcome is, in almost every case, exactly what it would have been if there had been no separately-stated rule: *quod erat demonstrandum*.

C. EQUITABLE OBLIGATIONS

As indicated above, difficulty surrounds any attempt to show how the domestic rules and principles of equity coexist with the rules of conflict of laws. A related difficulty arises with the accommodation of foreign principles of equity. This may have been a problem for some time, but it received scholarly attention only in the last few years.

I. CHOICE OF LAW ACCORDING TO THE COMMON LAW

One suggestion would stake out the position that the domestic law distinction between common law and equity is wholly irrelevant to the conflict of laws, and that claims founded on obligations in or analogous[53] to those found in English equity are to be located within existing characterization categories. Or, to put it another way: equity follows the choice of law. According to this, some equitable claims would be regarded as torts, or wrongs, to be dealt with by the *lex delicti*: examples may include misuse of confidential information or breach of confidence, and aiding and abetting another's breach of trust. These impose remedies[54] for dishonesty, fault, wrongdoing: the remedies may differ[55] from those generally awarded for torts at common law, but this should not be decisive. And if the definition of 'tort' for the purpose of the statutory choice of law rule in the Private International Law (Miscellaneous Provisions) Act 1995 is taken to be wider than its meaning in English domestic law, the statutory choice of law rules for torts may already have supervened to bring some equitable claims within its scope. Other forms of claim should be regarded as contractual, or as based on agreement: examples may be the breach by an agent of his fiduciary duty, or breach of the duty not to act unconscionably in relation to contractual rights or the holding of office. The basis for liability is disloyalty to or unconscionable dealing with another

[53] This form of words is meant to denote causes of action arising under a foreign law but which are analogous to those found in English equity.

[54] It is probably irrelevant whether this is assessed by reference to the claimant's loss or the defendant's gain, but if this *is* critical, loss-based recovery would be a wrong, and gain-based recovery would be restitutionary.

[55] Although the difference between equitable compensation and common law damages is not substantial.

with whom one had an agreement, and the difference between the remedies will diminish if an account of profits may be ordered for a breach of contract. Yet others may be restitutionary,[56] because the aim is to ensure that its victim is not depleted, even if what is handed over is technically the property of the defendant: an example would be the knowing[57] receipt of trust property; and the choice of law will therefore reflect the distinction between relational and non-relational restitution.[58] Those of equity's rules which are specific to remedies would apply as part of the procedural *lex fori*; and the overall result would be the denial of a separate characterization category for equity, and the disappearance of a distinct choice of law rule.

The advantages of this approach are obvious: there would be a simplification of the law, the echoes of historical irrelevancies[59] would become inaudible, and a basis would also have been established for dealing with claims based on foreign laws but which are claimed to be enforceable in an English court.[60] There is another, compelling, advantage. The account just given proceeds by taking English equitable causes of action and asking how they fit within the characterization categories. But this places the cart before the horse. It is the characterization category which identifies the choice of law rule, and thus which identifies the cause of action: if it points to English law it may also point to English equity. But not until this point is reached should there be any mention of equity. If the price to be paid is a measure of dissonance between domestic and private international law, it is worth the expense.

An alternative view of the matter proceeds from the proposition that the operation of equity is, in effect, dependent only upon the court's having personal jurisdiction over the defendant and his conscience, and that choice of law is not material to the application of English equity by an English court. The extreme, ultramontane, even scary form of the argument maintains just that: a claimant who formulates a claim by reference to English[61] equity—that is, any claim which would be brought in equity's exclusive jurisdiction if all the facts were domestic—may rely on English

---

[56] But in the light of the previous section, this would simply result in their reallocation to another classification category.

[57] On the footing that liability does not depend on (dis)honesty, but knowledge.

[58] There is some basis for this distinction: *Kuwait Oil Tanker SAK v Al Bader* [2000] 2 All ER (Comm) 271 (CA).

[59] In the sense that whatever the doctrinal history of equity may impose in other areas, it has no relevance in this context.

[60] It is also supported by Yeo, *Choice of Law for Equitable Doctrines* (2004).

[61] As *lex fori*. In fact, the most significant cases in this line are decisions of the Australian courts.

equity even though some or all of the facts are foreign. Or, to put the same point another way, the equitable obligations contained in English domestic law are applicable, either as part of the *lex fori*, binding on and applicable to anyone subject to the personal jurisdiction of the court,[62] or as mandatory laws, by which judges are directed to apply equitable principle to any case before them, no matter the choice of law which might otherwise have applied. If equitable obligations were seen as a crystallization of English public policy, this might, just possibly, be acceptable, but this would be an ambitious claim to make for the whole of equity. After all, equity enforces standards of good faith and acts against fraud; the common law enforces duties of care and acts against deceit: it is simply unrealistic to regard the one but not the other as manifesting English public policy. That one but not the other should operate without regard to choice of law is incredible. Both should depend on the *lex causae* being English to begin with.

A slightly less extreme version of this approach recognizes that there may be cases when an undiluted dose of English equity would be a little too strong. On this view, notice will be taken of a foreign law if it has a significant connection to the case.[63] But on this view, the maximum role of the foreign law will be to contribute data for the purpose of helping decide what English equity requires—if it requires proof of dishonesty, standards prevailing in the place where the defendant acted will shine a light by which to evaluate his conduct as honest or dishonest—or expects of a defendant in a given case. If this is correct, the availability to a claimant of English equitable doctrines would again depend not upon the prior application of choice of law rules, but only upon the existence of personal jurisdiction. So far as can be deduced from cases on dishonestly assisting a breach of trust, in particular,[64] this is approximately the basis of liability as it is currently understood: as long as the foreign law (usually in practice the place where the defendant acted) imposes a form of liability resembling the nature of the English action, the claim will proceed on the basis of English law; were it to be shown that under the foreign law there was no ground for even arguing that there would be liability, this would be a

---

[62] *National Commercial Bank v Wimborne* (1978) 5 Butterworths Prop Rep 11958 (NSW SC); *United States Surgical Corporation v Hospital Products International Pty Ltd* [1982] 2 NSWLR 766, 797–8, aff'd [1983] 2 NSWLR 157 (CA), rev'd on different grounds (1984) 156 CLR 41; *Paramasivam v Flynn* (1998) 160 ALR 203, 214–18 (Fed Ct); cf *Macmillan Inc v Bishopsgate Investment Trust plc (No 3)* [1995] 1 WLR 976, 989, aff'd without reference to this point [1996] 1 WLR 387 (CA).

[63] *Grupo Torras SA v Al Sabah* [2001] CLC 221 (CA); *Kuwait Oil Tanker SAK v Al Bader* [2000] 2 All ER (Comm) 271 (CA).

[64] ibid.

weighty factor in denying that there was dishonesty for the purposes of the English claim. In other words, English equity would apply, without regard to choice of law, but with notice taken of foreign law. It is a possible answer, but it is not the right answer.

In the context of anti-suit injunctions, however, there is a subtle difference. An applicant may obtain an anti-suit injunction by relying exclusively on English equity and its law on vexation and oppression: no observable part is played by the law of any other country in deciding whether the applicant has made out the cause of action which justifies the relief. But the court will not use English equity to adjudicate on the application unless England is the natural forum for the underlying claim.[65] In other words, the precondition to the application of English equity is not one cast in terms of choice of law, but the closeness of connection of the underlying dispute with England.[66] It is perhaps surprising that whereas this may be true for anti-suit injunctions, there is no trace of it as a limitation when claims have been brought, say alleging dishonest assistance of a breach of trust. In other words, in the context of anti-suit injunctions, English equity applies as long as, but only if, England is the natural forum for the litigation.

If the forum-centric approach represents the present state of the law, it is difficult to look on it as being satisfactory. It seems particularly strange that, when equity enforces common law rights, such as under contracts, choice of law first decides whether there is a legal right on which to base the remedy, but where a remedy is sought on the basis of an equitable obligation there is no similar process: it is as if equity sits above choice of law, as if choice of law were a creature of the common law alone. Whilst the restrictions on the application of English equity in its pure and undiluted form, described above, are better than nothing, they are not a lot better than nothing; and it is very hard indeed to explain why English equity should not, like English common law and English legislation, generally depend on choice of law pointing to English domestic law as the *lex causae*.[67] And if that is so, the view that there is no separate choice of law category for equity represents the way ahead. It would certainly be

---

[65] *Airbus Industrie GIE v Patel* [1999] 1 AC 119.

[66] As a country, not with English as a law, or so it seems.

[67] cf Supreme Court of Judicature Act 1873 s 25, which provided, in effect, that where the rules of equity and the common law conflicted, those of equity were to prevail. If the rule of equity were one which operates without regard for, or despite, choice of law, one might regard the (common law) choice of law as prevailed over. But it is not apparent that this reasoning was ever adopted to justify the proposition that equity did not depend on choice of law rules pointing to English law in the first place.

wrong to regard all equitable claims and obligations as restitutionary, for many are not; but it would be equally strange to say that they are above and beyond the reach of choice of law. The approach which assimilates them into the characterization categories of contract, tort, and restitution does no real damage to the law; and it removes the suggestion of characterization being unnecessary where the claimant relies on an equitable claim. The approach to anti-suit injunctions can be explained and justified as a procedural, remedial, issue, governed by the *lex fori*. But until this happens, the role of equity in the conflict of laws will be anomalous and unstable.

2. CHOICE OF LAW UNDER REGULATION (EC) 864/2007

It goes without saying that insofar as the claim in question is founded on the law of obligations, the fact that it may be equitable in nature is wholly irrelevant to the rules for choice of law established by the Rome II Regulation.

8

Property

The private international law of property is a large topic, or several topics, covering transactions *inter vivos* and devolution of property upon death. It can raise difficult questions about the relationship between jurisdiction and choice of law, and between property and the law of obligations. In most cases in which a court is called upon to adjudicate it is asked to settle a dispute about title, and to make an order which is good and reliable against the world, not just as between the parties to the action. As a result, a court will generally be entitled[1] to apply any foreign law which its rules tell it to in its *renvoi* sense, that is, as the law would be applied by a judge sitting in the foreign country and hearing the case himself. Even though parties will frequently place no reliance on the principle of *renvoi*, this cannot be taken as a decision that the doctrine is inadmissible in the context of property law.

The law of property divides into immovable and movable property, and movables sub-divide into tangible and intangible property. Whether a thing is an immovable is determined by the law of the place where it is, the *lex situs*.[2] It may be thought that this offends against the principle that characterization is a matter for the *lex fori*, and that in cases of potential disagreement, such as where the property is an oil rig, a pontoon bridge, the interest of a mortgagee in the property mortgaged, an interest under a trust of land, and so on, this question should be answered by the law of the forum. But in a context in which, as will be seen, the *lex situs* is broadly applicable, and *renvoi* applies also, it would be self-defeating to distort the very law which a court is seeking to apply with particular faithfulness. The result is that the question whether property is movable or immovable is determined by the *lex situs*.

A. IMMOVABLE PROPERTY

So far as the common law was concerned, an English court had no jurisdiction to determine questions of title to immovable property situated

---

[1] If the rules of foreign law are pleaded and proved to the satisfaction of the court.
[2] Dicey, ch 22; *Re Hoyles* [1911] 1 Ch 179, 185.

outside England, nor to entertain tort claims in which such an issue would arise for decision.[3] So where a claim was brought which alleged trespass to a hotel, and to chattels in the hotel, in the northern part of the island of Cyprus by defendants claiming authorization by the authorities of the *soi-disant* and illegal 'Turkish Republic of Northern Cyprus', the court had no jurisdiction to entertain the action concerning the land, but did have jurisdiction over the claim alleging conversion of the chattels. The decision shows the width of the rule, for under the *lex situs*, a connecting factor defined by English law and which acknowledged only the laws of the Republic of Cyprus, there was no dispute about title: the illegal ordinances of the non-state were without effect. But the exclusionary rule still operated to deny jurisdiction. The common law rule was amended by statute to confer jurisdiction over tort claims where the issue of title is not a principal one[4] but otherwise the jurisdictional preclusion prevails.[5] So a claim alleging trespass can be defeated on jurisdictional grounds if the defendant pleads that the land was his. It is probably correct to read the reference to 'title' as being broad: if the same defendant alleged a licence to enter or remain, this too should be seen to raise a dispute about title. The historical basis of the rule lay in the common law principle that such actions were 'local', and had to be tried in the place where the land was situated, but a more pragmatic, private international legal, reason is that most laws impose the same limitation for reasons of public policy. Moreover, as titles to land are increasingly recorded on a register, only the court with personal jurisdiction over the registrar has any sensible basis for accepting jurisdiction over an action which may result in the registrar being told to amend the register of title. It follows that disputes about title to foreign immovables must be tried in the courts of the *situs*, no matter how inconvenient this is, and notwithstanding that the parties are willing to submit to the personal jurisdiction of a different court. By parity of reasoning, foreign judgments which purport to adjudicate title to English immovables will not be recognized in England.[6]

Moreover, if the land is in another Member State of the European Union to which the Brussels Regulation[7] applies Article 22(1) denies jurisdiction to the English court where the proceedings have as their object

---

[3] *British South Africa Co v Companhia de Moçambique* [1893] AC 602; *Hesperides Hotels Ltd v Aegean Turkish Holidays Ltd* [1979] AC 508.

[4] *Re Polly Peck International plc (in administration) (No 2)* [1998] 3 All ER 812, 828 (CA).

[5] Civil Jurisdiction and Judgments Act 1982, s 30.

[6] Although for the possibility that they may be recognized between the parties as judgments binding them *in personam*, see *Pattni v Ali* [2006] UKPC 51, [2007] 2 AC 85.

[7] Regulation (EC) 44/2001, [2001] OJ L12/1.

a right *in rem* in, or a tenancy of, that land.[8] A different issue arises where the land is in a non-Member State but the court has personal jurisdiction over the defendant under the Regulation. One view is that it may not have recourse to its national conflicts rules to decline to exercise it, on the basis that this common law jurisdictional principle would, in effect, negate a provision of the Regulation.[9] An alternative view would be that the absence of subject matter jurisdiction is unaffected by the Regulation, or that a court should be able to exercise a procedural discretion to stay proceedings which would be incompetent if the land were in a Member State. Given the state of the national laws, this seems by far the better solution.

A common law exception to the exclusionary rule exists. If a claim may be brought as one to enforce a personal obligation, albeit one relating to a foreign immovable, there is no jurisdictional impediment to it, even though it may appear to some that the court is doing indirectly what it cannot do directly. The exception derives from the ancient case of *Penn v Baltimore*,[10] concerning an agreement to demarcate the boundary of two American proto-states, and which the court was willing and able to enforce as an agreement which the parties to it could be ordered to perform. Despite its unlikely origins, the principle is plain enough: if the claim is brought to enforce a contract or in respect of a pre-existing equitable obligation, such as a trust, between the parties, the court does not lack jurisdiction even if the obligation derives from, or is created by, a transaction relating to land;[11] a similar principle applies if a court is administering an estate which includes foreign land. (It is only because there is no contract or equity between trespasser and proprietor that the statutory amendment mentioned above was required to bring the law of tort into line with this principle.) So if the claim is that the defendant seller has failed to perform his contract for sale of land, or as bare trustee should convey legal title to the claimant beneficiary, the court has jurisdiction to make an order against the seller or trustee in person, capable of being backed up by the court's considerable coercive powers, requiring the conveyance of the land; or awarding damages for the breach. Likewise, a court should have jurisdiction to assess shares in the equitable ownership of foreign land to the purchase of which the parties have contributed, and to

---

[8] See above; and Chapter III of the Regulation requires the non-recognition of judgments which conflict with this.

[9] cf Case C–281/02 *Owusu v Jackson* [2005] ECR I–1383; *Pearce v Ove Arup Partnership Ltd* [2000] Ch 403 (CA).

[10] (1750) 1 Ves Sen 444.

[11] cf Case C–294/92 *Webb v Webb* [1994] ECR I–1717 (a case on what is now Art 22(1) of the Regulation).

decree the performance of the duties of any trust. The court is not doing indirectly what it cannot do directly; it is doing, directly, exactly what it is asked to do.

As regards choice of law in those cases in which the court does have jurisdiction, the inevitable choice is the *lex situs* as this would be applied in a court at the *situs* to any question concerning immovable property: this may, of course, result in the application of the domestic law of country other than that of the *situs*. The usual justification for this is the futility of doing otherwise than what a local judge would do, for he alone has control of the immovable, and his view on the correct answer is inevitably destined to prevail. This is not as convincing as it may seem. The real question for the foreign judge (as, were the roles reversed, it would be for an English judge) is whether to acknowledge that a judge in another country had jurisdiction to make any order concerning local land at all, rather than whether that judge got the right substantive answer: he may still refuse to recognize a foreign judgment, even though the reasoning and the result appear to be unimpeachable; and the recognition of a judgment does not usually depend on the conclusion that the adjudicating judge decided correctly. But, that said, it is impossible to maintain a serious argument for the application of anything other than the *lex situs* where the question is properly one concerning title to the land.[12] Where the court has jurisdiction under the *Penn v Baltimore* exception, the law governing the contractual issue may not be the *lex situs* of the land.[13] But this will be the presumed governing law for contracts concerning land;[14] and only on issues of formality or personal capacity, for example, is there any real prospect of applying a law other than the *lex situs*.

B. TANGIBLE MOVABLE PROPERTY

The reason for the application of the *lex situs* in the case of immovables is that, because the land cannot be moved, the *lex situs* combines expectation with reality. By contrast, movables move: the clue is in the name. True as this is, it does not affect the choice of law, only the justification for it. Disputes concerning title to, or the right to possession of, tangible movable property are generally governed by the *lex situs* of the movable at the

---

[12] *Bank of Africa v Cohen* [1909] 2 Ch 129 (CA). But the paucity of authority reflects the fact that jurisdiction will be rare.

[13] Likewise, where there is jurisdiction under Civil Jurisdiction and Judgments Act 1982, s 30, the *lex delicti* need not be the *lex situs* of the land, although it probably will be, whether the question arises under the 1995 Act or under the Rome II Regulation.

[14] Contracts (Applicable Law) Act 1990, Sch 1, Art 4(3).

date of the event which is alleged to have affected title to it.[15] It is accepted that certainty and security of title are paramount, and these aims are best achieved by the general application of the *lex situs*. Recognizing this, the courts have resisted the invitation to develop even limited exceptions to add to those established by authority. So if the parties are together in one place, but the thing is elsewhere the law of the place of the transaction, the *lex loci actus*, will not be applied, but the *lex situs* will.[16] True, if the parties have made a contract which specifies when property will pass, this may be effective, but only if its validity and effect are acknowledged by the *lex situs* applying (one presumes[17]) its own choice of law rule to appraise the contract. The *lex situs* prevails. As to whether *renvoi* does, the principle of security of title would suggest that our concern is with law as a local judge would apply it to the matter at hand; and if it is pleaded, *renvoi* should be apply in order more perfectly to support the policy underpinning the choice of law rule itself.[18]

But by way of difference from dealings with land, there are many cases in which a succession of transfers of, or other dealings with, a movable takes place, and in a series of countries with conflicting laws. There are two basic possibilities which may have been used to underpin the law. Suppose that X delivers a car to Y on hire purchase, according to the terms of which X remains owner during the period of hire, but that Y drives the car to a second country where he sells the car to Z. Let us also suppose that under the law of the second country, a person in possession of a chattel with apparent ownership of it can confer a good title on a buyer in good faith, but that under the law of the first country, the governing principle of *nemo dat quod non habet* would mean that Y had no title to give, nor capacity to confer the same. Under the law of the first country X had an indefeasible title, which could not be affected by a purported sale by a non-owner, Y. Under the law of the second country, the principle of indefeasible titles does not prevail, and a buyer in good faith, Z, may acquire a title which was not the seller's to give. If one were to adopt a strictly chronological view, and regard each *lex situs* as having sole control over the issues as arose

---

[15] *Cammell v Sewell* (1860) 5 H & N 728; *Winkworth v Christie, Manson & Woods* [1980] Ch 496.

[16] *Glencore International AG v Metro Trading Inc* [2001] 1 Lloyd's Rep 283.

[17] The argument to the contrary is that the Rome Convention, Art 15, does not allow for this. The response should be that as the Convention does not apply to proprietary issues, it does not infect the operation of the *lex situs* in its full, *renvoi*, sense.

[18] In this respect the methodology is that of *Neilson v Overseas Projects Corp of Victoria* (2005) 223 CLR 331. The contrary decision in *Iran v Berend* [2007] EWHC 132 (QB), [2007] 2 All ER (Comm) 132 is, from this perspective, wrong.

within its territory, one might say that the transaction in the first country
reserved to X an indefeasible title to the car; and that when it was taken to
the second country, that second law must have taken the indefeasibility of
X's title as given, with the result that Y will have been unable to defeat the
indefeasible by conferring title on Z: anything else allows the law of the
second country to trespass on the role of the first country's law.

It is evident that the analysis can be stood on its head, by pointing out
that the law of the first country is purporting to dictate to the second in
relation to a transaction taking place in the second. An alternative analysis
would be that the eventual question, who owns the car, is as to the legal
effect of the second transaction; that this is exclusively governed by the
law of the second country, and any anterior questions are answered by
looking through the eyes of this eventual *lex situs*, leaving it to the law
of obligations to remedy, as best it may, any losses sustained along the
way. This is the solution adopted by the English conflict of laws. It therefore follows that the main question will be answered by the *lex situs* of the
final disposition, and any earlier issues will be regarded as incidental, and
resolved by looking at them through the lens of the law governing the
main question.

As a result, the question whether A obtained good title to a camera
which he bought in Ruritania is governed by Ruritanian law, even if the
camera had been delivered on hire purchase terms or under a conditional
sale to A's seller in England; whether B lost his title to a painting stolen
from him in England and sold by auction in Italy is governed by Italian
law, even though the theft took place in England,[19] whether C succeeded
in reserving and retaining title to steel after its use or on-sale by D is
answered by the *lex situs* at the time of D's dealing with it, which law will
also decide whether it is still steel or is a completely different thing.[20]

The rule as it applies to transfers allows for one exception. If the goods
are in transit and[21] their *situs* unknown there is a case for applying instead
the law which governs the transaction which is alleged to have affected
title.[22] By contrast, where a disposition of goods is effected by document,
it is not yet, and may never be, established that the *lex situs* of the goods
can be by-passed by the application of (say) the law of the place of the

[19] *Winkworth v Christie, Manson & Woods Ltd* [1980] Ch 496.
[20] *Re Interview Ltd* [1975] IR 382, *Armour v Thyssen Edelstahlwerke AG* [1991] 2 AC 339; but
both cases are weak authority for the proposition advanced in the text.
[21] In its established form, this is conjunctive, not disjunctive. Although there is a case for
restating the exception in disjunctive form, the increased scope for uncertainty which this
would create will make it unlikely to be adopted.
[22] Dicey, Rule 124, exception.

documents. In principle, the answer should be that if the *lex situs* of the goods accepts the purported disposition by transfer of documents as effective, that will be conclusive; but that if it does not, that is conclusive also.[23] Any uncertainty in the minds of those involved will presumably be reflected in the price or in the taking of insurance.

Although the rule was established in the context of derivative titles, that is, transfers, in principle it will also apply to original modes of acquisition, to establish the claim of title to things found (*occupatio*), new things made (*specificatio*), things incorporated into something else (*accessio*); and to mixing and blending (*commixtio* and *confusio*).[24] But the simple moving of a chattel from one country to another will not have any effect upon its title; to hold otherwise would be most inconvenient. So if goods are transported by train across several countries, and under the law of one of them an existing title is not recognized, it would be unhelpful for the thing thereafter to be regarded as ownerless and as available for *occupatio*. It may be necessary to adapt the exception, described in the last paragraph, to produce this result.

The choice of law rule for tangible movables also applies to negotiable instruments.[25] As the instrument, being negotiable, is as good as the right to which it is the key, transfers of the document are, in effect, transfers of the thing. The same principle applies to bearer shares, which are treated as tangible things, and where transfer of the instrument is effective to transfer all rights or property inherent in it.

C. INTANGIBLE MOVABLE PROPERTY

Choice of law in relation to intangible property—the rights arising from a debt owed by a bank to an account-holder, the rights under a policy of insurance, the rights of an investor in a unit trust, and so forth—raises issues of some complexity, for three among many reasons. First, it is sometimes difficult to see why or on what basis intangibles are characterized under the common law as property at all, as distinct from their being the simple contractual or analogous rights which they almost always are. If[26] the question of who is now entitled to an intangible, and who may

---

[23] There will be consequential contractual claims.

[24] *Glencore International AG v Metro Trading Inc* [2001] 1 Lloyd's Rep 283. The *situs* rule also applies to seizure by way of nationalization or confiscation of property by governments; see below.

[25] Whether the document is negotiable is determined by its *situs* at the time of its purported negotiation.

[26] The issue of whether this is correct is considered below.

therefore enforce the obligation against the debtor or obliged party, is really to ask no more than who stands in a relationship equivalent to privity with the debtor or obliged party, there will be no substantial distinction between owning a debt and being owed a debt. This analysis would suggest that the issues which arise are neither more nor less than facets of the law of contract, albeit with a particular gloss supplied by laws regulating security and insolvency, but which may be got up to look like something else. Secondly, the universe of intangible things is almost certainly too wide for a uniform choice of law rule to be applied to everything in it. A rule developed in the 19th century for the assignment of insurance policies and interests under family trusts and dynastic settlements was not designed for, and may not adapt to, dealings with interests in financial instruments held in indirect holding systems, or for delocalized or dematerialized securities of the sort which now serve to underpin the global financial market. Either a choice of law rule has to allow for pragmatic exceptions, so that mindless dogmatism does not defeat the expectations of commerce, or the law must develop new (sub-)rules for choice of law.

Thirdly, when dealing with choice of law for the assignment of intangibles, the common law authorities were remarkably opaque, Dr Morris asserted, in the face of some really dreadful case law, that the law governing the underlying obligation would determine its assignability; the law governing the actual assignment would govern the effect of that transaction; and if the two answers were combined, the answer would emerge. Article 12 of the Rome Convention now provides a statutory rule for choice of law in voluntary assignments which is to similar effect.[27] Article 12(2) states that the law governing the right assigned determines its assignability, the relationship between assignee and debtor, the conditions for invoking the assignment against the debtor, and the discharge of the debtor; and Article 12(1) that the mutual obligations of assignor and assignee are governed by the law applicable to the contract between them. In other words, issues involving the debtor and enforcement against him are governed by the law which governs the thing assigned; any residual or consequential issues between the creditors, or between those trading in the debt owed by another, are for the law governing their relationship. This has the basic elements of good sense about it, for it accords due weight to the law which created the thing being dealt with; it defends the expectation of the parties who created the obligation that it has all, but has only, the characteristics with which they endowed it, thereby reflecting the essentially contractual

---

[27] Contracts (Applicable Law) Act 1990, Sch 1.

nature of the thing assigned; and it invites the conclusion that, as Article 12 embraces these matters within the Rome Convention as matters relating to contractual obligations in the autonomous sense, it precludes any argument that they are, in any exclusionary sense, proprietary.

It is possible to read down Article 12, by contending that while it regulates contractual issues, it is irrelevant to the proprietary aspects of intangibles. The difficulties with this argument were many, but for reasons set out in the discussion of the meaning of contractual obligations, it is hard to see that it is tenable today.[28] On the other hand, this analysis causes problems for those who trade in bundles of debts (receivables), and for whom the task of ascertaining the law under which each separate debt was created is disproportionate. From this perspective the property which is transferred from one to another may be seen not as the debt, as such, but as the right to have the debtor instructed to discharge the debt by paying to A or to B or to C as the case may be. If an 'assignment of the debt' is understood as a transfer of the right to give instructions to the debtor, giving the assignee the right to tell the assignor to direct the debtor to pay the assignee, it is much less obvious that this 'property', if that is what it is, needs to make any reference to the law governing the underlying debt. The differences in approach are fundamental, and it is hard to see how they may be reconciled. For practical purposes, however, the 'contractual' approach seems to be more easily reconciled with the Rome Convention.

If Article 12 is inapplicable, which will be the case where the right assigned is not contractual,[29] the Convention does not preclude the common law reflecting the basic structure of Article 12 as the basis of the law on assignment; and as Article 12 is probably a reflection of the state of the common law as it was best understood, in the rare cases where the common law rules on assignment of intangibles apply they may well be indistinguishable from Article 12.

I. SPECIAL CASES

Assignments of registered shares are governed by the *lex incorporationis* for the pragmatic reason that any solution which departs from the law of the place of the share register is futile. In such cases, the general rule in Article 12 of the Rome Convention is inapplicable.[30] This may be deduced from the exclusion in Article 1(2)(e) or, rather more persuasively, from

---

[28] *Raiffeisen Zentralbank Österreich AG v Five Star Trading LLC* [2001] EWCA Civ 68, [2001] QB 825.

[29] Such as the right to sue a defendant in respect of a tort.

[30] *Macmillan Inc v Bishopsgate Investment Trust plc (No 3)* [1996] 1 WLR 387 (CA).

the argument that it is inaccurate to say that shares are ever assigned: as they are a bundle of duties and obligations as well as rights, simple assignment of them is impossible. The process misdescribed as 'share transfer' is in fact the surrender and new-grant of rights in the company. If this is accepted, then the nomenclature of 'share transfer' should be abandoned. For shares and other instruments held in holding systems, according to the terms of which a 'shareholder' in fact has only an interest as investor in a pool of similar assets registered in the name of someone else (a process which may be replicated upwards through several levels of holding), it seems reasonable to accept that a mechanical solution derived from a rule intended for cases of much less complexity is inappropriate, especially where this would, for no obviously good reason, defeat the expectations of all those who participate in the system. Private international legal science appeared unlikely to produce a universal solution convenient to those whose business is founded on such trades. As a result, in 2003 a Convention was concluded at The Hague which would, when adopted, apply a dedicated, if rather complicated, rule for choice of law. It does not 'look through' to the law under which the ultimate or original intangible was issued, but treats the rights of an investor against the entity with which he holds a securities account as the property or thing with which one deals. The Convention has not yet been adopted or brought into force and its future does not look bright.

2. INTELLECTUAL PROPERTY

In relation to intellectual property rights, to the extent that a question is not governed by convention or statute, and is not outside the jurisdiction of an English court, patents, copyright, and trade mark rights are governed by the law of the place of the right of protection (*lex protectionis*), and that law will determine whether and on what terms they are assignable. This seems inevitable. The question of jurisdiction is complicated by the fact that the traditional understanding, that there was no jurisdiction to determine the validity of a foreign intellectual property right, was not supported by significant English authority.[31] As the issue of validity would frequently be raised by a defendant sued in proceedings alleging infringement, it was arguably inconvenient that a court could be deprived of jurisdiction over a tort claim, especially in relation to a defendant over whom it had personal jurisdiction under the Brussels Regulation. So far as the common law was concerned, the principle of *Penn v Baltimore*[32] was held

---

[31] *Potter v Broken Hill Pty Co* (1906) 3 CLR 479.
[32] (1750) 1 Ves Sen 444.

to apply, to provide a partial way around the jurisdictional impediment;[33] so far as the Brussels Regulation was concerned, the Court of Appeal was doubtful of the continued operation of any common law exclusionary rule.[34] However, where the right in question is granted by the law of a Member State, the Brussels Regulation gives exclusive jurisdiction, even where the issue simply arises as a defence to a claim alleging infringement, to the Member State of deposit or registration.[35] At present, the jurisdictional rule is therefore in a bit of a mess.

As to choice of law for infringement and other non-contractual claims, the Rome II Regulation applies the *lex protectionis* to non-contractual obligations, and excludes the right of the parties to choose another law.[36]

D. SEIZURE AND CONFISCATION OF PROPERTY

The treatment of nationalization or other expropriation or seizure of property by governments requires little more than an application of the general *lex situs* rule set out above. If the property is within the territorial jurisdiction of the state, the *lex situs* rule will lead to the recognition of the title acquired by this legislative act by reference to local law.[37] There is no question of an English court being called upon to 'enforce' the foreign law: once that law, the *lex causae* according to the rules of the English conflict of laws, has done what it set out to do and has vested title in the state, there is nothing left in it to require enforcing.[38] Accordingly, if property is seized by a state pursuant to a confiscatory decree, and is then sold by the authorities to a buyer who gets good title under that law and who then brings the property to England, the former and dispossessed owner has no maintainable claim for its return from the person who, as a matter of the English conflict of laws, has a complete title: the transfer of ownership and loss of the right to possession were both completed under the *lex situs* of the property at the time of the act, and any claim which asserts a right which follows from the claimant's ownership will be defeated. Likewise, if a government passes a decree to acquire ownership of shares in a company incorporated and registered under its law, it may, as new controlling shareholder, direct the management of the company to recover

---

[33] *Griggs (R) Group Ltd v Evans (No 2)* [2004] EWHC 1088 (Ch), [2005] Ch 153.
[34] *Pearce v Ove Arup Partnership Ltd* [2000] Ch 403.
[35] Case C–4/03 *GAT v LüK* [2006] ECR I–6509.
[36] Article 8.
[37] *Luther v Sagor* [1921] 3 KB 532 (CA); *Princess Paley Olga v Weisz* [1929] 1 KB 718 (CA).
[38] *Williams & Humbert v W & H Trade Marks (Jersey) Ltd* [1986] AC 368.

debts and property abroad.[39] But, by contrast, had the law provided that overseas property vested in the state, the ordinary application of the *lex situs* rule would mean that title to the property in England, at least, would be unaffected or changed by this legislative act, and that any action in the English courts would be founded on an irrelevant law, not part of the *lex situs* at the time of the relevant act. If a foreign state purports to confiscate English copyright, its law will be ineffective.[40] Not only that, but the action would in such a case be for the enforcement of a penal, revenue, or other public law, and prohibited from enforcement on that ground too. The result is less clear where the property lies outside the territory of the legislating state, but the law of the *situs*, the (to it) foreign legislation would be regarded as effective in the particular case:[41] where the *lex situs* rule collides with the rule against the enforcement of penal laws, one or the other has to give way. It seems, in principle at least, that if the *lex situs* accepts that the legislative decree has operated to alter the ownership, there is nothing left to enforce, and nothing to which enforcement can be denied. Only if the law is so abhorrent that it will be refused even recognition,[42] so that title acquired by reference to it and the *lex situs* rule will not be simply and conclusively applied, will the result be different. The same may be true where the Human Rights Act 1998 directs an English court not to give effect to its usual choice of law rule in a way which would place the English court in breach of its obligations under the European Convention on Human Rights. But whether the Convention applies to this effect is hard to tell. One might have thought that an English court was now precluded from giving a judgment which would have the effect of condoning behaviour, wherever committed, which violated the standards of the European Convention; but when faced with a submission in those terms, the House of Lords has required that the offending conduct amount to a 'flagrant' breach.[43] It seems probable that this question will need to be revisited. In the meantime, unless the Convention is interpreted as giving rise to a statutory one, there is no rule of English private international law which withholds recognition from an expropriatory law

---

[39] ibid.

[40] *Peer International Corp v Termidor Music Publishers Ltd* [2003] EWCA Civ 1156, [2004] Ch 212.

[41] Such as where the law is regarded as being effective in relation to nationals of the expropriating state.

[42] *Kuwait Airways Corp v Iraqi Airways Co (Nos 4 and 5)* [2002] UKHL 19, [2002] 2 AC 883, refusing to recognize an Iraqi law dissolving Kuwait and assuming ownership of Kuwaiti-owned property.

[43] *Barnette v United States* [2004] UKHL 37, [2004] 1 WLR 2241.

unless compensation is paid for the acquisition;[44] the fact that there may be such an obligation in public international law is of no general relevance in private law.

It is sometimes suggested that the answer is more complicated if the property is removed from the territory of the seizing state before it has been taken into the possession of the authorities. In cases where the *lex situs* requires possession to be taken as a precondition to the acquisition of title under it, this is uncontroversial.[45] There is, however, no general justification for imposing such a requirement as a condition which limits the ability of the state to enforce its title when this has been established under its own law, at least where the property in question was ownerless when the state legislated to vest title in itself.[46] On the other hand, where the state has demanded and acquired its title by expropriating a former owner, or has nationalized the property of an individual, the rule against the enforcement of foreign public laws will probably be interpreted to mean that unless the state has already taken possession of the property, it will not be entitled to ask the English court for an order that the property be delivered up to the claimant state to give the state possession which it had not previously enjoyed.[47]

The rules about seizure apply to immovable property, and to tangible property. In relation to intangible property it plainly applies to shares situated where the company is incorporated.[48] It is less obvious how it will apply to simple contractual intangibles, but the *situs* of a debt is in general the place of residence of the debtor, for it is there that he may be sued as a matter of right; and the *situs* rule will therefore apply to this. Article 12 of the Rome Convention, dealing as it does only with voluntary assignments, is irrelevant to the issue.

E. TRUSTS

The private international law of trusts is substantially contained in the Hague Convention on the Recognition of Trusts, given force in England by the Recognition of Trusts Act 1987.[49] From the perspective of English law, however, the Convention has much more to do with the

---

[44] *Williams & Humbert Ltd v W & H Trade Marks (Jersey) Ltd* [1986] AC 368.

[45] *AG for New Zealand v Ortiz* [1984] AC 1.

[46] *Islamic Republic of Iran v Barakat Galleries Ltd* [2007] EWCA Civ 1374.

[47] ibid explaining *Brokaw v Seatrain UK Ltd* [1971] 2 QB 476 (CA) *AG for New Zealand v Oritz* [1984] AC 1, 20 (CA); aff'd on different grounds, 41.

[48] *Williams & Humbert Ltd v W & H Trade Marks (Jersey) Ltd* [1986] AC 368.

[49] Dicey, ch 29.

identification of the governing law than with the recognition of foreign trusts. The Convention defines a trust as the legal relationship, created (*inter vivos* or on death) voluntarily and evidenced in writing, when the settlor places assets under the control of a trustee for the benefit of a beneficiary or for a specified purpose.[50] However, the Act extends this Convention definition to encompass trusts of property arising under the law of any part of the United Kingdom, and to trusts created by judicial decision;[51] and applies it to trusts falling within its definition whatever the date of their creation.[52] Its application to implied, resulting, and constructive trusts is therefore clear. Accordingly, the implied or constructive trust arising from the joint purchase of property will fall squarely within the scope of the Act; but where a constructive trust is sought against or imposed upon a defendant found answerable to an equitable claim, the relevant choice of law rules are probably those examined in the context of equitable obligations.[53]

A trust is governed by the law chosen by the settlor; in default of such a demonstrable choice it is governed by the law with which it is most closely connected.[54] In identifying the latter regard is to be had to the place of administration of the trust, the *situs* of the assets of the trust, the place of residence of the trustee, and the objects of the trust and the places where they are to be fulfilled. The governing law regulates the trust, its construction, effect, and administration;[55] but gives way to mandatory and conflicts rules of the *lex fori*, and to public policy.[56]

F. PERSONAL STATUS AND PROPERTY RIGHTS

I. MARRIAGE AND PROPERTY RIGHTS

The impact of marriage on property rights is only a fragment of a larger picture.[57] Where a marriage is annulled or dissolved, many systems of law

---

[50] Article 2.
[51] Recognition of Trusts Act 1987, s 1(2).
[52] Article 22.
[53] Chapter 7 above.
[54] Articles 6, 7. Note that it is the connection to a law, and not to a country, which is the determining factor.
[55] Article 8.
[56] Article 18.
[57] Dicey, ch 28. It is liable to become larger still as the European Union is in the early stages of proposing legislation to regulate choice of law for matrimonial property. At present, property rights arising from a matrimonial relationship fall outside the Brussels Regulation, Rome Convention, and Rome II Regulation.

allow the court to make orders in relation to the property of the spouses which override rights created or existing prior to or independently of the marriage;[58] and where a marriage is terminated by death, many systems proceed by use of rules of succession, perhaps modified by limiting the testamentary freedom of a deceased. Others, more commonly civilian systems, employ the institution of a matrimonial property regime, often but not always community of property, to deal with the property rights of the quick and the dead. Our concern at this point is with the effect which marriage has on the property rights of spouses; it appears that civil partnership regimes as identified by the 2004 Act will be treated in the same way.[59]

Where the parties on their marriage make a matrimonial contract the proper law of that contract governs its creation, validity, interpretation, and effect.[60] Such contracts are excluded from the Rome Convention, but the choice of law principles of the common law are not substantially different: the proper law may be chosen. In the absence of choice it will be that with which the marriage has its closest and most real connection, the matrimonial domicile:[61] there was a historical preference for this law being that of the husband's domicile, but this has been indefensible at least since the abolition of the wife's dependent domicile in 1974. The capacity of a person to make a marriage contract is governed by his or her domicile at the date of marriage.[62] It is consistent with the principle that once a matrimonial contract has been made, a change in matrimonial domicile cannot alter its content and the rights created under it;[63] but there is nothing in principle, or probably in law, to prevent the spouses varying their contract by agreement. Where the parties do not make a matrimonial contract it was once thought that the foundation of the proprietary relationship was different, and a distinct set of answers was applicable. It was proposed that the law by reference to which they married (the law with which the marriage had its closest connection; the matrimonial domicile) applied to determine the proprietary consequences of marriage,[64] but that this original regime did not necessarily survive a change of spousal domicile. The better view[65] is,

---

[58]   eg Matrimonial Causes Act 1973, s 24(1)(c).

[59]   Civil Partnership Act 2004. The regimes of foreign law which the Act regards as civil partnership are listed in Sch 20.

[60]   *Re Fitzgerald* [1904] 1 Ch 573 (CA).

[61]   *Duke of Marlborough v AG* [1945] Ch 78 (CA). The connection is to a law, not to a country.

[62]   *Re Cooke's Trusts* (1887) 56 LT 737; *Cooper v Cooper* (1888) 13 App Cas 88.

[63]   *De Nicols v Curlier* [1900] AC 21.

[64]   *Re Egerton's Will Trusts* [1956] Ch 593.

[65]   Goldberg (1970) 19 ICLQ 557.

however, that on marriage the spouses simply accept the scheme which is imposed by the law of the matrimonial domicile, and which may be a system of community of property, or separation of property, or some other variant. Whether or not this is conceptualized as a tacit contract or default provision is an irrelevance: it continues to apply after a change in personal domicile, and for the same reasons, as where there is an express contract.

A seeming problem may arise when two systems of provision come into contact and become entangled. If spouses marry into a system of community, when one dies the community rules will determine what portion of the marital property accrues to the survivor, and what falls into the estate of the deceased. But if the deceased dies domiciled in a country where separation of property, and particular provision for inheritance, is the basis of the law, that law may give the survivor a claim to a portion of the estate of the deceased, with the result that, in principle at least, the survivor can claim more than either system would have provided. A practical solution would be for characterization to lead to the result that only one of these schemes applies, but all the while it is seen that there are two, sequential, issues—what did the deceased own when he died? who succeeds to the estate of the deceased?—each having its own choice of law rule, this will be hard to achieve. And in any case, can one really be certain that this generosity to the survivor was not what the parties sought to bring about?

2. DIVORCE AND PROPERTY RIGHTS

The private international law rules for (post-)matrimonial property orders, which, as a matter of domestic law, give a court very wide powers to adjust and override property rights, and which, for the purposes of private international law, is closely related to the dissolution of marriage, is best examined as part of family law.

3. BANKRUPTCY AND PROPERTY RIGHTS

The private international law rules for personal bankruptcy form an important part of the law on change of status and property rights. However, because of the tendency of states to legislate for bankruptcy and corporate insolvency together, is best examined as part of the law of corporations. It is not logical, but for convenience of exposition, it will appear in the final chapter of this book.

4. DEATH AND PROPERTY RIGHTS

When someone dies and the question arises of the ownership of his or her property, it is necessary to separate two issues, each having its own rules for choice of law.[66] The first stage is the administration of the estate of the deceased: the interim process during which the assets are identified and collected, the proven debts paid in the order of their priority, and the balance of the estate calculated. If the deceased was subject to a regime of community of property, the effect of this on his estate will be calculated at this stage of administration. During this period, legal systems differ on the question of who owns the property: in some, the property vests immediately in those who will ultimately take it, but in England it vests in those charged with the administration of the estate. The second stage is the substantive devolution of the estate: once the administration is complete, a further set of rules determines who actually takes which property. Substantive devolution sub-divides into three kinds: testate succession, where devolution is governed by a will left by the deceased and proved in the administration; intestate succession, where the deceased left no valid will or a will which left some of his estate ungifted, where the law steps in to allocate the property according to a formula which usually incorporates a descending scale of relationship; and *bona vacantia* where, because there is no succession (because there is no will and according to the rules on intestacy there is no relative to whom the property will pass by operation of law), the property is regarded as truly ownerless and will be taken by the state as a matter of last resort.

(a) Administration of deceased estates

The administration of estates is the process by which the estate of a deceased person is organized and settled prior to its distribution to those to whom the assets will pass by way of succession. As a matter of English law, it requires an order of the court to empower a person to deal with the assets of a deceased, whether by proving a will in order to appoint a named and willing executor or by obtaining a grant of letters of administration.[67] Although the court may make a grant of representation of any deceased, only rarely will it do so if there is no property of the deceased in England. The making of a grant confirms or vests the property of the deceased in the grantee. Where the deceased died domiciled in a foreign country, the court will usually make a grant to the person who, under the law of the domicile, has been or is entitled to be appointed to administer the estate.[68] The representative may take all steps to get in all property, wherever situated, of the deceased. The substance of the administration is governed

---

[66] Dicey, ch 26.
[67] *New York Breweries Co v AG* [1899] AC 62.
[68] Supreme Court Act 1981, s 25(1).

by the law of the country under which the grant of representation was made.[69] As a matter of English law, in the paying of the deceased's debts foreign creditors and English creditors are treated alike; the admissibility of and priority between claims is governed by English law as *lex fori*.

A foreign grant of representation has, in principle, no effect in England: the person appointed must obtain an English grant.[70] This stands in curious contrast to the fact that the status of a foreign-appointed trustee in bankruptcy is recognized without the need for further order. It has been said that this is the best way to secure the interests of English creditors, but this cannot explain the difference in treatment between different types of representation.

(b) Succession to property

Except where its rules lead to the conclusion that there was no valid will and no relative of the deceased to take on the intestacy, it is the law of succession which determines who takes the property of a deceased who may have died with or without leaving a will.[71] When disputes about succession arise, if a duly appointed representative is before the court, an English court has jurisdiction to determine a question of succession.[72] A foreign court is regarded as having jurisdiction to determine succession to the property, wherever situated, of a deceased dying domiciled in that country, and its decision will be recognized in England;[73] it also has jurisdiction to determine succession to all property within its territorial jurisdiction, regardless of the domicile of the deceased. The potential overlapping of decisions will require the principles of estoppel by *res judicata* to regulate it.

Where the deceased died having left a will, any question of his testamentary capacity is governed by his domicile at the date of making the will,[74] and the capacity of a legatee to take is conferred by the law of either his own or the testator's domicile.[75] The formal validity of the will is satisfied if it is formally valid according to the law of the place when and where it was executed, or the law of the place (at the time of either execution or death) where the deceased died domiciled or habitually resident, or of

---

[69] *Re Kloebe* (1884) 28 Ch D 175; *Re Lorillard* [1922] 2 Ch 638 (CA).

[70] *New York Breweries Co v AGen.* [1899] AC 62.

[71] Dicey, ch 27.

[72] *Re Lorillard* [1922] 2 Ch 638 (CA).

[73] *Re Trufort* (1887) 36 Ch D 600; *Ewing v Orr-Ewing* (1883) 9 App Cas 34; *Ewing v Orr-Ewing* (1885) 10 App Cas 5.

[74] *Re Fuld's Estate (No 3)* [1968] P 675.

[75] *Re Hellmann's Will* (1866) LR 2 Eq 363.

which he was a national.[76] The same laws govern the formal validity of a will revoking an earlier will.[77] Wills of immovables are formally valid if they conform to the *lex situs*.[78] The material validity of a will is governed by the law of the testator's domicile at death,[79] except for immovables, where this is governed by the *lex situs*.[80] It follows that if it is argued that the testator was limited as regards the fraction of his estate over which he had testamentary freedom, as is the case in systems which provide a statutory portion for spouses and children, this question will be treated as one of the material validity of the will. But the interpretation of the will is governed by the law of the domicile at the date of making the will.[81] The validity of an act of revocation is governed by the domicile of the testator at the date of revocation.[82] So the question whether subsequent marriage, or the tearing up or burning of a will, serves to revoke an earlier will is determined by the *lex domicilii* of the testator at the date of the marriage or other event.

Where the deceased dies without leaving a valid will or fails to will a part of his estate, the intestate succession is governed by the domiciliary law of the deceased at the date his death, except that succession to immovables is governed by the *lex situs*.[83] It is inherent in the nature of intestate succession that it means the taking of property, by operation of law, but by a relative of the deceased who did not make a will.

Where there is no will and no person to take by way of intestate succession, the property still has to pass. In this case the principles can no longer be those of succession, for there is no-one to succeed to it. Instead, a state will assume title to local ownerless property as *bona vacantia*, and the question of which state is governed in all cases by the *lex situs* of the property. An illusory problem arises when the application of the law of the domicile would vest the property of an intestate deceased in the state of his domicile, it being provided that the state is the 'final heir' of a deceased. It has been said that in this context it is necessary to characterize the rule of law relied on by the claiming state to determine whether it is a succession rule or a rule about *bona vacantia*, and that this is a matter of ascertaining the

---

[76] Wills Act 1963, s 1.
[77] ibid s 2(1)(c).
[78] ibid s 2(1)(c).
[79] *Whicker v Hume* (1858) 7 HLC 124; *Re Groos* [1915] Ch 572; *Re Ross* [1930] 1 Ch 377.
[80] *Nelson v Bridport* (1846) 8 Beav 547; *Freke v Carbery* (1873) LR 16 Eq 461.
[81] *Ewing v Orr-Ewing* (1883) 9 App Cas 34.
[82] *In bonis Reid* (1866) LR 1 P & D 74.
[83] *Balfour v Scott* (1793) 6 Bro PC 550.

substance of the foreign rule rather than being persuaded by its form.[84] This is misguided. Quite apart from the fact that the process of characterization is directed at issues as distinct from rules of law, the law requires a characterization line to be drawn to separate intestate succession from the devolution of *bona vacantia*, to which a different choice of law rule, the *lex situs*, applies. The court must first decide whether the issue concerns property which is owned by way of succession, or is ownerless for failure of succession: only in the latter case does an issue arise of its devolution as *bona vacantia*. Thus understood, there is no need to characterize rules rather than issues. The misunderstanding arises where the process of taking property upon death is seen in every case as succession. Once it is accepted that the true characterization category is the devolution of property on death, which in turn sub-divides into three possibilities, each with its own choice of law rule, there is no real difficulty.

It may finally be noted that the European Union is giving consideration to legislation in this area: in 2005 it published a Green Paper on succession and wills. It will be of comfort to some to know that legislation in the field of private international law to secure the free movement of the dead is necessary to complete the internal market. Should it come to pass (whereupon it will be known, no doubt, as Rome IV[85]) the justification which will be recited as the legal basis for such a nonsense will be worth reading.

---

[84] *Re Maldonado's Estate* [1954] P 233 (CA).

[85] Rome III is intended to be the successor to Brussels II*bis*, which is discussed in the following chapter.

9

Family Law

A. ADULTS

Family law, and the private international law of marriage in particular, is the one area in which the *lex domicilii*, the law of the domicile, still has a significant role to play. Not every issue is answered by recourse to it, and statutory reform has encroached on its hegemony. But family law is largely about status; status is generally determined by the personal law; and as a matter of English conflict of laws, the personal law is the *lex domicilii*, the law of the domicile. It should not be supposed, however, that this means that there will be international agreement on the status of an individual. For although most systems agree that status is a matter for the personal law, there is no agreement about which law—domicile, nationality, law of the religious group, and so on—actually is the personal law; and even as between countries which use the *lex domicilii* as the personal law, there are differences in its definition. In the context of family law, the reference to *law* usually indicates the whole law, including the rules of the conflict of laws, which would be applied by a judge hearing the case in his own court: the principle of *renvoi* is relevant to those family law cases in which it is pleaded and proved.

The plan of this chapter is to examine adult relations: marriage, matrimonial causes, and financial provision, and to offer an outline, inevitably brief, of the highly complex law relating to children.

B. MARRIAGE

The validity or invalidity of marriage requires a preliminary distinction to be drawn between formal validity, capacity to marry, and other impediments to marriage.[1] The first is concerned with the ceremony and its components, the second with whether the person is in law entitled to marry, or entitled to marry the other, and the third with a miscellany of issues of validity which are not within the scope of the other two. The advantage

---

[1] Dicey, ch 17.

of this division is that it reflects the plausible and legitimate interest of a number of countries in the validity of marriage, but seeks to limit that interest to those particular matters with which they are most closely concerned. On the other hand, reference to a number of laws may make for complexity, and it may tend to increase the likelihood of the marriage being invalidated as more laws are given the opportunity to make an objection. If this were valid as a criticism, it might be preferable to have marriage governed by a single law, say that with which the marriage is most closely connected. It is generally assumed that this should not be the law of the place of celebration, although this is not without significant support in the laws of the United States and elsewhere. On the other hand, such a rule, by focusing on the marriage as if it were a self-contained contract as opposed to a step in a chain of status-determining events, would weaken the idea of status as an enduring, organic concept.

From time to time it is said that English law makes a presumption of the validity of marriage.[2] All this appears to mean is that where there is room for any flexibility in the rules for choice of law, and the parties believe that they have gone through a valid ceremony of marriage, any doubt should be resolved in favour of validity. This does not mean that marriage is a higher and more developed state of human existence, but reflects the sensible fact that where there has been a wedding ceremony, and reliance has been placed on its validity, there needs to be good reason to surprise the parties and any interested third parties by regarding it as having been invalid all along.

Once an issue has been characterized, and the relevant choice of law rule invoked, it is necessary to decide what precise question is to be formulated for answer by reference to the chosen law. Suppose facts are characterized as raising an issue of formal validity, and that this requires reference to a foreign law which, in the particular case, governs formal validity. The question to be referred to the foreign law for answer will be either 'is this marriage formally valid despite . . . ?' or 'is this marriage valid despite . . . ?', the difference being whether the characterization which led to the choice of law remains as a constraint on the formulation of the question. It was proposed above[3] that it does not: that where the English court may be trying to decide the case as the foreign judge would, there is no sense in pre-empting the foreign law on the first stage of the analysis which it would have to undertake.

---

[2] eg *Radwan v Radwan (No 2)* [1973] Fam 35.
[3] At p 18.

I. FORMAL VALIDITY OF MARRIAGE

The formal requirements of a marriage ceremony and the effects of non-compliance are governed by the law of the place of celebration of the marriage, the *lex loci celebrationis*.[4] The question whether there is need for a public, civil, or religious ceremony,[5] whether particular words need to be read or spoken in the course of the ceremony, whether the ceremony must be held in the particular building or in none, whether a priest need be present, whether it is necessary for either party to be present in person or by proxy,[6] or whether it is necessary for the parents or other third parties to give their consent,[7] are all characterized as issues of formal validity. They are all answered by recourse to the *lex loci celebrationis*, and the consequences in terms of nullity or otherwise are determined by it as well. If the marriage would be invalid by the domestic law of the place of celebration, but would be valid by reference to the law to which a judge at the *locus celebrationis* would look if he were trying the issue, the marriage will be formally validated via the principles of *renvoi*.[8] Although theoretically possible, it is improbable that the reverse proposition would invalidate a marriage, for all systems of family law are likely to regard compliance with local forms as sufficient.

There is an exception to the proposition that a marriage is formally valid only if it complied with the *lex loci celebrationis*. In two cases a marriage will be formally valid by having complied with the rudimentary formal requirements of the English common law as this stood prior to 1753. This extraordinary proposition—that a completely foreign marriage may be formally valid if it complied with the requirements of a law prior to its alteration by statute over 250 years ago—is only a little less startling if it is remembered that this is in fact a reference to the canon law which prevailed across much of Europe, and in England until 1753. The requirements of the pre-1753 common law involve no more than the public declaration of intention to marry in the presence of witnesses with no need for a priest,[9] which comes close to saying that there are no formal requirements at all. This suffices to establish formal validity where it was impossible for the parties to comply with local forms, or where the place of celebration was

---

[4] *Simonin v Mallac* (1860) 2 Sw & Tr 67; *Berthiaume v Dastous* [1930] AC 79 (PC).

[5] *Taczanowska v Taczanowski* [1957] P 301 (CA).

[6] *Apt v Apt* [1948] P 83 (CA); *McCabe v McCabe* [1994] 1 FLR 257 (CA).

[7] *Simonin v Mallac* (1860) 2 Sw & Tr 67; *Ogden v Ogden* [1908] P 46 (CA) (both parental consent); cf *Sottomayor v De Barros (No 1)* (1877) 2 PD 81 (CA) (papal consent, although this may instead be a question of personal capacity).

[8] *Taczanowska v Taczanowski* [1957] P 301 (CA).

[9] *Wolfenden v Wolfenden* [1946] P 61; *Penhas v Tan Soo Eng* [1953] AC 304 (PC).

under belligerent occupation and the parties belonged to or were associated with those occupying forces.[10] Impossibility may be found where two persons wish to marry in a place where civil order has wholly broken down, or where there is no human population; but it is much less clear that it applies if the parties have ethical objections to the form—say, that only religious marriage is permitted—of local marriage ceremony. It is hard to see why parties should be able to opt out of the local law, especially where international travel is not difficult. But if the parties do not come within the local formality criteria for marriage, it is hard to deny that marriage is impossible for them, there. As regards belligerent occupation, it would have been revolting to common sense to require Poles or other victims of barbarism, who married while serving in forces in belligerent occupation of enemy territory in 1945 or in groups associated with them, to comply with the formal requirements of German or other axis laws, even if the marriage would not have been technically impossible: the exception allows decency to prevail over dogmatism. Statutory provision is made for members of HM forces to marry while serving abroad, and for consular marriages.[11]

2. CAPACITY OF PERSONS TO MARRY

Each party is required to have capacity to marry the other according to the law of his or her ante-nuptial domicile, the *lex domicilii*.[12] The reason is said to be that whether and when someone is ready for marriage is determined by the society in which he or she has grown up. Some authorities suggest that the law of the intended matrimonial home might be a more appropriate test, but none has so decided, and the inherent uncertainty of such a test makes it difficult to support, at least when the question arises prospectively.[13] But it must be admitted that there is much to be said for the view that the law of the society in which the spouses are going to live has the most obvious interest in saying whether they have capacity to live there as husband and wife. The characterization category of capacity includes the age of marital capacity[14] and the prohibited degrees of relationship.[15] But the distinct issue of the effect of a previous marriage arguably dissolved or annulled by decree is examined below, as it deals with a more complex conflict of laws and of judgments.

---

[10] *Taczanowska v Taczanowski* [1957] P 301 (CA); *Preston v Preston* [1963] P 411 (CA).

[11] Foreign Marriage Act 1892, ss 22 (as amended) and 1, respectively.

[12] *Brook v Brook* (1861) 9 HLC 193; *Sottomayor v De Barros (No 2)* (1879) 5 PD 94.

[13] For its use retrospectively, see *Radwan v Radwan* [1973] Fam 35.

[14] The Marriage Act 1949, s 2, applies to any marriage in England, and requires that neither party be under 16.

[15] *Brook v Brook* (1861) 9 HLC 193.

The concurrent role of the *lex loci celebrationis* in the regulation of capacity is also a bit of a puzzle. The first question is whether it is necessary to comply with the capacity rules of the *lex loci* as well as with those of the personal laws. If the marriage takes place in England it is probable that the parties must also satisfy the capacity requirements of English law,[16] at least if the issue arises prior to the celebration of the marriage, in the form of judicial review of a registrar's refusal to license the marriage. So if the registrar refuses to permit the marriage of two foreign-domiciled persons, one of whom is under 16, he will not be ordered to marry them even though each has domiciliary capacity. But if the marriage has taken place in England, the parties having had capacity by their personal laws, and subject to what is said about marriages celebrated overseas, it is hard to see the interest of English law in then regarding it as invalid. If the marriage takes place overseas, the dominant, although questionable, view is that the parties do not need capacity under the *lex loci* in addition to satisfying their personal laws, even though one case did assume that such capacity was required.[17] Even so, there is a respectable argument that capacity by the *lex loci*, whether English or overseas, ought generally to be required for a marriage to be valid. It is unconvincing to maintain that the law of the place is uniquely concerned with formal validity, and completely unconcerned with capacity. Moreover, if the law under which the celebrant is vested with authority considers that, on account of the parties' lack of capacity to marry, his purported act of marriage was a nullity, it is hard to see why English law should disagree. If it is correct to understand marriage as something which is done by a marriage officer, rather than something done by the parties themselves, the law which defines the officer's powers appears to be acutely interested in the question whether he has altered the capacity of the parties, even though reference to an additional law will tend to increase the invalidity of marriages.

By contrast with the possibility that the *lex loci* may invalidate a marriage, otherwise valid, for lack of capacity, it may also validate a marriage even though one of the parties lacks domiciliary capacity. If the marriage takes place in England, one party being domiciled in England, it suffices for the other to have capacity according to English domestic law, even though he or she lacks capacity under the foreign domiciliary law.[18] This is a controversial principle, justified on the unconvincing basis that injustice would otherwise be done to an English domiciliary. Its weakness is

---

[16] There is no judicial authority to this effect, however.

[17] *Breen v Breen* [1964] P 144.

[18] *Sottomayor v De Barros (No 2)* (1879) 5 PD 94; *Ogden v Ogden* [1908] P 46 (CA) (alternative ratio).

magnified when it is observed that the foreign incapacities which the court indicated it was prepared to override were opposed to English public policy—prohibitions on inter-racial marriage, the need for the head of the Roman Catholic Church to consent—and which could have been better accommodated under that exceptional rule. Tellingly, the rule has no counterpart for a marriage taking place overseas in the domicile of one of the parties.

3. OTHER IMPEDIMENTS TO MARRIAGE

There remain a number of other factors which may lead to the invalidity of marriage, but which it is not helpful to see as raising issues of personal capacity, and which are not the subject of a uniform choice of law rule. They are grouped together for convenience. First, each party must consent to marry the other. Any argument that there was no consent, whether this is said to follow from mistake, fraud, concealment, or duress, will be governed by the *lex domicilii* of the party said not to have consented, as if this were a question of personal capacity.[19] Secondly, it is rational, although not clearly established by law, that physical impediments such as inability or refusal to consummate the marriage by sexual intercourse are referable to the law of the allegedly incapable party,[20] although contrary views are not untenable: it may be argued that if the willing-and-able party has no capacity to marry a refuser, that party's law should apply instead. But as absence of consent and refusal both render a marriage voidable rather than void, and as the evidence is likely to be problematic, there is room for the further alternative view that the case should be treated as though it were one of divorce, for which the appropriate choice of law would be the *lex fori*.

Thirdly, there are special rules which apply to the validity of polygamous marriages in so far as the polygamy is alleged to be an impediment. For the purpose of the rule, it is first necessary to identify when a marriage is polygamous. This will be the case[21] if two conditions are met: it is celebrated in polygamous form[22] and the husband's *lex domicilii* gives him personal capacity for polygamy.[23] The first condition means that a marriage celebrated in England is inevitably monogamous but, if celebrated overseas, the nature of the marriage will depend on the nature of the ceremony.

---

[19] *Szechter v Szechter* [1971] P 286, but cf *Vervaeke v Smith* [1983] 1 AC 145.

[20] *Ponticelli v Ponticelli* [1958] P 204.

[21] Subject to the Private International Law (Miscellaneous Provisions) Act 1995, s 5, a marriage is polygamous if actually or potentially so.

[22] *Lee v Lau* [1967] P 14.

[23] *Hussain v Hussain* [1983] Fam 26 (CA).

The second condition needs no further explanation, save that if the husband loses his personal capacity for polygamy, for example by changing his domicile, the nature of the marriage will be changed to monogamy.[24] When the matter was regulated by the common law, the second condition meant that a marriage celebrated overseas by an English domiciled man was not polygamous, for he lacked personal capacity for polygamy. But if celebrated by an English-domiciled woman it could be polygamous, as the husband may have personal capacity for polygamy, and it would on that account be invalid if her capacity to enter it was governed by English law as her *lex domicilii*. But it is now provided that if a potentially polygamous marriage is actually (in the sense of arithmetically) monogamous, an English woman does not lack capacity to enter it, and the domiciliary incapacity is restricted to actually polygamous marriages. Moreover, while a woman domiciled in a country which permits polygamy may contract a polygamous marriage, and an Englishwoman has no personal capacity for actual polygamy,[25] it has been held, in a decision ostensibly designed to uphold the validity of a marriage which had endured for 20 years, that her personal capacity to have contracted a polygamous marriage should be governed by the law of what was the intended matrimonial home.[26]

Fourthly, if a previous marriage has been dissolved or annulled by a decree recognized by English law otherwise than under Regulation (EC) 2201/2003,[27] the subsequent remarriage of either party is not invalidated by the refusal of some other system of law to recognize the decree.[28] So if a Maltese domiciliary is divorced by a decree recognized by the Family Law Act 1986 but denied recognition under Maltese law, the remarriage will be valid even though Maltese law, as the law of the domicile, would regard the first marriage as subsisting and the second marriage as bigamous and void: this result is brought about by legislation, and the deduction that a divorce is not really being recognized in accordance with Parliament's instruction if it still leaves the spouse incapable of marriage. In this it reverses the understanding of the common law which, although allowing the recognition of a divorce to break the bonds of matrimony, accepted that capacity to remarry was a distinct issue having a different, and domiciliary, choice

---

[24] *Ali v Ali* [1968] P 564; *Parkasho v Singh* [1968] P 223. This still seems rather odd, especially if polygamy is seen as an institution which is quite different and distinct from monogamous marriage. After all, if a married man undergoes a change of sex, it is improbable that the marriage is turned into a civil partnership.

[25] Private International Law (Miscellaneous Provisions) Act 1995, s 5.

[26] *Radwan v Radwan (No 2)* [1973] Fam 35.

[27] [2003] OJ L338, discussed, at p 253 below.

[28] Family Law Act 1986, s 50.

of law. The inverse position, where the *lex domicilii* recognizes the validity of a decree which English legislation does not, is not provided for. But if the *lex domicilii* regards an individual as capable of remarriage it is hard to see the rational interest of English law in contradicting it just because English law would not recognize the decree.[29] On the other hand, the wording of the Family Law Act 1986, section 45, may stand in the way of this result, on the ground that to accept the remarriage as valid is to grant constructive recognition to the divorce; and section 45 states that a divorce may not be recognized except in accordance with the Act.

But where recognition of the decree of a court in a Member State is mandated by the Brussels II*bis* Regulation,[30] the provisions of the Family Law Act 1986 do not apply[31] and the impact of the decree on the parties' capacity to remarry is more uncertain. As the Regulation governs the dissolution of matrimonial ties, and disclaims any effect on related issues,[32] it may not mean that a spouse whose personal law refuses to recognize the decree is free to remarry. The choice is to regard the issue as governed by the law of the state which granted the decree and to give it the effect it had under that law;[33] or to discern the answer from the text of the Regulation; or to revert to the common law;[34] or to pretend that the Family Law Act 1986, section 50, had not been made inapplicable to such cases.[35]

Fifthly, public policy may intervene at the point when a rule of the *lex causae*, even after making allowance for different cultural and social traditions, offends the English conception of marriage, freedom to marry, and the equality of the sexes. For example, if the personal law of one of the parties denies marital capacity to a person on grounds which are capricious, penal, or discriminatory,[36] such an impediment will, or at any rate should, be ignored. And if the personal laws were to confer marital capacity at the age of five, or allow marriage to a dead person,[37] it is possible that public policy would deny recognition. But English law draws the limits of public

---

[29] *Schwebel v Ungar* (1963) 42 DLR (2d) 622 (Ont CA) supports the application of the *lex domicilii* over the non-recognition of the *lex fori*.

[30] Regulation (EC) 2201/2003, [2003] OJ L338; and see SI 2001/310, as amended.

[31] SI 2001/310, reg 9, amending the Family Law Act 1986, Pt III.

[32] Recital 10.

[33] cf Case 145/86 *Hoffmann v Krieg* [1988] ECR 645.

[34] Giving primacy to the personal law: *Schwebel v Ungar* (1963) 42 DLR (2d) 622 (Ont CA).

[35] Despite the wording of SI 2001/310, reg 9.

[36] *Scott v AG* (1886) 11 PD 128; cf *Sottomayor v De Barros (No 2)* (1879) 5 PD 94.

[37] Not as improbable as it sounds: certain laws may allow a person to marry, *post mortem*, a fiancé who was killed in war service but before the marriage had taken place.

policy tightly, with the result that marriages which are considerably different from the English domestic law model may be recognized.

4. CIVIL PARTNERSHIP

English courts did not have to decide whether any special rule applied to marriages celebrated between persons of the same sex. The conflicts issues which might have flowed from the fact that some countries allow marriage between persons of the same sex, without the skies falling in should not have been complex but could have been fascinating. After all, if the law could accommodate islamic polygamy within the pale of marriage, same-sex marriages provided for under the laws of western secular democracies should not have been too challenging. On the other hand, the states in question have legislated in various ways to permit marriage, as well as unions which, in varying degrees, resemble marriage; and issues of characterization could have been expected to arise. But before any such thing could happen, and to the professional disappointment of private international lawyers, legislation[38] supervened. It provided for the creation of English, and recognition of foreign, civil partnership on grounds functionally equivalent to those governing marriage, and stipulated that same-sex marriage contracted under laws which provided for it was to be seen, for the purposes of English law, as civil partnership. This saved English law from having to deal with arid distinctions between different types of same-sex marriage, according to whether the foreign law under which it was contracted defined it as marriage, quasi-marriage, or non-marriage. For practical purposes, the law on contracting and terminating civil partnership is the same as the law on marriage in England and overseas, although it is not certain whether the Brussels II*bis* Regulation applies of its own force and right to the dissolution of civil partnership: if it does not, English law can produce that effect itself.

C. MATRIMONIAL CAUSES

The private international law of matrimonial causes[39] has to juggle a number of laws which may all have some interest in the issues which arise. The result cannot avoid being messy. The laws which determine the initial validity of marriage may not be those which apply on its annulment or

---

[38] Civil Partnership Act 2004. Sch 20, as amended, lists the foreign institutions which are deemed to be civil partnerships for the purposes of the Act.

[39] The rules also cover judicial separation, but the infrequency of this form of decree justifies its omission from a book of this size.

dissolution; the laws which determine the effectiveness of an annulment or dissolution may not, as has been seen, be the ones which regulate the right to remarry. There are two parties who, by the time matters come to court, may have acquired separate domiciles and residences; there will be laws which had, laws which have, and laws which will have, a connection to the facts and to the parties themselves. There may be third parties with personal laws which also have an interest in being taken into account. Decrees of nullity and divorce may be obtained by civil proceedings which may or may not also be fully judicial, but also by reference to religious 'law'. A local policy of being disposed to grant recognition to divorces may clash with a foreign law's policy of not doing so; and all in all there is plenty of scope for a conflict of laws. Perhaps because of this, the role of the *lex fori* is still more prominent than one might expect it to be in the field of status; and the rules on jurisdiction are inevitably complex. Painting the picture by reference to principle is, therefore, rather difficult.

Outside the context of choice of law, the law does not draw a sharp distinction between divorce and annulment, for although the two forms of decree are conceptually distinct, the law is complicated enough without having entirely separate sets of rules for jurisdiction, choice of law, and recognition. Accordingly, they may be considered together as matrimonial causes.

Having been kept at bay until recently, the European Union has finally got its hoof through the door of family law, the better to complete the internal market.[40] A Regulation, known as 'Brussels II',[41] was made to govern, although only in part, the jurisdiction of Member States to grant matrimonial decrees and the recognition and enforcement of decrees granted in other Member States. This was remade, with amendment mainly confined to parental responsibility for children, by 'Brussels II*bis*'.[42] It follows that the law on jurisdiction to grant, and recognition of, decrees has become complex.

1. OBTAINING DECREES FROM AN ENGLISH COURT

The jurisdiction of an English court to grant a decree of divorce, legal separation, or annulment is governed in the first instance by the Brussels II*bis*

---

[40] See Recital 2. It is not quite as daft as it sounds. Disagreement between the laws of Member States on whether persons are regarded as married or not will certainly have its impact on the willingness of such persons to move freely and establish themselves within the single market.

[41] Regulation (EC) 1347/2000, [2000] OJ L160/19.

[42] Regulation (EC) 2201/2003, [2003] OJ L338.

Regulation[43] and depends on the respondent spouse.[44] If the respondent is habitually resident in a Member State[45] or is a national of a Member State other than the United Kingdom or Ireland, or is domiciled[46] in England, Scotland, Northern Ireland, or Ireland, jurisdiction may be taken only in accordance with Articles 2 to 7 of the Regulation.[47] Accordingly, the court has jurisdiction if both spouses are domiciled in England.[48] Alternatively, it has jurisdiction if England is where the spouses are habitually resident; or where they were last habitually resident, in so far as one of them still resides there; or where the respondent is habitually resident; or where (in the event of a joint application) either of the spouses is habitually resident; or where the applicant is, and for a year immediately before the application was made was, habitually resident; or where the applicant, who is domiciled in England, was habitually resident for six months immediately prior to the application.[49] If none of these provisions gives jurisdiction to the court, there is no jurisdictional basis for an application; where they give jurisdiction to the English courts and those of another Member State, Article 19 provides for a first-seised rule to settle any problem of *lis alibi pendens*.[50]

If the respondent is not so resident, domiciled, or a national, Article 8 of the Regulation provides that 'residual' jurisdiction is a matter for national law to determine.[51] In England this will require that either party to the marriage was domiciled in England on the date the proceedings were begun;[52] jurisdiction over proceedings for nullity is substantially the same,[53] save that a decree of nullity may also be granted if one party has died but at death was domiciled, or had for a year been habitually resident,

---

[43] [2000] OJ L160/19. Consequential amendments to statutes are made by SI 2001/310, as itself amended by SI 2005/265.

[44] In this respect the structure of the law is close to that of the Brussels Regulation, Regulation (EC) 44/2001 [2000] OJ L12/1, dealing with jurisdiction in civil and commercial matters, in which the domicile of the defendant is of principal concern.

[45] A state of the European Union excluding Denmark: Art 1(3).

[46] As a matter of the law of the UK: Art 41(b).

[47] Article 7.

[48] Article 2(1)(b). The corresponding rule for the other Member States except Ireland is framed in terms of nationality rather than domicile. 'Domicile' has its common law meaning: Art 4(2); and England is treated as if it were a Member State by reason of Art 41.

[49] Article 2(1)(a).

[50] *Bentinck v Bentinck* [2007] EWCA Civ 175, [2007] ILPr 391; *Prazic v Prazic* [2006] EWCA Civ 497, [2007] ILPr 381.

[51] Article 8.

[52] Domicile and Matrimonial Proceedings Act 1973, s 5(2) as amended by SI 2001/310, reg 3(4).

[53] Domicile and Matrimonial Proceedings Act 1973, s 5(3) as amended by SI 2001/310, reg 3(5).

in England.[54] But proceedings may also be brought in a foreign court. In relation to parallel proceedings, if the other court is that of another Member State, Article 19 will apply a first-seised rule to deny the jurisdiction of the second court, but the Regulation otherwise makes no provision for and takes no account of principles of *forum conveniens*. Subject to that overriding rule an English court has a statutory[55] power to stay proceedings. Accordingly, where jurisdiction is taken under Article 8, a stay may be obligatory given prior divorce proceedings in another part of the United Kingdom,[56] and is discretionary in all other cases. Although this statutory power is distinct from the inherent power to stay on grounds of *forum non conveniens*, any distinction between the two is more technical than substantial. It follows that if the foreign court is clearly and distinctly more appropriate than England for the resolution of the dispute, the fact that the petitioner will be disadvantaged by having to proceed in the foreign jurisdiction will not ward off a stay if substantial justice may be obtained there.[57] There is no[58] hard and fast rule that a stay should be granted if the foreign proceedings were begun first, but there will be a strong disinclination to allow later-begun proceedings to continue in a way which simply duplicates earlier ones.

On a petition for divorce, an English court applies English domestic law without exception. There is no rational doubting the rightness of this. Whenever there are proposals to alter the grounds upon which a divorce may be obtained, there is public debate and often sharp disagreement. In this sensitive context it cannot be right for some divorces, for which the English court has jurisdiction, to be granted on grounds insufficient in English domestic law, or for a petitioner to be denied a divorce although satisfying the criteria of English law. The general application of English law to everyone, equally and indiscriminately, is inevitable. A recent European proposal[59] to provide for the application of personal laws has attracted well-founded opposition, not least on account of its potential to require a court to apply the divorce (or non-divorce) law of some primitive, usually religious, law: it is hard to believe that anything will

---

[54] ibid.

[55] Domicile and Matrimonial Proceedings Act 1973, Sch 1, para 9, as amended by SI 2001/310, reg 4. Whether a court may stay its proceedings if jurisdiction is founded on Art 2 of the Regulation but the natural forum in a non-Member State is uncertain: cf *Re Harrods (Buenos Aires) Ltd* [1992] Ch 72 (CA).

[56] Domicile and Matrimonial Proceedings Act 1973, Sch 1, para 8.

[57] *De Dampierre v De Dampierre* [1988] AC 92.

[58] By contrast, the High Court of Australia does appear to have such a view: *Henry v Henry* (1996) 185 CLR 571.

[59] The proposal takes the form of a Draft Regulation, to be known as 'Rome III', to replace Regulation Brussels II *bis*, which is discussed below.

come of it. For decrees of nullity, the applicable law will be deduced from the grounds of invalidity examined in relation to the original validity of marriage: allegations of personal incapacity will be governed by the *lex domicilii*, and so on. If the marriage is plainly void, as distinct from being voidable or dissoluble, there is no need to obtain a decree to this effect, although it will usually be prudent to do so. Where the alleged defect relied on is one which is in substance unknown, either precisely or by analogy, to English law, no reported authority exists to confer the power to annul the marriage.[60] Such cases will be rare, and the chances must be that to grant a decree on such grounds would offend English public policy.

2. RECOGNITION OF FOREIGN JUDGMENTS

There are three main statutory schemes for the recognition of foreign judgments given in matrimonial causes. The principal distinction is the source of the judgment. A decree from Scotland, Northern Ireland, the Channel Islands, or the Isle of Man will be recognized on the same basis as an English decree, that is, that it was granted by a court.[61] A decree from a Member State bound by the Brussels II*bis* Regulation will be governed by that regime;[62] beyond that, recognition is governed by the Family Law Act 1986, Part III.

(a) The Brussels II*bis* Regulation

The law on recognition of matrimonial decrees from Member States is, pretty much, that such decrees will be recognized. The detail is contained in Chapter III of the Regulation, which tracks the corresponding provisions of the Brussels Regulation[63] on jurisdiction and judgments in civil and commercial matters, and which fact allows the discussion of it here to be abbreviated. The effect is to align civil, commercial, and matrimonial judgments from other Member States for the purposes of their recognition: this is a radical departure from the tradition of English law, which had kept them well apart. Recognition under Chapter III will apply to decrees obtained from a court in a Member State given in proceedings which were instituted after 1 March 2001.[64] Any divorce, legal

---

[60] cf *Vervaeke v Smith* [1983] 1 AC 145.

[61] Family Law Act 1986, s 44.

[62] Regulation (EC) 2201/2003. A proposal to extend the Regulation to cover choice of law for matrimonial causes has been made as a draft 'Rome III' Regulation. It is not discussed here.

[63] Regulation (EC) 44/2001.

[64] That it to say, according to the commencement date of the predecessor, Brussels II Regulation, with which Brussels II*bis* is materially identical.

separation, or annulment pronounced by a court[65] in a Member State is to be recognized without any procedure or formality.[66] Non-recognition is permitted[67] if recognition is manifestly contrary to public policy; if the judgment was given in default of appearance and there was no due and timely service, unless the respondent has unequivocally accepted the judgment; if the judgment is irreconcilable with a local judgment in proceedings between the same parties; or if it is irreconcilable with an earlier judgment from a non-Member State in proceedings between the same parties which qualified for recognition. But the jurisdiction of the adjudicating court may not be reviewed or subjected to the test of public policy;[68] recognition may not be withheld on the basis that the recognizing court would not itself have granted the decree;[69] and the substance of the judgment may not be reviewed.[70] Unexpectedly, perhaps, recognition is said not to affect the property consequences of the marriage, maintenance obligations, or other ancillary measures,[71] although it is difficult to see how these can remain wholly unaffected. As was pointed out above, it is not said whether it is implicit in the obligation to recognize a decree that the parties to the former marriage have restored to them their capacity to marry, even if the personal law of one of them would refuse to acknowledge it. The eighth recital suggests that recognition of the decree extends only to the dissolution of matrimonial ties, but there is English authority for the proposition that a decree can hardly be said to have been recognized if it does not carry with it the freedom to remarry.[72] The procedure for enforcement, where this is required as a separate legal effect, is set out in Articles 28 to 30, which corresponds to the provisions of Brussels Regulation.

(b) Family Law Act 1986, Part III

The Brussels II*bis* Regulation proceeds by reference to the court which granted the decree. This makes it easy to determine whether the decree

---

[65] Which includes all authorities with jurisdiction in these matters, so that non-judicial decrees are treated as if they were judicial decrees: Art 2(1). By way of derogation, it appears from recital 7 that 'purely religious procedures' are excluded from the scope of the Regulation, and decrees granted by such bodies are therefore recognized, if at all, under the Family Law Act 1986.

[66] Article 21.

[67] Article 22, on which see Art 34 of the Brussels Regulation, Regulation (EC) 44/2001.

[68] Article 24.

[69] Article 25.

[70] Article 26.

[71] Recital 8 to the Regulation.

[72] *Lawrence v Lawrence* [1985] Fam 106 (CA); Family Law Act 1986, s 50. But s 50 does not apply to decrees recognized under the Regulation: Family Law Act 1986, s 45(2) as inserted by SI 2001/310, reg 9.

is one to which the Regulation applies. The Family Law Act 1986[73] also draws a fundamental distinction, but according to where the decree was obtained: they are either divorces obtained in the British islands[74] or are overseas divorces. This would be rational if divorces were always obtained in a single country, as will be seen, the untidy reality does not conform to that template. Nevertheless, the point of departure is that divorces or annulments obtained in England must be obtained by means of judicial proceedings, otherwise they are of no effect.[75] 'Overseas divorces', which means divorces obtained in a country outside the British islands, will be recognized, according to section 45(1), only in accordance with sections 46 to 49; and according to section 46 it is necessary to decide whether they were obtained by means of proceedings (whether judicial or otherwise) or not.[76] The separate treatment of divorces obtained without proceedings requires the drawing of a peculiarly useless line of division. Were a distinction necessary, separate treatment of civil-judicial, and religious-non-judicial, divorces would have reflected the rather different procedures and assumptions underpinning each category of case. But this was not done and, for the recognition of foreign divorces, all now turns on whether the divorce was obtained by 'proceedings'.

The scheme put in place by sections 44 and 45(1) proceeds on the unspoken assumption that every divorce or annulment is obtained in a single country. Problems arise when a decree is obtained by means of proceedings whose components touch more countries than one. In relation to decrees presented for recognition as overseas divorces, the leading cases[77] were both ones where part of the procedure leading to the divorce—in each case a divorce obtained outside court and under religious 'law'—had taken place in England. In holding that this precluded recognition of the decree, the court did not limit its reasoning to a case where part of the procedure had taken place in England. Instead, it deduced from the statutory definition of an overseas divorce that to be recognized as such, all the elements required for it to be obtained must be located in one foreign country. So a Jewish religious divorce obtained by the formal writing and

---

[73] The legislation draws no distinction between divorces and annulments, and the term 'decrees' is used to encompass both. But for convenience of explanation, we will use the term 'divorce' to include divorce and nullity.

[74] This expression includes England, Scotland, Northern Ireland, the Channel Islands, and the Isle of Man (decrees from Ireland fall under the Regulation). Nevertheless, for convenience we will refer to English and overseas divorces.

[75] Family Law Act 1986, s 44.

[76] ibid s 46.

[77] *Berkovits v Grinberg* [1995] Fam 142, effectively following *R v Secretary of State for the Home Department, ex p Fatima* [1986] AC 527 (a case on earlier legislation).

delivery of a bill of divorce, or a modified Muslim divorce obtained by the writing of the words of repudiation and sending them to the wife and to a statutory body, will be denied recognition if any of the elements—often the sending or service of a document—was geographically separated from the others; and it appears to be irrelevant that the divorce would be recognized as effective in all of the countries in which a part of it happened. Why English law would deny recognition to a divorce, which is effective under the laws of all those countries which had a factual connection, on the ground that it did not all happen in the one place, is beyond rational explanation.

Daft as this undoubtedly is, it produces three further consequences of baffling absurdity. The first is that such a trans-national divorce, being excluded from the definition of an overseas divorce, is not one which section 45(1) requires to be recognized under the 1986 Act or not at all: this is true only for overseas divorces, which means those obtained in a country. No provision of the Act specifically proscribes the recognition of divorces which are not, in this particular sense, monoterritorial overseas divorces. As all other statutory schemes for recognition have been repealed, it appears to follow that such decrees fall to be recognized under the rules of the common law thought to have been abolished in 1971.[78] The second is that a divorce obtained from a Canadian court cannot be recognized as an overseas divorce if any of the procedural elements—such as the service of the petition on the respondent—took place outside Canada: it will no longer be a divorce obtained in Canada and it will no longer fall under section 45. The third is that where service of an English petition is made outside England, the divorce will, by parity of reasoning, not be seen as a divorce obtained in England, with the restrictions which the law places on such divorces. The result is quite impossible, but follows from the legislative categorization of divorces according to where they were obtained, and the judicial insistence that this means all elements must be concentrated in the one place. As a cautionary tale against legislation, private international law offers none more startling than this. It makes the case for European legislation seem almost unanswerable.

If the decree was obtained in a single country outside the British islands, the rules governing its recognition depend on whether it was obtained by judicial or other proceedings.[79] Judicial proceedings are not hard to

---

[78] The Recognition of Divorces and Legal Separations Act 1971, which abolished them, was itself repealed by the Family Law Act 1986. The rules recognized a divorce if granted by a court which had a real and substantial connection to the case.

[79] 1986 Act, s 54(1).

identify as such, but 'other proceedings' require the involvement of an agency of or recognized by the state, having a role which is more than merely probative.[80] Quite why this was considered to be a line worth drawing is a mystery,[81] and it requires some intricate analysis of religious and foreign law. A religious divorce conforming to the (Pakistani) Muslim Family Law Ordinance 1961 is obtained by proceedings,[82] because the requirement to notify the chairman of a statutory body and the imposition of a statutory timetable amount to proceedings. The same was held, but on rather less convincing grounds, in the case of a Jewish divorce: it was obtained by proceedings because, it seems, of the elaborate ceremonial involved in writing the bill of divorce.[83] But a purely religious Muslim divorce, brought about by unilateral words of repudiation spoken by the husband,[84] is not obtained by means of proceedings.[85]

If the decree was obtained by proceedings and is to be recognized, it must be obtained where either[86] party was domiciled, according either to English law or to the law of the place of the obtaining,[87] or was habitually resident, or was a national. The decree must be effective under that law to dissolve the marriage.[88] Where domicile or habitual residence is relied on as the jurisdictional connection, the decree must be effective in the relevant law district, such as Nevada as distinct from the United States; but in the case of nationality, it must be effective throughout the entire national territory,[89] a fact which may raise issues of constitutional law. Recognition of the decree may be denied[90] on grounds of lack of notice or of the right to be heard, or if the matter is already *res judicata*. It may also be denied on grounds of public policy, and the operation of that policy may vary according to whether the marriage or the spouses had a significant connection

---

[80] *Chaudhary v Chaudhary* [1985] Fam 19 (CA).

[81] Indeed, it may not have been intended as a line at all: its appearance in the Recognition of Divorces and Legal Separations Act 1971 may have been intended to clarify that *all* divorces, whether judicial or not, were within the Act. Only after it had been held that 'judicial or other proceedings' were not inclusive, but served to exclude some forms of divorce, did the idea take root that there was a line to be drawn, and this understanding, or maybe misunderstanding, was subsequently incorporated into the 1986 Act.

[82] *Quazi v Quazi* [1980] AC 744.

[83] *Berkovits v Grinberg* [1995] Fam 142.

[84] 'Talaq, talaq, talaq' ('I divorce you', again and again).

[85] *Chaudhary v Chaudhary* [1985] Fam 19 (CA).

[86] Husband or wife, petitioner or respondent.

[87] 1986 Act, s 46(5).

[88] ibid s 46(1); though not necessarily to reattribute marital capacity: s 50.

[89] ibid s 49(3)(a).

[90] ibid s 51.

to England.[91] Although the grounds upon which the decree was obtained are not specified as a ground of objection, they will, in an extreme case, be relevant, such as where a marriage is judicially[92] annulled for racial or religious reasons. Some may ponder how it can be correct for the law to recognize a form of divorce in which one spouse has no right to be consulted, never mind being represented and heard. Perhaps Article 6 of the European Convention on Human Rights will provide the only civilized answer, that recognition of such practice is inconsistent with several of the human rights secured by the Convention. The proposition that such behaviour is warranted by religious belief or other superstition is manifestly insufficient, and the fact that the law of another country may tolerate it is nothing to the point.

If the decree was obtained without proceedings, its recognition requires that it be obtained where both parties were domiciled when it was obtained, or where one was domiciled, with the country of domicile of the other party recognizing the decree. But it will be denied recognition in any event if either party had been habitually resident in the United Kingdom throughout the year prior to its being obtained.[93] The statutory grounds of non-recognition include those which may be raised against decrees obtained by proceedings but, in a final spasm of legislative caprice, recognition may also be denied if there is no official document certifying the effectiveness of the decree under the law of the foreign country.[94]

3. FINANCIAL PROVISION AND MAINTENANCE

The jurisdictional rules are particularly complex; and several bases need to be distinguished. The complexity reflects the fact that there are many reasons why an English court should be able to make such orders, and they make for an untidy list, the content of which is not susceptible to organization which will lay bare the principle which makes it rational. English courts may make an order for financial provision on or before granting a decree of divorce, nullity, or judicial separation.[95] Subject to the jurisdictional rules of the Brussels Regulation,[96] they also have jurisdiction to make an order for financial provision after a foreign decree

---

[91] cf *Chaudhary v Chaudhary* [1985] Fam 19 (CA).
[92] If a marriage is said to be dissolved by operation of law when one of the parties changes religion, this should not be seen as done by divorce.
[93] Family Law Act 1986, s 46(2).
[94] ibid s 51(4), a requirement read minimally in *Wicken v Wicken* [1999] Fam 224.
[95] Matrimonial Causes Act 1973, ss 22, 23 (as amended).
[96] The Brussels II*bis* Regulation has no application to financial provision: recital 8.

recognized in England if either party was domiciled in England when the divorce was obtained or when applying for leave to proceed, or if either party was habitually resident in England for the year preceding either of those dates, or if either has a beneficial interest in a dwelling house (once the matrimonial home) at the date of the application for leave to proceed.[97] A court may make an order for financial provision on the ground of failure to provide reasonable maintenance if either party is domiciled in England on the date of the application, or has been habitually resident for the year preceding that date, or if the respondent is present in England on that date.[98] A magistrates' court has jurisdiction to make a maintenance order if the respondent is resident in England,[99] or in a foreign country to which the Maintenance Orders (Facilities for Enforcement) Act 1920 extends,[100] or is resident in a country to which Part I of the Maintenance Orders (Reciprocal Enforcement) Act 1972 extends,[101] or in accordance with Part II of the same Act.[102] English courts may vary an order if each of the parties is domiciled or resident in England.[103] English courts may make the orders against anyone over whom personal jurisdiction is conferred by the rules of the Brussels Regulation.[104] Choice of law is, by contrast, straightforward: English courts still apply English law to claims for financial provision.[105]

So far as concerns foreign orders, a foreign divorce, even if recognized in England, does not automatically terminate an English maintenance order.[106] A foreign order for financial provision which is final and conclusive may be recognized and enforced in England at common law and under statute:[107] it is, after all, a judgment *in personam*. The provisions for recognition are largely reciprocal with the grounds of jurisdiction exercised by English courts; those from Member States to which the Brussels Regulation applies may be enforced under the provisions of those instruments.

---

[97] Matrimonial and Family Proceedings Act 1984, ss 12, 15, 27.
[98] Matrimonial Causes Act 1973, s 27 (as amended).
[99] *Forsyth v Forsyth* [1948] P 125 (CA).
[100] Domestic Proceedings and Magistrates' Courts Act 1978, s 30(3)(a).
[101] Maintenance Orders (Reciprocal Enforcement) Act 1972, s 3 (as amended).
[102] ibid ss 27A–28B.
[103] Matrimonial Causes Act 1973, s 35 (as amended).
[104] Chapter 2 above.
[105] *Sealey v Callan* [1953] P 135 (CA).
[106] *Macaulay v Macaulay* [1991] 1 WLR 179.
[107] Maintenance Orders Act 1950, Pt II, Maintenance Orders (Facilities for Enforcement) Act 1920, Maintenance Orders (Reciprocal Enforcement) Act 1972, Civil Jurisdiction and Judgments Act 1982, Council Regulation (EC) 44/2001, [2001] OJ L12/1.

D. CHILDREN

Leaving aside questions of legitimacy, which are even more archaic today than they used to be, the law of children is principally concerned with adoption, guardianship, and custody. The last of these has given rise to a substantial amount of legislation, local and international, to deal with the distressing problem of child abduction, which is a miserable consequence of the breakdown of certain kinds of family. Much has been accomplished by international convention, no doubt because the area is too delicate or sensitive to be left to national laws and the willingness of national courts to adopt an approach which other courts would see as being even-handed. It is all very well to start from the premise that the dominant concern is to make orders which are in the best interests of the child, but this is easier said than done. *Quot homines, tot sententiae* could have been formulated to describe the private international law of children.

The current starting point is the Brussels II*bis* Regulation. This applies in civil matters relating to the attribution, exercise, delegation, restriction, or termination of parental responsibility. This covers rights of access, rights of custody, guardianship, fostering, and the protection and preservation of a child's property. But it does not include disputes over parenthood, or adoption and the procedures leading up to it.[108] The basic rule is to give jurisdiction to the courts for the place of the child's habitual residence,[109] but where the child has moved lawfully from one Member State to another, the courts of the former retain a short period of exceptional jurisdiction as well.[110] If a court is exercising matrimonial jurisdiction under the Regulation, it may also have consequential jurisdiction over a matter of parental responsibility. It will do so if the child is habitually resident in England, at least one of the spouses has parental responsibility, and the jurisdiction has been accepted by the spouses and is in the best interests of the child.[111] Jurisdiction ceases once the matrimonial proceedings have terminated in dismissal or a final decree, or on final judgment in the responsibility proceedings. In a development which appears to be a novelty within the framework of European legislation, a court has a statutory power to ask a court in another Member State to assume jurisdiction in its place.[112] This reflects the truth that, no matter how detailed the rules of jurisdiction, there may still be cases which

---

[108] Article 1. [109] Article 8.
[110] Article 9. [111] Article 12.
[112] Article 15.

ought, in the interests of justice, be dealt with in another court which has jurisdiction and that jurisdiction is more appropriate. The jurisdictional rules of Brussels II*bis* are complex, and do not lend themselves to concise accurate summary. The reason is that there is no real principle at work, rather an attempt to set up a set of rules which is detailed and sufficiently balanced for courts to apply them and to respect orders made by courts in other Member States which they might not have made for themselves. The Regulation does not prescribe the choice of law. English courts therefore apply English law.

Where the Regulation does not ascribe jurisdiction to the courts of a Member State, it provides that each state shall exercise what may be described as its 'residual jurisdiction'.[113] So far as concerns orders for guardianship and custody, the English courts have jurisdiction to make an order otherwise than as regards care, education, and contact where the child is a British national or is present within the jurisdiction of the court.[114] Orders for contact, residence, or specific issues may be made in matrimonial proceedings;[115] also if the child is habitually resident in England or is present in England and not habitually resident in Scotland or Northern Ireland[116] (and on such basis, an order for care, education, or contact may also be made; this is also permitted if the child is present and the immediate exercise of the power is necessary for the protection of the child[117]). But if the matter of the proceedings has already been determined by a foreign court the English court may decline to act;[118] and if proceedings are pending in a foreign court the English court may stay its own if it is appropriate to do so.[119] Where they have jurisdiction the courts apply English law.[120] So far as concerns foreign orders, a guardianship order made by a court of a country of which the child was a national or in which it was present will usually be recognized in England;[121] but the power of the guardian will extend no further than the powers of a foreign parent. A foreign custody order does not prevent an English court making such order as it thinks fit in relation to the welfare of the child.[122]

---

[113] Article 14.
[114] *Re P (GE) (An Infant)* [1965] Ch 568 (CA).
[115] Family Law Act 1986, ss 1, 2 (as amended).
[116] ibid s 2(2) (as amended).
[117] ibid s 1(1)(d) (as amended).
[118] ibid s 5 (as amended).
[119] ibid.
[120] *J v C* [1970] AC 668.
[121] *Re P (GE) (An Infant)* [1965] Ch 568 (CA).
[122] *McKee v McKee* [1951] AC 352 (PC).

The private international law on child abduction is now largely derived from international convention. As a matter of common law, the power to order the return of a child who has been abducted is a particular example of orders generally made in the interests of the welfare of the child.[123] But this was superseded by the Luxembourg Convention on Recognition and Enforcement of Decisions Concerning Custody of Children 1980,[124] and the Hague Convention on the Civil Aspects of Child Abduction 1980.[125] The point of departure for these instruments is that a child who has wrongfully[126] been removed, or who is being wrongfully retained, outside the jurisdiction of the court of his or her habitual residence should be restored to custody[127] in the country of its habitual residence,[128] whether or not a prior court order has been made, for this will be the place in which it is most appropriate that decisions are made. The Conventions prescribe defences to the claim for restoration, such as acquiescence in the removal. The inclination of the English courts at one time appeared to be to read these as restrictive, only applicable in exceptional cases; but it is now clear that the Conventions' objectives of swiftly returning the child did not necessarily outweigh the need to give weight to the best interests of the child.[129] By contrast, in relation to non-Convention countries, the courts will give predominant weight to the principle of the welfare of the child, and will not approach its decision as though the principles of the Convention were applicable.[130] The principle of the welfare of the child gives rise to what are, in one respect, delicate questions where the country to which return is sought is one where Muslim religious 'law' is in force. In some cases the court has taken the robust and rational view that, in effect, the threat of damage done by religion cannot be allowed to prevail over the best interests of child, and a return to a country where this may result cannot be ordered.[131] Other courts, not surprisingly, have preferred the view that it is not their business to pass judgment on what is,

---

[123] *J v C* [1970] AC 668 (PC).

[124] Child Abduction and Custody Act 1985, Sch 2.

[125] ibid Sch 1.

[126] That is, in breach of custody rights attributed to a person, institution, or other body under the law of the state of habitual residence and which were actually exercised, or would have been exercised but for the removal: art 3 of the Hague Convention.

[127] Which may be of a person or, in appropriate cases, a court: *Re H (Child Abduction: Rights of Custody)* [2000] 2 AC 291.

[128] *Re J (a Minor) (Abduction: Custody Rights)* [1990] 2 AC 562; *Re F (a Minor) (Abduction: Custody Rights)* [1991] Fam 25 (CA).

[129] *Re M (Children) (Abduction: Rights of Custody)* [2007] UKHL 55, [2007] 3 WLR 975.

[130] *Re J (A Child) (Custody Rights: Jurisdiction)* [2005] UKHL 40, [2006] 1 AC 80.

[131] *Re JA (Child Abduction: Non-Convention Country)* [1998] 1 FLR 231 (CA), which was generally approved in *Re J (A Child) (Custody Rights: Jurisdiction)*.

in effect, the cultural structure of a foreign system.[132] It is an enormously delicate area for judicial decision. It has to be dealt with as part of the conflict of laws and conflict of jurisdictions, but in truth the conflict operates at a quite different level, and its resolution by the application of rules of law is challenging.

In relation to adoption, a court has jurisdiction to make an order if at least one of the applicants is domiciled in a part of the United Kingdom and the child is in England when the application is made;[133] and in deciding whether to make the order it will apply English law.[134] Foreign adoptions may be recognized under the Adoption Act 1976[135] or under the common law if the adopted child was domiciled in the foreign country at the time of the adoption.[136]

---

[132] *Osman v Elisha* [2000] Fam 62 (CA).
[133] Adoption Act 1976, ss 14, 15, 62.
[134] *Re B (S) (An Infant)* [1968] Ch 204.
[135] Adoption Act 1976, ss 38, 72.
[136] *Re Marshall* [1957] Ch 507 (CA).

10

Corporations and their Insolvency

It has been the tradition of English private international law to treat corporations and the laws of insolvency alongside each other, presumably as insolvency is a significant component of corporate activity, litigation, and legislative activity. As to choice of law, the *lex incorporationis* governed many of the issues raised under the law of corporations, whereas insolvency was dominated by the *lex fori*. But this ignored a problem which, in recent years, grew to alarming size. The uncoordinated nature of corporate insolvencies which had cross-border components came to seen as simply intolerable: for a court to insist on applying its own law, and taking jurisdiction whenever there was a local justification, was not designed to promote the orderly resolution of the cross-border issues raised by a large insolvency. Even where they were receptive to the idea, there was only so much that judges could do to manage the proceedings before them in a way which was sensitive to the fact that other courts were properly involved in a parallel enterprise.[1] Although domestic legislation made modest provision for rendering assistance in relation to foreign proceedings, the first attempt at harmonization took the form of a European Regulation,[2] which applies to corporate insolvency as well as to individual bankruptcy. A Model Law[3] on cross-border insolvency was given effect in English law in 2006: it has the aim of further developing the cross-border cooperation and coordination of insolvency procedures. These statutory steps taken to bring order to the administration of cross-border insolvency have, it is fair to say, been far more successful than anything national parliaments or individual judges could ever have achieved. Although the detail of the law is extremely complex, the field of cross-border insolvency is an excellent

---

[1] Even so, for a remarkably bold example of what a court considered might be done under its inherent jurisdiction, see *Cambridge Gas Transportation Corp v Committee of Unsecured Creditors of Navigator Holdings plc* [2006] UKPC 26, [2007] 1 AC 508.

[2] Council Regulation (EC) 1346/2000, [2000] OJ L160/1.

[3] UNCITRAL, 30th session, 1997. For the implementing legislation, see Insolvency Act 2000, s 14(4) and SI 2006/1030, in force 4 April 2006.

example of when legislation to improve the state of the law is the only way ahead.

We will look first at the private international law of corporations, and then at the law of insolvency. In substantial part, what is said about corporate insolvency will apply also to personal bankruptcy, which is mentioned only by way of postscript.

A. CORPORATIONS

I. CORPORATIONS IN PRIVATE INTERNATIONAL LAW

A corporation is an artificial creation, a legal person. The question whether, and with what powers, a body corporate has been created is determined by the law under which its creation took place, the *lex incorporationis*. Likewise, the question who is empowered to act on its behalf is a matter for the *lex incorporationis*, even though the consequences in law of an act which an officer or organ was not entitled to do may also be referred to another law.[4] The question whether an individual is liable for the acts of a corporation is also governed by the *lex incorporationis*; and, in principle, all issues having to do with the internal government and management of a corporation are for that law.[5] It is undeniable that this offers an incentive to incorporate under a law which offers advantages to those who may wish to create a corporation with wide powers but restricted liabilities, or to incorporate with no significant risk of allowing liability to affect individual officers or corporators.[6] This is, however, little more than a consequence of the doctrine of corporate personality and the fact that some laws are better than others for the disreputable corporator. Although it is sometimes suggested that the place of incorporation should not be decisive, and that the law of the place of daily or central management and control should assume a more prominent role;[7] or that the doctrine of separate corporate personality really needs to be countered by an analysis based on the economic realities of life and the need to assert effective

---

[4] *Janred v ENIT* [1989] 2 All ER 444 (CA).
[5] *Risdon Iron and Locomotive Works v Furness* [1906] 1 KB 49 (CA); *Bonanza Creek Gold Mining Co v R* [1916] 1 AC 566 (PC); *Lazard Bros v Midland Bank* [1933] AC 289; *National Bank of Greece and Athens SA v Metliss* [1958] AC 509; *Carl Zeiss Stiftung v Rayner & Keeler Ltd (No 2)* [1967] 1 AC 853; *JH Rayner (Mincing Lane) Ltd v Department of Trade and Industry* [1990] 2 AC 418.
[6] Although there is a persuasive view that the question whether the corporate veil will always protect whoever is hiding behind it will not necessarily be answered by the *lex incorporationis*: Tham [2007] LMCLQ 22.
[7] Drury [1998] CLJ 165.

control over multi-national enterprises,[8] these arguments have tended to be directed at jurisdiction over companies rather than at the hegemony of the *lex incorporationis* as the determinant of legal personality and power.

2. RECOGNITION AND DISSOLUTION OF FOREIGN CORPORATIONS

English law recognizes the creation of corporations, and the conferment of legal personality upon them, under the *lex incorporationis*. The recognition of corporations has been extended to those which are created under the ordinances of a non-state, such as Taiwan, or the *soi-disant* 'Turkish Republic of Northern Cyprus'.[9] Moreover, although English law does not recognize the legal personality of an international organization in the absence of domestic legislation to confer such status, where a foreign law has conferred such personality under its law, the resultant legal person will be recognized in England.[10] So the Arab Monetary Fund, an international organization of states of which the United Kingdom is not a member, had been given legal personality under the law of the United Arab Emirates, and was accordingly recognized as a person under English law. What would have happened if it had been given personality under the laws of more states than one raises questions to which no easy answers exist.

But what the law creates the same law can also destroy, so the question whether a corporation has been dissolved is likewise one for the *lex incorporationis*[11] alone. The validity of a dissolution may raise difficult questions when the law under which the corporation was created ceases to exist and in its geographical place a new law arises. But corporations created under the law of Russia were recognized as being dissolved under the law of the Soviet Union, and, later the same century, in a pleasing act of symmetry, *vice versa*.[12] A combination of the rules for creation and dissolution means that the amalgamation of corporations, the recognition of the new corporation, and whether it assumes the rights and liabilities of the dissolved corporation(s), are in principle all questions for the *lex incorporationis*,[13]

---

[8] Muchlinski (2001) 50 ICLQ 1.

[9] Foreign Corporations Act 1991, s 1.

[10] *Arab Monetary Fund v Hashim (No 3)* [1991] 2 AC 114; *Westland Helicopters Ltd v Arab Organisation for Industrialisation* [1995] QB 282.

[11] *Lazard Bros v Midland Bank* [1933] AC 289; *Russian and English Bank v Baring Bros* [1932] 1 Ch 435 (and if there is a branch in England it cannot sue after the corporation has been dissolved; it should be wound up).

[12] *The Kommunar (No 2)* [1997] 1 Lloyd's Rep 8.

[13] *National Bank of Greece and Athens SA v Metliss* [1958] AC 509; if the two corporations are incorporated in different countries it is probable that the *lex incorporationis* of each must

although the issue whether this process discharges liabilities incurred by the old corporation is a distinct and contractual one, governed by the law applicable to those obligations.[14] A court will naturally endeavour to give effect to a case of corporate succession, and will do what it can to ensure that it is effective in English private international law.[15] But corporate reconstruction can be untidy, and a court may reach the view in a particular case that the process is not a true succession or amalgamation notwithstanding the language used by the foreign legislator.[16]

3. DOMICILE OF CORPORATIONS

As a matter of common law, a corporation is domiciled at the place of its incorporation.[17] This, for example, means that its capacities[18] are governed by its *lex incorporationis*, and the general principle that legal capacity is governed by the law of the domicile is preserved. In other contexts, however, a statutory domicile may be conferred. In the context of jurisdiction under the Brussels Regulation, a corporation is domiciled where[19] it has its statutory seat or has its central administration or has its principal place of business.[20] It is obvious that this cannot be seen as 'the' domicile which determines corporate capacity, for a corporation may, under this slightly inelegant provision, have as many as three domiciles for jurisdictional purposes.

4. JURISDICTION OVER CORPORATIONS

Just as with individual defendants, a corporation can be sued in England when process can be served on it. In one respect, service on a corporation is more complex than service on individual defendants, for there can be no personal service on an artificial person. But the changes to the methods of service ushered in by the Civil Procedure Rules simplified matters

---

recognize the amalgamation. See also *Adams v National Bank of Greece and Athens SA* [1961] AC 255 for cases where there may not be a true and complete succession to the rights and liabilities of the former companies.

[14] *Adams v National Bank of Greece and Athens SA* [1961] AC 255.
[15] *Toprak Enerji Sanayi SA v Sale Tilney Technology plc* [1994] 1 WLR 840; *Eurosteel v Stinnes* [2000] 1 All ER (Comm) 964; *Astra SA Insurance and Reinsurance Co v Sphere Drake Insurance Ltd* [2000] 2 Lloyd's Rep 550.
[16] *The Kommunar (No 2)* [1997] 1 Lloyd's Rep 8.
[17] *Gasque v Inland Revenue Commissioners* [1940] KB 80.
[18] To some extent this will also determine its liability to pay taxes.
[19] In the sense of 'wherever'.
[20] See Art 60. For the purposes of the UK, 'statutory seat' means the registered office or, where there is no such office anywhere, the place of incorporation or, where there is no such place anywhere, the place under the law of which the formation took place: Art 60(2). The Regulation is at [2001] OJ L12/1.

considerably; and when the statutory changes made by the Companies Act 2006 enter into force,[21] statutory service will be less complicated as well.[22]

A company registered under the Companies Acts will be served by leaving the document at, or by posting it to, the company's registered office. An overseas company[23] which has registered statutory particulars with the registrar of companies may be served by leaving the document at, or sending it to, the address of the person authorized to accept service; but if that is not possible it may be left at 'any place of business of the company in the United Kingdom'.[24] In this context a place of business will be taken to mean somewhere fixed and definite and from which the business of the company is carried on. A general guide to whether the company carries on business at such a place is to ask whether it can make contracts there. If there is such a place of business, jurisdictional competence is not limited to the activities of the place of business.[25] Even so, if contracts are not made at the particular place, a court may still find that the activity carried on at the place in question constitutes the carrying on of business, for the statutory rule is not defined in terms of a principal place of business.[26]

As indicated above, in addition to statutory service under the Companies Acts, a company, including an overseas company,[27] may be served in accordance with Part 6 of the Civil Procedure Rules, at any place within the jurisdiction where it carries on its activities, or at any place of business within the jurisdiction. Service is made by leaving the document with a person holding a senior position[28] within the company.

Service is one thing; jurisdiction is another. Where the company is domiciled in a Member State for the purposes of the Brussels Regulation, Article 22(2) gives exclusive jurisdiction to the courts of the seat[29] of the corporation in proceedings having as their object the validity of the

---

[21] Sections 1139–42 will in practice be all that needs to be read. Until then, the relevant rules are in sections 691–5, and section 725, of the Companies Act 1985.

[22] For the separate nature of the Schemes, see *Sea Assets Ltd* v *PT Garuda International* [2000] 4 All ER 371.

[23] One incorporated outside the United Kingdom: Companies Act 2006, s 1044 (not yet in force). The extent of the obligation on such a company to register particulars is governed by ss 1045–8 (not yet in force).

[24] Companies Act 2006, s 1139 (not yet in force).

[25] *Okura & Co Ltd v Forsbacka Jernverks AB* [1914] 1 KB 715; cf *Adams v Cape Industries plc* [1990] Ch 433 (CA).

[26] *South India Shipping Corp Ltd v Export-Import Bank of Korea* [1985] 1 WLR 585 (CA).

[27] Service under CPR Pt 6 may be made as an alternative to statutory service: CPR 6.2(2).

[28] CPR r 6.4(4); for the definition of 'senior position', see the Practice Direction—Service, para 6.2(2).

[29] As defined by the national law of the court seised: Art 22(2), and not by Art 60.

constitution, the nullity or dissolution of companies, or decisions of their organs. This reflects the fact that the birth and death of a company, and the inherent validity of acts of its organs, can really only be dealt with in the one place. Of course, the consequences of acts which were based on decisions of corporate organs which were not valid are not comprehended by this rule.[30]

5. CONTRACTS MADE BY CORPORATIONS

The principal issue when dealing with contracts made by corporations is one of capacity: of the corporation to make the contract at all and of the organ or officer to bind it. As the private international law of agency is apparently incapable of reform by convention, the questions are mainly dealt with under common law choice of law rules. If the corporation had capacity under the *lex incorporationis* and the *lex contractus* to enter into the contract, no problems arise. But where it is alleged that it did not, the contract will be *ultra vires* the corporation. Even so, it may in a proper case be estopped by its own conduct from relying on its own incapacity,[31] although it is unclear whether the applicable estoppel principles will be those of the *lex fori* or of the *lex contractus*.[32] Where the corporation had capacity to enter the contract, but the person purporting to act on its behalf did not have authority to so act, the question whether the contract made between the agent and the third party binds or may be relied on by the company is a difficult one, though it may well be a matter for the *lex contractus* of that contract which was created.[33] The case law is difficult. It seems right that where an agent acts on behalf of a principal, a third party is generally entitled to assume that the agent has such power and authority as he would have under the law which governs the contract which they make. It is true that where the agent is the representative of a company, a third party will or should be aware that the *lex incorporationis* may place limits upon the extent to which a company can be bound, but this deemed awareness applies more obviously to the legal capacities of the company than to the powers which it has chosen to vest in a particular officer. It

---

[30] *Grupo Torras SA v Sheikh Fahad Mohammed Al-Sabah* [1996] 1 Lloyd's Rep 7 (CA); *Speed Investments Ltd v Formula One Holdings Ltd (No 2)* [2004] EWCA Civ 1512, [2005] 1 WLR 1936.

[31] *Janred v ENIT* [1989] 2 All ER 444 (CA).

[32] If there would be estoppel under the one but not the other, there is a conflict of laws; principle suggests that the *lex fori* should defer to the *lex contractus*.

[33] *Chatenay v Brazilian Submarine Telegraph Co* [1891] 1 QB 279; *Maspons v Mildred* (1882) 9 QBD 530 (CA); *Ruby SS Corporation v Commercial Union Assurance Co Ltd* (1933) 150 LT 38 (CA).

follows that there is no reason to make a special rule for contracts made by corporate agents who acted outside their authority: the extent to which the company is bound and entitled should be a matter for the law of the contract made between the agent and the third party. If a corporation has been dissolved and amalgamated with, or to create, another, the question whether dissolution terminates the contract as a source of obligation is a matter for the *lex contractus*. So although the amalgamation may provide for the vesting of all liabilities in the new corporation, it cannot discharge those liabilities, then or later, unless it is also the law applicable to them.[34]

6. WINDING UP OF COMPANIES

The dissolution of companies under the *lex incorporationis* is one thing, but the winding up of companies is more complex. Because of the impact of European legislation, it is necessary to distinguish between solvent and insolvent companies when dealing with winding up.[35] So far as solvent companies are concerned, English courts may wind up a company registered in England.[36] But a solvent company may not be wound up if it has a seat only in another Member State.[37] The regimes which apply to insolvent companies are more complex. The law on the winding up of insolvent companies has been made more complex as a result of the Insolvency Regulation,[38] in force since May 2002. The Regulation applies where the centre of main interests of the debtor is in a Member State; it does not apply where this is not so.

(a) Centre of debtor's main interest not in a Member State

Where the matter is not governed by the Insolvency Regulation, an English court may wind up a company formed under the Companies Acts.[39] Less expected, perhaps, is the fact that the court may wind up a company not formed under the Companies Acts so long as the company

---

[34] *Adams v National Bank of Greece and Athens SA* [1961] AC 255.

[35] See Fletcher, *Insolvency in Private International Law* (2nd edn, 2005).

[36] Insolvency Act 1986, s 117.

[37] Brussels Regulation, Art 22(2); [2001] OJ L12/1.

[38] Regulation (EC) 1346/2000, [2000] OJ L160/1. The Regulation lies outside the 'Brussels' or 'Rome' families, for it is concerned with jurisdiction *and* choice of law. The draft EC Convention, on which its text was closely based, was signed by all but one of the Member States at or after meeting in Madrid. The last signature, that of the United Kingdom, was never applied. It never came into force as a Convention, and there appears to be no wish to commemorate the ancestry of the Regulation by referring to it as the Madrid Regulation. The reasons which led the United Kingdom to refuse to sign the Convention are a story for our times: a witches' brew of mad cow disease and hypersensitivity over Gibraltar, of all ridiculous causes. For the account, read Fletcher, *Insolvency in Private International Law* (2nd edn, 2005) ch 7, and weep.

[39] Insolvency Act 1986, s 117.

has a sufficient connection with the jurisdiction and is insolvent, and it is not otherwise inappropriate to make the order.[40] A 'sufficient connection' will exist if there are persons in England who could benefit from a winding-up order and there is enough connection with England to justify making the order.[41] Most unexpected of all is that an insolvent company which has been dissolved under its *lex incorporationis* may be revived for the purpose of being wound up.[42] As Parliament can make any provision it cares to, this is not an impossible surprise. But it represents a significant victory for pragmatism over the principle that dissolution is the exclusive concern of the *lex incorporationis*. Upon making the order, the assets of the company subject to the order are bound by a trust for the benefit of those interested in the winding up. The liquidator is under an obligation to get in all the assets to which the company appears to be entitled, and is obliged to use them to discharge English and foreign liabilities. If there is also a foreign liquidation he is obliged to seek to secure equal treatment for all claimants, not just for English creditors.[43] Many provisions of the Insolvency Act 1986 dealing with orders which may be made in the course of administration or liquidation are unhelpfully silent about what their international scope is intended to be, but they will probably be interpreted as requiring a sufficient connection with England,[44] which is not very much more helpful, but which probably reflects the common sense of the view that if something cannot be defined well, it is better that it not be defined at all.

So far as concerns a foreign winding up, a liquidator appointed under the *lex incorporationis* is recognized by English private international law,[45] but there appears to be no authority on the recognition of a liquidator appointed under the law of a third country. The courts of the United Kingdom have a statutory obligation to assist each other in a winding up;[46] in relation to countries outside the United Kingdom the secretary of state may designate states whose courts (but not liquidators acting on their own authority[47]) may

---

[40] ibid ss 220, 221; *Re A Company (No 00359 of 1987)* [1988] Ch 210; *Re Paramount Airways Ltd* [1993] Ch 223 (CA).

[41] *Re A Company (No 00359 of 1987)* [1988] Ch 210; *Re A Company (No 003102 of 1991), ex p Nyckeln Finance Co Ltd* [1991] BCLC 539; *Stocznia Gdanska SA v Latreefers Inc* [2001] BCC 174 (CA).

[42] Insolvency Act 1986, s 225.

[43] *Re Bank of Credit and Commerce International SA* [1992] BCLC 570.

[44] *Re Paramount Airways Ltd* [1993] Ch 223 (CA); cf *Re Seagull Manufacturing Co Ltd (No 2)* [1994] Ch 91 (notice under the Company Directors Disqualification Act 1986).

[45] *Bank of Ethiopia v National Bank of Egypt and Ligouri* [1937] Ch 513.

[46] Insolvency Act 1986, s 426(4).

[47] *Re Bank of Credit and Commerce International SA (No 9)* [1994] 3 All ER 764.

request cooperation from an English court;[48] the court will assist if it can.[49] On the other hand, the extent to which an English court may 'dis-apply' some aspects of English insolvency legislation in order to cooperate with a foreign insolvency is distinctly limited.[50]

(b) Centre of debtor's main interest in a Member State

In insolvencies to which the Insolvency Regulation applies, the instrument prescribes and limits the jurisdiction of the courts of Member States in relation to the opening of insolvency proceedings; the choice of law for the insolvency proceedings; and the recognition of judgments from other Member States ordering the opening, conduct, and closure of such proceedings. Its purpose is to bring order to an area which was excluded from the original jurisdictional scheme of what was the Brussels Convention, and for which the coordination of the judicial function was particularly problematic.

The Regulation applies to debtors wherever they are domiciled, but the critical requirement is that a debtor's main interest is in a Member State. In the nature of things, this test is likely to be hardest to use in the cases in which its guidance is the most needed, for the kind of business for which this is a crucial definitional tool is likely to be cross-border in the first place. For a company, it is presumed to be the place of the registered office,[51] although it seems inevitable that scrutiny of the whole of a company's activities may be required where the issue of location is contested.

The Regulation applies to collective insolvency proceedings which involve the complete or partial divestment of a debtor and the appointment of a liquidator,[52] whether the debtor is an individual or a corporate body. It excludes insurance undertakings and credit institutions.[53]

The overall aim is to ensure that within the European Union, the lead role is given to a single court, and to relegate to a subordinate role proceedings in all other courts. Accordingly, 'main proceedings' may be opened

---

[48] Insolvency Act 1986, s 426(4), (11); SI 1986/2123. See also the reference to the UNCITRAL Model Law, below.

[49] *Hughes v Hannover Ruckversicherungs AG* [1997] 1 BCLC 497 (CA).

[50] *Re BCCI SA (No 10)* [1997] Ch 213; *Re HIH Casualty and General Insurance Ltd* [2006] EWCA Civ 732, [2007] 1 All ER 177.

[51] Article 3(1). The expression has an autonomous meaning. The presumption applies even though the debtor is a subsidiary of a company incorporated elsewhere, on the broad footing that it is the appearance to those dealing with the debtor which is the principal concern: Case C–341/04 *Re Eurofood IFSC Ltd* [2006] ECR I–3813.

[52] Including a trustee or an administrative receiver appointed under a floating charge: Art 1(1).

[53] Article 1(2).

only in the Member State in which the centre of a debtor's main interests is situated at the date of the request to open the proceedings, even if it later moved.[54] 'Secondary' or 'territorial' proceedings may be opened in any Member State in which the debtor has an 'establishment;[55] although their effect is confined to assets situated[56] in the Member State in which the secondary or territorial proceedings are opened; they may be opened before main proceedings are.[57] The law which is generally applicable to insolvency proceedings and their effects is the *lex fori*,[58] which governs most issues,[59] but exceptions are made for a list of other matters for which this would not be the appropriate choice of law.[60] An order from a court in a Member State opening insolvency proceedings must be recognized, from the time it becomes effective, in all other Member States, and be given the same effect as it has in the state of origin.[61] Judgments relating to the conduct and closure of insolvency proceedings are recognized in all other Member States,[62] and enforcement takes place under the Brussels Regulation. A liquidator appointed in the main proceedings is to be recognized in all other Member States[63] and accorded the powers which he has under the law of the state of his appointment. If there are secondary proceedings in another Member State, his powers are limited in relation to those assets; but the various liquidators are under an obligation to share information and to cooperate with each other.[64]

(c) UNCITRAL Model Law

In a similar development, the UNCITRAL produced a model law on cross-border insolvency. Regulations made under the Insolvency Act 2000[65] brought it into force in 2006. It does not provide a comprehensive scheme to regulate cross-border insolvency, but does aim to pave the way for states to enact legislation to provide for the recognition of foreign insolvency procedures, the right of foreign representatives to have access

---

[54] Case C–1/04 *Re Staubitz-Schreiber* [2006] ECR I–701.
[55] Any place of operations where the debtor carries out a non-transitory economic activity with human means and goods.
[56] Defined in Art 2(g).
[57] They are then known as territorial proceedings.
[58] Article 4.
[59] Article 4.
[60] Articles 5–15.
[61] Articles 10 and 17.
[62] Article 25.
[63] Article 18(1).
[64] Article 31.
[65] SI 2006/1030.

to courts, requests for cooperation, and judicial coordination of concurrent proceedings.

B.　PERSONAL BANKRUPTCY

I.　ENGLISH BANKRUPTCIES

We can deal with personal bankruptcy really by way of postscript. The Insolvency Regulation applies its regime of jurisdiction, choice of law, and recognition and enforcement of judgments to personal bankruptcy as well as to corporate insolvency. Accordingly, the summary of its provisions given above is equally applicable to bankruptcies, and for this reason those provisions are not repeated here. The account which follows is therefore of the law as it applies to bankruptcies to which the Regulation does not apply, which principally means cases where the centre of the debtor's main interests is outside the territory of the Member States.

The English courts have jurisdiction to declare bankrupt any debtor who is domiciled or present in England on the day of presentation of the petition.[66] They also have jurisdiction if he was ordinarily resident, or had a place of residence, or carried on business (or was a member of a partnership firm which carried on business) in England at any time within the three years prior to the presentation of the petition.[67] A debtor who has subjected himself to a voluntary arrangement submits to the jurisdiction by doing so.[68] In deciding whether to exercise their discretion to make the order, the courts will consider the location of assets, any foreign bankruptcy, and other issues of general convenience.[69] The bankrupt may be examined by order of the court, but the private examination of any other person is probably limited to those who are present within the jurisdiction to be served with the summons requesting their attendance.[70]

As to choice of law, an English court applies English law to the bankruptcy.[71] The making of the order operates as a statutory assignment of all of the debtor's property, wherever situated, to his trustee;[72] the bankrupt may be ordered to assist the trustee in recovering property outside the control of the court. A creditor subject to the personal jurisdiction of

---

[66] Insolvency Act 1986, s 265.
[67] ibid.
[68] ibid s 264.
[69] *Re Behrends* (1865) 12 LT 149; *Re Robinson, ex p Robinson* (1883) 22 Ch D 816 (CA).
[70] cf *Re Seagull Manufacturing Co Ltd* [1993] Ch 345 (CA).
[71] *Re Kloebe* (1884) 28 Ch D 175; *Re Doetsch* [1896] 2 Ch 836.
[72] Insolvency Act 1986, ss 283, 306, 436.

the court may be restrained from taking proceedings overseas, in order to safeguard the principle of equal division.[73] Foreign debts must be shown to be good by the law under which they arise, but the court will use its own rules to secure, as best it may, equality between creditors of the same class.[74] The power of the court to set aside an antecedent transaction is not subject to express limitation, but the defendant against whom reversal of the transaction is sought must be (or by service out with leave of the court, be made) subject to the jurisdiction of the court, and the test is whether it is just and convenient in all the circumstances of the case to make the order.[75]

An English discharge operates in relation to all the debts provable in the bankruptcy, irrespective of the law which governed the debt,[76] and a discharge under the law which governed the debt will be effective in England.[77]

2. FOREIGN BANKRUPTCIES

A foreign bankruptcy will be recognized if the debtor was domiciled[78] in or submitted[79] to the jurisdiction of the court; and the bankruptcy will vest English movables (but not land) in the assignee if this is the effect it has under the foreign law.[80] The result may be that the debtor no longer has property in England, and this will tell strongly against making an English order. A discharge from a foreign bankruptcy is effective in England only if it is effective under the law which governed the debt.[81] A court may not question the bankruptcy jurisdiction of a Scottish or Northern Irish court; and the effect of such an order extends to all property in England, not excluding land.[82]

---

[73] *Barclays Bank plc v Homan* [1993] BCLC 680 (CA).
[74] *Re Scheibler* (1874) 9 Ch App 722.
[75] *Re Paramount Airways Ltd* [1993] Ch 223 (CA).
[76] Insolvency Act 1986, s 281.
[77] *Gibbs and Sons v Soc Industrielle et Commerciale des Métaux* (1890) 25 QBD 399 (CA).
[78] *Re Hayward* [1897] 1 Ch 905.
[79] *Re Anderson* [1911] 1 KB 896.
[80] *Re Craig* (1916) 86 LJ Ch 62.
[81] *Gibbs and Sons v Soc Industrielle et Commerciale des Métaux* (1890) 25 QBD 399 (CA).
[82] Insolvency Act 1986, s 426.

Index